CLIMATE CHANGE LITIG

This examination of the role of litigation in addressing the problem of climate change focuses not only on how the massive and growing number of lawsuits influences regulation directly but also on how the lawsuits shape corporate behavior and public opinion. It provides readers with an understanding of how these lawsuits have shaped approaches to mitigation and adaptation and have been used to try to force and to block regulation. There is a particular emphasis on lawsuits in the United States and Australia, the two jurisdictions that have had the most climate change litigation in the world, and the lessons supply broader insights into the role of courts in addressing climate change.

Both authors are internationally recognized experts on climate change law. JACQUELINE PEEL is a professor of law at the Melbourne Law School, Australia. Her teaching and research interests lie in the areas of environmental law (domestic and international), risk regulation and the role of science, and climate change law.

HARI M. OSOFSKY is a professor of law and the 2014–15 Julius E. Davis Chair in Law at the University of Minnesota, where she is also faculty director of the Energy Transition Lab and director of the Joint Degree Program in Law, Science, and Technology. Her research focuses on energy transition and climate change.

CAMBRIDGE STUDIES IN INTERNATIONAL AND COMPARATIVE LAW

Established in 1946, this series produces high-quality scholarship in the fields of public and private international law and comparative law. Although these are distinct legal subdisciplines, developments since 1946 confirm their interrelations.

Comparative law is increasingly used as a tool in the making of law at national, regional, and international levels. Private international law is now often affected by international conventions, and the issues faced by classical conflict rules are frequently dealt with by substantive harmonization of law under international auspices. Mixed international arbitrations, especially those involving state economic activity, raise mixed questions of public and private international law, while in many fields (such as the protection of human rights and democratic standards, investment guarantees, and international criminal law), international and national systems interact. National constitutional arrangements relating to "foreign affairs," and to the implementation of international norms, are a focus of attention.

The series welcomes works of a theoretical or interdisciplinary character and those focusing on the new approaches to international or comparative law or conflicts of law. Studies of particular institutions or problems are equally welcome, as are translations of the best work published in other languages.

General Editors

James Crawford, SC, FBA
Whewell Professor of International Law, Faculty of Law, University of Cambridge

John S. Bell, FBA
Professor of Law, Faculty of Law, University of Cambridge

A list of books in the series can be found at the end of this volume.

CLIMATE CHANGE LITIGATION

Regulatory Pathways to Cleaner Energy

JACQUELINE PEEL AND HARI M. OSOFSKY

CAMBRIDGE
UNIVERSITY PRESS

CAMBRIDGE
UNIVERSITY PRESS

University Printing House, Cambridge CB2 8BS, United Kingdom

One Liberty Plaza, 20th Floor, New York, NY 10006, USA

477 Williamstown Road, Port Melbourne, VIC 3207, Australia

4843/24, 2nd Floor, Ansari Road, Daryaganj, Delhi - 110002, India

79 Anson Road, #06-04/06, Singapore 079906

Cambridge University Press is part of the University of Cambridge.

It furthers the University's mission by disseminating knowledge in the pursuit of education, learning and research at the highest international levels of excellence.

www.cambridge.org
Information on this title: www.cambridge.org/9781316641071

© Jacqueline Peel and Hari M. Osofsky 2015

First published 2015
First paperback edition 2017

A catalogue record for this publication is available from the British Library

Library of Congress Cataloging in Publication data
Peel, Jacqueline, author.
Climate change litigation : regulatory pathways to cleaner energy / Jacqueline Peel, Hari M. Osofsky.
pages cm. – (Cambridge studies in international and comparative law ; 116)
ISBN 978-1-107-03606-2 (hardback)
1. Climatic changes – Law and legislation – Australia.   2. Climatic changes –
Law and legislation – United States.   3. Actions and defenses – Australia.
4. Actions and defenses – United States.   5. Liability for environmental damages –
Australia.   6. Liability for environmental damages – United States.   I. Osofsky,
Hari M., 1972– author.   II. Title.
K3585.P44   2015
344.7304′633 – dc23   2014046696

ISBN 978-1-107-03606-2 Hardback
ISBN 978-1-316-64107-1 Paperback

To our children and the future generations that depend on
our addressing climate change adequately

CONTENTS

PREFACE AND ACKNOWLEDGMENTS

Courts have often been central battlegrounds in fights to address important social issues, from civil rights to the health effects of smoking. The latest such courtroom battlefront concerns efforts to deal with the problem of climate change. As we highlight in Chapter 1, lawsuits raising climate change issues have been brought across six continents and in eighteen different countries, as well as in international tribunals. In total, climate change cases worldwide now number close to seven hundred claims.

This book explores the consequences of that litigation explosion for regulatory action to deal with the climate change problem. In essence, *how* does litigation shape regulatory and behavioral responses to climate change, and, in the process, pathways toward a "cleaner energy" future – sustainable, low-carbon societies that will be resilient in the face of a changing climate?

The book examines this central question from a range of different perspectives: the roles of climate change litigation as a tool for (1) reducing greenhouse gas emissions and increasing adaptation to the effects of climate change, (2) changing social and business norms, and (3) providing a forum in which pro- and antiregulatory forces interact. It combines doctrinal analysis of the case law and associated regulatory development with unique insights about the significance of the litigation drawn from interviews with those actively involved in bringing, adjudicating, and responding to the lawsuits.

Two countries provide the main case studies for this examination: the United States and Australia. These are the nations in which the most climate change litigation has taken place. As major players in the global carbon economy, both countries also face significant challenges in transitioning away from reliance on fossil fuels like coal to foster a cleaner energy future.

We see this book as an important, novel contribution to the scholarship and practice of climate change litigation that has burgeoned in the past decade, including three major US Supreme Court decisions, *Massachusetts v. EPA* (2007), *American Electric Power v. Connecticut* (2011), and *Utility Air Regulatory Group v. EPA* (2014). The book moves beyond the first wave of scholarship analyzing individual cases and the second wave cataloging and classifying the types of climate change litigation. It tackles the regulatory significance of this case law and how it has, does, and is likely to influence the behaviors and choices that matter for climate change mitigation and adaptation. We hope that, by addressing these issues, the book will be a useful resource for both regulators and litigators in the field as well as for judges, activists, business organizations, academics, and students.

We have found our transnational collaboration to be a rich and rewarding experience. Each of us is an expert in climate change litigation and regulation in our home countries of Australia (Jacqueline Peel) and the United States (Hari Osofsky). As a result of writing the book, we both have a deeper appreciation for and understanding of climate change litigation–regulation dynamics in each other's home jurisdiction, but also in our own. The comparative analysis in the book illuminated many similarities between the climate change litigation experiences of the United States and Australia but also some surprising and interesting differences that have implications for the future trajectory of the litigation in each country; it also potentially offers lessons for claimants in other countries about the regulatory pathways that litigation can generate. As one example, the United States and Australia confront similar challenges in responding to climate change on both the mitigation and adaptation fronts. However, case law targeting greenhouse gas emissions has achieved far more substantial regulatory success in the United States than in Australia, whereas Australia leads the United States in adaptation litigation. In discussing and seeking to explain the relative regulatory significance of climate change case law in each jurisdiction, the book therefore offers a window into the particular social, political, and legal features that shape litigation's regulatory pathways.

Writing this book was our first substantial collaboration as coauthors. However, this work has drawn on and developed our previous publications, authored separately and together. We would particularly wish to acknowledge the prior work we have reproduced in edited form or on whose ideas we have built: William C. G. Burns and Hari M. Osofsky (eds.), *Adjudicating Climate Change: State, National, and International Approaches* (Cambridge University Press, 2009); Hari M. Osofsky, "The Intersection of Scale, Science, and Law in *Massachusetts v. EPA*,"

Oregon Review of International Law 9 (2007); Hari M. Osofsky, "Litigation's Role in the Path of U.S. Federal Climate Change Regulation: Implications of *AEP v. Connecticut*," 46 *Valparaiso University Law Review* (2012); Hari M. Osofsky and Jacqueline Peel, "Litigation's Regulatory Pathways and the Administrative State: Lessons from U.S. and Australian Climate Change Governance," 25 *Georgetown International Environmental Law Review* (2013); Hari M. Osofsky and Jacqueline Peel, "The Role of Litigation in Multilevel Climate Change Governance: Possibilities for a Lower Carbon Future," 30 *Environmental and Planning Law Journal* (2013); Jacqueline Peel, "Issues in Climate Change Litigation," 5 *Carbon and Climate Law Review* (2011); Jacqueline Peel, Lee Godden, and Rodney J. Keenan, "Climate Change Law in an Era of Multi-Level Governance," 1 *Transnational Environmental Law* (2012); Jacqueline Peel and Hari M. Osofsky, "Climate Change Litigation's Regulatory Pathways: A Comparative Analysis of the United States and Australia," 35 *Law and Policy* (2013); Alexander Zahar, Jacqueline Peel, and Lee Godden, *Australian Climate Law in Global Context* (Cambridge, 2013); Hari M. Osofsky, "*AEP v. Connecticut's* Implications for the Future of Climate Change Litigation," 121 *Yale Law Journal Online* (2011–12); and Jacqueline Peel and Hari M. Osofsky, "Sue to Adapt?," *Minnesota Law Review* (forthcoming).

In undertaking the research for this project, including the interview component, we benefited greatly from funding provided under an Australian Research Council grant: Discovery Project 130100500, "Transition to a Clean Energy Future: The Role of Climate Change Litigation in Shaping Our Regulatory Path" (2013–15). This grant funding facilitated workshops and attendance at conferences in Australia, the United States, and elsewhere to present our interim findings and receive feedback on our work. We would particularly like to thank colleagues at Minnesota Law School and Melbourne Law School for feedback on early stages of the research and draft chapters of the book provided at workshops held in each location. We also benefited greatly from feedback at the 2012 British Academy Conference on Climate Change Litigation, Policy and Mobilization; the 2013 American Society of International Law Annual Meeting; the 2013 Australian National Environmental Law Association Conference; the 2013 International Law Weekend – Midwest at Washington University School of Law; and the 2014 Law and Society Annual Meeting. Other colleagues who provided helpful feedback whom we would particularly like to acknowledge include Helen Anderson, Bradley Karkkainen, Michael Gerrard, Lee Godden, Kristin Hickman, Alexandra Klass, Alice Kaswan, Mark Poirer, J.B. Ruhl, Gerry Simpson, Lisa Vanhala, and Rob

Verchick. Australian Research Council funding also allowed us to employ research assistants – Lisa Caripis, Emma Cocks, and Nick Boyd-Caine at Melbourne University School of Law and Thomas Burman, Joseph Dammel, Drew McNeill, Justin Moor, and Sarah Schenck at the University of Minnesota Law School. We are indebted to these individuals for their research efforts and assistance with footnoting. Lisa and Nick, building on earlier efforts by Rachelle Downie, Mick Power, and Naomi Wynn, were also central to the establishment, updating, and maintenance of the web database of Australian climate change case law developed for the project. This database is housed with Melbourne Law School's Centre for Resources, Energy, and Environmental Law at www.law.unimelb. edu.au/creel/research/climate-change.

From the outset of this project, the editorial team at Cambridge University Press has been extremely supportive. We appreciate their editorial work, support for the project, and flexibility as the project evolved. In particular, we would like to acknowledge the support of series editor Professor James Crawford, commissioning editors Finola O'Sullivan and Elizabeth Spicer (and before Elizabeth, Nienke van Schaverbeke), and the marketing and editing team led by Richard Woodham.

We would also like to extend a sincere thank-you to our interviewees in the United States and Australia who undertook interviews with us for the purposes of this project. In accordance with the ethics procedures of our home institutions of the University of Melbourne and University of Minnesota, interviewees are not named in the book to protect the confidentiality of their responses. However, we wish to acknowledge their generosity in giving of their time, experience, and expertise. We appreciate the many wonderful insights they offered into climate change litigation in the United States and Australia and the influence it has had and may have in the future. We have included quotations from our interviewees throughout the book. In addition, two quotations – one from a US interviewee and one from an Australian interviewee – appear at the beginning of each chapter. We hope our readers enjoy and benefit from these pithy, honest, and perceptive comments on the regulatory pathways of climate change litigation as much as we did.

Last, but not least, we would like to thank our respective families for their love, support, and patience during the writing of this book. Jacqueline extends particular thanks to husband Michael Findlay, daughter Aly, and son Will. Hari would like to thank husband Joshua Gitelson, son Oz, and daughter Scarlet. As mothers of young children, we feel a particular responsibility to ensure that we are a constructive part of efforts to address the problem of climate change. We hope that this book sheds light on the role of litigation in regulatory progress and contributes to broader understanding of the necessary elements of effective climate change governance. We dedicate this book to our children and the future generations that depend on our addressing climate change adequately.

1

Why climate change litigation matters

Everything is litigated, everything will be litigated. And that's the starting point and the presumption. No matter how small the rule is or how big the rule is. It's going to be litigated. And it's going to be decided by the D.C. Circuit if it's a federal rule and if it's a state rule it's going to be decided somewhere else in some court. It's just the nature of America! I mean, I am gainfully employed, likely, because of the degree to which we rely upon law to guide regulatory development as opposed to other countries, which are policy-driven.

– US Interview Participant 5

I take a long-term view [of] climate litigation. I really think we are like lawyers in Alabama in 1950 fighting for black civil rights or... lawyers at the early stages of cigarette and asbestos litigation, trying to establish a causal link between cigarettes and lung cancer. And, you know, you get looked at like you've got two heads and you're green by the courts to start with and you get lots of bad decisions. But the issues are so enormous and the science is so strong; it's not like the problem is going away. So I take a long-term view to these cases that we will have many losses and it's about doing the right thing. Even if at the end of the day we don't change and our society just continues on this suicidal approach of burning fossil fuels, I think we have to do what we can now, with the tools we have, to try and protect the future.

– Australian Interview Participant 4

1.1   Introduction

Courtrooms have become a key battleground in the public debate over climate change around the world. Lawsuits over climate change have been brought in eighteen countries on six continents, as well as in international tribunals.[1] In the United States alone, which has more of these cases than

---

[1] For details, see Richard Lord, Silke Goldberg, Lavanya Rajamani, and Jutta Brunnée (eds.), *Climate Change Liability: Transnational Law and Practice* (2011, Cambridge University Press, Cambridge); Arnold and Porter LLP, "U.S. Climate Change Litigation Chart" and

any other country, more than five hundred cases under many different laws in state and federal courts have raised climate change mitigation and adaptation issues.[2] These lawsuits – brought by both those supporting climate change regulation and those fighting it – and the media attention surrounding them have shaped regulation in these countries directly through mandate and indirectly through influencing corporate behavior and social norms.

The most prominent example of climate change litigation is *Massachusetts v. EPA*, the first US Supreme Court decision on climate change, which provided the basis for federal regulation by the US Environmental Protection Agency (EPA) of motor vehicle and power plant greenhouse gas emissions.[3] This decision may be "the most important environmental case of the century, if ever," issued by the US Supreme Court.[4] For those working in the field of climate and energy law – such as the regulators, lawyers, judges, energy company representatives, planners, insurance risk managers, and environmental campaigners whom we interviewed for this book – the case is "bedrock by now."[5] It established that the Clean Air Act provides the US government with the authority to regulate greenhouse gas pollution, the principal contributor to global climate change.[6] No less momentous was the US Supreme Court's endorsement of climate change as a serious public policy issue. A decision like that "causes everybody to perk up and take notice; so, at least in the deliberations and corporate boardrooms, they say we can't completely dismiss this anymore."[7]

Because *Massachusetts v. EPA* was such an important decision, though, it tends to overshadow the fact that hundreds of other US cases have had a variety of impacts on the country's regulation of climate change. Moreover, litigation has also been an important influence on climate regulation in other major developed-country greenhouse gas emitters. Australia is one such nation; it has seen an enormous growth in climate

---

"Non-U.S. Climate Change Litigation Chart," www.climatecasechart.com; and Climate Justice Programme, "Cases," www.climatelaw.org/cases.

[2] A comprehensive database of climate change cases filed and decided in US courts, including links to judgments, is maintained by the Columbia Climate Change Law Center. See, further, Arnold and Porter LLP, "U.S. Climate Change Litigation Chart." Climate change "mitigation" refers to efforts to reduce greenhouse gas emissions from human sources, whereas climate change "adaptation" focuses on managing the impacts of climate change on communities, infrastructure, and the environment.

[3] *Massachusetts v. EPA*, 549 U.S. 497 (2007).

[4] In-person interview, US Participant 5 (Nov. 14, 2012).   [5] Ibid.

[6] The findings of the case and its subsequent impact on US climate regulation are described in depth in Chapter 3.

[7] Telephone interview, US Participant 8 (Nov. 26, 2012).

change litigation over the past decade and has the second most climate cases in the world.[8] As this litigation continues to expand around the globe, and particularly in these two countries, the need to understand its role in broader climate change efforts grows. This need is particularly strong in the United States and Australia because they are major carbon polluters and fossil fuel producers, disproportionately contributing to climate change. Both also face significant challenges – social, political, and economic – in their efforts to transition to cleaner energy from their currently carbon-dominated economies.

This book asks how litigation on climate change issues influences regulatory pathways to a cleaner energy future. It focuses on the United States and Australia because they have more of these lawsuits than any other countries, and enough commonalities in both their legal systems and approaches to climate change to provide useful points of comparison. The book attempts to understand the extent to which litigation in each country has affected government regulation and corporate behavior and the pathways by which these effects have occurred, and likely will occur, in the future. In this regard, we are interested in direct legal change brought about by cases and how the case law might help change social and business norms in ways that motivate action by governments and other key stakeholders.

To answer these questions, we not only examined cases and accompanying regulation but also talked with those bringing, adjudicating, and responding to these cases. Our interviewees from the United States and Australia provided valuable insights into the direct and indirect effects of the litigation. Throughout the book, we attempt to take a balanced approach that recognizes that litigation over climate change may have mixed effects on regulatory efforts. While the majority of the litigation in both the United States and Australia has been brought by pro-regulatory litigants who want to advance climate change regulation, a growing body of antiregulatory cases launched by business groups and the fossil fuel industry has emerged in response to decisions like *Massachusetts v. EPA* and the regulation it has spawned as well as proactive action by state governments.[9] The book considers how these antiregulatory cases, and

---

[8] For details of Australian climate change cases, see the database maintained by the Centre for Resources, Energy, and Environmental Law (CREEL) at Melbourne Law School: Jacqueline Peel, "Australian Climate Change Litigation," CREEL, www.law.unimelb.edu.au/creel/research/climate-change. Judgments in many of the cases are freely available online from the Austlii website: www.austlii.edu.au.

[9] David Markell and J.B. Ruhl, "An Empirical Assessment of Climate Change in the Courts: A New Jurisprudence or Business as Usual" (2012) 64 *Fla. L. Rev.* 15.

other barriers to and backlash against litigation, might limit the progress achieved by pro-regulatory lawsuits.

This chapter sets the scene for the book's discussion of these issues. We begin by describing what we mean by climate change litigation. This is a far from straightforward question because "when you're talking about climate change litigation it's very much a broad spectrum, so it really does depend on what your focus is."[10] Because the book is concerned with the regulatory significance of climate change litigation, our focus has been on cases that have the issue of climate change at the "core" and generally raise climate-specific arguments or contain judicial analysis referencing climate change.

The next part of the chapter discusses how climate change litigation fits into the broader picture of climate change governance. Climate change is a problem regulated at multiple levels – from the international to the local – that involves complex interactions among the activities of multiple actors, governmental and nongovernmental. Although climate change is a global issue in the sense that the accumulation of greenhouse gas emissions from human activities around the world causes impacts in every jurisdiction, many of the most important responses take place at the domestic level. Climate change litigation has tended to have its greatest impact at this level and is a mechanism that is especially well suited for bringing together different levels of government.

Chapter 4 introduces our two national case studies – the United States and Australia – and explains why litigation in these two countries, and the role it plays in shaping their respective regulatory paths, is particularly important in assessing domestic efforts to move toward cleaner energy. We also discuss how the common challenges that Australia and the United States face in transitioning away from fossil fuels and preparing their communities for the effects of climate change make them good subjects for comparative study. The final part of the chapter provides an outline of the remainder of the book.

1.2   What is climate change litigation?

As noted earlier, climate change is a complex problem that cuts across multiple levels of governance, areas of law, and sectors of the economy. Taking a broad approach, then, "virtually all litigation could be conceived of as [climate change litigation]," given that "climate change is the

---

[10] Skype interview, Australian Participant 6 (Apr. 5, 2013).

consequence of billions of everyday human actions, personal, commercial, and industrial."[11] However, the climate change litigation that has arisen in countries like the United States and Australia tends to have a much more direct link to climate change, by addressing either the greenhouse gas emissions that cause the problem (mitigation-related litigation) or the predicted impacts of climate change on ecosystems, communities, and infrastructure (adaptation-related litigation). Litigants in such cases may be seeking to promote climate change regulation (proactive litigation) or to oppose existing or proposed regulatory measures (antiregulatory litigation).

More difficult to classify are cases at the edges of these categories. A good example is the many claims that have been brought – both in the United States and Australia – concerning the environmental effects of hydraulic fracturing ("fracking") for unconventional energy sources such as shale or coal seam gas.[12] As we discuss further in Chapter 3, the explosion in natural gas production facilitated by fracking has major implications for the future of clean energy. Although many in the industry argue that "we're advancing the cause for climate change by our emissions being less than other fossil fuels, like coal," the relationship between fracking and climate change is more complex.[13] This expansion may decrease emissions in the short term through coal-to-gas substitution in energy systems. Over the longer term, though, reliance on natural gas – without major technological shifts – will still result in rising greenhouse gas emissions.[14]

[11] Chris Hilson, "Climate Change Litigation in the UK: An Explanatory Approach (or Bringing Grievance Back In)" in F. Fracchia and M. Occhiena (eds.), *Climate Change: La Riposta del Diritto* (2010, Editoriale Scientifica, Naples), 421. Hilson also makes the point that litigation itself is a broad concept that can connote many different things. It extends from the formal resolution of a dispute by a court or tribunal on the basis of adjudicative procedures to more informal proceedings before an independent decision maker, as well as to judicial proceedings that have been commenced but settle before they reach the stage of a full hearing and judgment. Because our focus is on the regulatory impact, direct and indirect, of climate change litigation rather than on its form, we have taken a broad view of what litigation involves and include decided cases, cases before administrative tribunals, and settled cases in our discussion.

[12] US fracking cases are tracked in Arnold and Porter LLP, "Hydraulic Fracturing Case Chart," "US Climate Change Litigation Chart." For examples of cases over fracking and coal seam gas exploitation in Australia, see Peel, "Australian Climate Change Litigation." In the United States, coal seam gas is referred to as coal bed methane.

[13] Skype interview, Australian Participant 7 (Apr. 11, 2013).

[14] International Energy Agency, "Are We Entering a Golden Age of Gas? Special Report" in *World Energy Outlook 2011* (2011, OECD/IEA, Paris), 8 ("An increased share of natural gas in the global energy mix is far from enough on its own to put us on a carbon emissions path consistent with an average global temperature rise of no more than 2°C"). See

Fracking cases have not (yet) been litigated on an explicit climate action platform, with plaintiffs instead favoring arguments about the impacts on water resources and wildlife.[15] Nonetheless, at least some groups bringing antifracking claims in the United States and Australia are doing so as part of broader climate change campaigns.[16]

Other scholars who have evaluated climate change litigation, such as Professors J.B. Ruhl and David Markell, have been hesitant to rely on the motivation of litigants bringing claims as a basis for categorizing cases as "climate change litigation." They worry that this approach requires uninformed judgments about litigants' mental state. Hence, in their empirical studies of climate change litigation in the United States, these authors have limited their analysis to "any piece of federal, state, tribal, or local administrative or judicial litigation in which the party filings or tribunal decisions directly and expressly raise an issue of fact or law regarding the substance or policy of climate change causes and impacts."[17] As Markell and Ruhl acknowledge, this approach "has some limiting effects on the pool of cases included."[18] For instance, their definition excludes challenges to coal-fired power plants that are motivated by a concern over climate change but litigated on other grounds, such as the plants' contribution to air pollution or their impacts on water. Markell and Ruhl argue that such cases are likely to influence the law and policy of climate change only "in the broadest sense" and "would not be contributing to any discrete body of law bearing a direct connection to climate change issues."[19]

In our view, however, this approach is too narrow where the purpose is to understand the linkage between litigation and climate change

also recent scientific evidence suggesting that fugitive methane emissions associated with unconventional gas exploitation may outweigh any climate benefits from its substitution for coal. See Robert W. Howarth, Renee Santoro, and Anthony Ingraffea, "Methane and the Greenhouse-Gas Footprint of Natural Gas from Shale Formations" (2011) 106 *Clim. Change* 679.

[15] See, e.g., *Fullerton Cove Residents Action Group Incorporated v. Dart Energy Ltd.* (No. 2) (2013) NSWLEC 38.

[16] See, e.g., Center for Biological Diversity, "California Fracking," available at www.biologicaldiversity.org/campaigns/california_fracking/. In an Australian context, see "Lock the Gate Alliance," www.lockthegate.org.au/.

[17] David Markell and J.B. Ruhl, "An Empirical Survey of Climate Change Litigation in the United States" (2010) 40(7) *Environ. L. Rep.* 10644, 10647. See also Markell and Ruhl, "A New Jurisprudence or Business as Usual," 27.

[18] Markell and Ruhl, "A New Jurisprudence or Business as Usual," 27.

[19] Markell and Ruhl, "An Empirical Survey," 10647; Markell and Ruhl, "A New Jurisprudence or Business as Usual," 26–27.

regulation. Although discerning a climate change–related motivation for litigation is not always straightforward when the parties' pleadings or the judgment do not mention it directly, a range of other materials, including case briefings and media releases, can aid in identifying the ultimate reasons behind particular litigation.[20] Our interviews with litigants, particularly those from environmental groups, also indicate that the way a case is framed in argument is often dictated by what are perceived to be the strongest legal points for a claim, which may not be the climate change issue at stake. Nonetheless, the litigation itself is designated within the organization or by the litigants concerned as contributing to a climate change or anticoal campaign.[21] Taken on an individual basis, a case focused on challenging a particular fossil fuel project is often relatively small scale and narrow in scope, which tends to limit its discrete impact. However, excluding these cases from consideration may miss their cumulative regulatory influence. No single case may achieve a "home run," but collectively they work to "forc[e] coal plants to account for some of their unrealized externalities."[22]

At the opposite end of the spectrum from cases motivated by climate concerns but litigated on alternative non–climate grounds are lawsuits that only peripherally touch on climate change issues. In some of these cases, climate-related concerns may be thrown into pleadings as another plausible argument, but without such concerns being the main focus of the litigation.[23] In others, responses to climate change created the regulatory issue being litigated, but climate change itself is not central to the case. Interviewees mentioned private litigation over carbon trading contracts as an example of this category of cases. Although such litigation is a by-product of carbon trading schemes under climate regulatory instruments such as the Kyoto Protocol[24] or the European Emissions

---

[20] Hilson, "Climate Change Litigation in the UK."

[21] See, e.g., in-person interview, Australian Participant 1 (Mar. 7, 2013) ("The contribution of coal to climate change was one of our motivations for taking on the litigation and discussing the issue, even though the cases did not directly address climate change issues").

[22] Telephone interview, US Participant 1 (Oct. 20, 2012).

[23] Skype interview, Australian Participant 18 (Jul. 18, 2013). Another interviewee gave the example of cases against animal factories: "there the hook was smog forming pollution from big dairies or a big meat chicken factory. But the same processes at the dairies that emit a lot of smog forming emissions also emit a lot of methane. So there's this two-for-one aspect sometimes in some cases." In-person interview, US Participant 10 (Jan. 14, 2013).

[24] This international treaty, discussed further later, provides for trading of emissions units between nations that are Protocol parties.

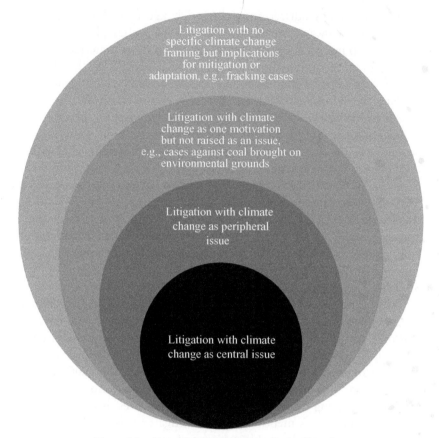

Figure 1.1   Conceptualizing climate change litigation.

Trading Scheme,[25] climate change as such is not an issue in the disputes, which largely concern the interpretation of contractual terms.[26]

In Figure 1.1, we represent our concept of climate change litigation in terms of a series of concentric circles. At the core are cases where climate change – whether relating to mitigation or adaptation and brought by pro- or antiregulatory claimants – is a central issue in the litigation. These

---

[25] For details of the European Emissions Trading Scheme, see European Commission, "Climate Action," http://ec.europa.eu/clima/policies/ets/index_en.htm. See also Michael Faure and Marjan Peeters (eds.), *Climate Change and European Emissions Trading: Lessons for Theory and Practice* (2008, Elgar, Cheltenham).

[26] Skype interview, Australian Participant 6 (Apr. 5, 2013).

cases tend to have some element of deliberate framing of the arguments or judgment in climate change terms. As Professor Chris Hilson points out, "climate change framing of claims is a relatively new phenomenon."[27] Challenges to fossil fuel projects or other greenhouse gas–intensive developments have been brought in both the United States and Australia for many years. But it is only in the last decade that a substantial portion of these cases has used the contribution to climate change as part of the argument or motivation for the case.[28] At the outer limits of the boundaries of climate change litigation lie cases that are not explicitly tied to specific climate change arguments but which have clear implications for climate change mitigation or adaptation. In between are cases where (1) climate change is raised, but as a peripheral issue in the litigation, and (2) concerns over climate change motivate the lawsuit, at least in part, but are not raised explicitly in the claims or decision.

As our interest lies in how litigation may serve as a pathway to improved climate change regulation, and in the process influence mitigation and adaptive behaviors, the majority of our case examples in the following chapters are drawn from the core of this broader sphere. However, on occasion, cases further from the core may have a significant regulatory impact, usually in combination with other cases or through the indirect effects they have on government or corporate behavior.

1.3 Why climate litigation matters as part of climate governance

This book examines climate change litigation and the extent to which these cases mandate, foster, or facilitate improved regulation. It moves beyond describing or cataloging the cases that have emerged to evaluate the impact of climate change litigation on government regulation of climate change and the behavior of other key actors, such as major corporate emitters. We are thus fundamentally concerned with the real-world consequences of climate change litigation for the achievement of mitigation and adaptive outcomes.

This choice of focus may invite several questions from readers; after all, the realm of climate change governance is increasingly acknowledged to

---

[27] Hilson, "Climate Change Litigation in the UK."

[28] Many cases against coal in both the United States and Australia continue to pursue only non-climate-related grounds, such as environmental, health, or air quality impacts.

be both complex and multidimensional.[29] Why, then, focus on litigation rather than other pieces of the governance puzzle, such as international agreements or national regulatory programs? Moreover, given that litigation is fact intensive and jurisdiction specific, can it have any broader regulatory role, especially in addressing a problem of global dimensions such as climate change? In the following sections, we argue that there are at least three reasons why climate change litigation matters as a component of the overall system of climate governance: (1) international regulatory efforts are failing, increasing reliance on domestic regulatory solutions to which litigation can contribute; (2) climate governance operates across multiple scales and involves many actors, and litigation can be a useful means of connecting these different elements; and (3) mitigation and adaptive outcomes rely on the cumulative effect of numerous smaller-scale decisions, many of which come before courts and through which litigation can play an effective shaping role.

1.3.1   Regulatory gaps created by struggling international climate negotiations

As is widely acknowledged, international solutions to the climate change problem have been slow to emerge.[30] The international climate change

---

[29] Among others, see Steven Bernstein and Benjamin Cashore, "Complex Global Governance and Domestic Policies: Four Pathways of Influence" (2012) 88(3) *Int. Affairs* 585; Frank Biermann, Philipp Pattberg, and Fariborz Zelli, *Global Climate Governance beyond 2012: Architecture, Agency and Adaptation* (2010, Cambridge University Press, Cambridge); Daniel C. Esty, "Climate Change and Global Environmental Governance" (2008) 14 *Global Governance* 111; Neil Gunningham, "Confronting the Challenge of Energy Governance" (2012) 1(1) *Transnatl. Environ. L.* 119; Ellen Hey and Andria Naudé Fourie, "Participation in Climate Change Governance and Its Implications for International Law" in Rosemary Rayfuse and Shirley V. Scott (eds.), *International Law in the Era of Climate Change* (2012, Edward Elgar, Cheltenham), 254; Kati Kulovesi, "Exploring the Landscape of Climate Law and Scholarship: Two Emerging Trends" in Erkki J. Hollo, Kati Kulovesi, and Michael Mehling (eds.), *Climate Change and the Law* (2013, Springer, Dordrecht), 31; Jacqueline Peel, Lee Godden, and Rodney J. Keenan, "Climate Change Law in an Era of Multi-Level Governance" (2012) 1(2) *Transnatl. Environ. Law* 245; Joanne Scott, "The Multi-level Governance of Climate Change" (2011) 5(1) *Carbon Clim. L. Rev.* 25.

[30] In the wake of the Copenhagen COP, the failures of the UNFCCC regime prompted serious discussion of the future of international climate law: see, e.g., Daniel Bodansky, "The Copenhagen Climate Change Conference: A Postmortem" (2010) 104 *Am. J. Intl. L.* 230; Sebastian Oberthür, "Global Climate Governance after Cancun: Options for EU Leadership" (2011) 46(1) *Intl. Spectator* 5; Elinor Ostrom, *A Polycentric Approach for Coping with Climate Change: Background Paper to the 2010 World Development Report* (Policy Research Working Paper 5095) (2009, World Bank, New York); Gwyn Prins et al., *The Hartwell Paper: A New Direction for Climate Policy after the Crash of 2009* (2010,

regime as it stands consists of the two-decades-old United Nations Framework Convention on Climate Change (UNFCCC) – which establishes the basic global infrastructure for climate change mitigation and adaptation actions and seeks to stabilize atmospheric greenhouse gas concentrations "at a level that would prevent dangerous anthropogenic interference with the climate system"[31] – and the supplementary Kyoto Protocol.[32] The 1997 Kyoto Protocol established binding emissions reduction targets for participating developed-country parties (which did not include the United States) over the first commitment period running from 2008 to 2012.[33] At the UNFCCC Conference of the Parties (COP) meeting in 2012, parties to the Protocol agreed to institute a second commitment period for 2013 to 2020, but the necessary treaty amendment has not yet received sufficient support to come into force.[34]

Although countries acknowledged at the 2009 COP in Copenhagen the urgency of deep cuts in greenhouse gas emissions and agreed that global temperature rise should be limited to two degrees Celsius (2°C) to avoid the worst impacts of climate change,[35] subsequent international actions to reduce emissions and prepare for impacts have been feeble.[36] International climate negotiators are currently engaged in another round of negotiations pursuant to the so-called Durban Platform that emerged from the 2011 COP. These negotiations aim to reach agreement by late

Institute for Science, Innovation, and Society, University of Oxford; LSE for the Study of Long Wave Events; MacKinder Programme, Buckinghamshire).

[31] United Nations Framework Convention on Climate Change (UNFCCC), New York, May 9, 1992, entered into force Mar. 21, 1994, 1771 UNTS 107, article 2.

[32] Kyoto Protocol to the United Nations Framework Convention on Climate Change (Kyoto Protocol), Kyoto, Dec. 11, 1997, entered into force Feb. 16, 2005, 2303 UNTS 148.

[33] Kyoto Protocol, article 3 and Annex B. The Protocol includes no binding emissions reduction targets for developing countries even though some such countries, including China and India, have emerged as major emitters.

[34] Doha Amendment to the Kyoto Protocol, Doha, Dec. 8, 2012, C.N.718.2012.TREATIES-XXVII.7.c (not yet in force). The amendment requires support from three-quarters of the Protocol's parties to enter into force. So far only nine of the Protocol's 192 parties have ratified the amendment: see UNFCCC, "Doha Amendment," https://unfccc.int/kyoto_protocol/doha_amendment/items/7362.php. Australia, under the Gillard government, was a supporter of the Doha amendment, but with the Abbott government now in power, it is unlikely that Australia will join a second commitment period under the Protocol. See, further, Chapter 3.

[35] Decision 2/CP.15, "Copenhagen Accord," in UNFCCC/CP/2009/11/Add.1 (Mar. 30, 2010), paragraphs 1 and 2.

[36] A significant gap remains between emissions reduction pledges submitted by countries under the Copenhagen Accord and Cancun Agreements that emerged from the 2010 COP and the emissions cuts necessary to meet the 2°C target. See UNEP, *The Emissions Gap Report 2013* (2013, UNEP, Geneva).

2015 on "a protocol, another legal instrument or an agreed outcome with legal force under the Convention applicable to all Parties."[37]

The parties made progress toward that goal in the 2014 negotiations with the Lima Call for Action, but the commitments by all nations to make voluntary commitments likely will still fall substantially short of what scientists say are needed. Even if the Durban Platform negotiations are successful in producing a robust, comprehensive, and universal climate change agreement (i.e., one that would bind all UNFCCC parties, including major emitters outside the Kyoto Protocol, regime such as the United States and China), the agreement would only come into effect from 2020.[38] This timetable is seriously at odds with the information emerging from scientific organizations such as the Intergovernmental Panel on Climate Change (IPCC). In its latest 2014 report, the IPCC stresses that

> continued emissions of greenhouse gases will cause further warming and changes in all components of the climate system. Limiting climate change will require substantial and sustained reductions of greenhouse gas emissions.[39]

Other reports have been more explicit about the urgency of action in the next few years. For instance, in 2011, the Australian Climate Commission warned that 2011 to 2020 is the "critical decade" for turning around rising emissions of greenhouse gases and putting us on the pathway to stabilizing the climate system.[40] Likewise, the United Nations Environment Programme – in its successive Emissions Gap reports since 2010,

---

[37] Decision 1/CP.17, "Establishment of an Ad Hoc Working Group on a Durban Platform for Enhanced Action, 2011," in FCCC/CP/2011/9/Add.1 (Mar. 15, 2012), paragraph 2 (Durban Platform).

[38] Durban Platform, paragraph 2; Lima Call for Action, Decision -/CP.20, Dec. 14, 2014, http://unfccc.int/files/meetings/lima_dec_2014/application/pdf/auv_cop20_lima_call_for_climate_action.pdf; Coral Davenport, "A Climate Accord Based on Global Peer Pressure," *N.Y. Times*, Dec. 14, 2014, http://www.nytimes.com/2014/12/15/world/americas/lima-climate-deal.html?emc=edit_na_20141214&nlid=52930963&_r=0.

[39] IPCC, "Summary for Policymakers" in T. F. Stocker et al. (eds.), *Climate Change 2013: The Physical Science Basis. Contribution of Working Group I to the Fifth Assessment Report of the Intergovernmental Panel on Climate Change* (2013, Cambridge University Press, Cambridge), 19. The IPCC found that to have a greater than 66 percent chance of limiting the warming caused by anthropogenic carbon dioxide emissions to less than 2°C, cumulative emissions from all anthropogenic sources will need to stay below 1 trillion tonnes of carbon. Of this carbon budget, around 531 billion tonnes (over half) was already emitted by 2011. This accords with scientific literature suggesting that to stay within the available carbon budget, less than half the proven oil, gas, and coal reserves can be exploited. See Malte Meinshausen et al., "Greenhouse-Gas Emissions Targets for Limiting Global Warming to 2°C" (2009) 458 *Nature* 1158.

[40] Climate Commission, *The Critical Decade: Science, Risks and Responses* (2011, Australian Government, Canberra).

assessing emissions pathways necessary to give the world a more than even odds chance of staying below the 2°C warming target – has repeatedly emphasized that this will require a peak in global annual emissions before 2020.[41]

The failures of the international climate treaty regime in adequately reducing emissions[42] and improving adaptive capacity[43] have focused attention and hope on regulatory efforts at the subglobal and even sub-national levels, especially in countries that are major carbon emitters.[44] At these federal, state, and local levels, in both countries, litigation clearly has a vital role to play, both as a gap-filler and as a potential catalyst for regulatory action.[45]

1.3.2 Litigation as an element of multidimensional climate governance

Even if a more effective treaty regime were to emerge from current inter-national climate negotiations, it would still struggle to capture the ways in which both mitigation and adaptation require regulatory interactions among public and private stakeholders at individual, local, state, national, and interstitial regional scales. Climate change is a problem that cuts across many levels of governance and types of law, implicates the com-petencies of different agencies, and involves a wide range of public and private actors.[46] For this reason, some have described climate change

---

[41] See, e.g., UNEP, *Emissions Gap Report 2013*.

[42] Emissions are steadily growing, and according to the International Energy Agency, current energy consumption puts the world on track for a long-term global average temperature rise of at least 3.6°C, far in excess of the 2.0°C aim. See International Energy Agency, *World Energy Outlook 2013* (2013, OECD/IEA, Paris).

[43] IPCC Working Group II, *Summary for Policymakers – Final Draft, Climate Change 2014 – Impacts, Adaptation, and Vulnerability* (2014, IPCC, Geneva), describing "a growing adap-tation deficit."

[44] See, e.g., Kirsten H. Engel and Scott R. Saleska, "Subglobal Regulation of the Global Com-mons: The Case of Climate Change" (2005) 32 *Ecol. L. Q.* 183; Ann E. Carlson, "Iterative Federalism and Climate Change" (2009) 103 *Northwestern Univ. L. Rev.* 1097; Daniel Farber, "Carbon Leakage versus Policy Diffusion: The Perils and Promise of Subglobal Climate Action" (2013) 13 *Chicago J. Intl. L.* 359; Hari M. Osofsky, "Suburban Climate Change Efforts: Possibilities for Small and Nimble Cities Participating in State, Regional, National, and International Networks" (2012) 22 *Cornell J. L. Public Policy* 395; Peel et al., "Climate Change Law in an Era of Multi-Level Governance."

[45] Hari M. Osofsky, "The Continuing Importance of Climate Change Litigation" (2010) 1 *Clim. L.* 3.

[46] Hari M. Osofsky and Jacqueline Peel, "Litigation's Regulatory Pathways and the Admin-istrative State: Lessons from U.S. and Australian Climate Change Governance" (2013) 25 *Georgetown Intl. Environ. L. Rev.* 207.

as a "super-wicked" problem – one that is not only enormously complicated but also poses problems of timing, incentives, and massive scope.[47]

An emerging scholarly literature conceptualizes what governance models capable of capturing these complexities might look like.[48] This literature often draws from theories of international law, such as polycentric governance and global legal pluralism, which have an inclusive vision of lawmaking. Such theories treat treaties between nation-states as important but also look to the contributions of a diverse set of actors at multiple levels to climate change governance. These models provide possibilities for valuing the role of litigation in climate change regulation. If a vision of climate change governance views treaties among nation-states as only one piece of a regulatory puzzle, even if the most important one, that opens an inquiry into how other approaches to regulation fit into an overall scheme.

Although scholars and policy makers have devoted significant attention to evolving climate change litigation, especially in the United States, much of the focus has been on the analysis of particularly significant cases on an individual basis[49] or, alternatively, on creating typologies for the case law and quantifying the number of cases in different categories.[50] In these first and second waves of climate litigation scholarship, less attention has been paid to the part courts can play in helping to create and develop

---

[47] Richard Lazarus, "Super Wicked Problems and Climate Change: Restraining the Present to Liberate the Future" (2009) 94 *Cornell L. Rev.* 1153.

[48] See particularly Hari M. Osofsky, "Climate Change Litigation as Pluralist Legal Dialogue" (2007) 26A *Stanford Environ. L. J.* 181, and Ostrom, "A Polycentric Approach."

[49] The *Massachusetts v. EPA* case alone generated a massive number of law review articles, as noted in Elizabeth Fisher, "Climate Change Litigation, Obsession and Expertise: Reflecting on the Scholarly Response to *Massachusetts v. EPA*" (2013) 35(3) *L. Policy* 236. Of the many examples, see, particularly, Jody Freeman and Adrian Vermule, "Massachusetts v EPA: From Politics to Expertise" (2007) *Supreme Court Rev.* 51; Hari M. Osofsky, "The Intersection of Scale, Science, and Law in *Massachusetts v. EPA*" in William C. G. Burns and Hari M. Osofsky (eds.), *Adjudicating Climate Change: State, National, and International Approaches* (2009, Cambridge University Press, New York), 129; Kathryn A. Watts and Amy J. Wildermuth, "*Massachusetts v. EPA*: Breaking New Ground on Issues Other Than Global Warming" (2008) 102 *Nw. Univ. L. Rev.* 1029.

[50] For prominent examples, see Markell and Ruhl, "An Empirical Survey" and "A New Jurisprudence or Business as Usual"; Navraj S. Ghaleigh, "'Six honest serving men': Climate change litigation as legal mobilization and the utility of typologies" (2010) 1 *Clim. L.* 31, and Tim Stephens, "International Courts and Climate Change: Progression, Regression and Administration" in Rosemary Lyster (ed.), *In the Wilds of Climate Change Law* (2010) 53.

regulatory responses to the complex climate change problem.[51] This ever-growing body of cases, however, may serve as a generative source of regulation well suited to the complexity of the problem. It provides a mechanism for fluid, multilevel interests to interact among relatively fixed legal structures situated at different scales.[52] In addition, courts are forums accessible, in the main, to a wider range of actors than are other government institutions.[53] As one interviewee explained, litigation offers the chance of

> actually doing something to try and deal with a massive issue that at an individual level is hard to [do] because the decisions are made by government and internationally that individuals can't influence very much. But two or three, or maybe half a dozen key people can run a really good court case. Half a dozen people can't normally influence national policy or international policy.[54]

This combination of bringing together key stakeholders at multiple levels and of accessibility has made, and likely will continue to make, courts an important place for shaping climate change regulation.

1.3.3 Role of court decisions in shaping smaller-scale decision making

Although the accumulation of greenhouse gases in the atmosphere ultimately causes the climate change problem, many billions of individual

---

[51] We situate the work in this book as part of a new "third wave" of climate litigation scholarship concerned with litigation's regulatory role. We believe that this concept of waves has value in differentiating our work from what has gone before, while acknowledging the important contribution made by previous research to developing our understanding of climate change litigation. These waves represent conceptual rather than chronological development; some third wave scholarship, including articles we have authored, was published several years ago, and some first and second wave scholarship continues to be produced. However, thinking of these types of scholarship as a progression helps to clarify how they fit together.

[52] Hari Osofsky, "Diagonal Federalism and Climate Change: Implications for the Obama Administration" (2011) 62 *Alabama L. Rev.* 237 (arguing that litigation has an important "diagonal quality" that can create intersections between different levels of government and different actors – public and private – concerned with a climate issue).

[53] Nonetheless, climate litigants, like other public interest claimants, face access to justice barriers. These barriers and the extent to which they have been addressed in climate litigation are examined in Chapter 7.

[54] Skype interview, Australian Participant 4 (Mar. 20, 2013). See also David B. Hunter, "The Implications of Climate Change Litigation: Litigation for International Environmental Law-Making" in William C. G. Burns and Hari M. Osofsky (eds.), *Adjudicating Climate Change: State, National, and International Approaches* (2009, Cambridge University Press, New York) 357.

decisions and actions impact global efforts to reduce emissions or adapt to climate change effects. Examples include whether a city's plan opts for denser development and integrated public transport over urban sprawl; whether new coal-fired power plants are allowed to be built or existing ones extended; whether insurers provide policies for homes in areas that could be inundated or are otherwise at risk in the future as a result of sea level rise and climate change; and whether investors and banks decide to invest in fossil fuel assets or alternatives. These are the kinds of decisions that regularly come before local decision makers and that may subsequently be challenged or reviewed in the courts. Courts can play a significant role in shaping individual decisions at this level, both through the direct legal changes their judgments bring about and through the indirect influence they exert over broader social norms and values. Moreover, over time, a series of judicial opinions can aid in providing coherence to policies and decision making through courts' consistent application of legal principles and consolidation of a body of case law.

In sum, climate change litigation matters in overall climate governance because of the significant part it can play, is playing, and is likely to play in shaping decision making and the regulatory landscape relating to climate change across various levels of governance. Its impact to date has been felt most prominently at the national, subnational, and local levels. Given the failures of top-down, international models of climate change governance in recent years, it is likely that regulatory action at these levels will continue to make a critical contribution in addressing the larger, globalized problem of climate change.

1.4   Climate litigation and regulatory pathways in the United States and Australia

Climate change litigation has been initiated in many countries around the world, including Argentina, Australia, Canada, the Czech Republic, France, Germany, Greece, India, Israel, Japan, New Zealand, Nigeria, Poland, Spain, Ukraine, the United Kingdom, Uruguay, and, most prominently, the United States.[55] In the book, we focus on the United States

---

[55] This listing is based on records of climate change cases in Richard Lord et al. (eds.), *Climate Change Liability: Transnational Law and Practice* (2011, Cambridge University Press, Cambridge), Arnold and Porter LLP, "U.S. Climate Change Litigation Chart" and "Non-U.S. Climate Change Litigation Chart," available at www.climatecasechart.com,

and Australia as two national case studies of the ways in which litigation shapes climate regulatory pathways.

The United States as a central case study in investigating the regulatory role of litigation is an obvious choice. The United States has been, and remains, the epicenter of the climate change litigation phenomenon. As we discuss further in Chapter 3, the country's uneven regulatory response to climate change, including its failure to ratify the Kyoto Protocol and to enact comprehensive national climate legislation, has been a major driver of climate change litigation in the United States. The United States also has a far more litigious culture compared to other nations, as the opening quotation for this chapter highlights.[56]

Litigation has played a key role in shaping the US regulatory response to climate change at multiple levels. Most significantly, as discussed further in Chapter 3, the Obama administration has justified Clean Air Act

and Climate Justice Programme, "Cases," www.climatelaw.org/cases. In common law countries, half a dozen cases each have been brought in Canada and New Zealand. Several Canadian cases have focused on the necessity of considering greenhouse gas emissions and climate change impacts in development, including fossil fuel extraction and power generation projects. Other cases have sought to question Canada's compliance with duties under legislation implementing the Kyoto Protocol and the decision of the Canadian government in 2011 to withdraw from the Protocol. Lisa Vanhala, "The Comparative Politics of Courts and Climate Change" (2013) 22(3) *Environ. Politics* 447. The New Zealand cases raising climate change issues have done so in challenges to power stations and in defence of renewable energy wind farm projects. Greenpeace Briefing, "History of Climate Change Litigation," New Zealand, June 2007. For its part, the United Kingdom has seen more than twenty cases, with many likewise involving wind farm proposals. Other UK climate change cases have concerned the adequacy of government decision making on proposals with significant, associated greenhouse gas emissions (e.g., airport expansions), contractual claims relating to carbon trading, the compatibility of investment decisions by Treasury with the United Kingdom's climate change commitments, and "reactive" litigation where climate change activists are prosecuted for their involvement in allegedly unlawful direct action. Hilson, "Climate Change Litigation in the U.K." Climate change litigation at the European Union level has mainly focused on the operation of the EU emissions trading scheme. These actions have been brought by the private sector, or member states lobbied by the private sector, seeking to protect economic interests. Sanja Bogojević, "EU Climate Change Litigation, the Role of the European Courts and the Importance of Legal Culture" (2013) 35(3) *L. Policy* 184. There have also been a handful of cases brought at the international level as petitions to human rights bodies (e.g., the petitions to the Inter-American Commission on Human Rights by the Inuit and on black carbon emissions from Canada) and the World Heritage Committee (with the latter seeking "in danger" listings for world heritage sites imperiled by climate change), as well as noncompliance actions under the Kyoto Protocol and disputes over renewable energy subsidies before the World Trade Organization.

[56] In-person interview, US Participant (Nov. 14, 2012).

regulation of motor vehicle and power plant emissions as flowing from the US Supreme Court's decision in *Massachusetts v. EPA*. However, the diversity of the several hundred legal claims that have been brought, by both pro- and antiregulatory claimants, illustrates the many different pathways by which litigation can impact regulation, and their relative strengths and weaknesses.

Australia, to some, might seem a less obvious choice as a focus for comparative study of the regulatory role of climate change litigation. In contrast to the massive greenhouse gas emissions of the United States, Australia is a small nation of 23 million people whose domestic emissions make a relatively modest contribution to global greenhouse gas pollution.[57] However, the country is second only to the United States in the number of decided climate cases and so also offers considerable data for analysis. Indeed, taken on a per capita basis, Australia has seen the most climate change cases brought.[58]

More importantly, Australia is a major player in the global carbon economy as a result of its substantial fossil fuel reserves. For instance, the country is the world's second largest coal exporter, with the majority of this coal supplying the Asian market in China and India.[59] The local decisions made in Australia about coal projects thus have significance for the development of cleaner energy beyond its shores. In addition to its significant mitigation litigation, Australia has the most well-developed adaptation litigation in the world. It thus provides a useful model for the United States and other countries for how lawsuits might influence evolving systems of adaptation regulation.

The following sections outline key details about the climate change litigation that has been brought in the United States and Australia. They then address why these two countries are good comparators. As explored in more depth subsequently, important similarities in their legal systems and domestic climate change politics allow for an especially fruitful comparative analysis of litigation's regulatory influence.

---

[57] As discussed in Chapter 3, Australia's domestic emissions account for 1.2 percent of the global total. This figure, however, does not take into account exported emissions associated with Australian coal and other fossil fuels shipped overseas.

[58] The relative ratio in Australia is around 1 case per 300,000 people compared with 1 case per 600,000 people in the United States. Our study thus encompasses the country with the highest absolute number of climate change cases and the country with the highest per capita number of cases. We are grateful to Michael Findlay (Jacqueline Peel's husband) for identifying this important point.

[59] Australia's "carbon economy" is discussed further in Chapters 3 and 5.

1.4.1 Climate change litigation in the United States

Climate change cases filed in US courts currently number more than five hundred.[60] The earliest US climate change case was *City of Los Angeles v. National Highway Transportation Safety Administration* (NHTSA), decided by the DC Circuit Court of Appeals in 1990.[61] That litigation involved a challenge by cities, states, and environmental groups to the failure of the NHTSA to prepare an environmental impact statement under the National Environmental Policy Act (NEPA) considering the adverse climatic effects of lowering fuel economy standards for motor vehicles. Although the petitioners were unsuccessful in their argument before the DC Circuit, the case has served as a "prototype" for the vast majority of US climate change litigation brought subsequently.[62] This litigation gained steam around 2006 – the year when the US Supreme Court heard oral argument in *Massachusetts v. EPA* – and has grown exponentially since then.[63] Because the United States has failed to pass comprehensive climate change legislation, and has no prospects of doing so in the near future, litigation has played a particularly important role in its regulatory approach to climate change.

US litigants have used a wide variety of legal avenues in pursuing climate change–related claims. Charts prepared by Professor Michael Gerrard's Center for Climate Change Law at Columbia University detail the numerous statutory and common law claims that have been brought in state and federal courts raising climate change issues.[64] Suits have been brought, for example, to attempt to force or prevent federal and state governmental regulation of greenhouse gas emissions under environmental statutes, to require consideration of climate change in the review of power plant projects, and to portray climate change as a public nuisance. Although much of the US climate change litigation started out as progressive action designed to force or spur regulatory reform by governments or behavioral

---

[60] Arnold and Porter LLP, "Types of Climate Cases Filed" (Oct. 3, 2012), at www.climatecasechart.com/. See also Arnold and Porter LLP, "Climate Chart Case Index," at www.climatecasechart.com. This case index divides up cases as active (310 claims), inactive or resolved (78 claims), or unknown (251 claims) (figures as of May 15, 2014).

[61] 912 F.2d 478 (D.C. Cir. 1990).

[62] Markell and Ruhl, "An Empirical Assessment," 10649: ("Based on sheer number of cases, the prototype of climate change litigation in the United States involves an environmental NGO suing a federal agency in federal court to prevent the agency from taking action by alleging that the agency violated NEPA.")

[63] Markell and Ruhl, "An Empirical Assessment," 10647.

[64] Arnold and Porter LLP, "U.S. Climate Change Litigation Chart."

change by polluters, an increasingly substantial body of antiregulatory cases seeking to delay, limit, or invalidate climate regulatory actions by different levels of government has emerged over the last few years.[65]

Both pro- and antiregulatory climate change litigation in the United States has been predominantly directed at issues of mitigation, with a particular focus on stopping coal-fired power and tightening regulatory requirements applicable to fossil fuel energy sources.[66] As we discuss further in Chapter 4, adaptation concerns – such as the management of coastal climate hazards and planning for weather-related disasters – are also beginning to emerge in the US case law, although this adaptation-specific litigation is far less developed in the United States than it is in Australia. A smaller number of US climate lawsuits have sought to regulate private conduct (e.g., by requiring corporate disclosure of climate change–related risks to assets and investments) and to defend (or attack) protestors or scientists who advocate action to address climate change.

1.4.2   Climate change litigation in Australia

The United States has not been alone in experiencing a surge in climate change litigation since the mid 2000s. Besides the United States, the other country that stands out as having experienced a significant amount of climate change litigation is Australia. Our database of Australian climate change litigation compiled in the research contains more than sixty cases, which is more than double the number of climate-related lawsuits in larger common law countries, such as the United Kingdom.[67]

Like in the United States, climate change litigation in Australia first surfaced in the 1990s. In 1994, Greenpeace Australia challenged a development consent issued for the Redbank Power Station in New South Wales on the basis of the plant's greenhouse gas emissions and its "contribution to the human enhanced greenhouse effect."[68] Justice Pearlman of

---

[65] This antiregulatory litigation is discussed further in Chapter 7.

[66] Michael B. Gerrard, "Coal-Fired Power Plants Dominate Climate Change Litigation" (2009) 242(61) *N.Y. L. J.* 25.

[67] Peel, "Australian Climate Change Litigation." See also Arnold and Porter LLP, "Non-US Climate Change Litigation Chart."

[68] *Greenpeace v. Redbank Power Company* (1994) 86 LGERA 143; see also Tim Bonyhady, "The New Australian Climate Law" in Tim Bonyhady and Peter Christoff (eds.), *Climate Law in Australia* (2007, Federation Press, Sydney) 8, 11–13. The Redbank project was not a traditional coal-fired power station as it was proposed to be fueled by coal washery tailings. Hence the environmental benefits of reducing coal mining waste were an important consideration in the case.

the New South Wales Land and Environment Court – a state-level, specialist environmental court – recognized the national and international concern over climate change. However, Her Honor ultimately ruled that whether individual power stations should be prohibited as a result was "a matter of government policy" and not for the court to decide.[69]

Although unsuccessful, the Redbank Power Station case provided a model for much of the Australian climate change litigation that followed. As in the United States, a significant proportion of Australian climate change cases have focused on greenhouse gas–intensive energy sources, with challenges to coal-fired power and coal mining proposals. Australia's rejection of the Kyoto Protocol during the ten-year tenure of the Howard federal government (1997–2007), coupled with resistance to mandatory national regulation to reduce domestic greenhouse gas emissions over that period, provided drivers for Australian climate change litigation similar to those in the United States.[70]

Like the United States, Australia has also had litigation addressing adaptation issues.[71] Compared with the adaptation lawsuits in the United States, which have only emerged in the past few years, Australia has a far more developed adaptation jurisprudence, which has significantly shaped government policies and the behavior of actors in the land use and development sector.[72] It is likely that Australia's experience of early climate change effects over the past decade – including severe droughts, wildfires, floods, and intense storms – has been a factor precipitating this earlier consideration of adaptation issues in its courts.

Under the administration of the Rudd and Gillard Labor federal governments (2007–13), Australia's climate regulatory path diverged from that of the United States. The Rudd government ratified the Kyoto Protocol in 2007, and in 2011, the Gillard government passed legislation – the Clean Energy Act – to introduce a national carbon pricing mechanism

---

[69] *Greenpeace v. Redbank Power Company* (1994) 86 LGERA 143, 153.
[70] Jacqueline Peel, "The Role of Climate Change Litigation in Australia's Response to Global Warming" (2007) 24 *Environmental & Planning Law Journal* 90.
[71] Brian J. Preston, "The Role of the Courts in Relation to Adaptation to Climate Change" in *Adaptation to Climate Change: Law and Policy* (2010, Federation Press, Sydney). Several of the international climate change actions brought to date, such as the petitions submitted to the Inter-American Commission on Human Rights and the World Heritage Committee, have a similar focus on the impacts of climate change for sensitive communities and ecosystems. It is noteworthy that such cases have particularly targeted the United States and Australia.
[72] Jacqueline Peel and Hari M. Osofsky, "Sue to Adapt?" 2015 *Minn. L. Rev.* (forthcoming).

regulating major greenhouse gas emitters.[73] The introduction of this legislation might have seen Australia's climate change litigation develop in
a significantly different direction from that of the United States, with a
greater focus on enforcement of the statutory regime. However, the Clean
Energy Act, and the carbon pricing mechanism it established, proved to
be short-lived. Australian's current government, led by Prime Minister
Tony Abbott, has repealed the Clean Energy Act and is seeking to do
away with other clean energy institutions.[74] Australia is thus once again
facing a similar climate regulatory landscape to the United States – or,
arguably, a worse one, given the Obama administration's substantial regulation of greenhouse gas emissions under federal environmental statutes –
with limited short-term prospects for comprehensive national climate
legislation.

1.4.3 How the United States and Australia compare

In terms of the clean energy and adaptation challenges they face, and
the use of litigation to address those challenges, the United States and
Australia share the most commonalities of any developed countries.[75]
On the mitigation side, the United States and Australia have faced many
similar policy and political challenges. As we discuss further in Chapter 3,
both have energy, industrial, and transportation sectors that are heavily
dependent on coal and other fossil fuels, and consequently, the two countries are among the world's highest per capita emitters. Coal and other
fossil fuel companies based in the United States and Australia have been
active in opposing climate regulation at both the domestic and international levels, though this opposition has not been uniform. Responses

---

[73] Clean Energy Act 2011 (Cth). On the nature of the carbon pricing mechanism, see
further Lisa Caripis et al., "Australia's Carbon Pricing Mechanism" (2011) 2(4) *Clim. L.*
1; Jacqueline Peel, "The Australian Carbon Pricing Mechanism: Promise and Pitfalls on
the Pathway to a Clean Energy Future" (2014) 15(1) *Minn. J. L. Sci. Technol.* 429.

[74] Clean Energy Legislation (Carbon Tax Repeal) Act 2014 (Cth). Ongoing negotiations
between the government and senators who hold the balance of power suggest other
legislation designed to dismantle clean energy institutions such as the Climate Change
Authority or the Clean Energy Finance Corporation may be blocked in the Senate. For
details of the government's "Carbon Tax Repeal" legislation and other associated legislation, see Australian Government, Department of the Environment, "Repealing the Carbon
Tax," at www.environment.gov.au/climate-change/repealing-carbon-tax.

[75] Canada is another similarly placed country, but its climate litigation has been far more limited than the litigation of either the United States or Australia. Vanhala, "The Comparative
Politics of Courts and Climate Change."

to climate change have varied across sectors of the energy industry and among different companies within each sector, as explored in Chapter 5. Each country also has experienced a recent boom in fossil fuel exploration and exploitation, especially with respect to the oil and gas that fracking and deepwater drilling have opened up, and the two nations are major contributors to coal exports that fuel greenhouse gas emissions in other parts of the world.

Both the United States and Australia also face similar, albeit not identical, challenges in adapting to climate change impacts. Their substantial coastlines, containing their most politically and financially important cities, paired with susceptibility to drought, flood, fire, and severe storms, could place them among the developed countries most vulnerable to the effects of rising seas and a changing climate.[76] In both countries, greater awareness of the impacts of climate change and the need for adaptation measures has been heightened by an increasing frequency and severity of extreme weather events in recent years.[77] In response, governments are beginning to engage more earnestly with issues of coastal hazard management, disaster planning, and improving the resilience of cities, agriculture, and infrastructure.[78]

Parallels between the social and environmental contexts of the United States and Australia with respect to climate change policy and litigation patterns are supplemented by similar governance and legal traditions. Each country's legal system rests on a common law foundation. This is overlaid with a federal structure anchored in a national constitution prescribing the powers and functions of the federal government. Both countries have a multi-tiered system of federal and state courts as well as a tradition of judges shaping the content of the law through their decisions within the framework of a separation of powers among the judicial and other government branches. In comparative method terms, this constellation of similarities means that the United States and Australia conform to what is known as the "most similar cases" logic.[79] Accordingly,

[76] IPCC Working Group II, *Summary for Policymakers – Final Draft, Climate Change 2014 – Impacts, Adaptation, and Vulnerability* (2014, IPCC, Geneva).

[77] Notable events in the United States include Hurricane Katrina, Superstorm Sandy, and the 2013–14 Midwest and Californian droughts. In Australia, standout events include the Millennium Drought, the Black Saturday Bushfires, and the Queensland 2010–11 floods.

[78] Government responses to adaptation issues in the United States and Australia are discussed further in Chapter 4.

[79] Ran Hirschl, "The Question of Case Selection in Comparative Constitutional Law" (2005) 53 *Am. J. Comp. L.* 125; Ran Hirschl, "On the Blurred Methodological Matrix of Comparative Constitutional Law" in Sujit Choudhry (ed.), *The Migration of Constitutional Ideas*

comparison of the climate change litigation–regulatory linkages in these two jurisdictions opens up opportunities for testing explanations of the broader regulatory impact of climate change case law. It can assist in identifying those pathways that are the most well traveled in the case law, those that are emerging, and those pathways that – based on the experience of litigants in the two countries – are likely to encounter significant roadblocks that will ultimately reduce their effectiveness.[80]

At the same time, differences in litigation patterns and regulatory pathways in the United States and Australia can help predict future trajectories of climate change litigation. These two countries' comparative experiences can also provide lessons, positive or cautionary, for each other and for countries around the world. For example, as adaptation case law continues to develop in the United States, petitioners potentially have much to learn from the Australian experience, as we discuss in Chapter 4. Both successful and unsuccessful cases can help litigators develop future approaches. Cases that fail in their direct goals may provide a learning opportunity. Australian nongovernmental organizations might consider (and some are actively doing so) mounting a US-style tort claim against fossil fuel industries if they think they can avoid the pitfalls that have befallen US cases pursuing this pathway. Likewise, investor groups in both countries may look to the successes and failures of each other's efforts in using litigation to promote greater corporate disclosure around issues of climate investment risk.

A comparative examination of regulatory pathways through climate change litigation provides a window into the benefits and limitations of courts as sites for advancing regulation and accompanying social and behavioral change. Commentators discussing climate change litigation often embrace courts rather uncritically as forums for progressive climate action. The case examples and interview data presented in this book provide substantial evidence for this belief, pointing to the many ways that courts can be flexible, deliberative, and participatory sites for discussions of climate change science, policy, and regulation. In a number of instances, court decisions have led directly to climate change regulation that might not otherwise have emerged from legislative and executive processes. Moreover, the authority and respect accorded to court

---

(2011, Cambridge University Press, Cambridge), 39, 48–51; Mathias Siems, *Comparative Law* (2014, Cambridge University Press, Cambridge), 288–92.

[80] Jacqueline Peel and Hari M. Osofsky, "Climate Change Litigation's Regulatory Pathways: A Comparative Analysis of the United States and Australia" (2013) 35(3) *L. Policy* 150.

decisions in societies like the United States and Australia, whose legal systems are underpinned by rule-of-law principles, have allowed claimants to use litigation in a variety of ways to change the regulatory environment for addressing climate change.

However, the case law and interviews also reinforce that efforts to use litigation as a regulatory tool do not uniformly yield positive outcomes. Not only can litigation be deployed in an antiregulatory manner to delay, frustrate, or invalidate governmental initiatives but litigants bringing climate change cases can also face problems of courts' information deficits (e.g., regarding climate science), access barriers such as separation-of-powers doctrines and costs, and complex positionality with respect to policy consequences. Such barriers, which we discuss further in Chapter 7, help to shape and constrain the regulatory influence of these cases.

A key finding that emerges from this book's comparative analysis is that the type of court hearing the claim itself exercises a strong influence over the kinds of claims brought and the regulatory pathways that flow from this litigation. For instance, the availability of specialist environmental and planning courts at the state level in Australia – where the majority of the country's climate cases have been decided – has shaped the types of lawsuits litigated, the way climate science is received, and the extent of the case law's regulatory impact. In the United States, the lack of such courts and the focus of the litigation on interpreting the extent of mandates for climate regulation under existing, broadly framed environmental laws have generated a different set of litigation-regulatory dynamics. These include a greater diversity in the causes of action pursued, a more complex interaction between courts and climate science, greater attention to separation-of-powers concerns, and a stronger emphasis on antiregulatory litigation as industry groups seek to undo statutory mandates under environmental laws found in previous cases.

1.5 Outline of the book

In this book, we tell the story of climate change litigation and its regulatory impact through the lens of the case law that has arisen in the United States and Australia. Each chapter draws on doctrinal materials and insights from interviewees to elaborate different facets of the regulatory significance of climate change litigation.

Chapter 2 presents the model we have developed for understanding the ways in which climate change litigation can serve as a pathway for achieving regulatory outcomes regarding climate change. This model distinguishes between the direct and indirect impacts of litigation on regulation. Direct effects of the case law flow from its capacity to produce legal change through the interpretation of constitutional provisions, statutory mandates and requirements, or common law doctrines. Indirect effects arise, not from climate change decisions themselves, but as a result of the motivations cases provide for different choices around mitigation or adaptation. We focus on two types of indirect effects that seem most critical to making progress on climate change: alterations in corporate behavior and social norms. The chapter illustrates these direct and indirect pathways with examples drawn from US and Australian climate change case law.

Chapters 3 and 4 consider how climate change litigation influences regulatory efforts to mitigate and adapt. In Chapter 3, we discuss the substantial impact of litigation on greenhouse gas regulation in the United States and, to a lesser extent, in Australia. In Chapter 4, the narrative is reversed: we relate the development of adaptation litigation in Australia and consider what lessons this case law offers for the United States as adaptation lawsuits begin to emerge there too.

Whereas Chapters 3 and 4 are primarily concerned with government responses to climate change litigation and direct regulatory change, Chapters 5 and 6 focus on impacts on other actors. Chapter 5 examines corporate responses to climate change, canvassing the reaction of companies in the energy, land use, insurance, financial, and professional advising sectors to ongoing litigation and future litigation risk. Chapter 6 looks at how climate change litigation has influenced public attitudes, social norms, and values around climate change. The chapter also examines the ways in which public debates over climate change science and appropriate regulation play out in courts.

As we have already noted, although climate change litigation originally began as an effort by progressive actors to advance regulatory goals using the courts, litigation can equally be used as a tool by antiregulatory interests. Antiregulatory litigation has expanded significantly in the United States in reaction to efforts by the federal Environmental Protection Agency (EPA) to regulate greenhouse gas emissions from motor vehicles and power plants in line with the Clean Air Act authority found by the US Supreme Court in *Massachusetts v. EPA*. Progressive state climate change regulation, such as actions taken by California agencies under AB32, the Global Warming Solutions Act, has also attracted a number of lawsuits. Antiregulatory litigation has not been as prominent in Australia, notwithstanding the introduction (and demise) of national climate change legislation. However, climate change litigation is clearly producing some antiregulatory reactions as conservative governments move to over-turn proactive case outcomes via legislation or to limit avenues for chal-lenging government decisions approving fossil fuel projects. In Chapter 7, we assess these antiregulatory trends in conjunction with other potential barriers to climate change cases achieving pro-regulatory impact, such as costs and separation-of-powers issues expressed in doctrines of standing, political question, and displacement.

Chapter 8 evaluates the overall impact of climate change litigation in promoting regulation and discusses the potential future of the litigation in the United States and Australia – and elsewhere. We draw on insights provided by our interviewees to track the likely future directions in which the litigation may evolve. The chapter concludes with reflections on the roles that climate change litigation might play as regulatory strategies for mitigation and adaptation continue to develop. It is clear that, both now and in the future, litigation is not a panacea for addressing the climate change problem. But unlike many other regulatory efforts focused on distant milestones, climate change litigation has the distinct advantage of responding to the urgency of now in choosing our energy and climate future.

2

Model for understanding litigation's regulatory impact

> We always view litigation as *a* tool and not *the* tool. And the value of litigation often extends beyond the legal victory that you can secure. Sometimes litigation is a great organizing tool. Sometimes litigation is a great public relations tool.
>
> – US Interview Participant 10

> When Christopher Stone said in his article about "Should Trees Have Standing?," and he said in the article that some ideas are *frightening* when they're first raised. But as you talk about it, and analyze it and show some of that, the shock of the new disappears. That's where I think it is important that there be discussion of [climate change] issues and particularly in judgments because then some of the shock of the new disappears and it does become more accepted.
>
> – Australian Interview Participant 7

2.1   Introduction

The goal of this book is not simply to track an expanding area of litigation. Although these cases are quite interesting from a doctrinal perspective – sometimes breaking new ground in the way in which they frame legal issues – the book is primarily interested in this litigation as part of multilevel climate change governance. Lawsuits attempting to force climate action often aim to influence law and policy, change corporate behavior, or focus public attention;[1] this book explores whether they actually do so. Has the use of the courts to raise climate change issues been effective in producing responses by governments, corporations, community actors, and others that will improve outcomes on mitigation and adaptation? What is the evidence that would allow us to

---

[1] In-person interview, US Participant 6 (Nov. 14, 2012).

28

"connec[t] the dots" between climate change litigation and regulatory responses?[2]

As the international treaty regime continues to fail to obtain binding nation-state commitments adequate to prevent serious risks of impacts, the current and potential role of courts in forcing and limiting climate action is an important piece of the overall regulatory puzzle. Understanding the ways in which litigation serves as regulation, mandates regulation, and fosters regulation – as well the limits to it doing so – helps to provide a more complete view of how litigation has, is, and could help to produce more effective approaches to mitigation and adaptation. Both successful cases and "ostensibly unsuccessful" cases, brought at times by those who want to strengthen regulation, and at times by those who want to challenge or weaken it, can transform or tweak the regulatory landscape.[3]

This chapter presents a conceptual framework for the book's exploration of these issues. It begins with a discussion of how litigation – conventionally viewed as a tool of law enforcement – may also serve as a regulatory tool, including an explanation of what we mean by "regulation" in this context. The chapter then presents our model for understanding the pathways that litigation provides for shaping climate change regulation. This model focuses not only on the direct ways in which litigation leads to regulation – a relatively straightforward doctrinal inquiry – but also the indirect ways in which it influences the behavior of key stakeholders.[4] The rest of the book builds on this chapter's model to explore the various direct and indirect impacts of climate change litigation on mitigation and adaptation behaviors and choices.

2.2 Litigation as a regulatory tool

This section provides conceptual groundwork for the rest of the chapter by analyzing what it means to treat litigation as a regulatory tool in this context. It considers the ways in which advocates use litigation in the

---

[2] David Markell and J.B. Ruhl, "An Empirical Assessment of Climate Change in the Courts: A New Jurisprudence or Business as Usual" (2012) 64 *Fla. L. Rev.* 15, 83.

[3] Brian J. Preston, "The Influence of Climate Change Litigation on Governments and the Private Sector" (2011) 2 *Clim. L.* 485.

[4] This categorization of direct and indirect impacts from climate change litigation draws from previous scholarship; see Jolene Lin, "Climate Change and the Courts" (2012) 32(1) *Legal Stud.* 35; Hari M. Osofsky, "The Continuing Importance of Climate Change Litigation" (2010) 1 *Clim. L.* 3. In the book, this categorization is extended by elaborating different pathways for litigation's direct/indirect regulatory influence and by exploring specific case examples.

United States and Australia to try to force and limit climate action. It then examines the complexity of assessing litigation's regulatory impact.

2.2.1 Proactive and antiregulatory litigation

Litigants in common law countries primarily use courts to interpret and enforce laws rather than to develop regulation. However, both the United States and Australia have traditions of activists using lawsuits to try to influence the shape of the law and regulation in addition to assisting their clients in a particular case.[5] Governmental and nongovernmental actors seeking greater or lesser regulation may use lawsuits to clarify an agency's regulatory authority under a statute, to change how an agency exercises that authority, or to enforce that authority. In a climate change context, litigation has also been used in a strategic fashion as a response to inadequate lawmaking activity by government in an effort to prompt wider policy change.[6]

In both the United States and Australia, coal has been a core focus of such strategic litigation efforts. In Australia, for example, a leaked Greenpeace campaign document revealed plans for the extensive use of legal challenges to coal mining projects as part of a wider strategy of "stopping the Australian coal export boom."[7] The document describes several benefits from proactive litigation:

> Legal challenges can stop projects outright, or can delay them in order to buy time to build a much stronger movement and powerful public campaigns. They can also expose the impacts, increase costs, raise investor uncertainty, and create a powerful platform for public campaigning.[8]

Similar campaigns operate in the United States targeting coal-fired power stations and seeking to "quit coal" in favor of clean energy sources.[9]

---

[5] This strategy, which takes many forms, is at times referred to in the United States as "impact litigation." For a discussion of different impact litigation strategies, arguing for the value of large numbers of small claims in addition to class action approaches, see Andrew D. Freeman and Juli E. Farris, "Grassroots Impact Litigation: Mass Filing of Small Claims" (1992) 26 *U.S.F. L. Rev.* 261.

[6] Jacqueline Peel, "The Role of Climate Change Litigation in Australia's Response to Global Warming" (2007) 24 *Environ. Planning L. J.* 90.

[7] John Hepburn, Bob Burton, and Sam Hardy, *Stopping the Australian Coal Export Boom: Funding Proposal for the Australian Anti-Coal Movement*, Greenpeace, Nov. 2011, available at www.abc.net.au/mediawatch/transcripts/1206_greenpeace.pdf.

[8] Hepburn et al., *Stopping the Australian Coal Export Boom*, 6.

[9] See, e.g., Quit Coal (http://quitcoal.org/), Coalswarm (http://coalswarm.org/), Beyond Coal (http://content.sierraclub.org/coal/).

Although litigation is by no means the only mechanism available for social mobilization and activism on climate change,[10] litigation is unique in being able to harness the apparatus of the state (i.e., courts as the third branch of government) to achieve regulatory change. As one interviewee commented, "in a way climate change litigation is much more radical than traditional activism because you're trying to challenge the establishment through the processes of the establishment."[11]

Professor Navraj Ghaleigh, in his typology of climate change litigation, describes litigation of this kind – that seeks to "promote positive environmental outcomes by way of regulatory intervention sanctioned or even required by the courts" – as "promotive."[12] In reaction to "promotive" or proactive climate change litigation and regulation resulting from it, as well as regulatory initiatives by state and local governments, a body of "antiregulatory" lawsuits has developed, particularly in the United States.[13]

Both promotive and antiregulatory climate change lawsuits involve many diverse actors, including subnational governments, not-for-profit environmental groups, corporations, business organizations, community groups, and individuals. Climate change cases thus can function as a forum for diverse actors to engage in a dialogue about the appropriateness of particular regulation. As discussed in Chapter 6, the disagreements often have scalar dimensions, with antiregulatory parties arguing that

---

[10] For discussion of the range of social mobilization mechanisms used to address climate issues, see Mark Diesendorf, *Climate Action: A Campaign Manual for Greenhouse Solutions* (2009, UNSW Press, Sydney).

[11] In-person interview, Australian Participant 3 (Mar. 8, 2013).

[12] Navraj S. Ghaleigh, "'Six Honest Serving Men': Climate Change Litigation as Legal Mobilization and the Utility of Typologies" (2010) 1 *Clim. L.* 31, 45. Ghaleigh identifies three further categories: defensive (or antiregulatory), boundary testing (concerned with challenging the limits of an existing regulatory regime for climate change), and perfecting (seeking improvements in an existing regulatory regime for climate change). See also Chris Hilson, "Climate Change Litigation in the UK: An Explanatory Approach (or Bringing Grievance Back In)" in F. Fracchia and M. Occhiena (eds.), *Climate Change: La Riposta del Diritto* (2010, Editoriale Scientifica, Naples), 421, discussing "proactive" versus "reactive" litigation, where the latter involves criminal proceedings brought against climate change activists involved in alleged unlawful direct action.

[13] Markell and Ruhl, "A New Jurisprudence or Business as Usual," 65–70. Ghaleigh labels this category "defensive" in that "it defends the status quo of a regulatory vacuum." Ghaleigh, "Six Honest Serving Men," 44. We prefer Markell and Ruhl's term "antiregulatory" as the goal of these lawsuits is more clearly to delay or dismantle existing or emerging regulatory measures for climate change.

climate change is too big a problem for regulation at a particular level and pro-regulatory parties demonstrating state and local impacts.[14]

Moreover, the issues that courts are asked to address in climate change cases, although framed in the context of specific legal requirements and factual settings, often reflect common themes.[15] These include questions around what amounts to a significant or meaningful contribution to global climate change; what level and type of evidence is needed to establish such a contribution; and whether impacts should be assessed in a cumulative, holistic fashion or on a project-by-project basis. The rulings issued by courts in climate change cases, across various jurisdictions and at different levels of governance, can therefore be seen to play an important role in articulating forms of "transnational climate change regulation."[16]

2.2.2   Regulatory impact

In evaluating the direct and indirect ways in which litigation contributes to mitigation and adaptation outcomes, the diverse goals of those bringing climate change litigation point to the need for a broad understanding of its regulatory impact. At its narrowest, "regulation" connotes rules developed by government departments or independent agencies to implement a legislative mandate.[17] Although we certainly see such rulemaking as a form of regulation, our analysis throughout this book is grounded in a sociolegal tradition that treats a wide range of formal and informal action by diverse actors as "regulatory" and as part of an overall governance process. This tradition takes a variety of forms across the relevant scholarly literature – such as legal pluralism,[18] polycentric

---

[14] Hari M. Osofsky, "Is Climate Change 'International'? Litigation's Diagonal Regulatory Role" (2009) 49(3) *Va. J. Intl. L.* 585. The role of litigation in scalar dialogue on climate change science and regulation is considered further in Chapter 6.

[15] Jacqueline Peel, "Issues in Climate Change Litigation" (2011) 5(1) *Carbon Clim. L. Rev.* 15.

[16] Osofsky, "Continuing Importance of Climate Change Litigation," 27.

[17] Bronwen Morgan and Karen Yeung, *An Introduction to Law and Regulation: Text and Materials* (2007, Cambridge University Press, Cambridge).

[18] Global legal pluralism treats multiple normative, and sometimes legal, communities as operating in a shared social space and considers the implications of having simultaneous valid orders. For examples of this scholarship, see Robert B. Ahdieh, "Dialectical Regulation" (2006) 38 *Conn. L. Rev.* 863; Diane Marie Amann, "Abu Ghraib" (2005) 153 *U. Pa. L. Rev.* 2085; Diane Marie Amann, "Calling Children to Account: The Proposal for a Juvenile Chamber in the Special Court for Sierra Leone" (2001) 29 *Pepp. L. Rev.* 167; Elena A. Baylis, "Parallel Courts in Post-Conflict Kosovo" (2007) 32 *Yale J. Intl. L.* 1; Paul

governance,[19] new governance,[20] and regulatory institutions theory,[21] just to name a few. In line with these approaches, regulation can be broadly conceived as "the intentional activity of attempting to control, order or influence the behaviour of others."[22] On this basis, regulatory impacts may manifest as the introduction of targeted rules, policies, or decision-making procedures but equally may encompass situations where climate change litigation "influence[es] the flow of events."[23] The actors involved in regulatory activity linked to a climate change case or cases are often governments or their agencies located at the same level

Schiff Berman, "Global Legal Pluralism" (2007) 80 *S. Cal. L. Rev.* 1155; William W. Burke-White, "International Legal Pluralism" (2004) 25 *Mich. J. Intl. L.* 963; Janet Koven Levit, "A Bottom-Up Approach to International Lawmaking: The Tale of Three Trade Finance Instruments" (2005) 30 *Yale J. Intl L.* 125; Ralf Michaels, "The Re-State-Ment of Non-State Law: The State, Choice of Law, and the Challenge from Global Legal Pluralism" (2005) 51 *Wayne L. Rev.* 1209. Hari Osofsky has explored a legal pluralist view of climate change litigation in Hari M. Osofsky, "Climate Change Litigation as Pluralist Legal Dialogue?" (2007) 26A *Stanford Environ. L. J.* 181. Similarly, the New Haven School views law as "a process of authoritative decision by which the members of a community clarify and secure their common interests": Harold D. Lasswell and Myres S. McDougal, *Jurisprudence for a Free Society: Studies in Law, Science and Policy* (Martinus Nijhoff, Dordrecht, 1992), xxi.

[19] Daniel H. Cole, "From Global to Polycentric Climate Governance" (EUI Working Paper No. 2011/30, 2011), available at http://cadmus.eui.eu/bitstream/handle/1814/17757/RSCAS_2011_30.pdf; Elinor Ostrom, *A Polycentric Approach for Coping with Climate Change* (World Bank Research Working Paper No. 5095, 2009).

[20] For examples of new governance scholarship, see Gráinne de Búrca and Joanne Scott (eds.), *Law and Governance in the EU and US* (Hart Publishing, London, 2006); Bradley C. Karkkainen, Reply, "'New Governance' in Legal Thought and in the World: Some Splitting as Antidote to Overzealous Lumping" (2004) 89 *Minn. L. Rev.* 471; Orly Lobel, Surreply, "Setting the Agenda for New Governance Research" (2004) 89 *Minn. L. Rev.* 498; Orly Lobel, "The Renew Deal: The Fall of Regulation and the Rise of Governance in Contemporary Legal Thought" (2004) 89 *Minn. L. Rev.* 342; J.B. Ruhl and James Salzman, "Climate Change, Dead Zones, and Massive Problems in the Administrative State: A Guide for Whittling Away" (2010) 98 *Cal. L. Rev.* 59.

[21] For a discussion of this theory generally, see Valerie Braithwaite, "Ten Things You Need to Know about Regulation and Never Wanted to Ask," RegNet Occasional Paper No. 10 (2006), available at http://ctsi.anu.edu.au/publications/occasionalpapers.htm. For a comparative law application, see Charlotte Wood, Mary Ivec, Jenny Job, and Valerie Braithwaite, "Applications of Responsive Regulatory Theory in Australia and Overseas," RegNet Occasional Paper No. 15 (2010), available at http://ctsi.anu.edu.au/publications/occasionalpapers.htm.

[22] Julia Black, "Decentring Regulation: Understanding the Role of Regulation and Self-Regulation in a 'Post-Regulatory' World" (2001) 54(1) *Current Legal Prob.* 103, 142.

[23] Christine Parker and John Braithwaite, "Regulation" in Peter Cane and Mark Tushnet (eds.), *The Oxford Handbook of Legal Studies* (2003, Oxford University Press, Oxford), 119.

(horizontal effects) or different governance levels (vertical effects).[24] However, regulatory pathways flowing from litigation may also arise due to the incentives provided for behavioral change by private, nongovernmental, and community actors.

Viewing litigation as having a potential regulatory impact of this kind in the climate change sphere opens up complicated questions about the appropriate role of courts.[25] Various criticisms have been advanced, for instance, that courts lack the necessary expertise to determine questions of climate change regulation, that policy decisions should be left to elected politicians, and that, ultimately, climate change litigation will be ineffective as a mechanism for advancing mitigation and adaptation goals given hurdles posed by technical legal rules around standing, costs, political question, and other separation-of-powers issues. These factors certainly may act as restraints on the capacity of litigation to contribute to climate change regulation and require serious attention in any project concerned with climate change litigation's broader regulatory impact.[26] However, whether or not one views this litigation as appropriate, it is important to understand the potential for the evolving case law to generate legal and behavioral change, which may in turn influence some of the existing barriers claimants face.[27]

Underlying many critiques of climate change litigation as a regulatory tool is a concern that the focus of regulatory efforts should be on developing national and international laws to address climate change in a top-down, coordinated fashion. Bottom-up or polycentric modes for generating legal and behavioral change are seen as running the risk of being piecemeal, uncoordinated, and even contradictory.[28] In our view, this criticism simultaneously overestimates the appetite for concluding far-reaching, timely climate change measures at the national and international levels and underestimates the complex, multidimensional

---

[24] Hari Osofsky, "Diagonal Federalism and Climate Change: Implications for the Obama Administration" (2011) 62 *Alabama L. Rev.* 237.

[25] For a prominent critique, see Shi-Ling Hsu, "A Realistic Evaluation of Climate Change Litigation through the Lens of a Hypothetical Lawsuit" (2008) 79(3) *Univ. Colo. L. Rev.* 701.

[26] Hari M. Osofsky, "The Intersection of Scale, Science, and Law in *Massachusetts v. EPA*" (2007) 9 *Oreg. Rev. Intl. L.* 233.

[27] Access barriers such as costs and separation-of-powers issues are discussed further in Chapter 7.

[28] Hsu, "A Realistic Evaluation of Climate Change Litigation," 704; Laurence H. Tribe, "Too Hot for Courts to Handle: Fuel Temperatures, Global Warming, and the Political Question Doctrine" (Washington Legal Foundation, 2010), 12.

character of climate change regulation. These lawsuits – both pro- and antiregulatory – help influence the extent of emissions and what options are selected in response to impacts. Whether or not treaty or statutory approaches would be preferable, courts serve as an important forum for debating climate change regulation, and the cases influence behavior in a variety of ways beyond the mandates contained in opinions. Understanding the roles that courts play is therefore important to a comprehensive view of multilevel climate change governance.

2.3   Regulatory pathways for climate change litigation

Increasing acceptance of the view that litigation forms part of a multi-dimensional system of climate change governance[29] has led to growing interest in the ways that climate change litigation shapes not just mitigation and adaptation outcomes, but also the extent and form of regulation. The groundwork for this assessment has been laid in the contributions of various scholars who have sought to catalog and categorize the burgeoning case law.[30] In the United States, such efforts over the past decade include – among others – climate change litigation charts for US and non-US case law prepared by Professor Michael Gerrard and the Columbia Center for Climate Change Law, scholarship by Professor Hari Osofsky starting in 2005 to understand this litigation's regulatory role, and empirical assessments undertaken by Professors David Markell and J.B. Ruhl that classify and quantify US climate change case law. For the Australian case law, Professor Jacqueline Peel has constructed a web database based at Melbourne Law School's Centre for Resources, Energy and Environmental Law that undertakes a similar breakdown of the case law into categories based on the focus of the claim (mitigation, adaptation, access to justice, or regulation of private conduct).[31]

---

[29] See, e.g., Lin, "Climate Change and the Courts"; Osofsky, "The Continuing Role of Climate Change Litigation"; Jacqueline Peel, Lee Godden, and Rodney J. Keenan, "Climate Change Law in an Era of Multi-Level Governance" (2012) 1(2) *Transnatl. Environ. L.* 245; Markell and Ruhl, "A New Jurisprudence or Business as Usual"; Jody Freeman and Adrian Vermule, "Massachusetts v EPA: From Politics to Expertise" (2007) *Supreme Court Rev.* 51.

[30] In the United States, see particularly Michael Gerrard et al., "Climate Change Litigation in the U.S.," Arnold and Porter LLP, www.climatecasechart.com, and Markell and Ruhl, "A New Jurisprudence or Business as Usual."

[31] See "Australian Climate Change Litigation," Centre for Resources, Energy and Environmental Law, Melbourne Law School, www.law.unimelb.edu.au/creel/research/climate-change.

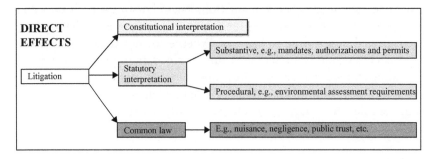

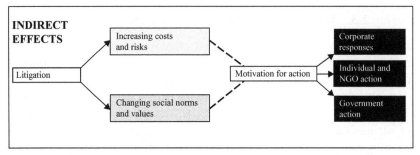

Figure 2.1   Conceptual model of regulatory pathways for climate change litigation.

Although these important scholarly contributions demonstrate the quantity of litigation and the multiple forms it is taking, as well as some of its direct regulatory effects, they do not address the broader questions of how climate change litigation might influence behavior and norms and whether it is effective as a strategy for changing mitigation and adaptive outcomes. This book attempts to fill this gap.

These questions, however, are difficult to analyze as there is no widely agreed method for assessing the link between regulatory development and a particular case or cases, especially when considering indirect effects. The book tackles these questions by employing a mixed-method approach that comprises (1) a comprehensive review of case law from two similarly placed jurisdictions, the United States and Australia, together with (2) qualitative evaluation of the extent to which climate change cases influence subsequent regulatory outcomes, drawing on insights from a series of semistructured interviews with US and Australian participants involved in the litigation. On this basis, we have developed a conceptual map of possible regulatory pathways for climate change litigation, depicted in Figure 2.1. Though some of the individual pathways have been previously identified in the literature,[32] this is the first work to map, comprehensively, the variety of pathways and their links to climate change litigation.

The regulatory impact pathways in the model are divided into direct and indirect categories, although we recognize that a firm dividing line between the two does not always exist. Like all models, there is a degree of simplification involved. For example, some cases, especially high-profile ones such as *Massachusetts v. EPA*, will have a mix of direct and indirect effects along multiple pathways. In addition, in identifying how litigation acts as a pathway toward greater regulation of the causes or impacts of climate change, and toward greater mitigation and adaptive behaviors, we are not attempting to prove the existence of a definitive causal link between observed regulatory changes and particular cases.[33] Judicial decisions are not issued in a social vacuum, and hence the extent to which litigation influences or serves as regulation in any particular case will be affected by contextual and background factors, including the prevailing political environment, the interaction between courts and other branches of the government, legal requirements governing the right to sue, economic or market forces, and the state of public opinion concerning climate change. Nonetheless, our interview data provide insights into how those most closely involved with and affected by the litigation perceive its regulatory significance, which in turn can be an important factor in influencing behavior, motivations, and actions.

Some of the pathways identified in the model are already well traveled in the case law; some are emerging; and yet others are indications of where future case law may arise. In the following sections, we provide a brief description of each pathway with illustrative examples.

2.3.1   Direct regulatory impacts

The book treats regulatory pathways as direct when litigation results in a formal change in climate change law and policy. Proactive climate change litigation's direct regulatory impacts involve forcing regulatory action, whereas antiregulatory litigation generally aims to prevent or stall such action. These varying cases affect efforts to regulate climate change by

---

[32] See particularly Markell and Ruhl, "A New Jurisprudence or Business as Usual," and David Markell and J.B. Ruhl, "An Empirical Survey of Climate Change Litigation in the United States" (2010) 40(7) *Environ. L. Reporter* 10644.

[33] Indeed, sociolegal literature on this issue has not resolved an appropriate methodology for doing so.

altering the regulatory landscape, both in terms of who can regulate and what regulation they can create.

In common law systems with a constitutional separation of powers – like the United States and Australia – pathways for climate change litigation to exert a direct regulatory impact are constrained by the limited power of the judiciary vis-à-vis the other branches of government. Nonetheless, even within the framework of a limited judicial power, litigation can provide direct pathways for climate change regulation through the traditional functions of the courts concerned with construing constitutional doctrine and statutory law and with developing the common law. The book therefore considers three primary direct pathways that exist – constitutional, statutory, and common law – while acknowledging that only the statutory one has had substantial direct impacts in the two countries. Specifically, most direct impacts thus far have occurred through courts interpreting statutory law in a way that includes climate change considerations, though some cases have attempted to use common law causes of action to address climate change harms, and others have raised constitutional issues.

2.3.1.1   Constitutional interpretation

Constitutional claims potentially could take two forms: (1) people have rights being violated by climate change or (2) regulatory action to address climate change implicates constitutionally protected rights or exceeds the bounds of federal power. However, only claims in the second category have actually been brought in the United States and Australia.

In theory, the first type of action might rely on constitutional rights to life or to a healthy environment. Such rights could serve as a basis for affected citizens to challenge government action responsible for contributing to climate change and its effects.[34] However, the federal constitutions of both countries – while conferring judicial review authority on the US Supreme Court and the Australian High Court, respectively, to invalidate legislation or executive actions that are judged

---

[34] Brian J. Preston, "Climate Change Litigation (Part 2)" (2011) 2011/2 *Carbon Clim. L. Rev.* 244. Human rights claims have already been taken at the international level. E.g., "Petition to the Inter-American Commission on Human Rights Seeking Relief from Violations Resulting from Global Warming Caused by Acts and Omissions of the United States" (Dec. 7, 2005). For discussion of a possible human rights climate change claim by Aboriginal and Torres Strait Islanders in Australia, see Owen Cordes-Holland, "The Sinking of the Strait: The Implications of Climate Change for Torres Strait Islanders' Human Rights Protected by the ICCPR" (2009) 9(2) *Melb. J. Intl. L.* 40.

unconstitutional – do not contain broadly framed right-to-life or environment provisions (as exist in some other national constitutions). In the US context, more possibilities for such constitutional rights claims exist at the state level, given the presence of formally entrenched provisions providing protection to the environment and natural resources in some state constitutions.[35] As Professors Markell and Ruhl note, if constitutional/civil rights cases were to emerge, they might offer courts the opportunity "to forge a special jurisprudence for climate change."[36] But this jurisprudence – though perhaps more promising than one based on federal constitutional rights – has yet to emerge.

Although claims that climate change violates constitutional rights have not yet been brought in either country at federal or state levels, courts in both countries have been presented with claims that climate regulation implicates such rights. The most common constitutional claims regarding climate change in both countries are antiregulatory ones; they argue that mitigation or adaptation legislation or implementing regulations violates constitutional protections. For example, a writ filed in the Australian High Court in May 2013 on behalf of mining entrepreneur Clive Palmer challenged the constitutionality of aspects of the federal carbon pricing mechanism dealing with compensation provided to trade-exposed, emissions-intensive industries.[37] In the US context, federal constitutional issues – namely, compliance with the dormant Commerce Clause – are also at the center of ongoing litigation over California's Low Carbon Fuel Standard, Colorado's Renewable Energy Standard, and the Minnesota Next Generation Energy Act. As discussed in depth in Chapter 7, the US federal constitution is here used as a tool to try to block state-level efforts to address climate change or support the transition from coal to other fuels, including renewables. Thus far, one of these claims has succeeded and the other two have failed.[38]

---

[35] E.g., Montana Const. art. XI, § 1.

[36] Markell and Ruhl, "An Empirical Assessment of Climate Change in the Courts," 85.

[37] *Queensland Nickel Pty Ltd v. Commonwealth of Australia*, Writ of Summons, No. 1325 of 2013, May 16, 2013, High Court Registry, Brisbane. This claim is not being pursued following election of the Abbott government and repeal of the carbon tax. Clive Palmer himself was elected as a member of parliament at the September 2013 elections that installed Tony Abbott as the new prime minister.

[38] *Rocky Mountain Farmers Union v. Corey*, 730 F.3d 1070 (2013) (remanding to lower court to determine if the regulation discriminates in fact); *Rocky Mountain Farmers Union, et al. v. Corey*, No. 12–15131 (9th Cir. Jan. 22, 2014) (denying rehearing en banc); *North Dakota v. Heydinger*, __ F.Supp.2d __, 2014 WL 1612331 (D. Minn. Apr. 18, 2014); *Energy and Environmental Legal Institute v. Epel* __ F.Supp.2d __, 2014 WL 1874977 (D. Colo., May 9, 2014).

Some constitutional claims regarding climate change–related regulation do not involve the validity of the regulation but rather the question of appropriate compensation. For instance, as discussed in more depth in Chapter 4, the US state of New Jersey's supreme court decided that the adaptive benefits of a sand dune should be taken into account when deciding just compensation under the US Constitution's Fifth Amendment Takings Clause.[39] As a consequence, homeowners received only one dollar in compensation, an approach that is being relied on in other cases in that state.[40] Some scholars and practitioners have argued that the Takings Clause may be used in more climate change regulatory contexts over time, including challenges to the constitutionality of land use–related climate change regulation.[41]

2.3.1.2 Statutory interpretation

The most significant direct regulatory pathway for climate change litigation to date involves statutory interpretation cases focused on spurring or limiting governmental action. In both Australia and the United States, the most important of such cases involve reinterpretation of long-standing pollution control and environmental statutes to encompass newer climate change concerns. These cases have addressed substantive and procedural provisions.

Substantive statutory interpretation. Many cases have been brought under existing environmental statutes to force or limit action under them. Referred to by Professors Markell and Ruhl as "substantive mitigation regulation" claims,[42] action-forcing suits in this category seek to "require a legislature or agency to promulgate a statute, rule, or policy establishing new or more stringent limits on [greenhouse gas] emissions by regulating direct or indirect sources."[43] Where successful, the result of such cases is to establish a mandate for the legislature or executive branch agencies to undertake climate change regulation.[44] Even ostensibly unsuccessful

---

[39] The Australian Constitution contains a similar Just Compensation Clause in respect of property acquisition by the federal government, but no federal case has been brought on these grounds.

[40] *Borough of Harvey Cedars v. Karan*, 43 ELR 20149, No. A-120–11 (N.J., Jul. 8, 2013).

[41] For a discussion of takings and climate change, see J. Peter Byrne, "Rising Seas and Common Law Baselines: A Comment on Regulatory Takings Discourse on Climate Change" (2010) 11 *Vermont J. Environ. L.* 625 (2010); A. Dan Tarlock, "Takings, Water Rights, and Climate Change" (2012) 36 *Vermont L. Rev.* 731.

[42] Markell and Ruhl, "A New Jurisprudence or Business as Usual," 30.   [43] Ibid., 33.

[44] In Australia, there is not the same tradition, as in the United States, of independent executive agencies operating under legislative mandates, because, by and large, laws are

cases, which do not produce a statutory mandate for regulation, may see courts using "prods and pleas" in an attempt to push other branches of the government to act.[45] By contrast, action-limiting suits seek to undermine the legal basis for mandates or constrain their application.

The most prominent example of this kind of regulatory pathway for climate change litigation is the mandate established via the US Supreme Court's interpretation of the federal Clean Air Act in *Massachusetts v. EPA*.[46] As discussed in the previous chapter, this decision found that the US Environmental Protection Agency (EPA) had statutory authority under the Clean Air Act to introduce regulations limiting greenhouse gas emissions from new motor vehicles. The EPA has since engaged in a number of rulemaking exercises in response to this decision, including issuing an Endangerment Finding regarding the public health and welfare impacts of motor vehicle emissions, establishing greenhouse gas emissions standards for light- and heavy-duty vehicles, and creating limits on emissions from stationary sources such as power plants.[47] As discussed further in the next chapter, these regulations make up the bulk of climate change law at the federal level in the United States and have put the nation firmly on a path of administrative regulation of emissions levels rather

---

administered by government departments that are beholden to government ministers (members of the executive) and through them to the legislature. Where independent executive agencies have been established in the climate change field, as in the case of the Climate Change Authority, their role is generally limited to one of advising responsible ministers (although from a political standpoint, such advice may be difficult to ignore).

[45] Benjamin Ewing and Douglas A. Kysar, "Prods and Pleas: Limited Government in an Era of Unlimited Harm" (2011) 121 *Yale L. J.* 350. Ewing and Kysar conceptualize prods and pleas as the converse of checks and balances in a system of limited government. Faced with regulatory inertia on the part of other branches of government, courts may prod those institutions "by taking action that makes further avoidance of the issue unpleasant or infeasible"; pleas take a softer form, involving courts "calling attention to a problem of social need and asking for its resolution" (at 361). Markell and Ruhl point to the US decision in *Re Otter Tail Power Company* 744 N.W.2d 594, 603 (S.D. 2008) as an example of a court exercising this plea function in the climate change context. Markell and Ruhl, "An Empirical Assessment of Climate Change in the Courts." In that case, the South Dakota Supreme Court refused to overturn a decision of the Public Utility Commission to issue a power plant permit but commented in its judgment on the "momentous and complex threat to our planet" presented by global warming, the difficulty of resolving such complex issues in judicial proceedings, and the need for policy decisions to be taken by the state executive and legislative branches on the question.

[46] *Massachusetts v. EPA*, 549 US 497 (2007).

[47] For discussion, see Markell and Ruhl, "A New Jurisprudence or Business as Usual," 49–50. See also Hari Osofsky, "Diagonal Federalism and Climate Change."

than one of adopting a market-based cap-and-trade approach through comprehensive climate change legislation.

The EPA regulations have attracted an array of antiregulatory lawsuits, which focus on challenging the extent of the Clean Air Act mandate established by the Supreme Court's decision. To date, the Supreme Court has not been receptive to challenges to the EPA's motor vehicle regulations. However, in a June 2014 decision, it partially upheld and partially struck down the agency's stationary source regulations. As a practical matter, though, the part that the Supreme Court upheld will allow the EPA to proceed with regulating most of the stationary source greenhouse gas emissions that it had planned to address.[48]

When statutory authority and accompanying rules already exist, the substantive statutory interpretation pathway also includes agencies using their legislatively based mandates in courts. For example, the entry into force of the Australian carbon pricing legislation on July 1, 2012, opened up opportunities for a new kind of litigation there concerned with maintaining and policing the statutory regime.[49] In addition, the federal competition regulator, the Australian Competition and Consumer Commission (ACCC), brought enforcement actions pursuant to its statutory mandate against companies making false claims about increases in the prices of goods and services due to the carbon tax.[50] Following the repeal of the national Clean Energy Act, these avenues will no longer be pursued. Instead, the Abbott government has conferred new statutory powers on the ACCC to pursue companies that issue misleading price claims as a

---

[48] For the DC Circuit opinion that the Supreme Court reversed in part, see *Coalition for Responsible Regulation v. EPA*, 684 F.3d 102 (DC Cir. June 26, 2012) (No. 09-1322, 10-1092). In October 2013, the Supreme Court granted six petitions for writ of certiorari filed by industry and state petitioners on the following single issue: "Whether EPA permissibly determined that its regulation of greenhouse gas emissions from new motor vehicles triggered permitting requirements under the Clean Air Act for stationary sources that emit greenhouse gases." For its decision in that case, see *Utility Air Regulatory Group v. EPA*, 134 S.Ct. 2427, 2449 (June 23, 2014). The *Utility Air Regulatory Group* decision is discussed further in Chapter 3.

[49] The Clean Energy Act 2011 (Cth) gave enforcement powers to the Clean Energy Regulator but made no provision for actions by third parties (citizen suits). It was consequently not expected to be a site of significant climate litigation, and in any event, the legislation has now been repealed: see Clean Energy Legislation (Carbon Tax Repeal) Act 2014, available at www.environment.gov.au/climate-change/repealing-carbon-tax.

[50] See, e.g., *ACCC v. GM Holden* [2008] FCA 1428 (Sep. 16, 2008). For discussion of the ACCC's efforts in this regard, see Brian J. Preston, "Climate Change Litigation (Part 1)" (2011) 5(1) *Carbon Clim. L. Rev.* 3, 12–14.

result of failing to factor in cost decreases associated with repeal of the carbon tax.[51]

A further category of substantive statutory interpretation cases involves lawsuits that seek to prevent, overturn, or limit a legislative or executive branch decisions regarding mitigation and adaptation.[52] The mitigation cases largely focus on governmental decisions to carry out, fund, or authorize a project that will produce substantial greenhouse gas emissions. Claims seeking judicial review of permits issued for greenhouse gas–emitting projects, such as coal-fired power stations or coal mines, are the most common example of this category in both countries.[53] These mitigation-oriented challenges have been complemented by ones focused on adaptation decision making, both pro- and antiregulatory. For example, some lawsuits have challenged development permits for including new or more extensive adaptation requirements,[54] whereas others have critiqued the failure to impose such requirements to protect against adaptation risks (e.g., sea level rise, wildfire, flooding). Such adaptation cases are just beginning to emerge in the United States[55] but, as discussed in Chapter 4, make up a substantial portion of the climate change litigation brought in Australia. In both mitigation-related and adaptation-related examples, judicial extension of existing environmental statutes to cover climate change issues directly expands the scope of climate change regulation.

A key difference between US and Australian cases in this latter substantive statutory interpretation category reflects the greater availability of "merits review" to challenge many planning, development, and mining-related decisions made by governments in Australia. Unlike judicial review, which is restricted to examining the legality of administrative

---

[51] These new powers are the result of amendments to the ACCC's governing statute made by the Clean Energy Legislation (Carbon Tax Repeal) Act 2014. For information on the ACCC's new powers, see ACCC, "Carbon Tax Repeal," www.accc.gov.au/business/carbon-tax-repeal/our-role-in-carbon-tax-repeal.

[52] Markell and Ruhl, "A New Jurisprudence or Business as Usual," 30.

[53] Markell and Ruhl, "A New Jurisprudence or Business as Usual," 39. See also Peel, "Australian Climate Change Litigation," www.law.unimelb.edu.au/creel/research/climate-change (mitigation).

[54] Markell and Ruhl, "A New Jurisprudence or Business as Usual," 31. Markell and Ruhl's 2012 typology does not anticipate the latter type of adaptation claim, that is, one challenging a decision as inadequately adaptive. However, this has been a significant focus of adaptation case law in Australia and is an emerging area of case law in the United States. See, further, Chapter 4.

[55] Jacqueline Peel and Hari M. Osofsky, "Sue to Adapt?" (forthcoming) *Minn. L. Rev.*

decisions, merits review (or nonjudicial review) permits an evaluation of the merits of the decision concerned. In merits review, the task of the reviewing court or tribunal is to determine what is "the correct or preferable decision" on the factual, scientific, and legal material before the reviewer.[56] The availability and scope of merits review for a particular decision will be determined by the statute pursuant to which the decision is made. At the state level in Australia, environmental, energy, and planning legislation offers numerous opportunities for litigants to challenge not just the legality but also the merits of particular decisions authorizing projects with potential climate change impacts or adaptation risks.[57]

Procedural statutory interpretation. The bulk of climate change cases that have been brought or are being litigated in US and Australian courts do not seek a direct reduction in greenhouse gas emissions or the implementation of specific adaptation measures. Rather, their goal is to ensure that greenhouse gas emissions and climate change impacts are routinely taken into account and adequately evaluated in planning and environmental assessment processes under long-standing state and federal environmental laws. Litigation of this kind involves statutory interpretation focused on procedural requirements, such as the scope of environmental assessment processes or relevant considerations in decision making. Many of our interview participants identified the significant impact of case law in "mainstreaming" the consideration of climate change issues in both government and corporate planning and development processes.

In the United States, a suite of such cases have been launched under the national environmental impact assessment legislation – the National Environmental Policy Act (NEPA)[58] – along with state equivalents such as the California Environmental Quality Act.[59] In Australia, a similar pattern has emerged of cases being litigated under environmental impact assessment legislation at the state and federal levels.[60] Cumulatively, these cases have firmly established the relevance of greenhouse gas emissions and

---

[56] *Drake v. Minister for Immigration and Ethic Affairs (No. 1)* (1979) 46 FLR 409; 24 ALR 577, 589.

[57] Philippa England, "The Legal Basis for Australian Environmental Planning and Governance" in Jason Byrne, Neil Sipe, and Jago Dodson (eds.), *Australian Environmental Planning: Challenges and Future Prospects* (2014, Abingdon, Routledge), 39.

[58] National Environmental Policy Act, 42 U.S.C. § 4321 (1969); e.g., *Border Power Plant Working Grp. v. Dep't of Energy*, 260 F. Supp. 2d 997 (SD Cal. 2003).

[59] California Environmental Quality Act, Cal. Pub. Res. Code § 21000 (1970); e.g., *Communities for a Better Env't v. Richmond*, 108 Cal Rptr. 3d 478 (Cal. Ct. App. 2010).

[60] See, further, Peel, "The Role of Climate Change Litigation," and discussion of the Australian mitigation case law in Chapter 3.

climate change issues to environmental assessment exercises conducted for a range of development projects. Some environmental impact assessment cases have also had additional regulatory flow-on effects, such as the development of governmental planning policies requiring the inclusion of greenhouse gas emissions in environmental assessments.[61] More broadly, cases requiring assessment of greenhouse gas emissions or climate change impacts as part of new development proposals may generate changes in business risk management practices whereby the disclosure of such information becomes routine and/or efforts are made to offset impacts in project design to minimize the likelihood of litigation. As discussed later in the context of indirect impacts, litigation may also increase the cost of doing business for coal companies and other greenhouse gas–intensive businesses – and make financing more difficult – particularly when fulfillment of environmental assessment requirements (or challenges to the adequacy of such assessments) delays projects.[62]

2.3.1.3   Common law interpretation

In common law jurisdictions, interpretation of common law obligations relating to nuisance, negligence, or public trust to encompass climate change is also a possible pathway by which litigation can directly influence climate change regulation. Substantial commentary on climate change litigation, particularly in the United States, has focused on this potential avenue of court-led regulatory change, especially in the context of significant greenhouse gas emissions as a public nuisance.[63] The appeal is understandable. A successful nuisance case could create significant regulatory momentum in the United States and internationally by exposing large emitters to liability for damages caused by climate change to which their emissions contributed. Moreover, regardless of the legal success, or lack thereof, of such claims, they may also have a broader symbolic significance. Commenting on the state of California's attempt in 2007 to hold various automobile manufacturers accountable for the climate change effects of motor vehicle emissions, one of our interviewees was of the following view:

---

[61] Preston, "The Influence of Climate Change Litigation."

[62] Skype interview, Australian Participant 4 (Mar. 20, 2013).

[63] See, e.g., David A. Grossman, "Tort-Based Climate Litigation" in William C. G. Burns and Hari M. Osofsky (eds.), *Adjudicating Climate Change: State, National, and International Approaches* (2009, Cambridge University Press, New York), 193; David A. Grossman, "Warming Up to a Not-So-Radical Idea: Tort-Based Climate Change Litigation" (2003) 28 *Colum. J. Environ. L.* 1.

[A]s a legal attack and a legal doctrine – it didn't work. Having said that, the litigation itself was beneficial. I think it raised the issue. It forced companies and industries to think more about their exposure. I hope that it got the attention of insurance companies to evaluate risk. And it made it to the Supreme Court and it was a theory that actually won in the lower court. So I think it was a valiant effort and worth doing. In the end it didn't fully work, but I think it moved forward on having companies and others have to confront these issues.[64]

Nonetheless, the fact remains that common law climate change cases to date have not exerted a direct influence on the regulatory landscape. None of the US cases seeking to extend common law causes of action to climate change harms have yet been adjudicated on the merits, and many have not proceeded that far. As discussed further in Chapters 3 and 7, the Supreme Court's decision in one of these common law cases – *American Electric Power (AEP) v. Connecticut* – also places substantial limits on further development of this pathway in the nuisance context in the United States.[65]

The lack of success of common law climate change claims in the United States seems to have dissuaded similar actions in other common law countries, or at least led to such cases not being prioritized. For instance, in Australia, all of the climate change litigation has been statutorily based, despite the nation's common law tradition.[66] If common law suits raising public nuisance and negligence grounds were to emerge in Australia, these suits would be more likely to occur in an adaptation than a mitigation context; there is active discussion both in policy circles and in the literature of whether decisions of Australian local governments and other corporate entities that take insufficient account of climate change impacts, and thus lead to damage to private property and public infrastructure, could give rise to future liability on these grounds.[67] Australian environmental

---

[64] In-person interview, US Participant 6 (Nov. 14, 2012).

[65] The *AEP* decision found that the EPA's authority to regulate greenhouse gases – even if the EPA chose not to assert that authority – displaced the possibility for a claim under common law public nuisance. The opinion explained that if the EPA acted inadequately, it should be challenged through an administrative lawsuit under the Clean Air Act rather than through nuisance claims. The displacement doctrine and its role in climate cases is discussed further in Chapter 7.

[66] The closest example was the case of *Gray v. Macquarie Generation*, which raised a quasi-nuisance claim in litigation over the extent of authority granted under a statutory licence for a power station to emit greenhouse gases. This case is discussed further in Chapter 3.

[67] See, e.g., Baker and McKenzie, *Local Council Risk of Liability in the Face of Climate Change – Resolving Uncertainties*, a report for the Australian Local Government Association, Jul. 22,

nongovernmental organizations (NGOs) are also observing with interest novel common law claims in the United States, such as some of the lawsuits seeking to apply the public trust doctrine in a climate change context.[68] As discussed in more depth in Chapter 3, these lawsuits claim that governmental entities are violating their public trust duties by failing adequately to protect the atmosphere through their approach to climate change.[69]

2.3.2   *Indirect regulatory impacts*

In contrast to direct pathways, the indirect ones in our model focus on behavioral and norm change that influences choices of key actors. These pathways map how responses of governments, corporations, community groups, environmental organizations, or individuals alter the regulatory environment. Cases may provide a stimulus for regulatory change through increasing costs or reputational risks associated with particular projects or business practices, raising public awareness of the climate change problem or generating shifts in public opinion or social norms.

These indirect pathways may not resemble regulation in the formal sense; unlike the direct pathways, indirect pathways do not involve courts and other governmental entities mandating the changed behavior. But these pathways are regulatory in the broader conception of the term discussed earlier because of the ways in which they motivate different choices to decrease emissions or advance adaptation than would have otherwise occurred. Cases that help to mobilize nongovernmental actors, in particular, are likely to be an important factor in producing the cultural and

2011; Jan McDonald, "A Risky Climate for Decision-Making: The Liability of Development Authorities for Climate Change Impacts" (2007) 24(6) *Environ. Planning L. J.* 405; Nicola Durrant, *Legal Responses to Climate Change* (2010, Federation Press, Sydney), 289–306; Productivity Commission, Report No. 59, *Barriers to Effective Climate Change Adaptation* (Productivity Commission, Canberra, 2012).

[68] In-person interview, Australian Participant 1 (Mar. 7, 2013).

[69] For a listing of these cases, see Gerrard et al., "U.S. Climate Change Litigation Chart." Examples include *Bonser-Lain v. Texas Commission on Environmental Quality* (Dist. Ct. of Travis Cty, Tx, Aug. 2, 2012) (holding that the public trust doctrine applies but that the petition is denied on the basis that defendant is exercising reasonable rulemaking discretion in light of pending litigation); *Sanders-Reed v. Martinez* (N.M. Dist. Ct., Jul. 14, 2012) (N.M. Dist. Ct., filed Mar. 2012) (granting in part and denying in part motion to dismiss). For a discussion of these cases, see Alexandra Klass, "Federalism at Work: Recent Developments in Public Trust Lawsuits to Limit Greenhouse Gas Emissions," *CPRBlog*, Jul. 13, 2012, www.progressivereform.org/CPRBlog.cfm?idBlog=8092FA68-ADF9-7258-98BF80BAC5FA4AA7.

behavioral shifts necessary for realization of a sustainable, low-carbon future over the longer term. Indeed, to the extent that climate change litigation can tie into the broader corporate social responsibility movement, including sustainability indices and global reporting networks, these indirect pathways may prove an especially effective route for achieving change.

2.3.2.1   Increasing costs and risks

An important set of indirect regulatory pathways followed by many climate change cases involves increasing the costs and other business risks of emitting greenhouse gases for major corporate emitters. In the United States, the large volume of cases over coal-fired power plants may make each project a little more expensive, with an aggregate economic influence. As discussed in Chapter 3, these costs may come through courts imposing conditions on permits or licenses for emitting activities.[70] In addition, suits involving insurance often have significant financial implications, as they may create the necessity to obtain liability insurance or the potential for rising insurance premiums.[71]

In Australia, the volume of litigation directed against coal-fired power stations and coal mines – much lower than in the United States – has not been so great as to increase substantially the cost of such projects.[72] Nonetheless, coal companies do monitor decisions issued around mineral and mining projects that have the potential to be stopped on a greenhouse gas basis. From their perspective, "it only takes one [project] to get knocked down around greenhouse that sets a precedent."[73] As the economic conditions for coal production have become less favorable in Australia in recent times,[74] there is also the possibility that legal challenges and the associated delays will render projects economically unviable. While their focus remains on stopping coal projects on legal

---

[70] See, e.g., *Hunter Envtl. Lobby Inc. v. Minister for Planning* (2011) NSWLEC 221 (Nov. 24, 2011); *Hunter Environment Lobby Inc v. Minister for Planning (No 2)* (2012) NSWLEC 40 (Mar. 13, 2012); *Dual Gas Pty Ltd & Ors v. Environment Protection Authority* (2012) VCAT 308 (Mar. 29, 2012). These cases are discussed further in Chapter 3.

[71] See, e.g., *AES Corp. v. Steadfast*, Va. S. Ct. No. 100764 (2011), discussed further in Chapter 5.

[72] Skype interview, Australian Participant 16 (May 30, 2013).

[73] Skype interview, Australian Participant 13 (May 23, 2013).

[74] Mike Seccombe, "Coal? It's Over," *The Global Mail* (online), Oct. 29, 2012, www.theglobalmail.org/feature/coal-its-over/448/; Bernard Lagan, "Coal's Over. Anyone for Wine and Cheese?," *The Global Mail* (online), Jul. 12, 2013, www.theglobalmail.org/feature/coals-over-anyone-for-wine-and-cheese/657/.

grounds, environmental NGOs recognize that project delays and associated financial problems may be the "indirect impact" of lawsuits that often take a year or more to wind their way through the court system.[75]

2.3.2.2 Changing social norms and values

Many decisions – and the publicity associated with them – influence social norms and values surrounding climate change. Changes in these norms and values may in turn boost the campaigning efforts of NGOs, increase the profile of the climate change issue for government actors, or raise the reputational stakes for businesses that disregard climate change risks. For instance, the US Supreme Court decision in *Massachusetts v. EPA* – important in terms of the direct pathways it created for federal climate change regulation in the United States – also has had significant indirect regulatory influence. It has served to legitimize the climate change issue in the eyes of some portion of the general public and has induced companies to incorporate greenhouse gas emissions reductions into their business practices and planning.[76] One interviewee involved with the case described its impact as follows:

> I do think when the Supreme Court comes out and says, climate change is a concern and EPA should be doing something about it, it's harder for a lot of companies to ignore it anymore because they know, whether they want it or not, there's going to be legal requirements. So they have the choice to participate in that affirmatively or to put their head in the sand and wait for this to happen. So I do think for a number of companies, a number of industries, it did cause them to take a more proactive position in supporting climate change legislation.[77]

Cases often have a complicated relationship with the public debates over climate change science, with courts influencing evolving views of the science and the political climate appearing to influence courts. For example, the clear endorsement given by the majority of the US Supreme Court to climate change in *Massachusetts v. EPA* and decisions of other courts following its approach[78] were also described by interviewees as a judicial

---

[75] Skype interview, Australian Participant 4 (Mar. 20, 2013).

[76] For further discussion of these indirect effects of the litigation in changing social norms and values, see Chapter 6.

[77] Telephone interview, US Participant 9 (Dec. 12, 2012).

[78] E.g., *Coalition for Responsible Regulation v. EPA*, 684 F3.d 102 (D.C. Cir. Jun. 26, 2012) (No. 09-1322, 10-1092); *Coalition for Responsible Regulation v. EPA*, 2012 WL 6621785 (D.C. Cir. Dec. 20, 2012) (No. 09-1322, 10-1024, 10-1025, 10-1026, 10-1030, 10-1035, 10-1036, 10-1037, 10-1038) (denying rehearing en banc).

imprimatur conferring considerable legitimacy. Court decisions "saying that the science is substantial" help to counteract skeptical press reports maintaining "that all the science is baloney."[79] However, the US Supreme Court's discussion of science in dicta a few years later in *AEP v. Connecticut* had a different tone that conveyed greater skepticism about the appropriate role of courts in addressing complex scientific issues, perhaps to some extent representing a similar public evolution since the time of *Massachusetts v. EPA*.[80]

Some climate change cases filed by environmental NGOs or other community groups have been brought explicitly with an expressivist – that is, a social norm changing – purpose. In such cases, petitioners may recognize limited possibilities for direct regulatory impact and instead aim to change perceptions and values. The Inuits' 2005 petition to the Inter-American Commission on Human Rights alleging violations of the human rights of Inuit peoples as a consequence of US policy inaction on climate change is one such example. Then-chair of the Inuit Circumpolar Conference Sheila Watt-Cloutier acknowledged how unlikely formal success was and discussed the case as a basis for starting a human rights dialogue over climate change with the United States.[81]

The nuisance cases brought in the United States seem designed, at least partially, to serve a similar role. They have yet to succeed formally, and the US Supreme Court's decision in *AEP v. Connecticut* makes such success even more unlikely. However, their characterization of climate change as a public nuisance potentially influences how greenhouse gas emissions, and greenhouse gas–emitting products like coal, are viewed. As one coal company representative put it, "It's becoming a bit like – and I hesitate to use this – coal, in particular, I think is becoming like tobacco, big tobacco."[82] Cases such as the *Kivalina v. Exxon Mobil* case, brought by an Indian tribe in Alaska to seek damages for the impacts of rising greenhouse gas concentrations and resulting climate change on property, livelihood, and way of life, can also play a role in changing public perceptions.[83]

---

[79] Telephone interview, US Participant 8 (Nov. 26, 2012).

[80] *American Electric Power v. Connecticut*, 131 S. Ct 2527 (2011).

[81] Hari M. Osofsky, "The Inuit Petition as a Bridge? Beyond Dialectics of Climate Change and Indigenous People's Rights" (2007) 31(2) *Am. Indian L. Rev.* 675.

[82] Skype interview, Australian Participant 13 (May 23, 2013).

[83] David B. Hunter, "The Implications of Climate Change Litigation: Litigation for International Environmental Law-Making" in William C. G. Burns and Hari M. *Osofsky* (eds.), *Adjudicating Climate Change: State, National, and International Approaches* (2009, Cambridge University Press, New York), 357.

Through such cases, the human dimension of climate change becomes visible: "more people know about the situation that Kivalina is facing because of the case."[84]

The indirect pathways associated with changing norms and increasing costs often interact, as worries about litigation and rising costs influence business norms. For example, lawsuits may provide incentives for corporate actors to adopt more climate-friendly practices, whether to minimize the potential for litigation against them or to avoid reputational damage to their business. Even for an energy company that is not "in the crosshairs of the lawsuit or the litigation," the necessity to report the occurrence of greenhouse-related litigation to shareholders could provide a motivation for the adoption of cleaner energy strategies. Discussing litigation risk and the link to cleaner energy profiles that could allow businesses to avoid future litigation, a private attorney interviewed for the book described the effect as follows:

> I don't think it gets expressed in the actual statements issued to shareholders but it might be that, "while these lawsuits have targeted traditionally fossil-fuelled energy companies, because of our clean generating profile, we do not anticipate significant impacts associated with this litigation." And basically what you're saying is, no, we're not in their crosshairs, we're clean, we've made the right investment decisions.

In the private sector sphere, this effect may be augmented by the activities of attorneys and legal professional organizations.[85] Through the advice they provide to commercial clients, coupled with their generally risk-averse attitude, these practitioners and groups can play a substantial role in shaping the perception of and response to climate change litigation by other actors. In the same way, environmental groups are key communicators and mediators of the effects of court decisions in the public sphere.[86] Climate change litigation is often used by NGOs in conjunction with more traditional campaigning techniques to raise the public profile of climate change, generate community interest in action, and put pressure on businesses to alter "dirty" energy practices.

---

[84] In-person interview, US Participant 10 (Jan. 14, 2013).

[85] E.g., Jones Day, "Climate Change," www.jonesday.com/climate_change/; Van Ness Feldman LLP, "Climate Change," www.vnf.com/climate-change; Allens Linklaters, "Services: Climate Change Law," www.allens.com.au/services/cc/.

[86] See, e.g., the updates on climate case law published by groups such as the New South Wales Environment Defenders Office (www.edonsw.org.au/climate_change_energy_cases) and Climate Justice (www.climatelaw.org/).

2.4 Conclusion

This chapter's survey of the pathways by which litigation shapes regulation underscores the fundamental nature of climate change as a complex, multidimensional regulatory problem. These cases interact with both mitigation and adaptation law and policy at local, state, national, and international levels. The claims involve many areas of law and interface with social norms and the voluntary choices of corporations, NGOs, other branches of government, and individuals. The pathways described in this chapter's model provide an important tool for understanding the nuances of these many interactions.

Moreover, the variety of ways in which climate change litigation influences regulation reinforces the importance of a concept of climate change governance that includes litigation.[87] Though, for many, government regulation at national and international levels remains the preferable option, action at those levels has been inadequate to achieve the policy response that climate scientists and organizations such as the Intergovernmental Panel on Climate Change say is critical. Proactive climate change litigation has emerged, at least in part, as a response to inadequate regulation and aims to bridge the gap between those efforts and the goal of a sustainable, clean energy future. As the volume of litigation reflects, concerned NGOs and governmental officials have used litigation as a tool to push for regulatory action that was failing to emerge from legislative and planning processes.[88] Antiregulatory cases also play an important role in this push and pull around climate action. These cases often have resulted when those who stand to lose from greater regulation challenge government action. The challenged action at times constitutes the government response to the proactive litigation, bringing these conflicting uses of courts together in a complex dance.

However, characterizing litigation as merely debates over what gaps should be filled misses the full spectrum of its regulatory significance.

---

[87] Acknowledging the important role of litigation does not resolve what one's model of governance would be. One could view cases as helping to constitute a country's regulatory approach in a top-down, treaty-focused governance model, or alternatively, one could adopt a more pluralist or polycentric approach in which various formal and informal activities at multiple levels of government are all viewed as part of climate change governance. See Hari M. Osofsky, "The Geography of Climate Change Litigation Part II: Narratives of *Massachusetts v. EPA*" (2008) 8 *Chicago J. Intl. L.* 573.

[88] See the series of subnational and national case studies discussed in William C. G. Burns and Hari M. Osofsky (eds.), *Adjudicating Climate Change: State, National, and International Approaches* (2009, Cambridge University Press, New York).

Litigation is not simply an adjunct to regulation or an enforcement tool but also an integral part of the multilevel climate governance system that creates fluid pathways for interactions among regulation at subnational, national, and international levels. Some of these pathways lead to direct changes in the legal regime applicable to the assessment and regulation of climate change. Other pathways involve a more indirect effect on social and business norms that in turn helps to motivate different choices in relation to mitigation and adaptation than would otherwise have occurred. Exploring the many direct and indirect ways in which litigation interacts with regulation assists a more systematic understanding of its impact in establishing and altering approaches to mitigation and adaptation. Both proactive and antiregulatory cases, through their successes and failures, can help to reshape the regulatory landscape.

The rest of the book examines these pathways in more depth. In Chapters 3 and 4, we explore the regulatory impacts of litigation for mitigation and adaptation. We show how litigation has been a key tool for enhancing laws and spurring regulation of greenhouse gas emissions in the United States and Australia and is an emerging tool for addressing adaptation challenges in both jurisdictions. Then, Chapters 5 and 6 draw from our interviews to consider each of the indirect pathways. These chapters illuminate the ways in which climate change cases have changed corporate behavior and influenced social norms and values in this context. Finally, Chapters 7 and 8 focus on the ways in which these pathways – and responses to them – have been used to advance both pro- and antiregulatory aims. These chapters consider the overall regulatory influence of these cases and what the future may hold.

3

Litigation as a mitigation tool

The first question is whether litigation has achieved much at all. And I think the answer is yes. I get kind of cynical because things are very slow and they don't feel, in some ways, as if we've gotten very far. On the other hand, when you kind of step back a little bit, I would say, at least in California, we are in a different place than we were ten years ago, five years ago, and some of that is because of those . . . cases. . . . So *Massachusetts v. EPA* – it said that the existing Clean Air Act covers greenhouse gas emissions. It's obviously a two- or three-step process to get from there to actual regulation and that has been phenomenally slow at the federal level. But it did end the debate about it. . . . So that's no small thing to have an existing statute that can submit emitters to litigation and subject emitters to rules and regulations. It's frustratingly slow and we haven't seen much progress on the regulations but it has – it changed a part of the discussion and hopefully it will allow some additional laws to move forward.

– US Interview Participant 6

The [New South Wales] Department of Planning which is responsible for recommending or issuing [development] consents has woken up to the fact that judges in the Land and Environment Court . . . take the view that climate change is real, the science is in, and as a consequence this is a fact that ought to be weighed up and assessed in any planning approval. So that's why, nowadays, director-general's requirements for coal-fired power stations or the like, all include a climate change assessment and/or require preparation of a greenhouse gas mitigation plan, which I now sense is a bit woolly, but that didn't exist five or ten years ago. That's a reasonably recent invention. And I'd suggest a lot of that has come out of cases . . . where climate change arguments have been agitated, not always successfully. I think it's now mainstream. I think that's now much more mainstream. For the Department of Planning to insist on that sort of stuff adds another layer of complexity and risk of cost to getting planning approvals for big industrial undertakings.

– Australian Interview Participant 8

3.1   Introduction

A primary goal of much of the climate change litigation brought in the United States and Australia has been to spur greenhouse gas emissions regulation and thereby contribute to the mitigation of climate change. The US Supreme Court case of *Massachusetts v. EPA* is the leading example of this kind of litigation.[1] It has had significant direct and indirect regulatory effects in the United States; the case has not only formed the basis for extensive federal government regulation but has also brought more public attention to the problem in a variety of ways.[2] President Obama even used the decision in international negotiations as an example of US action when his efforts at comprehensive climate legislation failed.[3]

However, *Massachusetts v. EPA* is only the most well-known and important example. Hundreds of climate change cases have been brought in the United States, involving both statutory and common law claims, spanning state and federal courts, which address aspects of the mitigation challenge. These include lawsuits concerning transportation emissions, the regulation and permitting of coal-fired power stations, renewable energy projects and programs, and the adequacy of environmental assessments for greenhouse gas–intensive projects.[4]

Australia has not had a high-profile "*Massachusetts v. EPA* moment" in its mitigation jurisprudence but also has a significant body of cases seeking to improve the regulation of greenhouse gas emissions and to promote clean energy outcomes.[5] Most of the Australian litigation has involved the interpretation of existing environmental laws to include climate change considerations, a pathway that has also been pursued in a considerable number of lawsuits in the United States.

This chapter considers mitigation-related litigation in the United States and Australia and its regulatory impacts on each country's pathway toward

---

[1] *Massachusetts v. EPA*, 549 U.S. 497 (2007).

[2] The impact of the case on social norms and values around climate change is discussed further in Chapter 6.

[3] Michael M. Mian, "The Road to Copenhagen: The Role of the Obama Administration in Shaping the Political Climate of Climate Change Leading to COP 15," Fellows Papers, 2010, Center for the Study of the Presidency and Congress, available at www.thepresidency .org/storage/documents/Fellows2010/Mian.pdf.

[4] See Arnold and Porter LLP, "U.S. Climate Change Litigation Chart," at www. climatecasechart.com, for a comprehensive list.

[5] See Jacqueline Peel, "Australian Climate Change Litigation," Melbourne Centre for Resources, Energy and Environmental Law, at www.law.unimelb.edu.au/creel/research/ climate-change, for a comprehensive listing.

cleaner energy at international, national, and subnational levels. This mitigation-focused litigation in both countries is taking place against the backdrop of a rapidly evolving global energy system[6] and strongly divided political views as to the necessity for, and form of, domestic mitigation action. Although the much-publicized *Massachusetts v. EPA* case focused on motor vehicle emissions, much of the mitigation-related litigation in both countries targets coal – focusing on the facilities that use coal to produce power and the mines where coal is extracted.[7] The chapter provides an overview of how the two countries fit into the global energy economy before turning to the regulatory influence of mitigation-related litigation in the United States and Australia.

For each country, the chapter draws from doctrinal materials and interviews to consider how the litigation has influenced the country's mitigation efforts at international, national, and subnational levels. It then compares the role of this type of litigation in the two countries and considers possibilities for its future evolution. As explored in Chapter 4 as well, we see opposite comparative patterns in mitigation and adaptation; the US mitigation jurisprudence is far more extensive than that of Australia, but the Australian adaptation jurisprudence is much more developed than that of the United States. Given those patterns, we see particularly strong opportunities for the US mitigation jurisprudence and Australian adaptation jurisprudence to influence the future course of litigation in the other country.

3.2   The "carbon economy" in the United States and Australia

Mitigation-related litigation has developed in the United States and Australia because they are major emitters with significant fossil fuel industries. In both countries, the fossil fuel economy is in transition, due in part to technological developments, such as hydraulic fracturing, that have caused a boom in oil and natural gas production and in part to climate change and other environmental regulation – at times stemming from litigation – that makes coal more expensive. But even with these

---

[6] See generally International Energy Agency, *World Energy Outlook 2013* (2013, OECD/IEA, Paris).

[7] Michael B. Gerrard, "Coal-Fired Power Plants Dominate Climate Change Litigation" (2009) 242(61) *N.Y. L. J.* 25; Brad Jessup, "Dragging Coal through the Courts: An Alternative Emissions Reduction Strategy," *The Conversation*, Nov. 14, 2011, at http://theconversation.edu.au/dragging-coal-through-the-courts-an-alternative-emissions-reduction-strategy-4275.

shifts and the increasing commercial viability and market integration of renewable sources, both countries remain major users and producers of fossil fuels, the combustion of which contributes to climate change. This section describes that contribution to provide context for explaining the litigation that has taken place.

The United States plays a pivotal role in global efforts to reduce greenhouse gas emissions because of its massive total and per capita contribution. The United States is the second biggest total emitter in the world, surpassed only by China, with high per capita emissions as well compared to other developed countries.[8] However, recently, US emissions have decreased. In 2014, the US Environmental Protection Agency (EPA) reported that total US greenhouse gas emissions decreased by 3.4 percent from 2011 to 2012 and that 2012 emissions were 10 percent below 2005 levels.[9] These decreases accompanied the economic downturn; people's diminished budgets made them try to use less electricity and vehicle fuel. However, other factors were relevant as well. The EPA reported a mix of decreased electricity use, increased vehicle efficiency, and weather fluctuations as important contributors to the lower numbers. Nonetheless, even with this recent decline, relative to 1990 levels, total US greenhouse gas emissions as of 2014 increased by 4.7 percent.[10]

Carbon dioxide emissions, most of which are related to fossil fuel production, made up 82.5 percent of total US emissions as of 2012. Fossil fuel carbon dioxide emissions increased at an average annual rate of 0.3 percent between 1990 and 2012 owing to a combination of a generally growing economy over that twenty-year period (despite recessionary periods), growth in emissions from electricity generation and transportation, and a general decline in the carbon intensity of fuels combusted for energy in recent years across most sectors of the economy. In 2012, electricity generation accounted for 32 percent, transportation accounted for 28 percent, and industrial emissions accounted for 20 percent of total

---

[8] US Energy Information Administration, "International Energy Statistics," at www. eia.gov/cfapps/ipdbproject/iedindex3.cfm?tid=90&pid=45&aid=8&cid=all,&syid=2007 &eyid=2011&unit=MTCDPP. See also Larry Parker and John Blodgett, Cong. Research Serv. RL32721, *Greenhouse Gas Emissions: Perspective on the Top 20 Emitters and Developed versus Developing Nations* (2010); Mark McCormick and Paul Scruton, "World Carbon Dioxide Emissions Data by Country," *The Guardian*, Jan. 31, 2011, available at www. guardian.co.uk/news/datablog/2011/jan/31/world-carbon-dioxide-emissions-country-data-co2?intcmp=239.

[9] EPA, *Inventory of U.S. Greenhouse Gas Emissions and Sinks: 1990–2012* (2014).

[10] Ibid.

US greenhouse gas emissions. Agricultural, commercial, and residential sectors provided the other 20 percent of emissions.[11]

Energy in the United States comes from various sources in constantly changing combinations. In 2012, these were 36 percent oil, 26 percent natural gas, 18 percent coal, 8 percent nuclear, and 9 percent renewable energy.[12] The World Energy Council's 2011 data put US supply and use of coal in global perspective during this growth period for climate change litigation. US recoverable coal resources, 237,295 million tonnes, were by far the largest in the world and 26 percent of the global total; the United States was also second in the world for coal production and eleventh in the world for coal used in energy generation.[13] With technological developments around hydraulic fracturing in recent years, the United States has massively expanded exploitation of unconventional energy sources such as shale gas and shale oil. In 2013, US oil and gas production from shale saw it surpass other countries to become the world's top producer of these resources.[14]

Central to the Australian climate change regulatory story is also the country's economic dependence on fossil fuel production and exports, particularly coal. Coal is Australia's largest energy export, earning the country around AUD$77 billion in 2011–12.[15] Australia has the fourth largest proved recoverable coal reserves and is currently the second largest coal exporter in the world.[16] It is also the fastest growing exporter of liquefied natural gas.[17] Emissions from exported coal are not included in emissions inventory processes as they occur offshore.[18] When current

---

[11] Ibid.

[12] US Energy Information Administration, "Energy in Brief: What Are the Major Sources and Users of Energy in the United States," at www.eia.gov/energy_in_brief/article/major_energy_sources_and_users.cfm. Similar figures apply in 2014: see "Evaluating the U.S. Energy Market," *Resource Investing News,* May 8, 2014, at http://resourceinvestingnews .com/70506-infographic-evaluating-the-us-energy-market.html.

[13] World Energy Council, *World Energy Resources: 2013 Survey* (World Energy Council, 23rd ed., 2013).

[14] US Energy Information Administration, "U.S. Expected to Be Largest Producer of Petroleum and Natural Gas Hydrocarbons in 2013," Oct. 4, 2013, at www.eia.gov/ todayinenergy/detail.cfm?id=13251.

[15] Bureau of Resources and Energy Economics, *Energy in Australia 2013* (Australian Government, Canberra, 2013). This accounted for 34 percent of the total value of Australia's commodity exports over this period.

[16] World Energy Council, *World Energy Resources: 2013 Survey* (World Energy Council, 23rd ed., 2013), 5, 11, and 1.6.

[17] International Energy Agency, *Medium-Term Gas Market Report* (IEA, Paris, 2013).

[18] In other words, these emissions are not counted in Australia's total energy-related emissions, instead being assigned to the country where the coal is burned.

exported emissions are added to domestic emissions, Australia jumps from the fifteenth to the sixth largest global carbon polluter.[19] In coming years, these exported emissions are likely to grow substantially as Australian governments and companies seek rapid expansion of coal and other fossil fuel exports.[20]

Within Australia, energy production is also heavily dependent on fossil fuel energy sources. In the financial year 2011–12, brown and black coal supplied 34 percent of Australia's energy consumption, whereas petroleum products (oil, diesel, and liquefied petroleum gas) supplied 39 percent and natural gas 23 percent. Despite an abundance of available renewable energy sources, such as solar and wind, renewable energy sources accounted for only 4 percent of energy consumption during the same period.[21] Although coal use decreased in 2011–12 by 5 percent, overall fossil fuel consumption in Australia is increasing, driven by strong growth in the use of natural gas and petroleum products in the transportation and mining sectors.[22] Total carbon dioxide emissions associated with energy consumption in Australia were 392.286 million tonnes in 2011.[23] This represents a relatively modest 1.2 percent of the total global emissions from energy consumption in the same year.[24] On a per capita basis, however, Australia produces just over 18 tonnes of carbon dioxide emissions per person (compared to 17.621 tonnes in the United States, 6.52 tonnes in China, and 1.451 tonnes in India). This makes Australia one of the

---

[19] Fergus Green and Reuben Finighan, *Laggard to Leader: How Australia Can Lead the World to Zero Carbon Prosperity* (2012, Beyond Zero Emissions Inc., Melbourne), at 16.

[20] Recent reports examining the extent of Australia's fossil fuel resources and corporate coal holdings reveal the massive tonnage of greenhouse gas emissions that would be released if those resources were to be fully exploited. For instance, the independent national Climate Commission (now the Climate Council), in a report released in 2013, found that Australia's untapped fossil fuel resources equate to around 51 billion tonnes of greenhouse gas emissions. To put this in context, this is about one-twelfth of the world's carbon budget – the amount of carbon scientists estimate can be burned by 2050 if we are to prevent a global temperature rise of more than 2°C. See William L. Steffen and Lesley Hughes, *The Critical Decade 2013: Climate Change Science, Risks and Responses* (2013, Climate Commission Secretariat, Department of Industry, Innovation, Climate Change, Science, Research and Tertiary Education, Canberra), 85.

[21] Nhu Che et al., *2013 Australian Energy Update*, Bureau of Resources and Energy Economics, Australian Government, Jul. 2013, at 5–6. Australia has no nuclear power supply.

[22] Ibid., at 1.

[23] U.S. Energy Information Administration, "International Energy Statistics," at www.eia.gov/cfapps/ipdbproject/iedindex3.cfm?tid=90&pid=45&aid=8&cid=all,&syid=2007&eyid=2011&unit=MTCDPP.

[24] Ibid. Total global CO_2 emissions for 2011 were 32,578.645 million tonnes.

highest per capita emitters in the world, rivaling oil-producing countries such as Saudi Arabia.[25]

As the most recent report from the Intergovernmental Panel on Climate Change highlighted, the international community has not yet made or committed to adequate mitigation. However, such mitigation must happen soon to avoid the greatest risks of major climate change.[26] Both the United States and Australia are important parts of this problem and must be part of its solution. The rest of the chapter explores the role that courts have played in the regulatory dialogue about how to proceed in each country, and lessons from that comparative experience.

3.3   US mitigation litigation–regulation linkages

This section traces how US mitigation litigation has influenced the country's regulatory path at multiple levels. Although international climate change litigation has not had significant regulatory impacts, litigation has influenced US mitigation choices substantially at national and subnational levels. Interviewees recounted the many ways in which both statutory and common law suits have shaped not only what regulation has occurred but also the decision-making processes around regulation and projects.

3.3.1   International-level litigation–regulation linkages

The United States is party to the United Nations Framework Convention on Climate Change (UNFCCC) and plays an active role in ongoing international climate change negotiations. However, it has lagged behind other major emitters in its willingness to make binding commitments on emissions reduction. Although President Clinton's administration helped to shape the Kyoto Protocol through US negotiating positions, the US Senate provided such clear opposition to ratification that President Clinton did not even submit the treaty to that body. Specifically, the Senate unanimously passed a resolution stating that the United States should not become party to the Kyoto Protocol owing to its exclusion of developing

---

[25] U.S. Energy Information Administration, "International Energy Statistics: Per Capita emissions," at www.eia.gov/cfapps/ipdbproject/iedindex3.cfm?tid=90&pid=45&aid= 8&cid=all,&syid=2007&eyid=2011&unit=MTCDPP.

[26] See IPCC, "Summary for Policymakers" in T. F. Stocker et al. (eds.), *Climate Change 2013: The Physical Science Basis. Contribution of Working Group I to the Fifth Assessment Report of the Intergovernmental Panel on Climate Change* (2013, Cambridge University Press, Cambridge).

country major emitters like China and India.[27] Under President George W. Bush's leadership, the United States further reinforced its unwillingness to participate in the Kyoto Protocol.[28]

President Obama brought the United States back into more active participation in the UNFCCC and played a pivotal role in negotiating the 2009 Copenhagen Accord that incorporates soft emissions reduction pledges from major emitters.[29] Even so, the US international-level position has not changed fundamentally. The nation remains outside of the Kyoto Protocol regime, even as some parties agreed to a second commitment period at the 2011 Durban and 2012 Doha negotiations.[30] Instead, the United States continues to press for a universal regime and has made voluntary commitments in the lead up to and during recent negotiations, such as its 2014 bilateral agreement with China weeks before its pledges at the Lima UNFCCC negotiations. These positive steps, however, still amount to less in total emissions reductions than its Kyoto Protocol commitments would have.[31]

Litigation at this level has not influenced the US international posture substantially. The 2005 petition by the Inuit peoples to the Inter-American Commission on Human Rights, arguing that climate policy failures in the United States were contributing to climate change damage in the Arctic, was rejected and does not appear to have changed the formal US position.[32] However, the petition probably has had some indirect regulatory influence, particularly in terms of changing norms and values through increasing the public profile of Arctic climate change impacts. In contrast, domestic litigation, discussed in more depth later in the chapter, has fundamentally shaped the US national-level approach. These national-level regulatory impacts affect the global emissions contribution

---

[27] S. Res. 98, 105th Cong. (1997).

[28] George W. Bush, Pres., United States of America, Speech Discussing Global Climate Change (2008) (transcript on file with authors).

[29] Mian, "The Road to Copenhagen."

[30] Doha Amendment to the Kyoto Protocol, Doha, Dec. 8, 2012, C.N.718.2012.TREATIES-XXVII.7.c (not yet in force).

[31] On the November 2014 US-China bilateral deal under which the United States pledged to reduce emissions by 26 to 28% below 2005 levels by 2025, which amounts to 4 to 5% below 1990 levels, see Philip Bump, "The Politics of the U.S.-China Deal," *Wash. Post*, Nov. 12, 2014, http://www.washingtonpost.com/blogs/the-fix/wp/2014/11/12/the-politics-of-the-big-u-s-china-climate-deal/; e-mail from William Burns to Environmental Law Professors Listserv, Nov. 12, 2014 (on file with authors).

[32] Petition to the Inter-American Commission on Human Rights Seeking Relief from Violations Resulting from Global Warming Caused by Acts and Omissions of the United States (Dec. 7, 2005). In 2013, a further petition was filed with the commission targeting Canada's failure to regulate black carbon emissions.

of the United States and its domestic regulatory framework but have not for the most part been connected directly to the US negotiating position or commitments under climate change treaties. The closest tie has been the Obama administration announcing regulatory action pursuant to *Massachusetts v. EPA* just before the 2009 Copenhagen negotiations that took place in the aftermath of comprehensive climate change legislation failing in the US Congress. Since then, the Obama administration has continued to use the opinion as a basis for executive action under the Clean Air Act that it uses to meet its international commitments.[33]

3.3.2   National-level litigation–regulation linkages

Although the United States has had statutes addressing climate change explicitly since the late 1970s, these laws primarily deal with research and measurement. The 1978 National Climate Program Act sought to forward scientific understanding of climate change, and President Carter commissioned a National Research Council Report under that Act.[34] The 1987 Global Climate Protection Act built on the 1978 law, with a focus on establishing "coordinated national policy," forwarding US international leadership on climate change and supporting additional data collection.[35] Neither of these laws requires specific mitigation action, and efforts to pass comprehensive climate change legislation beyond these statutes have failed repeatedly.[36]

Despite this limited legislation directly focused on climate change, the United States has a long-standing robust regime of broader environmental law, including – most relevant to climate change – the Clean Air Act, the Clean Water Act, the Endangered Species Act, and the National Environmental Policy Act (NEPA). Advocates for greater mitigation have pushed for regulation through lawsuits under these broad environmental laws. This litigation has served as a primary direct pathway for federal climate change regulation. For the foreseeable future, the United States seems likely to continue along this regulatory path focused on existing

---

[33] John M. Broder, "Greenhouse Gases Imperil Health, EPA Announces," *N.Y. Times*, Dec. 8, 2009, at A18, www.nytimes.com/2009/12/08/science/earth/08epa.html?r=1&emc=eta1; Hari M. Osofsky, "The Continuing Importance of Climate Change Litigation" (2010) 1 *Clim. L.* 3, at 7.

[34] US National Climate Program Act, 15 U.S.C. §§ 2901-07 (2006); Climate Research Bd., *Carbon Dioxide and Climate: A Scientific Assessment* (1979, National Academies Press, Washington, DC).

[35] Global Climate Protection Act of 1987, 15 U.S.C. § 2901 (1992).

[36] Hari Osofsky, "Diagonal Federalism and Climate Change: Implications for the Obama Administration" (2011) 62 *Alabama L. Rev.* 237.

environmental statutes, with some variation as administrations change. The ongoing lack of consensus in Congress over comprehensive climate change legislation makes it unlikely a direct statutory solution is "going to be a palatable option anytime soon."[37] This section explores how litigation under these environmental statutes has shaped emerging regulation of motor vehicle and power plant greenhouse gas emissions.

3.3.2.1   Clean Air Act

The US Clean Air Act, the statute under which the most significant and publicized litigation and regulation has occurred, was first passed in 1963.[38] It built on the 1955 Air Pollution Control Act and has been amended many times, most significantly in the 1970 amendments that brought it into its modern formulation.[39] As noted, significant recent US regulation of motor vehicles and power plants under the Clean Air Act stems from the US Supreme Court's 2007 decision in *Massachusetts v. EPA*.[40] Interviewees cited this decision, and related litigation under the Clean Air Act, as "critical" to moving forward mitigation regulation at the federal level: "I mean I don't think it would have happened on the timeframe that it is happening without that litigation."[41]

In *Massachusetts v. EPA*, petitioners challenged the US EPA's denial of a petition requesting that it regulate motor vehicles' greenhouse gas emissions under Section 202(a)(1) of the Clean Air Act. The Supreme Court decided that the Clean Air Act's broad definition of air pollutant applied to greenhouse gas emissions despite their substantial differences from the types of pollutants, such as those contributing to smog, that were the act's initial focus. It found that the EPA had abused its discretion through the manner in which it justified not regulating greenhouse gas emissions and required it to "ground its reasons for action or inaction in the statute."[42] The parties to the petition mirrored the subnational divisions in the United States. Twelve states, a US territory, three cities, and thirteen nongovernmental organizations (NGOs) pushed for the regulation, while the EPA, ten other states, and nineteen industry and

---

[37] In-person interview, US Participant 5 (Nov. 14, 2012).
[38] US Clean Air Act of 1963, 42 U.S.C. §§ 7401–7671q (2006).
[39] US Clean Air Act of 1963, 42 U.S.C. §§ 7401–7671q (2006) § 7401; US Air Pollution Control Act of 1955, 42 U.S.C. §§ 7401–7671q (2006); see also Osofsky, "Diagonal Federalism and Climate Change."
[40] *Massachusetts v. EPA*, 549 U.S. 497 (2007).
[41] Telephone interview, US Participant 11 (Oct. 10, 2013).
[42] *Massachusetts v. EPA*, 549 U.S. 497, 535 (2007); see also Hari M. Osofsky, "Is Climate Change 'International'? Litigation's Diagonal Regulatory Role" (2009) 49(3) *Va. J. Intl. L.* 585.

utility groups opposed it. The states wanting stronger regulation were largely coastal, whereas those siding with the EPA tended to be states with large energy industries in the middle of the country.[43]

According to our interviewees, for many in the EPA, the Supreme Court's decision "came as a big surprise and triggered a current of consequences in terms of regulations and legislation and litigation that resulted from the decision."[44] Prior to the decision, the EPA had taken the position that it did not have the legal authority to regulate greenhouse gas emissions under the Clean Air Act. What flowed from the decision was a mandate for EPA regulatory action: "*Massachusetts v. EPA* didn't say [the EPA] had to do it, but they have the authority to do it, and they at least have to consider it."[45] An interviewee who was at the EPA at the time of the decision explained that the judgment

> was welcomed by the career staff who, by and large, wanted to see EPA expand into the realm of addressing greenhouse gases and saw that as a new program for the agency to be addressing and a new way to address the environment. I think that the political staff who were Bush administration officials at the time had the opposite reaction. That this was not something that regulatory agencies should be doing but something that Congress should be legislating.... At the end of the day, everybody reads the decision. When the Supreme Court issues a mandate, everybody follows the Supreme Court mandate. So whether people agreed with it or disagreed with it didn't really become very relevant. It was what was the agency going to do about it? At first EPA was going to regulate and actually proposed internally to do regulations, but then the agency changed its mind and decided to do something called an "advance notice of proposed rulemaking" which provided an opportunity for all stakeholders to advise EPA on how they think they should regulate. It wasn't until the Obama administration when both the political staff and the career staff were aligned that everyone decided to go ahead.[46]

Beyond the direct impacts flowing from its substantive statutory interpretation, *Massachusetts v. EPA* also had a notable indirect regulatory influence, both in terms of changing the nature of the public debate about climate change in the United States[47] and of its allowing access to the courts on a climate change claim. Most significantly regarding threshold issues like standing, it decided that the state of Massachusetts had sufficient interest in the case to have standing before the Court and that

---

[43] Osofsky, "Is Climate Change 'International'?"
[44] Telephone interview, US Participant 9 (Dec. 3, 2012).
[45] Ibid.   [46] Ibid.   [47] See, further, Chapter 6.

the state had made claims that could satisfy the requirements of injury, causation, and remedy. This ruling made it easier for governments to establish standing in subsequent climate change cases, although, through its focus on the special sovereign nature of Massachusetts, the Court created substantial uncertainty regarding nongovernmental petitioners' standing.[48]

In the several years since the *Massachusetts v. EPA* decision, Congress has passed neither legislation to eliminate this Clean Air Act regulatory authority nor additional legislation directly addressing climate change. As a result, EPA regulation pursuant to this decision – often in collaboration with other federal agencies, state governments, and relevant industries – has served as the core of the US federal efforts on climate change. Although the Bush administration did not act in any significant way on the *Massachusetts v. EPA* decision in its final months in office, the Obama administration began taking steps pursuant to the decision immediately on entering office. It commenced considering both whether greenhouse gas emissions from motor vehicles endanger public health and welfare and whether California should receive a waiver to regulate motor vehicle emissions at the state level (a waiver that had been denied by the Bush administration, resulting in litigation by California and other states that wished to follow California's approach).

Since making the Endangerment Finding and granting the waiver,[49] the EPA has created substantial new regulations for both motor vehicles and major stationary sources of greenhouse gas emissions.[50] The Obama administration's most significant accomplishment with respect to motor vehicles and climate change thus far is its National Program for emissions and fuel economy standards for new vehicles. Under this program, the EPA and Department of Transportation have promulgated joint rules on fuel economy and tailpipe greenhouse gas emissions, bridging the

---

[48] The Court's rulings on standing and subsequent federal case law are discussed further in Chapter 7.

[49] EPA, Endangerment and Cause and Contribute Findings for Greenhouse Gases under Section 202(a) of the Clean Air Act, Final Rule, Dec. 15, 2009, 74(239) F.R. 66496; EPA, California State Motor Vehicle Pollution Control Standards; Notice of Decision Granting a Waiver of Clean Air Act Preemption for California's 2009 and Subsequent Model Year Greenhouse Gas Emission Standards for New Motor Vehicles, Jul. 8, 2009, 74(129) F.R. 32744.

[50] These are discussed in depth later. For an overview of the EPA's evolving rulemaking efforts on motor vehicles and power plants, see www.epa.gov/climatechange/EPAactivities/regulatory-initiatives.html.

statutory and agency divide between applicable energy and environmental law. The plan – which emerged from the Obama administration's efforts to forge a compromise between automakers[51] and California[52] – allows manufacturers "to build a single light-duty national fleet that would satisfy

[51] For the reaction of automakers, see Letter from Frederick A. Henderson, CEO of General Motors Corporation, to Lisa P. Jackson, EPA Administrator, and Raymond H. LaHood, Secretary of Transportation, EPA (May 17, 2009), available at www.epa.gov/otaq/climate/regulations/gm.pdf; letter from Stefan Jacoby, President and CEO of Volkswagen Group of America, to Lisa P. Jackson, EPA Administrator, and Raymond H. LaHood, Secretary of Transportation, EPA (May 17, 2009), available at www.epa.gov/otaq/climate/regulations/vw.pdf; letter from James E. Lentz, President of Toyota Motor Sales, to Lisa P. Jackson, EPA Administrator, and Raymond H. LaHood, Secretary of Transportation, EPA (May 17, 2009), available at www.epa.gov/otaq/climate/regulations/toyota.pdf; letter from Dave McCurdy, President and CEO of the Alliance of Automobile Manufacturers, to Raymond H. LaHood, Secretary of Transportation, and Lisa P. Jackson, EPA Administrator, EPA (May 18, 2009), available at www.epa.gov/otaq/climate/regulations/alliance-of-automobile.pdf; letter from John Mendel, Executive Vice President of Automobile Sales for American Honda Motor Company, to Raymond H. LaHood, Secretary of Transportation, and Lisa P. Jackson, EPA Administrator, EPA (May 17, 2009), available at www.epa.gov/otaq/climate/regulations/honda.pdf; letter from Alan R. Mulally, President and CEO of Ford, to Raymond H. LaHood, Secretary of Transportation, and Lisa P. Jackson, EPA Administrator, EPA (May 17, 2009), available at www.epa.gov/otaq/climate/regulations/ford.pdf; letter from Robert L. Nardelli, Chairman and CEO of Chrysler LLC, to Raymond H. LaHood, Secretary of Transportation, and Lisa P. Jackson, EPA Administrator, EPA (May 17, 2009), available at www.epa.gov/otaq/climate/regulations/chrysler.pdf; letter from James J. O'Sullivan, President and CEO of Mazda North American Operations, to Raymond H. LaHood, Secretary of Transportation, and Lisa P. Jackson, EPA Administrator, EPA (May 18, 2009), available at www.epa.gov/otaq/climate/regulations/mazda.pdf; letter from Norbert Reithofer, Chairman of the Board of Management of The BMW Group, to Lisa P. Jackson, EPA Administrator, and Raymond H. LaHood, Secretary of Transportation, EPA (May 18, 2009), available at www.epa.gov/otaq/climate/regulations/bmw.pdf; letter from Dieter Zetsche, Chairman of the Board of Management of Daimler AG and Head of Mercedes-Benz Cars, and Thomas Weber, Member of the Board of Management, Group Research, and Mercedes-Benz Cars Development, to Raymond H. LaHood, Secretary of Transportation, and Lisa P. Jackson, EPA Administrator, EPA (May 18, 2009), available at www.epa.gov/otaq/climate/regulations/daimler.pdf.

[52] For California's pledge to adopt the less stringent federal standards for Model Years (MY) 2012 to 2016, see letter from Edmund G. Brown Jr., Attorney General of California, to Lisa P. Jackson, EPA Administrator, and Raymond H. LaHood, Secretary of Transportation, EPA (May 18, 2009), available at www.epa.gov/otaq/climate/regulations/calif-atty-general.pdf; letter from Mary D. Nichols, Chairman of the California Air Resources Board, to Lisa P. Jackson, EPA Administrator, and Raymond H. LaHood, Secretary of Transportation, EPA (May 18, 2009), available at www.epa.gov/otaq/climate/regulations/air-resources-board.pdf; letter from Arnold Schwarzenegger, Governor of California, to Lisa P. Jackson, EPA Administrator, and Raymond H. LaHood, Secretary of Transportation, EPA (May 18, 2009), available at www.epa.gov/otaq/climate/regulations/calif-gov.pdf.

all requirements under both programs and would provide significant reductions in both greenhouse gas emissions and oil consumption."[53]

The EPA regulations focus on tailpipe emissions pursuant to the Clean Air Act, whereas the National Highway Traffic Safety Administration (NHTSA) regulations take the form of CAFE standards under the Energy Independence and Security Act and the Energy Policy Conservation Act. But they are coordinated for the first time out of an understanding that "the close relationship between emissions of CO_2 [carbon dioxide] – the most prevalent greenhouse gas emitted by motor vehicles – and fuel consumption, means that the technologies to control CO_2 emissions and to improve fuel economy overlap to a great degree."[54] Both agencies measure compliance based on fleet average performance calculated at the end of each model year.[55] The government then issues credits to manufacturers that exceed the fleet average CO_2 or CAFE standard and debits to those that fail to meet the standard.[56] A manufacturer is able to use credits to offset past or future debits, to transfer them among the vehicles in its fleet, or to trade/sell credits to other companies.[57]

The agencies finalized their first set of rules for light-duty vehicles in 2010, covering model years 2012–16.[58] The Obama administration has built on this initial step with frequent new rulemaking efforts to address post-2017 model years of light-duty vehicles and emissions from medium and heavy vehicles.[59] In January 2011, the EPA announced, together with the US Department of Transportation and California, further unification of national and Californian approaches through a single timeframe for proposing those 2017–25 standards. These more stringent rules were finalized in 2012.[60] The two agencies complemented this progress on cars and light trucks with final rules in 2012 for medium- and heavy-duty vehicles. The Heavy Duty National Program establishes fuel economy

---

[53] Notice of Upcoming Joint Rulemaking to Establish Vehicle GHG Emissions and CAFE Standards, 74 Fed. Reg. 24,007, 24,007 (May 22, 2009).

[54] Ibid., at 24,009 n.7.   [55] Ibid., at 24,010.   [56] Ibid.   [57] Ibid.

[58] See Light-Duty Vehicle Greenhouse Gas Emission Standards and Corporate Average Fuel Economy Standards; Final Rule, 75 Fed. Reg. 25,324 (May 7, 2010); also President Barack Obama, Remarks on National Fuel Efficiency Standards in the Rose Garden (May 19, 2009), available at www.whitehouse.gov/the_press_office/Remarks-by-the-President-on-national-fuel-efficiency-standards/ (the Rose Garden agreement).

[59] Notice of Intent, 75 Fed. Reg. 62,739 (Oct. 13, 2010).

[60] Press Release, "EPA, DOT and California Align Timeframe for Proposing Standards for Next Generation of Clean Cars," Jan. 24, 2011, available at http://yosemite.epa.gov/opa/admpress.nsf/1e5ab1124055f3b28525781f0042ed40/6f34c8d6f2b11e5885257822006f60c0!OpenDocument.

and greenhouse emissions standards that the administration claims have the potential to reduce greenhouse gas emissions by nearly 250 million metric tonnes over the life of vehicles sold from 2014 to 2018.[61]

The Obama administration is pairing these efforts on motor vehicles with mandates that push major industrial emitters to reduce their greenhouse gas emissions under Section 111 of the Clean Air Act. These regulations have emerged more slowly, though, owing to the more contentious politics surrounding them. In February 2010, in response to political pressure regarding the economic impact of planned mandates, the EPA modified its plans to slow down the regulatory process. Then-administrator Jackson indicated that the EPA would begin to phase in permitting for large stationary sources in 2011 and for the smallest sources after 2016.[62] In May 2010, the EPA began this process by issuing a final rule that established threshold greenhouse gas permit requirements for new and existing power plants, refineries, and other major industrial emitters under the New Source Review Prevention of Significant Deterioration and Title V. These thresholds help to ensure that only the most significant emitters, which produce 70 percent of stationary source greenhouse gas emissions, are covered under the rule; they tailor the permitting process to make it appropriate for greenhouse gases and to prevent overburdening smaller emitters and state regulators.[63]

The EPA has engaged in additional rulemaking since to refine these requirements further and to account for the varying regulatory conditions in different states.[64] It also announced a settlement of two additional climate change lawsuits that helped shape the EPA's schedule for promulgating National Source Performance Standards for greenhouse gas emissions by power plants and refineries.[65] Most controversially, though,

---

[61] Greenhouse Gas Emissions Standards and Fuel Efficiency Standards for Medium- and Heavy-Duty Engines and Vehicles, 75 Fed. Reg. 74152 (Nov. 30, 2010). For correction to proposed rules, see Greenhouse Gas Emissions Standards and Fuel Efficiency Standards for Medium- and Heavy-Duty Engines and Vehicles, 75 Fed. Reg. 81952 (Dec. 29, 2010).

[62] See letter from Lisa P. Jackson, EPA Administrator, to Hon. Jay D. Rockefeller, IV, US Senator (Feb. 22, 2010), available at http://media.washingtonpost.com/wp-srv/special/climate-change/documents/post-carbon/022210adm-letter.pdf.

[63] Prevention of Significant Deterioration and Title V Greenhouse Gas Tailoring Rule, 75 Fed. Reg. 31,514 (Jun. 3, 2010), available at www.gpo.gov/fdsys/pkg/FR-2010-06-03/pdf/2010-11974.pdf#page=1.

[64] US EPA, Clean Air Act Permitting for Greenhouse Gas Emissions – Final Rules, Fact Sheet, Dec. 23, 2010, available at www.epa.gov/NSR/ghgdocs/20101223factsheet.pdf.

[65] See press release, "EPA to Set Modest Pace for Greenhouse Gas Standards" (Dec. 23, 2010), available at http://yosemite.epa.gov/opa/admpress.nsf/6424ac1caa800aab85257359003f5337/d2f038e9daed78de8525780200568bec!OpenDocument.

in September 2013, the EPA proposed a "Carbon Pollution Standard" for new power plants under Clean Air Act Section 111(b) that coal-fired power plants could only meet through partial carbon sequestration and storage.[66] In a speech at the University of Michigan that fall, EPA administrator Gina McCarthy explained that this decision represents a compromise between the most emissions-limiting option – full carbon sequestration and storage – and technological and economic reality.[67] Then, in June 2014, the EPA took the next contentious step with its "Clean Power Plan," through which the "EPA is proposing emission guidelines for states to follow in developing plans to address greenhouse gas emissions from existing fossil fuel-fired electric generating units."[68] The Clean Power Plan complements EPA's Section 111(b) regulation of new power plants with regulation under Clean Air Act Section 111(d) of existing power plants. Through its plan, the EPA aims to reduce carbon dioxide emissions from the power sector by 30 percent from 2005 levels by 2030.[69]

Heated debate over EPA greenhouse gas regulations, especially with respect to power plants, continues to take place in the public sphere, and both motor vehicles and stationary sources regulations have been challenged through litigation.[70] To date, the motor vehicle greenhouse gas regulations have withstood the challenges, but the Supreme Court has partially struck down stationary source regulations.

Initially, it looked like all of the Obama administration's greenhouse gas emissions regulation under the Clean Air Act might survive the challenges. The DC Circuit's June 2012 opinion in *Coalition for Responsible Regulation v. EPA* rejected numerous aspects of industry challenges to

---

[66] See EPA, Carbon Pollution Standards, 2013 Proposed Carbon Pollution Standard for New Power Plants, www2.epa.gov/carbon-pollution-standards/2013-proposed-carbon-pollution-standard-new-power-plants.

[67] Gina McCarthy, "Keynote Remarks at the University of Michigan Environmental Law and Public Health Conference," (2014) 3 *Mich. J. Environ. Admin. L.* __. For a discussion of these issues as well as property rights concerns, see Alexandra B. Klass and Elizabeth J. Wilson, "Climate Change, Carbon Sequestration, and Property Rights" (2010) *Univ. Ill. L. Rev.* 363; Alexandra B. Klass and Elizabeth J. Wilson, "Carbon Capture and Sequestration: Identifying and Managing Risks" (2009) 8 *Issues in Legal Scholarship*, no. 3, art. 1.

[68] EPA, "Carbon Pollution: Emission Guidelines for Existing Stationary Sources: Electric Utility Generating Units," 13, 40 CFR Part 60, EPA-HQ-OAR-2013-0602; FRL-xxxx-xx, Jun. 2, 2014, www2.epa.gov/sites/production/files/2014-05/documents/20140602proposal-cleanpowerplan.pdf.

[69] EPA, Carbon Pollution Emission Guidelines for Existing Statutory Sources, 14.

[70] Antiregulatory litigation challenging EPA rulemaking is discussed further in Chapter 7.

the EPA's rulemaking efforts.[71] The court held that "1) the Endangerment Finding and Tailpipe Rule are neither arbitrary nor capricious; 2) EPA's interpretation of the governing CAA provisions is unambiguously correct; and 3) no petitioner has standing to challenge the Timing and Tailoring Rules."[72] One interviewee explained that the DC Circuit opinion "signified a strong endorsement of EPA's use of the Clean Air Act as a regulatory tool" and that the "Court basically said, look, *Massachusetts v. EPA* required this, we're not going back."[73]

However, in its June 2014 decision in *Utility Air Regulatory Group v. EPA*, the Supreme Court partially reversed the DC Circuit with respect to the stationary source regulation. The Supreme Court granted certiorari on the relatively narrow question of "whether EPA permissibly determined that its regulation of greenhouse gas emissions from new motor vehicles triggered permitting requirements under the Clean Air Act for stationary sources that emit greenhouse gases."[74] The Supreme Court thus did not address the Endangerment Finding or tailpipe rule in its grant.

The Court allowed one pathway and rejected another for stationary source regulation. It held that the

> EPA exceeded its statutory authority when it interpreted the Clean Air Act to require PSD and Title V permitting for stationary sources based on their greenhouse gas emissions. Specifically, the Agency may not treat greenhouse gases as a pollutant for purposes of defining a "major emitting facility" (or a "modification" thereof) in the PSD context or a "major source" in the Title V context. To the extent its regulations purport to do so, they are invalid. EPA may, however, continue to treat greenhouse gases as a "pollutant subject to regulation under this chapter" for purposes of requiring BACT [best available control technology] for "anyway" sources.[75]

The practical effect of this decision for the EPA's greenhouse gas regulatory regime is relatively limited. The opinion notes the solicitor general's claim that "'anyway' sources account for roughly 83% of American stationary source greenhouse gas emissions, compared to just 3% for the additional,

---

[71] *Coalition for Responsible Regulation v. EPA*, 684 F.3d 102 (D.C. Cir. Jun. 26, 2012).
[72] Ibid., at 113.   [73] In-person interview, US Participant 5 (Nov. 14, 2012).
[74] *Coalition for Responsible Regulation v. EPA*, 684 F.3d 102, 113–14 (D.C. Cir. June 26, 2012) (No. 09-1322, 10-1092), *rehearing en banc denied*, 2012 WL 6621785 (D.C. Cir. Dec. 20, 2012) (No. 09-1322, 10-1024, 10-1025, 10-1026, 10-1030, 10-1035, 10-1036, 10-1037, 10-1038), certiorari granted in part and denied in part, *Utility Air Regulatory Group v. EPA*, 2013 WL 1155428, 81 USLW 3560 (U.S. Dist. Col. Oct. 15, 2013) (No. 12-1146).
[75] *Utility Air Regulatory Group v. EPA*, 134 S.Ct. 2427, 2449 (Jun. 23, 2014).

non-'anyway' sources EPA sought to regulate at Steps 2 and 3 of the Tailoring Rule."[76] But the opinion does constrain the EPA's regulatory approach.

Regardless of this somewhat limiting 2014 Supreme Court decision, the direct and indirect impacts of *Massachusetts v. EPA* have been substantial. The decision has undergirded the US federal approach to climate change during a time of congressional gridlock on these issues. Moreover, as discussed further in Chapters 5 and 6, the opinion has had a host of indirect regulatory impacts on public perceptions of climate change and on corporate behavior.

3.3.2.2 Other environmental statutes

Although *Massachusetts v. EPA* and the Clean Air Act have received more recognition, numerous other environmental statutes have served as a basis for lawsuits over climate change. For example, advocates have used NEPA[77] – and its state-level counterparts – to incorporate climate change concerns into environmental review processes. Actions under the Endangered Species Act have led to the listing of species as threatened or endangered based on climate change.[78] Lawsuits addressing fuel economy standards issued under the Energy Policy and Conservation Act (EPCA) have played a role in increasing the stringency of these standards.[79] Indeed, looking across the spectrum of these federal statutes, some US environmental groups see the key to improved climate change regulation as better enforcement and full implementation of general environmental laws rather than the enactment of national climate change legislation. As one of our interviewees stressed, "it's not the law that has to change; we need the political will to actually implement it."[80]

This section highlights actions under NEPA and the Endangered Species Act as examples of how additional litigation under major environmental statutes has influenced US mitigation pathways. These two examples are particularly illustrative because of the ways in which they complement the Clean Air Act efforts described earlier. While the Clean

---

[76] *Utility Air Regulatory Group v. EPA* at 2438–39.
[77] National Environmental Policy Act 1969, Pub. L. No. 91-190, 83 Stat. 852 (codified as amended at 42 U.S.C. § 4321) (NEPA).
[78] Endangered Species Act 1973, Pub. L. No. 93-205, 87 Stat. 884 (codified at 16 U.S.C. § 1531).
[79] Energy Policy and Conservation Act of 1975, Pub. L. No. 94-163, §§ 501–12, 89 Stat. 871, 901–16 (codified as amended at 49 U.S.C.A. §§ 32,901–16 [West 2009].
[80] In-person interview, US Participant 2 (Oct. 22, 2012).

Air Act litigation and subsequent regulation focus on setting defined limits on mobile and stationary source greenhouse gas emissions, NEPA addresses the process by which projects are approved and thus illustrates the procedurally oriented statutory interpretation pathway introduced in Chapter 2. The Endangered Species Act cases add an interesting regulatory dimension through highlighting mitigation–adaptation linkages. The lawsuits focus on the need both to limit emissions to prevent harm to species and to address that harm when it occurs. We address each of these statutes and the regulatory influence of climate change litigation under them in turn.

As noted earlier, NEPA is a process-oriented statute; it governs the environmental review process for new projects that receive federal funding.[81] While often not ultimately successful in blocking greenhouse gas–intensive projects, NEPA cases and equivalent lawsuits under state assessment laws have consistently resulted in decisions affirming that climate change should be part of environmental assessment procedures.[82] Professors Markell and Ruhl refer to this NEPA litigation, somewhat disparagingly, as "judicial business as usual,"[83] but this view may underestimate the cumulative significance of litigation over environmental assessment in directly altering the regulatory landscape for greenhouse gas–emitting projects. One of our interviewees – a private attorney regularly engaged in NEPA litigation and advising in the climate change context – put it this way:

> I think you can definitely find support for the view that the requirement to consider climate change under NEPA is either a natural evolution or it's built on all the prior rulings in the law beforehand. Yes, that's correct.

[81] Lynton K. Caldwell, *The National Environmental Policy Act: An Agenda for the Future* (1998, Indiana University Press, Bloomington).

[82] See Michael Gerrard, "Climate Change and the Environmental Impact Review Process" (2008) 22(3) *Natural Resources and Environment* 20; Mark Squillace and Alexander Hood, "NEPA and Climate Change" in Albert M. Ferlo, Karin P. Sheldon, and Mark Squillace (eds.), *The NEPA Litigation Guide* (2nd ed., 2012, American Bar Association, Section of Environment, Energy and Resources, Chicago), 261. At state level, litigation under statutes such as the California Environmental Quality Act (CEQA) has had similar effects: Stephen Kostka and Michael Zischke (eds.), *Practice under the California Environmental Quality Act* (2013, California Continuing Education of the Bar, San Francisco); Dave Owen, "Climate Change and Environmental Assessment Law" (2008) 33 *Colum. J. Environ. L.* 57; Shute, Mihaly & Weinberger LLP, "CEQA/NEPA Litigation," at www.smwlaw.com/practice-areas/ceqa-litigation.

[83] David Markell and J.B. Ruhl, "An Empirical Assessment of Climate Change in the Courts: A New Jurisprudence or Business as Usual" (2012) 64 *Fla. L. Rev.* 15, 15.

But on the other hand I'd also say it's still significant and a bit of a watershed because you have now judicial recognition essentially that, and judicial acknowledgment, that potential climate change effects are real. And it seems like it could have just as conceivably been that the majority rule developed that climate change impacts were either too remote or too unquantifiable or just too speculative to be able to evaluate and you could almost see the contrary possibility that you could have had a line of cases and agency guidance, and maybe even leading to rules saying that, well, yeah, we recognize climate change effects may be occurring but they are too remote and too unquantifiable so NEPA's not supposed to be a crystal ball and it's not possible to consider every possible impact and so until there's better science or a better way to evaluate these and quantify them, they're not going to have to be considered in environmental impact assessment. But that's *not* what the courts did. They've gone the other way! So I think that is significant and, like I say, a bit of a watershed and not just incremental. And so to those plaintiffs that brought those cases they've accomplished a shift, incremental or not, in the policy and law in that area and have institutionalized broader consideration of climate change effects through the NEPA process.[84]

NEPA has played an important role not just in power plant projects but also in regulation of motor vehicle emissions for many years. For example, prior to the *Massachusetts v. EPA* decision and the regulations pursuant to it that brought together tailpipe emissions and fuel efficiency, *Center for Biological Diversity v. NHTSA* addressed environmental review in the context of fuel efficiency and climate change.[85] One interview participant explained,

This case was pre–*Mass v. EPA* so it was just under EPCA and NEPA. And the court ruled both that the agency had unlawfully failed to do an environmental impact statement under NEPA because of greenhouse gas emissions and that that was exactly the kind of cumulative impact that we need to look at. And that was significant because in a case called *City of LA* in 1990 the DC Circuit had actually ruled, then Judge Ginsberg, Justice Ginsberg, had actually ruled you don't have to do an EIS [environmental impact statement] to look at the impact of lowering fuel economy standards – that was standards from the 1980s that had actually gone backwards and they had ruled you didn't have to do an EIS even though it was a close call. So the Ninth Circuit, you know, after the passage of sixteen years and the increase in understanding of the seriousness of global warming said, well, they had to look at greenhouse gas emissions, and that really

---

[84] Telephone interview, US Participant 3 (Nov. 7, 2012).
[85] *Center for Biological Diversity v. National Highway Traffic Safety Administration* 508 F.3d 508 (9th Cir. 2007).

has changed, well, it has dramatically changed, the types of EISs that we're seeing. I would say we now see very lengthy EISs quantifying greenhouse gas emissions and talking about them a lot.

Cumulatively, these NEPA cases have created an expectation of litigation over projects that involve significant greenhouse gas emissions. As Chapter 5 explores in more depth, this litigation has become increasingly mainstream over time, resulting not only in direct court orders for greenhouse gas emissions to be included in environmental review but also in more indirect changes to corporate culture around project development. In addition, the NEPA cases help tie the national regulatory scale to the international one by at times addressing the Overseas Private Investment Corporation (OPIC) and Export-Import Bank's financing of US exports of fossil fuels and projects abroad.[86]

The Endangered Species Act cases provide an important illustration of statutory regulatory pathways because of their significant regulatory influence in both the mitigation and adaptation spheres. The Endangered Species Act is a federal environmental law, enacted in 1973, that seeks to protect and recover imperiled plant and animal species and the ecosystems on which they depend. Beginning in 2001, several petitions and associated litigation sought the listing of species as threatened or endangered under the Endangered Species Act on the basis of climate change impacts.[87] In general, these cases have been seen as part of the effort to promote federal government action on mitigation given the potential for Endangered Species Act listing to trigger emissions reduction obligations to limit climate change impacts on listed species. However, the Endangered Species Act litigation, according to some, can also be seen to be adaptation oriented because its focus is "what is climate change doing

---

[86] These NEPA cases are discussed further in Chapter 5. Their focus on the contribution of US agency decision making to exported emissions has parallels with the Australian case law, discussed later, addressing scope 3 emissions from coal mines. Increasing NEPA litigation in the United States is focusing on this question of how coal exports (and associated infrastructure like export terminals) contribute to greater coal use and increased emissions. See, e.g., Earthjustice Petition to the Army Corp of Engineers to Undertake Area-Wide Environmental Impact Assessment on All Proposed Coal Export Terminals in Washington and Oregon, May 22, 2013, www.powerpastcoal.org/wp-content/uploads/2013/05/Petition-Area-Wide-Coal-Export-EIS.pdf; *Climate Solutions v. Cowlitz Co.*, Petition for Review (Washington State Shorelines Hearings Bd, filed Dec. 13, 2010).

[87] For an overview of the main petitions, Brendan R. Cummings and Kassie R. Siegel, "Biodiversity, Global Warming, and the United States Endangered Species Act: The Role of Domestic Wildlife Law in Addressing Greenhouse Gas Emissions" in William C. G. Burns and Hari M. Osofsky (eds.), *Adjudicating Climate Change: State, National, and International Approaches* (2009, Cambridge University Press, New York), 145.

to the United States or to the world more broadly and how should that influence our decision-making."[88] This chapter focuses on the mitigation-oriented aspects of the Endangered Species Act cases, while Chapter 4 considers their influence on adaptation.

The best-known climate listing under the Endangered Species Act is for the polar bear, whose Arctic sea ice habitat is imperiled by rising temperatures and sea ice melt.[89] A petition under the Endangered Species Act for listing of the polar bear as either endangered (garnering the highest level of protection) or threatened was initially submitted by an NGO, the Center for Biological Diversity, in 2005. This petition subsequently became the subject of long-running litigation designed both to force action by the Bush administration (through the National Fish and Wildlife Service) and to resist challenges to listing of the species from the state of Alaska and various fossil fuel industry associations.[90] As a result of the legal pressure maintained by the Center for Biological Diversity and other NGOs through the litigation, the Bush administration eventually listed the polar bear under the Endangered Species Act in May 2008 as a threatened species on the basis of global warming impacts.[91]

Momentous as this listing – and the Bush administration's accompanying acknowledgment of the science of climate change – was at the time, its full regulatory impact for both mitigation and adaptation remains unclear. In conjunction with listing the polar bear as threatened, the Bush administration issued the "4(d) rule." This rule exempts all greenhouse gas–emitting projects from the ambit of Section 7 of the ESA, which requires agency actions to safeguard listed species' critical habitats. Subsequent litigation challenged the 4(d) rule and was partially successful on procedural grounds under NEPA – illustrating how major environmental statutes can work synergistically in this context – but the rule remains in place, following its readoption by the Obama administration.[92]

---

[88] Telephone interview, US Participant 12 (Dec. 2, 2013).

[89] Cummings & Siegel, "Biodiversity, Global Warming, and the United States Endangered Species Act."

[90] *In re Polar Bear Endangered Species Act Listing & § 4(d) Rule Litig.*, 2011 U.S. Dist. LEXIS 119476 (D.D.C., Oct. 17, 2011); *In re Polar Bear Endangered Species Act Listing & § 4(d) Rule Litig.*, 2011 U.S. Dist. LEXIS 70172 (D.D.C., June 30, 2011); *In re Polar Bear Endangered Species Act Listing & § 4(d) Rule Litig.*, No. 11–5219 (U.S. Court of Appeals, D.C. Cir., Mar. 30, 2013).

[91] Determination of Threatened Status for the Polar Bear (Ursus maritimus) throughout Its Range, 73(95) F.R. § 28212 (2008).

[92] Special Rule for the Polar Bear Under Section 4(d) of the Endangered Species Act, 50 C.F.R. § 17.40(q) (2013).

Other litigation challenging the substantive merits of the 4(d) rule has been unsuccessful notwithstanding apparent judicial sympathy for plaintiffs' arguments that protecting the polar bear requires deep greenhouse gas reductions.[93] For example, *In re Polar Bear Endangered Species Act Listing and 4(d) Litigation*, two judgments issued by Judge Sullivan of the U.S. District Court for the District of Columbia[94] – later upheld on appeal[95] – noted that "the Court is sensitive to plaintiffs' arguments for a strong mechanism to combat the effects of global climate change."[96] Nonetheless, the district court ruled,

> The question at the heart of this litigation – whether the [Endangered Species Act] is an effective or appropriate tool to address the threat of climate change – is not a question that this Court can decide based upon its own independent assessment, particularly in the abstract. The answer to that question will ultimately be grounded in science and policy determinations that are beyond the purview of this Court.[97]

This opinion has effectively limited the potential for Endangered Species Act litigation to contribute to mitigation action, at least in the context of the polar bear.[98] As explored in Chapter 4, though, the Endangered Species Act litigation has arguably had more significant direct and indirect regulatory influence in the adaptation sphere.

3.3.2.3   Common law approaches

In addition to lawsuits seeking to force or limit governmental regulation of greenhouse gas emissions through the interpretation of statutes, a smaller subset of claims in US federal courts have followed the common law pathway, focusing directly on major corporate emitters under the

---

[93] *In re Polar Bear Endangered Species Listing and 4(d) Litigation*, U.S. District Court for the D.C. Circuit, Misc. No. 08-764, Transcript, Feb. 23, 2011, Washington, DC, at 15.

[94] *In re Polar Bear Endangered Species Act Listing & § 4(d) Rule Litig.*, 2011 U.S. Dist. LEXIS 119476 (D.D.C., Oct. 17, 2011); *In re Polar Bear Endangered Species Act Listing & § 4(d) Rule Litig.*, 2011 U.S. Dist. LEXIS 70172 (D.D.C., Jun. 30, 2011).

[95] *In re Polar Bear Endangered Species Act Listing & § 4(d) Rule Litig.*, No. 11-5219 (U.S. Court of Appeals, D.C. Cir., Mar. 30, 2013).

[96] *In re Polar Bear Endangered Species Act Listing & § 4(d) Rule Litig.*, 2011 U.S. Dist. LEXIS 119476 (D.D.C., Oct. 17, 2011), 10.

[97] *In re Polar Bear Endangered Species Act Listing & § 4(d) Rule Litig.*, 2011 U.S. Dist. LEXIS 119476 (D.D.C., Oct. 17, 2011), 56–57.

[98] The potential to use the Endangered Species Act as a mitigation tool is potentially greater for endangered species to which the 4(d) rule does not apply. Several coral species have been listed as endangered on global warming grounds. As rulemaking efforts for protection and recovery of these corals move forward, the role of climate change mitigation may again come to the forefront.

federal common law nuisance doctrine. In June 2011, the US Supreme Court produced its second climate change ruling in one of these nuisance cases, *American Electric Power (AEP) v. Connecticut.*[99]

AEP v. Connecticut focused on whether the combined greenhouse gas emissions from several of the largest US power plants constituted a public nuisance. With respect to threshold issues, a four-justice plurality – with Justice Sotomayor recusing herself – reaffirmed *Massachusetts v. EPA*'s approach to standing and also held that no other threshold issues barred review. This decision on threshold issues did not analyze the political question doctrine – which had been an issue in lower courts – in any depth but indicated that it would not pose a barrier to review.[100] However, after finding that these public nuisance claims fell within the limited parameters of federal common law, the Court used the displacement doctrine to foreclose federal public nuisance as an avenue for climate change litigation so long as the EPA retained its authority to regulate greenhouse gas emissions under the Clean Air Act.[101] In the process of its analysis, the Court reinforced promotive statutory interpretation suits under the Clean Air Act and Administrative Procedure Act as an appropriate way to shape the path of climate change regulation. The Court did not reach the question of whether state law nuisance claims were preempted, an issue that has not yet been resolved in other courts.[102]

The Supreme Court's decision in *AEP v. Connecticut* – to view common law federal nuisance suits as displaced – precludes success in future such cases so long as the US EPA retains its regulatory authority.[103] The Court's continued reluctance to resolve the issue of nongovernmental standing regarding climate change, often relevant in nuisance actions, is currently resulting in splits among lower courts over the issue.[104] Chapter 7 discusses these and other separation-of-powers barriers in more depth. If one

---

[99] 131 S. Ct. 2527 (2011).

[100] The political question doctrine and its role in US climate litigation are discussed further in Chapter 7.

[101] The role played by the displacement doctrine in climate case law is examined further in Chapter 7.

[102] *American Electric Power v. Connecticut*, 131 S. Ct. 2527 (2011); see also Hari M. Osofsky, "Litigation's Role in the Path of U.S. Federal Climate Change Regulation: Implications of *AEP v. Connecticut*" (2012) 46 *Valparaiso Univ. L. Rev.* 447. For a summary of all US climate change nuisance cases, see Arnold and Porter LLP, "U.S. Climate Change Litigation Chart."

[103] Osofsky, "Litigation's Role in the Path of U.S. Federal Climate Change Regulation."

[104] See, further, the discussion of standing in Chapter 7.

of the still-pending nuisance cases were to be successful, it could create significant regulatory momentum in the United States and internationally by exposing large emitters to liability for damage caused by climate change to which their emissions contributed. However, such cases face many hurdles regarding proof of causation and contribution even if they establish standing and successfully address the preemption question that *AEP v. Connecticut* left open for the state law nuisance claims.

Thus, at the federal level in the United States, climate change regulation is proceeding along pathways directly shaped by the Supreme Court despite the lack of political will to produce comprehensive legislation. This approach leaves US mitigation regulation vulnerable to changes in presidential administrations that influence agency enforcement efforts and to ongoing legal challenges. However, the inertia in the US Congress that stymies the passage of comprehensive climate change legislation will also likely prevent legislative action to strip the EPA of its statutory authority to regulate greenhouse gas emissions.

3.3.3   State-level litigation–regulation linkages

Owing to the federal system of government in the United States, states and local governments have substantial powers relevant to climate change mitigation. Most land use planning and energy decision making occur at subnational levels. In addition, related federal statutes allow substantial scope for autonomous state and local action; US federal environmental statutes have numerous provisions that allow states implementation flexibility and, at times, opportunities to exceed federal standards.[105] As a consequence, state and local governments, along with interstitial regional entities, form an important part of the US regulatory landscape relevant to climate change mitigation.

Like at the federal level, litigation has played a crucial role in US state and local regulatory approaches on mitigation, mainly utilizing direct regulatory pathways.[106] States and localities have been parties in

---

[105] These provisions vary in whether they set a minimum standard for states (floor preemption), mandate particular standards for states (ceiling preemption), or defer to the states with minimal preemption.

[106] Hari Osofsky has discussed these roles of states and cities in depth in previous scholarship. See Hari M. Osofsky, "Climate Change Litigation as Pluralist Legal Dialogue" (2007) 26A *Stanford Environ. L. J.* 181; Osofsky, "Is Climate Change 'International'?"; Hari M. Osofsky, "Scaling 'Local': The Implications of Greenhouse Gas Regulation in San

lawsuits over federal regulation,[107] states have sued the federal government to have the ability to regulate greenhouse gases more stringently than federal agencies,[108] state and localities have faced lawsuits (both pro- and antiregulatory) over their climate change statutes and regulations,[109] states have sued their localities to force climate change regulation,[110] and state courts have heard a diverse set of claims involving climate change including numerous challenges to specific projects, particularly coal-fired power plants.[111] As these examples indicate, the deep divides among states and localities regarding climate change complicate the regulatory role of these lawsuits; some states and localities support stronger regulation and some oppose it.[112] Nonetheless, as noted in one of the introductory

Bernardino County" (2009) 30 *Mich. J. Intl. L.* 689; Osofsky, "Suburban Climate Change Efforts: Possibilities for Small and Nimble Cities Participating in State, Regional, National, and International Networks."

[107] For example, cities and states were parties in both *American Electric Power v. Connecticut,* 131 S. Ct. 2527 (2011), and *Massachusetts v. EPA,* 549 U.S. 497, 535 (2007).

[108] See, e.g., Petition for Review of Decision of the *United States Environmental Protection Agency, California v. EPA,* No. 08-70011 (9th Cir. Jan. 2, 2008), http://ag.ca.gov/cms_attachments/press/pdfs/n1514_epapetition-1.pdf. For the EPA's waiver denial under the Bush administration, see letter from Stephen L. Johnson, Adm'r, U.S. Envtl. Prot. Agency, to Arnold Schwarzenegger, Governor of Cal. (Dec. 19, 2007), available at http://ag.ca.gov/cms_attachments/press/pdfs/n1514_epa-letter.pdf.

[109] E.g., *Thrun v. Cuomo* litigation in the New York Supreme Court, which attempted to block the state's participation in the Regional Greenhouse Gas Initiative.

[110] E.g., California's suit against San Bernardino County and other local governments for omitting climate change from general plans. See Petition for Writ of Mandate at 12, *Ctr. for Biological Diversity v. County of San Bernardino,* No. 07 Civ. 293 (Cal. Super. Ct., County of San Bernardino Sept. 11, 2007), available at www.communityrights.org/PDFs/Petition_(00011023).PDF; Order Regarding Settlement, *People v. County of San Bernardino,* No. 07 Civ. 329 (Cal. Super. Ct., County of San Bernardino, Aug. 28, 2007), available at http://ag.ca.gov/cms_pdfs/press/2007-08-21_San_Bernardino_settlement_agreement.pdf; Petition for Writ of Mandate at 2, *People v. County of San Bernardino,* No. 07 Civ. 329 (Cal. Super. Ct., County of San Bernardino, Apr. 13, 2007), available at http://ag.ca.gov/globalwarming/pdf/SanBernardino_complaint.pdf.

[111] For a summary of these cases, see Arnold and Porter LLP, "U.S. Climate Change Litigation Chart" (Challenges to Coal-Fired Power Plants).

[112] Kirsten Engel, "State and Local Climate Change Initiatives: What Is Motivating State and Local Governments to Address a Global Problem and What Does This Say about Federalism and Environmental Law?" (2006) *The Urban Lawyer,* no. 38, 1015; Reid Ewing et al., *Growing Cooler: Evidence on Urban Development and Climate Change* (2007, Urban Land Institute, Chicago); Hari M. Osofsky and Janet Koven Levit, "The Scale of Networks: Local Climate Change Coalitions" (2008) 8 *Chicago J. Intl. L.* 409; Katherine A. Trisolini, "All Hands on Deck: Local Governments and the Potential for Bidirectional Climate Change Regulation" (2010) 62 *Stanford L. Rev.* 669.

quotations to this chapter, interviewees expressed the view that progress is being made.[113]

Project challenges constitute the vast majority of state court suits by volume. Lawsuits against coal-fired power plants, which often take place in state courts, form part of broader NGO campaigns to shift utilities away from coal. These campaigns, discussed further in Chapter 6, combine regulatory and permitting suits with media and public awareness efforts and so often involve both direct statutory interpretation and indirect influences on social norms and corporate behavior. As an NGO leader involved in these campaigns explained,

> I think that the success at the most general level has been because it is a campaign that's fully integrated and coordinated so that we have organizers on the ground, in pretty much every state; we have media people supporting them; we have lawyers; we do lobbying when appropriate. I don't think that you can take any one of those elements in and of itself and stop a new coal plant or shut down an existing coal plant – it takes the whole package.... So, we have been able to play this role of being a coordinator of the effort and a resource where we do this tracking [whether] a new proposal or proposed plant [for] all of the proposals and what the status was – we do the same thing with existing plants. We have a team of legal assistants who track all of these proposals and/or things that are happening with existing plants when they go through – if they have to have some sort of proceeding before a state public utilities commission – so that we're on top of all that.... So with each plant, I'd say, maybe we'll be in the public service commission involved in a reg case.... And then for this same plant, we most certainly will be doing organizing around it and going and having rallies and trying to get public support for shutting it down....
>
> We don't necessarily focus on every single coal plant – there are hundreds (something like 1500 units?). If the plant is relatively newer and well-controlled and big and runs all the time – that's not necessarily where we're going to put our resources because it's not likely that we're going to be able to shut the thing down....
>
> The other aspect of it is that we do have – it's a national campaign – so we do national media and we try and tie everything together and show people the big picture.[114]

As discussed in more depth in Chapter 5, these suits also have directly influenced public utility commission proceedings and put significant

---

[113] In-person interview, US Participant 6 (Nov. 14, 2012), citing in particular the state of California's involvement in *Massachusetts v. EPA*, litigation over California's Pavley standards for greenhouse emissions from vehicles, and the San Bernardino county litigation.

[114] Telephone interview, US Participant 13 (Dec. 9, 2013).

pressure on both the utility industry and coal-fired power plants to change their behavior.

Although the vast majority of state court suits involve projects with significant fossil fuel emissions, other suits at this level involve dynamics around mitigation between state and local governments. The state of California's action against San Bernardino County under the California Environmental Quality Act over the county's failure to incorporate greenhouse gas emissions in its general plan provides an example of an action-forcing suit that has been seen as very successful in advancing mitigation outcomes at a local level. Settlement of the litigation, which included San Bernardino County's agreement to develop a Climate Action Plan, had a variety of direct and indirect regulatory impacts. As one interviewee explained,

> what happened was the legislature actually made explicit what we had pursued in the litigation, which was that you basically do need to evaluate greenhouse gas emission impacts of plans and projects and now in the state of California there are literally hundreds of Climate Action Plans for local governments and the concept has moved to other states as well. So some jurisdictions take it more seriously than others, but there is now quite a number of very good local plans for reducing greenhouse gas emissions over the next planning period. So that, I think, allowed local governments that wanted to engage to do so in a very specific way, and it moved those that were not so keen on it to have to do it anyway. So I think that actually – you know, it's a different . . . it's a ground-up idea – but I think it has been fairly effective.[115]

Alongside these pro-regulatory, action-forcing suits, antiregulatory subnational litigation is also growing quickly, with states and localities facing lawsuits over their climate change statutes and regulations. California, in particular, has faced strong challenges to its state climate change laws as affected fossil fuel companies and business interests seek to block or limit programs such as cap-and-trade and California's Low Carbon Fuel Standard.[116] A significant motivation for involvement in these lawsuits seems to be the desire to prevent the spread of stringent climate change laws across the country:

> And it's just that, you know, California's the leading edge and they don't want this program to go forward or to succeed because that only makes it that much more likely that it would succeed on a federal level. And, believe

---

[115] In-person interview, US Participant 6 (Nov. 14, 2012).
[116] State-level antiregulatory litigation is discussed further in Chapter 7.

me, I'm very pessimistic that this [Californian cap-and-trade] program
would ever provide a model for a federal program just because it has so
many moving parts, but the mere example that it could move forward
and it could be done. And time and time again it's been proven that as
California goes, so the rest of the country goes. So if they could stop it,
they would.[117]

Although dormant Commerce Clause challenges have not been successful thus far in California or Colorado, a Minnesota district court ruled
the other way. As discussed in depth in Chapter 7, these cases have the
potential to pose barriers to states attempting to take action to address
climate change and promote energy transition.

In addition to this extensive litigation over statutes, cases involving
states, either as plaintiffs or defendants, have also sought to utilize common law pathways, albeit with mixed results. The case of *AEP v. Connecticut*, involving a public nuisance action brought by a coalition of cities,
states, and other parties, was discussed previously. In another example, an
Oregon-based nonprofit organization, Our Children's Trust, filed lawsuits
against all fifty US states and some federal agencies under the public trust
doctrine.[118] The public trust doctrine treats certain natural resources as
owned by the government, which has trust obligations to the public to
maintain them for public use and benefit. In the United States, this doctrine varies from state to state, based on their common law traditions,
and in some states is also viewed as part of constitutional or statutory law.
Although a number of these lawsuits have already been dismissed,[119] state
courts in both Texas and New Mexico held in 2012 that the public trust
protections could extend to the atmosphere.[120] The ultimate resolution of
these and other cases, and their regulatory influence, will become clearer
as they continue through the courts.

---

[117] In-person interview, US Participant 5 (Nov. 14, 2012).

[118] *Alec L. v. Lisa P. Jackson, U.S. Environmental Protection Agency*, 863 F. Supp. 2d 11
(D.D.C. May 31, 2012) (No. 1:11-cv-02235). For details of the most recent developments
in the case, see Our Children's Trust, Legal Action, at http://ourchildrenstrust.org/US/
Federal-Lawsuit.

[119] For full details of these lawsuits, see Arnold and Porter LLP, "U.S. Climate Change
Litigation Chart" (Common Law Claims – Public Trust Doctrine Lawsuits).

[120] *Bonser-Lain v. Texas Commission on Environmental Quality* (Dist. Ct. of Travis City, Tex.
Aug. 2, 2012); *Sanders-Redd v. Martinez* (N.M. Dist. Ct Jul. 14, 2012), but see the later
decision of the Court on July 4, 2013, in favor of the defendants. See further Alexandra
Klass, "Federalism at Work: Recent Developments in Public Trust Lawsuits to Limit
Greenhouse Gas Emissions," *CPR Blog*, Jul. 13, 2012, at www.progressivereform.org/
CPRBlog.cfm?idBlog=8092FA68-ADF9-7258-98BF80BAC5FA4AA7.

The variety of different pathways pursued by climate change litigation at the state level in the United States reflects a desire to test the scope of the law and clarify obligations for greenhouse gas emissions reduction. However, even with this diversity, as noted, a clear pattern emerges: by far the most common type of US climate change lawsuit is challenges to coal-fired power plants utilizing the statutory interpretation pathway in an attempt to require consideration of the greenhouse gas impacts of these projects. While some of these cases are litigated in federal courts, a substantial number take place in state-level tribunals owing to the critical state role in land use planning and energy regulation. As we discuss further in Chapter 5, this litigation, even when ultimately unsuccessful, has an indirect regulatory influence by creating delay or other impediments that increase the economic costs of projects involving coal-fired power plants and make future proposals of this kind less attractive. Such litigation has not been the only factor in the shift away from coal in the United States, but, in the aggregate, these cases have made an important contribution.

3.4   Australian mitigation litigation–regulation linkages

This section details Australian regulatory approaches at the international, national, and subnational levels and the ways in which litigation has helped to shape domestic regulatory pathways for emissions reduction. Australia parallels the United States in having a federal, multi-tiered structure of government and courts that has afforded litigants opposing coal numerous opportunities to seek regulatory influence. However, in contrast to the United States, this litigation has not had the same degree of impact on mitigation regulation and behavior in Australia. As outlined in the following sections, litigation has had a discernible impact on decision-making processes around coal and energy projects but has not dislodged entrenched political and economic attitudes that resist the displacement of coal in favor of clean energy sources.

3.4.1   International-level litigation–regulation linkages

Reflecting the complexity of its political and economic priorities around fossil fuel production and export, Australia's record of engagement with the international climate change regime has been extremely mixed. Although Australia was one of the first nations to ratify the UNFCCC, the negotiating posture adopted by the conservative Howard government (1996–2007) during the 1997 Kyoto Protocol negotiations focused on securing beneficial concessions in the Protocol's text.[121] The Howard government signed the Kyoto Protocol in 1998 but, following the lead of the Bush administration in the United States, later refused to ratify the treaty citing its potential to damage the Australian economy.[122] This situation persisted over the ten-year period of the Howard government. Only following the 2007 election of Prime Minister Kevin Rudd's government did Australia finally ratify the Kyoto Protocol, some two and a half years after its entry into force. Although Australia ratified later than other major developed-country emitters, this decision still differentiates Australia from the United States, which has yet to ratify the Kyoto Protocol.

During the term of the Labor governments led by Rudd and his successor Prime Minister Julia Gillard (2007–13), Australia emerged as a key supporter of the Kyoto process. At the 2009 Copenhagen conference, Australia – like the United States – advocated disbanding the Kyoto Protocol and replacing it with a new universal treaty that would impose binding emissions reduction cuts on both developed and developing countries. However, it later agreed to take part in the Protocol's contemplated second commitment period running from 2013 to 2020, unlike many of the original Kyoto Protocol parties.[123] The domestic emissions reduction target nominated by Australia for the second commitment period was a modest 5 percent reduction on 2000 levels by 2020 with the possibility of increasing the ambition of this target depending upon the level of action taken by other countries.[124] The carbon pricing mechanism, introduced by the Gillard government in 2011, was intended to be the primary measure by which Australia would meet its international emissions reduction commitments.[125]

---

[121] Clive Hamilton, *Scorcher: The Dirty Politics of Climate Change* (2007, Black Inc., Melbourne), 74. These concessions included a generous first commitment period emissions reduction target for Australia of 108 percent of 1990 levels and inclusion of the so-called Australia Clause (article 3.7) that allows land-clearing emissions to be included in the 1990 baseline calculation: C. Hamilton and L. Vellen, "Land-use Change in Australia and the Kyoto Protocol" (1999) 2(2) *Environ. Sci. Policy* 145.

[122] Guy Pearse, *High and Dry: John Howard, Climate Change and the Selling of Australia's Future* (2007, Penguin, Camberwell).

[123] Greg Combet and Mark Dreyfus, Joint Press Release, "Australia Joins Kyoto Protocol Second Commitment as World on Track to 2015 Climate Change Agreement, Dec. 2, 2012, at www.climatechange.gov.au/ministers/hon-greg-combet-am-mp/media-release/australia-joins-kyoto-protocol-second-commitment-world.

[124] Australia, Submission under the Kyoto Protocol: Quantified Emission Limitation or Reduction Objective, Nov. 2012, at http://unfccc.int/files/meetings/ad_hoc_working_groups/kp/application/pdf/awgkp_australia_qelro_26112012.pdf.

[125] Clean Energy Act 2011 (Cth) (repealed), s 3(a) (objects).

Before his election as the new Australian prime minister in September 2013, Tony Abbott indicated the Coalition Party's in principle support for Australia's participation in a Kyoto second commitment period.[126] However, the prospects for continuing robust Australian engagement with the UNFCCC look dim given that the new government's "first order of business" has been to dismantle the carbon pricing mechanism.[127] Under the Abbott government, Australia has yet to ratify the amendment to the Kyoto Protocol required to establish the second commitment period. The government was also "missing in action" at the 2013 UNFCCC Conference of the Parties in Warsaw, with the environment minister too busy introducing the carbon tax repeal legislation into federal parliament to attend the international meeting.[128]

Australia has been similar to the United States in the very limited direct influence litigation has had on its international negotiating positions, which have been driven more by evolving national laws for greenhouse gas emissions reductions and the political orientation of the federal administration of the day. The main international-level petitions relevant to Australia have concerned requests to the World Heritage Committee for listing of Australian World Heritage Sites, including the Great Barrier Reef, as "in danger" due to climate change.[129] As with the Inuit Inter-American petition in the US context, these petitions – which, with others focused on sites in additional countries, resulted in further study by the World Heritage Committee but no danger listing[130] – have not directly shaped

---

[126] The Climate Institute, Media Brief: Coalition Commitments to 5 to 25 percent emissions reduction targets, Sep. 5, 2013, at www.climateinstitute.org.au/verve/_resources/TCI_MediaBrief_Coalitiontargets_5September2013.pdf. Government websites relating to climate change suggest this remains the Abbott government's position, but no further statements on the Kyoto Protocol have been issued since the government came to power.

[127] Sid Maher, "Tony Abbott Locks in Death of Carbon Tax," *The Australian*, Oct. 16, 2013, at www.theaustralian.com.au/national-affairs/policy/tony-abbott-locks-in-death-of-carbon-tax/story-e6frg6xf-1226740606857.

[128] Tom Arup, "Coalition Turns Back on UN Climate Summit," *Sydney Morning Herald*, Nov. 7, 2013, www.smh.com.au/federal-politics/political-news/coalition-turns-back-on-un-climate-summit-20131107-2x2ur.html.

[129] Anna Huggins, "Protecting World Heritage Sites from the Adverse Impacts of Climate Change: Obligations for States Parties to the World Heritage Convention" (2007) 14 *Austr. Intl. L. J.* 121.

[130] Copies of the petitions are available from www.climatelaw.org/ and relate to World Heritage Sites in Belize, Peru, Australia, North America, and Nepal. See, further, Catherine Redgwell, "Climate Change and International Environmental Law" in Rosemary Rayfuse and Shirley V. Scott (eds.), *International Law in the Era of Climate Change* (2012, Edward Elgar, Cheltenham), 118, 130–32.

Australia's evolving approach to the UNFCCC regime. Nonetheless, the publicity they have generated, particularly with respect to impacts on the Great Barrier Reef, may have had an indirect regulatory impact by exposing government decisions around coal export facilities adjacent to the reef to greater public and international scrutiny.[131]

3.4.2   National-level litigation–regulation linkages

Under the Australian Constitution, the federal parliament has primary responsibility for enacting legislation implementing international treaty obligations such as those under the UNFCCC and the Kyoto Protocol.[132] Prior to 2007, federal climate change legislation in Australia was sparse, mirroring that of the United States. The conservative government of Prime Minister John Howard that maintained power from 1996 to 2007 resisted unilateral action to reduce national greenhouse gas emissions fearing potential costs for Australian industry and the domestic economy. This resistance helped to spur proactive lawsuits aiming to force greater regulation of greenhouse gas emissions and climate change.[133] However, these lawsuits followed somewhat different pathways than lawsuits with similar aims in the United States, given Australia's less extensive federal environmental laws.

After 2007, Australia's path diverged from that of the United States at a federal level, but shifts in the political winds are again leading to some convergence, with Australia arguably moving behind the United States owing to President Obama's extensive use of executive authority. Once the Labor Party took control in 2007, the road to climate change legislation began, which changed the regulatory role of litigation. But Australia is

---

[131]   As discussed further in Section 3.4.2.3, coastal development adjacent to the reef has been a particular concern generating national and international publicity. In April 2014, the World Heritage Committee issued a Draft Decision noting its "concern" over recent approvals given to coastal developments adjoining the reef. The committee also expressed its "regrets" about the federal government's decision green lighting the controversial Abbot Point coal terminal, including approval for "dumping 3 million cubic metres of dredge material inside the [World Heritage] property prior to having undertaken a comprehensive assessment of alternative and potentially less impacting development and disposal options" (in the face of public outcry, the company involved has since sought approval for land-based disposal). If recommended actions are not taken to improve the health of the reef, the committee will consider in 2015 including the World Heritage Site on the "in danger" list. See World Heritage Committee, Draft Decision 38 COM 7B.63, 38th sess., WHC-14/38.COM/7B, Paris, Apr. 30, 2014.

[132]   Australian Constitution, s 51(29).

[133]   Nick Minchin, "Responding to Climate Change: Providing a Policy Framework for a Competitive Australia," (2001) 24 *UNSW L. J.* 550.

once again entering a new period, with a political party leadership change to the Abbott government, which has repealed the Clean Energy Act and is working to dismantle the federal climate change statutory framework. This section traces that national evolution and litigation's role in it.

3.4.2.1 Climate litigation prior to national climate change legislation

Like in the United States, prior to 2007, most of the climate change mitigation measures introduced at the national level in Australia were voluntary in nature and focused primarily on "no-regrets" interventions such as promoting energy efficiency.[134] The most significant climate change legislation enacted during the term of the Howard government was the National Greenhouse and Energy Reporting Act 2007.[135] This legislation introduced a national scheme for the reporting of information about corporate greenhouse emissions, energy production, and energy consumption but did not require reporting corporations to decrease greenhouse gas emissions.[136] Frustration over the Howard government's refusal to ratify the Kyoto Protocol and to introduce national legislation addressing emissions spurred litigation over this period.[137]

Compared with the United States, this climate change litigation was "less risky and less big-ticket."[138] Climate change cases, for instance, have yet to reach Australia's highest court, the High Court. In addition, only a handful of climate change cases have been brought before federal courts in Australia, in contrast to the hundreds of actions at the national level in the United States. In large part, as noted earlier, this reflects the more limited nature of federal environmental law in Australia compared with the United States. There is no equivalent to the Clean Air Act, the Clean Water Act, or the Endangered Species Act.

---

[134] See, e.g., Energy Efficiency Opportunities Act 2006 (Cth). The only mandatory legislative scheme introduced by the Howard government was the Mandatory Renewable Energy Target (that continues as the Renewable Energy Target today). See Renewable Energy (Electricity) Act 2000 (Cth).

[135] National Greenhouse and Energy Reporting Act 2007 (Cth).

[136] The NGER Act's reporting obligations apply to businesses emitting more than 25,000 tonnes of carbon dioxide equivalent or consuming more than 25,000 megawatt hours of electricity or 2.5 million litres of fuel annually. Covered corporations are required to report on scope 1 (direct) emissions and scope 2 emissions resulting from their consumption of electricity.

[137] Tim Bonyhady, "The New Australian Climate Law" in Tim Bonyhady and Peter Christoff (eds.), Climate Law in Australia (2007, Federation Press, Sydney) 8; Jacqueline Peel, "The Role of Climate Change Litigation in Australia's Response to Global Warming" (2007) 24 Environ. Planning L. J. 90.

[138] In-person interview, Australian Participant 1 (Mar. 7, 2013).

The principal Australian federal environmental law – the Environment Protection and Biodiversity Conservation Act 1999 (EPBC Act), also enacted by the Howard government – is a NEPA-style law focused on environmental impact assessment. It requires environmental review for certain kinds of "actions" that have, or are likely to have, a significant impact on "matters of national environmental significance."[139] The EPBC Act identifies only a limited number of matters of national environmental significance. These include World Heritage properties (such as the Great Barrier Reef), internationally significant wetlands, and threatened species.[140] Notably, there has been, and remains, no requirement under the EPBC Act for environmental assessment based on the greenhouse gas intensity or potential climate change impacts associated with a project or activity.[141]

In the absence of national legislation directly addressing greenhouse gas emissions, litigation during this period attempted to force consideration of climate change under the available federal law, the EPBC Act. As this act does not create substantive standards for national environmental protection, the litigation instead pursued pathways designed to test the scope of the law's procedural environmental assessment requirements in the context of fossil fuel projects, such as new, export-oriented coal mines.[142] The direct greenhouse gas emissions of such mines are relatively small; the bulk of emissions and resultant climate change impacts derive from burning the coal in the importing country (termed "scope 3" emissions).[143] Litigants in these cases sought to draw a link between authorizing the mines, the scope 3 emissions to which they would give

---

[139] Environment Protection and Biodiversity Conservation Act 1999 (Cth) (EPBC Act), s 67.

[140] EPBC Act, Part 3. In mid 2013, the Gillard government introduced a new assessment requirement for coal seam gas projects or "large" mining proposals with significant impacts on water resources.

[141] This has been a source of criticism of the legislation: see Lisa Ogle, "The Environment Protection and Biodiversity Conservation Act 1999 (Cth): How Workable Is It?" (2000) 17(5) *Environ. Planning L. J.* 468.

[142] See *Wildlife Preservation Society of Queensland Prosperine/Whitsunday Branch Inc v. Minister for the Environment and Heritage* (2006) 232 ALR 510; *Anvil Hill Project Watch Association Inc v. Minister for Environment and Water Resources* (2007) ALD 398; *Anvil Hill Project Watch Association Inc v. Minister for Environment and Water Resources* (2008) 166 FCR 54.

[143] This terminology follows that of the Greenhouse Gas Protocol, the most widely used protocol in international accounting for greenhouse gas emissions (see, further, www.ghgprotocol.org/). Scope 1 emissions refer to direct emissions from an activity. Scope 2 emissions are indirect emissions from the generation of purchased energy. Scope 3 emissions are all other indirect emissions that occur in the value chain of the reporting entity.

rise, and the impacts of global climate change on matters protected by the EPBC Act. The lack of success with such arguments has resulted in these cases having a limited direct regulatory impact on Australia's national approach to the mitigation of scope 3 emissions.

The case of *Wildlife Preservation Society of Queensland Proserpine/ Whitsunday Branch Inc v. Minister for the Environment and Heritage* (the Wildlife Whitsunday case) underlines the difficulties litigants experienced in seeking to use the EPBC Act as a vehicle for forcing regulation of climate issues at the national level using a procedural statutory interpretation pathway.[144] The environmental NGO litigants in the case challenged decisions of the environment minister finding that two new coal mines in the state of Queensland did not require assessment under the EPBC Act as they would have no significant impacts on matters of national environmental significance. The litigants argued that, on the contrary, permitting the mines would have a very significant impact on the ecological health of the Great Barrier Reef World Heritage Area by facilitating the release of greenhouse gas emissions when the coal was burned, contributing to climate change and increasing ocean acidification. They relied on another Federal Court decision under the EPBC Act that held that both the direct and indirect effects of a proposal must be taken into account in evaluating its environmental impact.[145]

However, the Federal Court in the Wildlife Whitsunday case refused to apply this approach in the context of coal mining and its indirect climate change–related effects. In a concluding paragraph to his judgment, Justice Dowsett of the Federal Court declared that he was "far from satisfied that the burning of coal at some unidentified place in the world, the production of greenhouse gases from such combustion, its contribution toward global warming and the impact of global warming upon a protected matter, can be so described [as an impact of the proposed coal mines]."[146] Instead His Honor accepted an assessment carried out by the federal Environment

---

For coal mining, the principal source of scope 3 emissions comes from burning of the harvested coal.

[144] *Wildlife Preservation Society of Queensland Proserpine/Whitsunday Branch Inc v. Minister for the Environment and Heritage* (2006) 232 ALR 510; see also Chris McGrath, "Regulating Greenhouse Gas Emissions from Australian Coal Mines" in Wayne Gumley and Trevor Daya-Winterbottom (eds.), *Climate Change Law: Comparative, Contractual and Regulatory Considerations* (2009, Thomson Reuters, Sydney), 217.

[145] *Minister for Environment and Heritage v. Queensland Conservation Council* (2004) 139 FCR 24.

[146] *Wildlife Preservation Society of Queensland Proserpine/Whitsunday Branch Inc v. Minister for the Environment and Heritage* (2006) 232 ALR 510, 524.

Department that the "indirect impacts" on the Great Barrier Reef and other protected areas of the large export-oriented coal mines at issue were "extremely small" and "speculative."[147]

As noted by one of our interviewees, the notion that the climate-related impacts of coal mines are speculative and insignificant (in global terms) has since been used by federal environmental officials to thwart further attempts to seek judicial review of coal mine proposals under the EPBC Act:

> All they do to avoid this – there's no legislative change required – what they do is make findings of fact in their statement of reasons to say that the effects are speculative, unquantifiable and are not likely to be significant, and then that basically kills any judicial review opportunities. So basically we don't litigate anything on climate change under the EPBC Act now because the Commonwealth Environment Department's worked it out – and they've got a formulaic way they write their statement of reasons, based on Wildlife Whitsunday.[148]

While the direct regulatory impact of early mitigation-related climate change litigation at the national level was minimal, these cases – in conjunction with the international-level petitions taken to the World Heritage Committee – appear to have set the scene for a greater public focus on the effects of scope 3 emissions from coal mining and climate change on the Great Barrier Reef.[149] This focus has included additional litigation in response to federal decisions such as the Abbot Point approval, discussed further in Section 3.4.2.3.

3.4.2.2   Advent and demise of national climate legislation in Australia

As in the United States, a long-term goal of climate change litigation in Australia has been to promote regulatory action at the national level to address domestic greenhouse gas emissions. Such regulation took some time to materialize in Australia and saw several failed attempts before the eventual enactment of the Clean Energy Act in 2011.[150] The Clean

---

[147] *Wildlife Preservation Society of Queensland Prosperine/Whitsunday Branch Inc v. Minister for the Environment and Heritage* (2006) 232 ALR 510, 515 and 519–20.

[148] Skype interview, Australian Participant 4 (Mar. 20, 2013).

[149] These indirect impacts are discussed further in Chapter 6.

[150] Clean Energy Act 2011 (Cth) (repealed). For a discussion of previous attempts to introduce a national emissions trading scheme in Australia, see Alexander Zahar, Jacqueline Peel, and Lee Godden, *Australian Climate Law in Global Context* (2013, Cambridge University Press, Melbourne), 155–63.

Energy Act introduced a national "carbon pricing mechanism" that came into effect on July 1, 2012.[151] The mechanism established a fixed period carbon price – commonly known as the carbon tax – that was set to transition to a fully fledged emissions trading scheme from July 2015.[152] However, this elaborate legislative regime has quickly "enter[ed] history as one of the best-designed yet shortest-lived policies for climate change mitigation."[153] Australia's prime minister Tony Abbott came to power promising to "axe the carbon tax" and successfully passed legislation to repeal the Clean Energy Act.

If the Clean Energy Act had survived, the enactment of national climate change legislation – so elusive in the United States – might have signaled the start of a significant divergence between the US and Australian climate change litigation experiences. In the European Union (EU), for instance, the existence of the EU Emissions Trading Scheme has produced associated litigation focused largely on testing the boundaries and operation of the scheme.[154] This type of jurisprudence has not developed in Australia. The lack of such litigation likely reflects the short political lifespan of the carbon pricing mechanism as well as the limited scope for public interest litigation under the Clean Energy Act.[155] Early on the chair of the Clean Energy Regulator – the institution charged with administering the carbon pricing program – indicated her intention to pursue rigorous enforcement action against liable entities that failed to discharge requirements under the legislation to buy emission units to cover their greenhouse pollution.[156] Even before the repeal process began, however,

---

[151] Lisa Caripis et al., "Australia's Carbon Pricing Mechanism" (2011) 2(4) *Clim. L.* 1.

[152] The design and early experience with the carbon pricing mechanism is described in Jacqueline Peel, "The Australian Carbon Pricing Mechanism: Promise and Pitfalls on the Pathway to a Clean Energy Future" (2014) 15(1) *Minn. J. L. Sci. Technol.* 429.

[153] Frank Jotzo, "Australia's Carbon Price" (2012) 2 *Nat. Clim. Change* 475, 476.

[154] Sanja Bogojević, "EU Climate Change Litigation, the Role of the European Courts and the Importance of Legal Culture" (2013) 35(3) *L. Policy* 184; Navraj S. Ghaleigh, "'Six Honest Serving Men': Climate Change Litigation as Legal Mobilization and the Utility of Typologies" (2010) 1 *Clim. L.* 31.

[155] Civil penalties were specified for various contraventions, but only the Clean Energy Regulator was authorized to apply for civil penalty orders (s 253). There was no citizen suit provision. Certain decisions made by a delegate of the Clean Energy Regulator were reviewable (s 281) but only by a "person affected" by the decision (s 282). The term "person affected" is generally construed narrowly in Australian administrative law to afford standing only to those with a financial stake in a decision.

[156] David Wroe, "Carbon Cop to Pull out All Stops" *Sydney Morning Herald*, Jul. 2, 2012, www.smh.com.au/federal-politics/political-news/carbon-cop-to-pull-out-all-stops-20120701-21b58.html.

only one enforcement proceeding had been brought by the regulator and under legislation other than the Clean Energy Act.[157]

The federal antitrust regulator, the Australian Competition and Consumer Commission (ACCC), was more active in exercising its statutory mandate to address false and misleading business claims regarding the effects of the carbon tax.[158] In August 2012, a month after the carbon pricing scheme came into effect, the ACCC issued its first fine to a business for making a false claim about carbon pricing's impact on the cost of goods and services.[159] This litigation built on the ACCC's previous enforcement efforts against businesses misrepresenting the carbon and climate benefits of their products[160] and had seemed to be acting as an effective deterrent against noncompliance. According to one Australian climate lawyer interviewed for the project,

> what's happened is the ACCC's been very, very active in coming down on people for that sort of [conduct]. That, in itself, has made people really a lot more careful. And I think secondly, the [Clean Energy Act] itself has created a level of awareness that . . . is slightly different. So if a company is not compliant, we'll assume the regulator will be very aggressive.[161]

If the Clean Energy Act had survived, it also might have had a more significant impact on litigation patterns at the national level in Australia. Several of our interviewees noted this inverse relationship between litigation and the state of the national climate regulatory landscape.[162] One (speaking before the September 2013 election) remarked,

> If the Coalition does get in at a federal level, I think there's a fair chance that climate litigation will be ramped up. . . . But if the Coalition don't get in and the Clean Energy Act remains in place, and the [carbon] price starts

---

[157] *Clean Energy Regulator v. MT Solar* [2013] FCA 205 (enforcement action under the Renewable Energy (Electricity) Act 2000).

[158] Shortly after the introduction of the carbon pricing mechanism, the ACCC released a fact sheet about "carbon price claims" and its role in preventing misleading and deceptive conduct: see ACCC, Carbon Price Claims (Australian Government, Canberra, 2012).

[159] Judith Ireland, "Gym Fined for Pumping up Carbon Claims" *Sydney Morning Herald*, Aug. 1, 2012, at www.smh.com.au/federal-politics/political-news/gym-fined-for-pumping-up-carbon-tax-claims-20120801-23eb7.html.

[160] For discussion, see Brian J. Preston, "Climate Change Litigation (Part 1)" (2011) 5(1) *Carbon Clim. L. Rev.* 3, 10–14.

[161] Skype interview, Australian Participant 6 (Apr. 5, 2013).

[162] See also Skype interview, Australian Participant 7 (Apr. 11, 2013): "once the Federal Government passed its climate change legislation, the carbon tax and all this, people sort of said, 'Oh well, we've achieved some of our goals of the litigation. If it was meant to be action-forcing, we've got it.'"

doing its job to some extent then I think public interest litigation might, there might be a bit less urgency around it. So I think good climate change outcomes might lead to less litigation.[163]

With the election of the conservative Abbott government, Australia has now embarked on a different climate regulatory course that is likely to see a return to the voluntary, no-regrets approach that characterized the Howard government era.[164] Indeed, with the passage of the carbon tax repeal legislation, Australia has been left with no mandatory national policy to control carbon emissions "and no clear path forward as to when or how that will happen."[165]

As the Clean Energy statutory package was legislated by the federal parliament, the carbon pricing mechanism and institutions it established could only be removed by repealing legislation also enacted through the parliament. The carbon tax repeal legislation was passed by the federal parliament in July 2014.[166] Ongoing negotiations with senators who hold the balance of power in the upper house over the fate of other legislation designed to dismantle clean energy institutions such as the Climate Change Authority and the Clean Energy Finance Corporation suggest that these bodies may yet remain in place.[167] The government has been successful, however, in passing legislation for its alternative climate policy of

[163] In-person interview, Australian Participant 1 (Mar. 7, 2013).

[164] The Abbott government will replace the carbon pricing mechanism with an Emissions Reduction Fund that purchases emissions reductions below "business as usual" baselines made by participating businesses. Businesses are not required to participate in the program, and the coalition has indicated it does not intend to fine businesses for exceeding business as usual emissions levels. See further Australian Government, Emissions Reduction Fund – White Paper, 2014, at www.environment.gov.au/topics/cleaner-environment/clean-air/emissions-reduction-fund. Several independent assessments of the Direct Action policy have questioned its effectiveness and efficiency for achieving the 2020 emissions reduction target.

[165] Dan Harrison, "Clive Palmer Says Tony Abbott Is Not 'Evil' and Needs Time to Consider the PUP's Climate Change Stance" *The Age*, Melbourne, Jun. 26, 2014, at www.theage.com.au, quoting climate lawyer, Martjin Wilder.

[166] Clean Energy Legislation (Carbon Tax Repeal) Act 2014 (Cth).

[167] The Climate Change Authority is an independent advisory agency providing recommendations in relation to emissions reduction targets and trajectories. Its most recent report recommended that Australia should increase its 2020 emissions reduction target from 5 percent to 19 percent of 2000 levels for Australia to do its fair share in the global emissions reduction effort. While the Abbott government had slated for removal the Climate Change Authority, and other institutions like the Clean Energy Finance Corporation (that mobilizes public and private sector financing for clean energy projects) and the Australian Renewable Energy Agency, the necessary legislation to repeal their authorizing acts now faces an uncertain fate in the Senate. The Abbott government has already

"direct action" (which sets up a fund to pay major emitters to reduce their emissions), although it remains unclear whether this program will produce sufficient emissions savings to meet Australia's target of a 5 percent reduction by 2020.

Following the repeal of the Clean Energy Act, it is possible that there may be aggrieved groups, such as renewable energy producers or perhaps formerly liable entities that have purchased emissions permits under the scheme. Even so, interviewees did not anticipate an avalanche of private litigation in response to the demise of the carbon tax: "I don't see the courts being stampeded by people wanting to run lawsuits against the federal government."[168]

3.4.2.3   A new era of climate litigation in Australia?

With the changing political dynamics at the national level, public interest litigation may again be an option considered by pro-regulatory groups as a way to maintain the public profile of the climate issue and to force regulatory changes on mitigation. Even in the early days of the new federal administration, there are already signs of increased interest among environmental groups in using litigation as a tool for climate advocacy.

Some of this litigation seeks to influence regulation along the procedural statutory interpretation pathway. These cases build on early efforts – like the Wildlife Whitsunday case – challenging the procedural regularity of federal decision making that fails to take account of the detrimental environmental effects of Australian coal mining and associated infrastructure, especially on the Great Barrier Reef. For example, two lawsuits were commenced against approvals issued by the federal government and its agencies for expansion of the Abbot Point coal export terminal in North Queensland adjacent to the reef World Heritage area.[169] Expansion of this coal terminal is a key element in efforts to unlock the huge coal

abolished the Climate Commission, which provided scientific information on climate change to the public.

[168] Skype interview, Australian Participant 8 (Apr. 24, 2013).

[169] One claim filed by the Mackay Conservation Group sought judicial review of the Abbott government's decision under the EPBC Act approving dredging and the marine disposal of dredge spoil. The other claim brought by the North Queensland Conservation Council (NQCC) targeted a dredging permit granted by the Great Barrier Reef Marine Park Authority (GBRMPA) – the federal agency responsible for environmental management of the reef. This latter claim was filed with the Administrative Appeals Tribunal that conducts merits review of federal agency decision-making: see, further, http://nqcc.org.au/abbot-point-update/.

reserves of the Galilee Basin.[170] Both claims focus on the environmental effects of dredging the area and dredge spoil disposal, as well as the compliance of the Australian government's actions with its obligations under international environmental agreements. However, concern over the role of Abbot Point in facilitating coal exports and increased greenhouse gas emissions is clearly also a motivation of the environmental groups bringing the cases.[171]

Individual cases focused on particular projects are likely to be integrated into broader national climate change campaigns run by larger environmental NGOs. Prominent groups like the Wilderness Society have indicated that they are "gearing up for a series of court cases to 'hold the line' against ecologically damaging industrialisation."[172] In November 2013, the group announced that it would be shifting its focus to bring climate change lawsuits specifically against the fossil fuel export industry for the first time in its thirty-seven years in existence. National campaign director Lyndon Schneiders justified this new emphasis:

> Australia is now an emerging energy superpower and our argument is if you're serious about nature conservation, and if you're serious about climate change you can't just keep messing around with domestic issues; you've got to look at the export industry. We've got to make a decision as a country to keep large coal, oil and gas reserves actually in the ground. . . .
>
> As a longtime greenie, I was always more concerned with direct threats to nature – logging or land clearing or invasive species, river health – but watching the acceleration in the mining and export industry in the last four or five years, you can't be a nature conservationist in this country any more without saying we've got to get rid of this fossil fuel addiction.[173]

---

[170] Queensland Government, Department of State Development, Infrastructure and Planning, Galilee Basin Coal Infrastructure Framework, at www.dsdip.qld.gov.au/infrastructure-planning-and-reform/galilee-basin-infrastructure-framework.html.

[171] Speaking about the case against GBRMPA, NQCC campaigner, Jeremy Tager, remarked, "As far back as 2009, GBRMPA was warning that pressures on the Reef must be removed if the world heritage icon is to have a chance of surviving climate change. Yet not only does this dumping permit add pressure, it is being done so that vast quantities of climate change exacerbating coal can be exported through the Reef. This can only contribute to climate change." NQCC, at http://nqcc.org.au/protect-our-coral-sea-2/. See also Mackay Conservation Group, "Abbot Point a Disaster in the Making," at www.mackayconservationgroup.org.au/abbot_point_a_disaster_in_the_making.

[172] Oliver Millman, "Environmentalists Gear up for Legal Fights after Gas Hub Declared Illegal" *The Guardian*, Aug. 19, 2013, at www.theguardian.com/world/2013/aug/19/environmentalists-legal-fights-40bn-gas-hub-illegal.

[173] Jill Start, "Wilderness Society Plans Legal Fight over Fossil Fuels in Shift to Tackling Global Warming" *The Age*, Nov. 30, 2013, at www.theage.com.au/environment/climate-change/wilderness-society-plans-legal-fight-over-fossil-fuels-in-shift-to-tackling-global-warming-20131130-2yi3a.html.

This new shift toward litigation by national environmental groups may result in direct regulatory change but also could have significant indirect impacts with respect to how people view the problem, the role of corporate actors, and appropriate regulatory responses.

3.4.3   State-level litigation–regulation linkages

More limited possibilities for proactive climate change litigation at the federal level in Australia have helped focus activity at the state level. Like in the United States, state and local authorities exercise significant regulatory authority over decisions about land use, including the issue of permits for new energy projects.[174] State environmental and land use planning laws also offer a greater variety of avenues for administrative challenges to government decision making on projects than comparable federal laws. In addition, litigants bringing suit at the state level have options to bring claims before specialist environmental courts and tribunals, many of which offer relaxed standing provisions and merits review for a range of planning- and project-level decisions.[175]

The relative accessibility of many state-level courts and tribunals has been a significant factor shaping pro-regulatory litigants' choices about where to bring mitigation-focused cases. Plaintiffs have for the most part been resource-poor environmental NGOs or individual climate activists for whom cost is an important factor.[176] Local governments also have been involved as proactive litigants in some cases, mostly defending decisions to approve wind farms.[177] However, there have been no instances of states suing the federal government, similar to the situation in *Massachusetts v. EPA*.

---

[174] Proposals for new coal-fired power stations or large coal mines as well as other projects with a substantial carbon footprint often attract federal assessment and decision-making powers under the EPBC Act given their broader environmental effects. However, the EPBC Act, s 10, provides that the federal legislation operates concurrently with any state legislative requirements.

[175] As discussed in Chapter 2, merits review is a form of administrative review in Australia that involves the court standing in the shoes of the original decision maker to remake the decision, taking account of the applicable law and expert evidence.

[176] In-person interview, Australian Participant 2 (Mar. 8, 2013).

[177] See, e.g., *Thackeray v. Shire of South Gippsland* [2001] VCAT 922; *Perry v. Hepburn Shire Council* (2007) 154 LGERA 182; *Russell & Ors v. Surf Coast SC & Anor* [2009] VCAT 1324.

The predominance of environmental groups among pro-regulatory climate litigants also seems to have influenced the kind of lawsuits brought. "Harder" causes of action like nuisance – pursuing a common law regulatory pathway, as has been attempted in the United States – have been eschewed in favor of actions under environmental and planning statutes.[178] As one interviewee explained,

> [compared with the United States,] in Australia, we have perhaps easier options. You know, you can just go [to the] Land and Environment Court, you've got an open standing provision, you can whack on anything about a breach of the law and you've got so many environmental laws with so many provisions that it is easier. And that's what [litigants] take. And so why would you then try a much more difficult common law action in a perhaps less sympathetic, or certainly less environmentally literate court?[179]

Like in the United States, the focus of much of the state-level climate litigation brought in Australia has been on stopping greenhouse gas–intensive development and large fossil fuel projects, especially coal-fired power stations and coal mines, with a smaller subset of cases challenging (or defending) clean energy projects such as wind farms.[180] The most common pathway pursued in such litigation has been that of statutory interpretation relating to procedural requirements for environmental assessment under state land use and planning laws. The standard hooks for these cases are the concept and principles of "ecologically sustainable

---

[178] The solitary exception to this overall litigation pattern was the case of *Gray v. Macquarie Generation* [2010] NSWLEC 34; [2011] NSWLEC 3; *Macquarie Generation v. Hodgson* [2011] NSWCA 424 heard by the Land and Environment Court and the Court of Appeal in New South Wales. The case involved a direct challenge to the lawfulness of greenhouse gas emissions from a large power station on the basis that the power station was unlawfully disposing of "waste" in the form of carbon dioxide without authorization under a licence. The environmental litigants involved were inspired by the approach taken in the United States in *Massachusetts v. EPA*, which secured regulation of greenhouse gas emissions under general pollution laws. Justice Pain in the Land and Environment Court rejected the argument that the power station's licence did not authorize the emission of greenhouse gases but allowed an amended claim to go forward pleading that there was an implied limit to the emitting authority granted by the licence. An adverse judgment from the New South Wales Court of Appeal, overturning Justice Pain's decision, followed. According to interviewees, this result delivered a "devastating blow" to environmentalists' plans to use statutory interpretation action-forcing suits under pollution laws as a way to improve regulation of greenhouse gas emissions: in-person interview, Australian Participant 3 (Mar. 8, 2013); Skype interview, Australian Participant 14 (May 23, 2013).

[179] Skype interview, Australian Participant 7 (Apr. 11, 2013).

[180] For an overview of the mitigation-related cases, see Peel, "Australian Climate Change Litigation." See also Jacqueline Peel, "Climate Change Law: The Emergence of a New Legal Discipline" (2008) 32 *Melbourne Univ. L. Rev.* 922.

development" (ESD), which is a central element of Australian environmental law.[181] State environmental and planning statutes typically include ESD among their objectives and make reference to ESD principles, such as intergenerational equity (consideration of the interests of future generations), the precautionary principle (not postponing action on serious environmental threats due to scientific uncertainty), and the need to ensure the conservation of biodiversity. A suite of cases brought before state environmental courts and tribunals has sought to link ESD objectives and principles expressed in legislation to the need to take climate change issues into account in assessing development projects. Depending on the context, the argument made is that legislative ESD requirements should be interpreted to require assessment of the climate change impacts associated with a project's direct greenhouse gas emissions (e.g., for a coal-fired power plant) or its indirect greenhouse gas emissions (e.g., for a coal mine where the coal will be exported).

Prominent examples of cases in this vein include *Australian Conservation Foundation v. Latrobe City Council* (the Hazelwood case)[182] and *Gray v. Minister for Planning* (the Anvil Hill case).[183] The former case, decided in 2004, targeted plans for expansion of Australia's dirtiest coal-fired power station located in the Latrobe Valley in the state of Victoria. It was decided by the Victorian Civil and Administrative Tribunal (VCAT), which held that the decision on a planning scheme amendment necessary to enable the expansion should consider the "indirect" effects of the amendment in terms of the environmental impacts of the greenhouse gases likely to be emitted if the life of the Hazelwood plant was extended.[184] This ruling did not prevent the Victorian government from approving the Hazelwood extension. Nonetheless, publicity surrounding the case was seemingly a factor in its later conclusion of a Greenhouse Gas Reduction Deed, with the owner of the power station required to offset a portion of the power station's emissions.[185]

A similar approach to including the "indirect" environmental effects of fossil fuel projects in assessment processes was taken up and expanded by Justice Pain of the New South Wales (NSW) Land and Environment Court in the Anvil Hill case. In that case, Justice Pain construed ESD objectives

---

[181] Jacqueline Peel, "Ecologically Sustainable Development: More Than Mere Lip Service?" (2008) 12(1) *Austr. J. Nat. Resour. L. Policy* 1.

[182] (2004) 140 LGERA 100.   [183] (2006) 152 LGERA 258.

[184] (2004) 140 LGERA 100, 109.

[185] Brian J. Preston, "The Influence of Climate Change Litigation on Governments and the Private Sector" (2011) 2 *Clim. L.* 485.

in state planning legislation to find that indirect, downstream emissions from burning of extracted coal (i.e., scope 3 emissions) were a relevant factor in environmental assessment of a coal mine. What was particularly significant about this case was that it was brought before a decision on the mine proposal had been made. The focus instead was on the adequacy of the environmental assessment process overseen by the director-general of the NSW Planning Department: "what it actually stood for was we could get in really early to challenge proponents when they say 'we've satisfied the director-general's requirements.'"[186]

The Anvil Hill case ultimately did not prevent the coal mine going ahead (very few Australian cases challenging coal mines have had that result). However, on the heels of the case, the NSW government released a new State Environmental Planning Policy for mining activities that requires a consent authority determining a mining development application to "consider an assessment of the greenhouse gas emissions (including downstream emissions) of the development."[187] As one interviewee noted, the case "did get people really thinking in New South Wales about how we could do things better and made the Planning Department lift their game. Now we don't have an assessment in New South Wales for a coal project that does not include scope 1, 2, *and* 3 emissions."[188]

When we asked our interviewees about the overall regulatory impact of this case law, responses were mixed. On one hand, many interviewees noted the positive effect of the cases in requiring a fuller assessment of climate change concerns in environmental assessment processes. As one summarized the situation,

> a lot of Australian planning and environmental legislation and regulation requires consideration of ESD, but a lot of environmental regulation and legislation doesn't (or did not until recently) mandate specifically that you have to consider climate change when you're making a development or a pollution licensing decision, even if climate change is a relevant factor because the development is going to contribute to climate change or climate change is going to impact on it. But because of the case law around "ecologically sustainable development" and what that requires, it's

---

[186] Skype interview, Australian Participant 14 (May 23, 2013).

[187] Clause 14(2), State Environmental Protection Policy (Mining, Petroleum Production and Extractive Industries). The New South Wales government is currently seeking to amend this policy, apparently in response to the Warkworth mine decision, discussed later, which refused a coal mine expansion. However, Clause 14(2) is unaffected by the proposed amendments.

[188] In-person interview, Australian Participant 3 (Mar. 8, 2013).

now pretty much become a box that you do have to tick and you do have to consider because otherwise the decision is vulnerable to judicial review. And in the nonregulatory sense, it's been important for awareness raising, I think, and putting it more toward the forefront of decision makers' minds and those of applicants because then at least they then have to do an assessment of it (i.e., a proposal's contribution to climate change). . . . So I think that has kind of started happening as a matter of course and I don't know whether I would have said that was the case maybe five to six years ago.[189]

Despite this progress, a number of interviewees who act for environmental groups spoke of their frustration with the outcomes of the litigation for advancing goals of climate change mitigation. As one respondent put it,

it's great to know from scope 3 emissions [data] nowadays just how much destruction we're going to perpetrate with the amount of coal we are producing and exporting. It hasn't changed, you know, that litigation has not changed the behavior of either governments or the coal industry in terms of what they are trying to do.[190]

Consequently, some have argued that the case law – especially that based in judicial review of decision makers' compliance with statutory requirements – may have reached its limits as an avenue for improving regulation of greenhouse pollution.[191] In sum, the case law seems to have been important and useful in making climate change and greenhouse gas emissions a "mainstream" issue for consideration by decision makers assessing coal projects.[192] However, there is concern that consideration of the issue is not producing any real change in government decision-making processes, which invariably end up approving any new coal-fired power station or coal mine application.

In an effort to get to the question at the heart of Australia's climate mitigation debate – whether the country should continue its reliance

---

[189] In-person interview, Australian Participant 1 (Mar. 7, 2013).

[190] Skype interview, Australian Participant 14 (May 23, 2013).

[191] Kirsty Ruddock, "Has Judicial Review Killed ESD?" (2013) 28(6) *Austr. Environ. Rev.* 625. Judicial review mitigation cases in the NSW Land and Environment Court post–Anvil Hill seem to bear out this criticism. The Court continues to acknowledge the relevance and importance of ESD and climate change matters but – beyond assessing whether government decision makers have produced evidence to show these matters were fully considered in the assessment process – decisions have generally not scrutinized the reasonableness or sustainability of governmental approvals approving coal mines or coal-fired power stations with significant greenhouse gas emissions.

[192] Skype interview, Australian Participant 8 (Apr. 24, 2013).

on coal-fired power and coal mining in an increasingly carbon-constrained world – there has been a trend in recent state-level climate cases of litigants utilizing merits appeals to challenge decisions authorizing coal projects. Many of these cases have been unsuccessful, particularly those brought in the state of Queensland,[193] the state that has led the Australian coal mining boom. Others, like the Victorian case of *Dual Gas v. EPA*, have been partially successful, with VCAT there upholding an approval for a new power station incorporating a novel coal drying and gasification process as "best practice," but adding a condition preventing commencement of the project until such time as retirement of an equivalent amount of more greenhouse gas–intensive generation capacity was secured.[194] Another example of a partially successful case was the NSW Land and Environment Court decision in *Hunter Environmental Lobby v. Minister for Planning*, involving a proposal for a coal mine expansion. In the case, Justice Pain originally ruled that a condition attaching to the mine approval requiring the mining company to offset the mine's direct emissions would be appropriate, although Her Honor accepted the coal company's arguments that offsets should not extend to scope 3 emissions beyond its direct control.[195] However, with the enactment of the Clean Energy Act before finalization of the proceedings, the judge found that an offsets condition was no longer necessary, as the bulk of the mine's direct emissions would attract liabilities under the carbon pricing mechanism.[196]

---

[193] See *Re Xstrata Coal Queensland Pty Ltd & Ors* [2007] QLRT 33; *Xstrata Coal Qld Pty Ltd & Ors v. Friends of the Earth Brisbane and Department of Environment and Resource Management* [2012] QLC 013 (Wandoan coal mine case) and *Hancock Coal Pty Ltd v. Kelly & Ors and Department of Environment and Heritage Protection (No. 4)* [2014] QLC 12 (Alpha coal mine case). The latter case was successful on the grounds of water impacts but not on the argument relating to scope 3 emissions. It is being appealed by the NGO litigant.

[194] *Dual Gas Pty Ltd & Ors v. Environment Protection Authority* [2012] VCAT 308. As discussed further in Chapter 5, the delay occasioned by the case and funding uncertainty generated by the condition imposed by VCAT played a critical role eventually in the project not going ahead. The case also exposed significant tensions within the Victorian government between the premier's office and the Environment Protection Authority over emissions reduction policy that would seem to have had negative rather than positive effects for mitigation regulation in the state. The antiregulatory effects of the litigation are discussed further in Chapter 7.

[195] *Hunter Environment Lobby Inc v. Minister for Planning* [2011] NSWLEC 221.

[196] *Hunter Environment Lobby Inc v. Minister for Planning (No 2)* [2012] NSWLEC 40, para. 17 (finding that the new legislative scheme met "at a practical level the purpose of imposing a condition requiring the offsetting of Scope 1 GHG emissions").

In the (rarer) category of merits review decisions that have led to outright refusals of projects are cases like *Bulga Milbrodale Progress Association v. Minister for Planning* (the Warkworth mine case). In that case, Chief Justice Preston of the NSW Land and Environment Court rejected approval for the expansion of an existing coal mine in the Hunter Valley on the basis of its social and environmental impacts.[197] This decision was later upheld on appeal by the NSW Court of Appeal.[198] However, greenhouse gas emissions were only raised as a peripheral issue in the case, as part of an argument that the costs associated with burning the mine's coal should have been included in the benefit-cost analysis supplied to the court to assist with its decision making.[199]

To date, no Australian court has tackled head-on the issue of whether considerations of climate change dictate the refusal of further coal-fired power stations and coal mines. Perhaps this issue is one that is just too difficult for courts to broach. It would involve challenging the prevailing political and economic orthodoxy in Australia that maintains that coal is essential to the country's energy system and economic health. The depth of the problem was illustrated by the recent judgment of the Queensland Land Court in *Hancock Coal Pty Ltd v. Kelly* (the Alpha Mine case) considering an application for a new coal mine in the coal-rich Galilee Basin. If the Alpha coal mine and other Galilee Basin coal projects proceed, the associated carbon dioxide emissions from burning of the harvested coal could amount to more than 700 million tonnes, dwarfing the annual emissions of all but six countries in the world.[200] Yet the deciding member of the Land Court agreed with the mining company's submissions that

---

[197] *Bulga Milbrodale Progress Association Inc v. Minister for Planning and Infrastructure* (2013) 194 LGERA 347 (Warkworth mine case).

[198] *Warkworth Mining Limited v. Bulga Milbrodale Progress Association Inc* [2014] NSWCA 105.

[199] The success of this argument in the Warkworth mine case has already seen similar arguments included in other lawsuits challenging coal mines: Skype interview, Australian Participant 22 (Sep. 13, 2013). However, the case has also generated antiregulatory backlash discussed in Chapter 7.

[200] Jeremy Leggett, "Australia Has a Chance to Slow Global Warming Down – but Will It Take It?" *The Guardian*, Oct. 2, 2013, at www.theguardian.com/commentisfree/2013/oct/02/australia-mining-alpha. See also John Rolfe, "Carmichael Mine is a Game-Changer for Australian Coal" *The Conversation*, Jul. 29, 2014, at https://theconversation.com/carmichael-mine-is-a-game-changer-for-australian-coal-29839?utm_medium=email&utm_campaign=Latest+from+The+Conversation+for+30+July+2014+-+1816&utm_content=Latest+from+The+Conversation+for+30+July+2014+-+1816+CID_8ccdf08828e10936e4064f414d0c9b01&utm_source=campaign_monitor&utm_term=writes%20John%20Rolfe.

even if the mine were refused, the coal would just be sourced elsewhere, with no net benefit for global greenhouse gas levels,[201] an argument some have labeled the "drug dealers' defence."[202] According to the court, "it is the demand for coal-fired electricity, and not the supply of coal from coal mines, which is at the heart of the problem."[203]

The many failures encountered in litigation attempting to stop coal projects, and continued resistance to regulation of scope 3 emissions, have left some disheartened about the prospects for achieving direct regulatory change through litigation on clean energy issues in Australia. Others emphasize the need to keep pressing these claims in the hope that they will eventually cut through. As one lawyer put it,

> what these cases were about was actually saying, hang on, we don't have clean hands here. We're the producers, we're like the drug dealers. We're the ones that are sending these things out. We do have responsibility.[204]

As we discuss further in Chapters 5 and 6, raising the issue of scope 3 emissions in state courts would seem to have had several important indirect impacts. These include developing information quantifying the environmental effects of project-related greenhouse gas emissions, which in turn has assisted in campaign and public awareness activities. The steady stream of coal-related climate change cases brought by public interest litigants has also facilitated courts' development of a jurisprudence on access to justice issues that may encourage NGOs to bring future actions.[205] Given the extent of Australia's clean energy challenge and entrenched political positions favoring fossil fuel use and exploitation, it is unsurprising that litigants have encountered strong headwinds in their efforts to advance mitigation policy through the courts. It is encouraging, however, that this has not prevented the cases from exerting indirect regulatory influence that, in time, may prove more critical in shifting prevailing public and political attitudes.

---

[201] *Hancock Coal Pty Ltd v. Kelly & Ors and Department of Environment and Heritage Protection (No. 4)* [2014] QLC 12 (Alpha coal mine case), para. 229.

[202] See Graham Readfearn, "Is It Un-Australian to Be Driving on with Fossil Fuel Expansion Plans?" *Planet Oz* (hosted by *The Guardian*), Apr. 14, 2014, at www.theguardian.com/environment/planet-oz/2014/apr/14/ipcc-report-climate-change-queensland-alpha-coal-mine-liability.

[203] Alpha coal mine case, para. 231.

[204] Skype interview, Australian Participant 4 (Mar. 20, 2013).

[205] Access to justice issues are discussed further in Chapter 7.

3.5   Comparing mitigation litigation in the United States and Australia

Despite vast differences in their respective domestic contributions to global greenhouse gas emissions, the patterns of fossil fuel use and production in the United States and Australia mean the two countries face many shared challenges in transitioning to a clean energy future. These similarities have led to some convergences in the influence of mitigation-oriented litigation on regulation. In both jurisdictions, for instance, mitigation-related litigation has played a major role in mainstreaming the consideration of climate change in environmental assessment processes; there has been a constancy of opposition to coal projects voiced through litigation, although such lawsuits have been more extensive and diverse in the United States. On the less positive side for those who are pro-regulatory, constitutional and common law pathways have not yielded any significant direct regulatory change in either country. Although the tort and public trust cases may yet lead to more direct change in the United States, the results thus far, especially in the nuisance context, should sound a note of caution for Australian groups considering similar options.

Currently there are few new coal-fired power plants being built or planned in either the United States or Australia.[206] The likelihood of proposals for coal-fired power attracting legal challenges has undoubtedly played a part in this development, although litigation is by no means the only factor at work. In the United States, for instance, hydraulic fracturing has helped make available a large, cheap supply of natural gas, which – in conjunction with the power plant standards being developed by the EPA – has also made coal-fired power plants less appealing economically.[207]

---

[206] In the United States, Sierra Club's Proposed Coal Plant Tracker lists 34 plants as active or upcoming, 30 as progressing, and 134 as defeated as of June 2014: see http://content.sierraclub.org/coal/environmentallaw/plant-tracker. Retirement of existing coal plants is also accelerating: U.S. Energy Information Administration, "AEO2014 Projects More Coal-Fired Power Plant Retirements by 2016 Than Have Been Scheduled" *Today in Energy*, Feb. 14, 2014, at www.eia.gov/todayinenergy/detail.cfm?id=15031. For the situation in Australia, see Peter Hannam, "Australia Unlikely to Build New Coal-Power Stations" *Sydney Morning Herald*, Feb. 8, 2013, at www.smh.com.au/business/australia-unlikely-to-build-new-coalpower-stations-20130207-2e1c3.html. Aside from the now repealed carbon tax, major factors have been the reputational and other risks associated with coal that mean developers struggle to get financing for projects.

[207] The EPA's proposed rules for new coal plants are sufficiently stringent that they can only be met by a plant that captures a portion of its carbon dioxide emissions. See

With the urgency of opposing domestic coal-fired power diminishing, the focus of litigation is shifting from coal as an internal emissions issue to coal as a carbon leakage issue associated with growing fossil fuel exports from both countries. The Australian cases addressing scope 3 emissions from coal mines are instructive as to the difficult path that lies ahead. Courts may be persuaded to require regulators and government agencies to consider such emissions when making decisions on coal or other fossil fuel projects, but no court has yet been prepared to halt a project on the basis of its offshore effects. This reluctance is understandable given courts' constitutionally restricted powers and limited scope of jurisdiction, an aspect we explore further in Chapter 7. On the question of exported emissions, litigation may exercise some of its most significant regulatory impacts through indirect pathways. But to leverage this success, litigation needs to be integrated with a broader strategy focused on the activities of multinational energy corporations and their contribution to greenhouse gas emissions. Chapter 5 addresses the role that litigation can play in shaping corporate responses to climate change mitigation in more depth.

Despite these many similarities between the lawsuits relating to mitigation issues in the United States and Australia, divergences in the two countries' underlying laws and resulting litigation have also created important differences that could be instructive for future litigation. The United States has had, and likely will continue to have, high-profile federal statutory interpretation cases that are playing a major role in shaping its regulatory landscape on climate change. These mandate-forcing actions have served as a significant regulatory pathway at the federal level in the United States, combining strong environmental laws with actions under the Administrative Procedure Act.

Conversely, Australia's short-lived comprehensive climate change legislation was the result of divisive political battles rather than litigation. Beyond the now-repealed Clean Energy Act, Australia's principal federal environmental law is more limited in scope, with no real equivalents to the US Clean Air Act, Clean Water Act, or Endangered Species Act. This has made administrative actions under broad environmental statutes a less viable option for achieving regulatory change at the national level. This different federal environmental legal framework helps to explain why

"EPA Fact Sheet: Reducing Carbon Pollution from Power Plants," http://www2.epa.gov/sites/production/files/2013-09/documents/20130920factsheet.pdf; James E. McCarthy, *EPA Standards for Greenhouse Gas Emissions from Power Plants: Many Questions, Some Answers* (Nov. 15, 2013, Congressional Research Service, Washington, DC).

Australian cases have disproportionately been brought at the state level, where there are more stringent laws available and specialist environmental courts.

Moreover, even if Australian litigants were to bring statutory mandate-forcing suits, any results achieved would be more susceptible to being overturned than has been the case in the United States.[208] While the United States remains unable to pass comprehensive climate change legislation, that same deadlock makes significant rollbacks in its broader environmental laws unlikely. In contrast, Australia's parliamentary democracy political system means that executive governments – both at the state and federal levels – have much greater control over the legislative agenda and can pass legislation to overturn court decisions with which they do not agree.[209] This type of adverse government reaction has been evident following the Warkworth mine case described earlier, which refused a coal mine expansion (the first ever such refusal).[210] As discussed further in Chapter 7, the potential for such legislative backlash creates a significant barrier to progress through litigation on clean energy in Australia.

3.6   Conclusion

Overall, mitigation-related litigation looks likely to continue to be an important regulatory tool in both countries. The sheer volume of past and pending cases – much greater in the United States – reflects how much these cases have evolved from creative lawyering to a mainstream part of the climate change dialogue. Some of the promotive regulatory impacts will stem from the continuing implementation of past decisions, like *Massachusetts v. EPA* in the United States, and ongoing litigation over coal in both countries. Others may emerge from new theories outlined here and in Chapter 2. On the flip side, antiregulatory cases may yet have more success, especially as US statutory interpretation cases lead

---

[208] Interviewees also indicated that bold decisions by state specialist courts grounded in judicial review were susceptible to being overturned by higher courts: Skype interview, Australian Participant 14 (May 23, 2013), and Skype interview, Australian Participant 16 (May 30, 2013).

[209] Legislatures cannot overturn a constitutional law decision of the High Court, but there have been no such cases in the climate sphere.

[210] The New South Wales government not only joined the miner's appeal of the decision but also introduced legislation to repeal the citizen's suit provision that enabled the Warkworth mine case to go before the New South Wales Land and Environment Court. See, further, Chapter 7.

to additional administrative regulation that the fossil fuel industry in turn challenges. Cases may also create unforeseen statutory backlash, particularly in Australia and in US state legislatures, which are often more able to act than the deadlocked US Congress.

Interestingly, some of the patterns outlined here with respect to mitigation litigation are reversed when comparing the two countries in the adaptation context. The Australian adaptation jurisprudence is far more developed than the US cases with that direct focus. To some extent, this difference reflects Australia's greater, earlier adaptation challenges and its more specialized state-level courts. However, as extreme weather events in the United States have brought more attention to climate change impacts and the need for adaptation, new cases are rapidly emerging that could learn from the Australian experience. The book turns in Chapter 4 to these issues.

Litigation as an adaptation tool

I believe that [the coastal adaptation] cases really led the way in this country in causing governments to have their departments prepare coastal guidelines to improve the mapping of likely sea rise impacts. And I think you can see a direct correlation between the development of policy, which then of course evolved into modifications in the town planning zone, such that such applications don't have to come forward again without having had those impacts taken into account. . . . And I don't believe that those decisions would have been obtained were it not for the fact that the early cases led the way, encouraged governments to then change the coastal policies, and then for subsequent decision makers to take those into account.

– Australian Interview Participant 15

I think on the adaptation side, climate litigation is just going to become more and more relevant. Some will be sort of the mundane: the disputes over who owns the shoreline with the rising sea level, but those will interplay in everything from local planning and flood insurance, and all the myriad of ways that climate change is impacting society already. That field is going to be rife with litigation and some of it will hopefully be transformative and improve our planning, and . . . force decisions about infrastructure and development that are not just more resilient to climate change but also ideally are closer to being carbon neutral that get to the mitigation side as well.

– US Interview Participant 12

4.1 Introduction

Much of the focus of litigation and regulation on climate change has concerned the issues of mitigation discussed in Chapter 3. Emissions from major power plants and motor vehicles – and the need to transition from coal to cleaner energy sources – have dominated the policy and public discussion of climate change. Litigation attempting to force mitigation has had a substantial impact on regulation, particularly in the United States, where the Supreme Court has weighed in on more than one occasion.

But as failures of mitigation continue to amplify the risks of impacts, and severe weather events raise public awareness of those impacts, policy making and litigation increasingly have turned to adaptation concerns as well. Whereas mitigation considers how to limit human changes to the climate, adaptation focuses on how governments, businesses, communities, and individuals can manage the consequences of and reduce vulnerability to climate change impacts.[1] In both Australia and the United States, adaptation is receiving greater attention in the aftermath of weather-related disasters such as Hurricane Katrina, the Black Saturday Bushfires, and Superstorm Sandy. In his second inaugural address in January 2013, for example, President Obama notably promised to

> respond to the threat of climate change, knowing that the failure to do so would betray our children and future generations. Some may still deny the overwhelming judgment of science, but none can avoid the devastating impact of raging fires and crippling drought and more powerful storms.[2]

Since then, President Obama has announced numerous new climate change measures, which have included initiatives to support more adaptation planning at federal, state, and local levels. Similar planning frameworks exist in Australia, underpinned by an array of state and local policies for managing threats such as wildfires, sea level rise, and coastal hazards.

Paralleling this executive action in both countries has been the growth of a body of case law directly focused on adaptation planning. These cases address a variety of adaptation issues from management and planning for coastal hazards in development-related decision making, to resiliency of the electricity grid, to the deterioration of coastal waters and groundwater allocation in conditions of drought. In contrast to mitigation case law, adaptation litigation has been more extensive and influential in Australia than in the United States, with heightened public and political awareness around the issue of adaptation prompted by Australians' experiences of a succession of weather-related disasters over the past decade. US litigation focused directly on adaptation issues has only emerged in the last few years but looks set to grow quickly. Moreover, if the more developed US jurisprudence on climate change mitigation is any guide, courts

---

[1] J.B. Ruhl, "Climate Change Adaptation and the Structural Transformation of Environmental Law" (2010) 40 *Environ. L.* 343; Victor B. Flatt, "Adapting Laws for a Changing World: A Systemic Approach to Climate Change Adaptation" (2012) 64 *Fla. L. Rev.* 269.

[2] President Barack Obama, Inaugural Address (Jan. 21, 2013), available at www.whitehouse.gov/the-press-office/2013/01/21/inaugural-address-president-barack-obama.

are likely to be important players in fashioning regulatory responses to adaptation in the United States. As key stakeholders shape the future course of adaptation-related litigation and regulation, the Australian litigation experience may offer a source of ideas and strategies for US litigants seeking to use lawsuits to improve the nation's preparedness to deal with climate change impacts.

Although policy making and litigation on adaptation are developing rapidly in both countries, these efforts still face political and geographic constraints. To some extent, the past focus on mitigation rather than adaptation in the United States has been a political choice by environmental organizations and elected representatives. They have feared that a public conversation about adaptation might decrease pressure to mitigate.[3] Moreover, people in many developed countries – particularly the United States – have often believed that the risks posed by climate change are remote and only likely to affect others.[4] As inaccurate as this belief may be – the Third National Climate Assessment released by the US Global Change Research Program makes clear that "climate change, once considered an issue for a distant future, has moved firmly into the present" – such perceptions still have been influential.[5] Although these politics have begun to shift in the United States, years of focusing on mitigation rather than adaptation shows how nascent efforts are at many levels of US government and in its courts. In Australia, the political shift necessary to focus on future climate change impacts occurred earlier than in the United States, but the nation still struggles with more deeply rooted social and cultural barriers to adaptation, including people's desire to live in coastal areas that are vulnerable to sea level rise and coastal storms, and adherence to property rights structures that inhibit flexible action to address adaptation risks.

More fundamentally, a meaningful national-scale effort on adaptation in both countries is constrained by the diversity of local impacts and

---

[3] A. Dan Tarlock, "Now Think Again about Adaptation" (1992) 9 *Ariz. J. Intl. Comparative L.* 169. Similar concerns have prevailed in international climate negotiations. See R. Pielke et al., "Lifting the Taboo on Adaptation" (2007) 445 *Nature* 597; E. Lisa F. Schipper and Ian Burton, "Understanding Adaptation: Origins, Concepts, Practice and Policy" in E. Lisa F. Schipper and Ian Burton (eds.), *The Earthscan Reader on Adaptation to Climate Change* (2009, Earthscan, London), 1.

[4] Public attitudes to climate change are discussed further in Chapter 6.

[5] Jerry M. Melillo, Terese Richmond, and Gary W. Yohe (eds.), *Climate Change Impacts in the United States: The Third National Climate Assessment* (2014, U.S. Global Change Research Program, Washington, DC).

the largely state and local character of the applicable law. For example, coastal communities face risks of sea level rise, inundation, erosion, storm surge, and more intense storms.[6] For other communities, climate change may take the form of heat waves, drought, and increased wildfires or shifting snowpack melt, floods, and drastic ecosystem changes.[7] Because adaptation planning is much more locally specific than mitigation, large-scale coordination is harder, and high-profile federal cases are less likely. Effective adaptation at larger scales means fostering appropriate smaller-scale action rather than creating a unified national approach.

This chapter examines and compares adaptation litigation in Australia and the United States and explores the regulatory significance of, and future pathways for, this litigation. The chapter begins by presenting the situation in Australia and by examining the nation's greater exposure to early climate change impacts and the respective roles that government regulatory efforts and litigation have played in addressing that vulnerability. The comparatively more extensive adaptation litigation in Australia, focusing particularly on coastal impacts and disaster risks, offers insights into how litigation can influence proactive regulation positively, but also negatively in some cases.

The next part of the chapter analyzes the role of emerging adaptation litigation in the United States. It explores the climate impacts facing the United States, multilevel governmental actions to plan for these impacts, and the emerging US case law on adaptation issues. Apart from

---

[6] Intergovernmental Panel on Climate Change, *Climate Change 2007: Impacts, Adaptation and Vulnerability. Contribution of Working Group II to the Fourth Assessment Report of the Intergovernmental Panel on Climate Change* (2007, Cambridge University Press, Cambridge), Chapter 6, at 316–57. See also IPCC Working Group II, *Summary for Policymakers – Final Draft, Climate Change 2014 – Impacts, Adaptation, and Vulnerability* (2014, IPCC, Geneva).

[7] IPCC, *Summary for Policymakers* (2007), at 11–12. Some communities may even experience beneficial impacts from climate change, at least in the short term, as warmer weather and more favorable conditions for agriculture migrate toward higher latitudes. For instance, short-term climate change may be beneficial for grape growing areas in the Western United States but over the longer term, increased temperatures are likely to be detrimental. See G. V. Jones, "Climate Change in the Western United States Grape Growing Regions" (2005) 689 *Acta Hort.* (ISHS) 41 www.actahort.org/books/689/689_2.htm. In the Australian context see Leanne B. Webb, The Impact of Projected Greenhouse Gas Induced Climate Change on the Australian Wine Industry (2006, PhD thesis, Department of Agriculture and Food Systems, The University of Melbourne), available at http://dtl.unimelb. edu.au/R/8YJ2S7RAGP6L145V8FEIUPIYKFT9TFPIGL6DUN4X4U1Y66G98G-00229? func=dbin-jump-full&object_id=67182&local_base=GEN01&pds_handle=GUEST.

Endangered Species Act and tort cases – which may be viewed as a form of adaptation litigation[8] – most US cases directly addressing adaptation issues are newly decided or still under consideration by the courts.

The final part of the chapter draws from these comparative experiences to provide an assessment of the ways in which the more established body of Australian case law might serve as a model for US strategies as they evolve. It concludes with reflections about the future trajectory of this litigation in the two countries and possibilities for an enhanced focus on adaptation to complement each country's mitigation efforts.

4.2   The role of adaptation litigation in Australia

This section traces the ways in which the underlying geography of Australia has made it especially vulnerable to climate change and extreme weather events. That vulnerability has shaped government efforts and litigation addressing adaptation, with both more extensive than those in the United States. As noted in the introduction, adaptation planning in Australia has tended to take place at the state and local levels, reflecting the primary role of states in matters of land use planning, environmental protection, and disaster management (with states then delegating many decision-making powers to local government authorities).[9] Litigation over adaptation issues in Australia has thus interacted most directly with state and local governmental responses to adaptation risks, particularly risks posed by coastal hazards and climate-related disasters. As in the mitigation sphere, specialist environmental courts and tribunals at the state level have provided the most important arenas for the development of adaptation case law, primarily following the procedural statutory interpretation pathway outlined in Chapter 2.

Although litigation over adaptation in Australia is extensive, its regulatory role in spurring behavioral change has been mixed. Some cases have led to more effective planning responses, especially regarding coastal climate change hazards. However, uncertainty over the extent of liability for future climate harms has sometimes also prompted "maladaptive"

---

[8] See J.B. Ruhl, "Climate Change and the Endangered Species Act: Building Bridges to the No-Analog Future" (2008) 88(1) *Boston Univ. L. Rev.* 1 (discussing the role of the Endangered Species Act in climate change adaptation).

[9] See generally, Jacqueline Peel and Lee Godden, "Australian Environmental Management: A 'Dams' Story" (2005) 28(3) *UNSW L. J.* 668. In addition to its six states, Australia also has two self-governing territories. Territory legislation may be overridden by federal law.

reactions on the part of governments.[10] Both dimensions of this experience offer lessons for the evolution of adaptation lawsuits in other countries, particularly the United States, which faces many adaptation challenges in common with Australia.

4.2.1   Climate change impacts in Australia

Australia's comparatively more developed regulation and jurisprudence on adaptation emerge from its particular physical vulnerability to impacts. Australia is well known as a land of climatic extremes,[11] with a propensity for extreme weather that is inherent to its geography. A vast arid center traps heat, whereas ocean waters surrounding the island continent intensify the impacts of sea level rise, powerful storms, and flooding rains. The average annual rainfall across the continent is low but also extremely variable, with rainfall intensity highest in the tropical north and some coastal areas.[12] Australia's largely hot, dry climate means that wildfires are a frequent occurrence, and the native vegetation has developed characteristics that promote the spread of fire.[13]

The effects of this geography and naturally harsh climate are amplified by patterns of settlement in Australia. More than 85 percent of Australia's population of 23 million lives within fifty kilometers (thirty miles) of the coast and is on the front line of climate change impacts such as sea level rise, coastal inundation, and more intense storms.[14] Residential development pushes out from the major urban centers, such as Sydney, Melbourne, and Brisbane, into bushland areas, exposing residents to high

---

[10] "Maladaptation" refers to behaviors and decisions that fail to meet adaptation objectives and even serve to increase vulnerability to adaptation risks. See Jon Barnett and Saffron O'Neill, "Maladaptation" (2010) 20 *Global Environ. Change* 211.

[11] The early-twentieth-century poet Dorothy Mackellar famously described Australia as "a sunburnt country" with "droughts and flooding rains." Dorothea Mackellar, *My Country* (2010, Omnibus Books, Malvern). The preciousness, and danger, associated with water is also a motif that appears throughout the cultural creation myths of Australia's Aboriginal peoples, embodied by the figure of the Rainbow Serpent. See Oodgeroo Noonuccal and Kabul Oodgeroo Noonuccal, *The Rainbow Serpent* (1988, Australian Government Publishing Service, Canberra). See also Australian Government, Bureau of Meteorology "The Rainbow Serpent," at www.bom.gov.au/iwk/climate_culture/rainbow_serp.shtml.

[12] Ross Garnaut, *Garnaut Climate Change Review* (2008, Cambridge University Press, Melbourne), 107–9.

[13] CSIRO, "Bushfire in Australia," Feb. 14, 2008 (updated Oct. 26, 2012), at www.csiro.au/Organisation-Structure/Divisions/Ecosystem-Sciences/BushfireInAustralia.aspx.

[14] CSIRO, "Our Resilient Coastal Australia," Oct. 21, 2009 (updated Jul. 26, 2013), at www.csiro.au/Organisation-Structure/Flagships/Wealth-from-Oceans-Flagship/ORCA.aspx.

fire risk.[15] Inland, agriculture faces a persistent problem of low rainfall, which has led to a reliance on irrigation but also exacerbated problems of soil salinity and acidity.[16]

Dealing with extreme weather is a fact of life in Australia and even a matter of some national pride. During the heat wave experienced by most of the country in January 2013, Birdsville locals in the state of Queensland – where temperatures reached 50°C (122°F) – grinned and bore the heat despite their rubber "thongs" (flip-flops) melting on contact with the road.[17] In recent years, however, Australians have become less complacent about extreme weather as it has increased in frequency and severity. The first signs of change in public attitudes came with the "one in a thousand year drought" that stretched over more than a decade (1997–2009), ravaging agriculture and leading to severe water shortages, especially in the southeast of the country.[18] Public concern over the "millennium drought" and about climate change grew in concert in the mid 2000s, peaking in late 2006 to early 2007.[19] Heading into the 2007 Australian federal election, climate change policy was a major issue in the campaign and helped propel Kevin Rudd – who famously declared climate change the "great moral, environmental and economic challenge of our age"[20] – to the prime ministership.

Since 2007, Australia has experienced a multitude of other extreme weather events that have left few parts of the continent untouched. Several

---

[15] Michael Buxton et al., "Vulnerability to Bushfire Risk at Melbourne's Urban Fringe: The Failure of Regulatory Land Use Planning" (2010) 49(1) *Geogr. Res.* 1. See also K. Hennessy et al., *Climate Change Impacts on Fire-Weather in South-East Australia* (2006, CSIRO, Canberra).

[16] Pichu Rengasamy, "World Salinization with Emphasis on Australia" (2006) 57(5) *J. Exp. Bot.* 1017.

[17] Marissa Calligeros, "Thongs Melt on the Ground as Birdsville Withers in the Heat," *Brisbane Times* (online), Jan. 9, 2013, at www.brisbanetimes.com.au/environment/weather/thongs-melt-on-the-ground-as-birdsville-withers-in-the-heat-20130108–2ceub.html.

[18] The Climate Institute, *Climate of the Nation 2013: Australian Attitudes on Climate Change* (2013, The Climate Institute, Sydney).

[19] This coincided with other events, such as the release of Al Gore's climate change documentary *An Inconvenient Truth*, Sir Nicholas Stern's review undertaken for the British government on the "Economics of Climate Change," and the *Fourth Assessment Report* of the Intergovernmental Panel on Climate Change: *Climate Change 2007: Impacts, Adaptation and Vulnerability. Contribution of Working Group II to the Fourth Assessment Report of the Intergovernmental Panel on Climate Change* (2007, Cambridge University Press, Cambridge).

[20] Kevin Rudd, "Rudd Speech to the United Nations," extracted in full, *Sydney Morning Herald*, Sep. 24, 2009, at www.smh.com.au/federal-politics/political-opinion/rudd-speech-to-the-united-nations-20090924-g3nn.html.

disasters stand out, including the 2009 Black Saturday Bushfires in the state of Victoria; extensive floods in Queensland in 2010–11 and again in 2013; Severe Tropical Cyclone Yasi in 2011, which rivaled Hurricane Katrina in its intensity and destructive force; devastating wildfires during early 2013 in New South Wales, Victoria, and Tasmania and again in New South Wales in October 2013; and searing heat waves blanketing most of the country across the summers of 2012–13 and 2013–14.[21]

The increasing frequency and intensity of extreme weather events have been documented by the Australian Climate Council (formerly the Climate Commission) in a series of scientific reports.[22] In its 2013 report, "The Critical Decade: Extreme Weather," the commission concluded that "the severity and frequency of many extreme weather events are increasing due to climate change" and that "there is a high risk that extreme weather events like heatwaves, heavy rainfall, bushfires and cyclones will become even more intense in Australia over the coming decades."[23] A special report on intense heat waves in Australia issued in early 2014 by the council found that climate change is making heat waves more frequent and severe, with higher temperatures, a longer duration, and an earlier start to the season. Indeed, during the decade from 2000 to 2009, heat waves reached levels that were not anticipated to occur until 2030.[24] Prominent Australian climate scientist and author of the heat waves report, Professor Will Steffen, has remarked that Australia "seems to be on the firing line for a lot of this stuff. I think in terms of what actually matters for people and infrastructure, we could be the canary in the coal mine."[25]

Given its already highly variable climate and susceptibility to extreme weather events, predictions of the impacts of climate change for Australia are relatively severe compared with other developed countries.[26] They

---

[21] William L. Steffen, *The Angry Summer* (2013, Climate Commission, Canberra).

[22] The Climate Commission was disbanded by the incoming Abbott government in September 2013 but has reemerged with private funding backing as the Climate Council.

[23] Climate Commission, *The Critical Decade: Extreme Weather* (2013, Climate Commission Secretariat, Department of Industry, Innovation, Climate Change, Science, Research and Tertiary Education, Canberra), 5.

[24] Climate Council, "Press Release: Interim Findings on Heatwaves," Jan. 17, 2014, www.climatecouncil.org.au/interim-heatwaves.

[25] Quoted in Matt Siegel, "Is Australia the Face of Climate Change to Come?," *National Geographic Daily News*, May 24, 2013, http://news.nationalgeographic.com/news/2013/13/130524.

[26] Kevin Hennessy et al., "Australia and New Zealand," *Climate Change 2007*, chapter 11. See also IPCC Working Group II, "Australasia," *Climate Change 2014: Impacts, Adaptation, and Vulnerability*, AR5, Final Draft, Chapter 25.

include increases in temperature extremes and heat waves; decreased rainfall, increased drought threat, and more frequent extreme rainfall events; an increase in fire weather risk and a longer fire season; more intense tropical storms; and rising sea levels exacerbating coastal flooding and erosion from storm surges.[27] Serious ecological and social impacts for the continent are also predicted as a result of climate change. Significant ecosystem damage is projected as early as 2020, including mass coral bleaching on the Great Barrier Reef due to rising sea temperatures and ocean acidification.[28] In addition, the physical climatic and weather changes predicted to result from climate change would have consequential effects on ecosystems, such as biodiversity loss and changing habitat ranges for species.[29] Socioeconomic impacts are expected as climate change affects water supply, agriculture and fisheries, the provision and maintenance of infrastructure, and human health.[30] Moreover, with an increasing frequency and severity of extreme weather, financial costs associated with insuring for, and recovering from, such events are projected to rise substantially.[31]

4.2.2   Government action to address adaptation in Australia

Australia's vulnerability to climate change – paired with increasing evidence of the likelihood of severe social, economic, and environmental impacts – has led to heightened federal, state, and local government attention over the past decade to the question of adaptation risk management. To date, much of the activity has centered on vulnerability

---

[27] Senate Committee on Environment and Communications, *Recent Trends in and Preparedness for Extreme Weather Events*, Aug. 7, 2013, Parliament of Australia, Canberra. The Committee received 344 submissions, including from the main scientific and climate-related organizations in Australia, such as the Bureau of Meteorology, the CSIRO, and the Climate Commission.

[28] See Hennessy et al., "Australia and New Zealand," at 527, Box 11.3.

[29] Australian Centre for Biodiversity, Monash University, "Biodiversity and Climate Change," report commissioned for the Garnaut Climate Change Review, June 2008, available at www.garnautreview.org.au/CA25734E0016A131/WebObj/04Biodiversity/$File/04%20Biodiversity.pdf; Will Steffen et al., *Australia's Biodiversity and Climate Change* (2009, Canberra, CSIRO).

[30] Senate Committee on Environment and Communications, "Recent Trends," Chapter 3. See also the Climate Institute, *Coming Ready or Not: Managing Climate Risks to Australia's Infrastructure* (2012, Climate Institute, Sydney).

[31] Deloitte Access Economics, *Building our Nation's Resilience to Natural Disasters*, White Paper commissioned by Australian Business Roundtable for Disaster Resilience and Safer Communities, June 2013, at 19. For an attempt to estimate the economic costs of climate change for Australia, see Garnaut Climate Change Review, Chapter 11.

assessments (including regional vulnerability and vulnerability to specific impacts like sea level rise),[32] government reports and inquiries,[33] and the release of broadly framed policy documents, such as the 2007 National Climate Change Adaptation Framework[34] and the proposed National Adaptation Assessment Framework.[35] There is, however, no national legislation specifically dealing with adaptation or associated risk management. Instead, adaptation has largely been cast as the responsibility of state and local governments.[36] A key aspect of the localized nature of adaptive action in Australia is the concentration of control over land use and planning at the state level, with state governments in turn delegating many decision-making powers to local governments.

As a general matter, the overarching environmental and planning laws applicable in each of the Australian states do not contain explicit

---

[32] See, e.g., *OzCoasts Climate Change: Sea Level Rise Maps*, Geoscience Austl., www.ozcoasts.gov.au/climate/sd_visual.jsp (last visited Mar. 4, 2014). The Australian government's national science organization, the CSIRO, has also undertaken several vulnerability assessments for different sectors as part of its Climate Adaptation Flagship program. *Climate Adaptation*, CSIRO, www.csiro.au/en/Organisation-Structure/Flagships/Climate-Adaptation-Flagship.aspx (last visited Mar. 4, 2014).

[33] Productivity Commission, *Barriers to Effective Climate Change Adaptation* (2012, Productivity Commission Research Report, No. 59, Canberra); House of Representatives Standing Committee on Climate Change, Water, Env't and the Arts, *Managing Our Coastal Zone in a Changing Climate: The Time to Act Is Now* (2009), available at www.aph.gov.au/parliamentary_business/committees/house_of_representatives_committees?url=ccwea/coastalzone/report.htm.

[34] Council of Australian Governments, National Climate Change Adaptation Framework, 2007, available at www.climatechange.gov.au/sites/climatechange/files/documents/03_2013/nccaf.pdf. The framework focuses on building knowledge and capacity through research to enhance adaptive capacity and improve resilience. It touches only lightly on governance issues.

[35] Australian Government, Department of the Environment, Climate Adaptation Outlook, www.climatechange.gov.au/climate-change/adapting-climate-change/climate-adaptation-outlook (last visited Jul. 31, 2014).

[36] Under the Council of Australian Government's (COAG) 2012 framework on government, "Roles and Responsibilities for Adaptation," the primary responsibility for ensuring effective regulation and the incorporation of climate change considerations into decision making lies with state and local governments. In many parts of Australia, it has been local governments that have taken the lead in developing adaptation planning responses. By contrast, the federal government has fulfilled more general roles of information provision and research support. The COAG framework indicates the federal government is also expected to "provide leadership on national adaptation reform," which may encompass cooperative development of "a consistent approach in adaptation responses, where there is a need." See also Productivity Commission, "Barriers to Effective Adaptation," at 58; Lee Godden et al., "Law, Governance and Risk: Deconstructing the Public-Private Divide in Climate Change Adaptation" (2013) 36(1) *Univ. N.S.W. L. J.* 224.

requirements to take climate change into account in land use decisions.[37] Instead, litigants – just as in the mitigation context – have looked to incorporate climate change considerations through statutory interpretation of the laws' broadly framed objectives, which refer to goals such as encouraging "ecologically sustainable development" (ESD), seeking to achieve "ecological sustainability," or avoiding "significant effects" on or from the environment.[38] Specific directions to consider climate change adaptation risks in planning and development decisions have generally been included in policy instruments and guidance materials that supplement the main planning legislation.[39] These policies are usually formulated with respect to particular hazards (e.g., coastal climate change risks, flooding, wildfire risks). A number of state governments have also prepared adaptation plans to consider the longer-term needs of adaptation risk management.[40]

Beyond these general planning efforts and policies, recent disasters, such as the Black Saturday Bushfires in Victoria and the Queensland floods of 2010–11, have driven some reconsideration of standard design approaches such as the "1 in 100 year" standard for flood-proofing of development or requirements for vegetation management in fire-prone areas. For instance, in the wake of the Black Saturday Bushfires, which destroyed 2133 homes, burned 430,000 hectares of land, and claimed 173 lives,[41] the state of Victoria overhauled its planning requirements

---

[37] Productivity Commission, "Barriers to Effective Adaptation," at 173. An exception is the Sustainable Planning Act 2009 in Queensland discussed later. In Victoria, the Climate Change Act 2010 requires decision makers to have regard to climate change for certain decisions, but this consideration does not extend to the state's main land use laws.

[38] As discussed in the previous chapter, ESD is a central element of Australian environmental law that has been included – most usually as an objective – in a wide range of state environmental, planning, and land use legislation. See, further, Jacqueline Peel, "Ecologically Sustainable Development: More Than Mere Lip Service?" (2008) 12(1) *Austr. J. Nat. Resour. L. Policy* 1.

[39] For an overview of these policies, see Meredith Gibbs and Tony Hill (Blake Dawson lawyers), *Coastal Climate Change Risk – Legal and Policy Responses in Australia* (2011, Department of Climate Change and Energy Efficiency, Australian Government, Canberra).

[40] See, e.g., Vict. Gov't, Victorian Climate Change Adaptation Plan (2013), www.climatechange.vic.gov.au/adapting-to-climate-change/Victorian-Climate-Change-Adaptation-Plan; Queensl. Gov't, Coastal Management Plan (2014), www.ehp.qld.gov.au/coastalplan; see also Andrew Macintosh, Anita Foerster and Jan McDonald, *Limp, Leap or Learn? Developing Legal Frameworks for Climate Change Adaptation Planning in Australia* (2013, National Climate Change Adaptation Research Facility, Gold Coast).

[41] 2009 Victorian Bushfires Royal Commission, *Final Report – Summary* (2010, Victorian Government, Melbourne); Rachel Naylor, "Planning to Mitigate the Impact of Bushfires in Victoria" (2012) 27(10) *Austr. Environ. Rev.* 328.

applicable to the management of wildfire risks in land use planning.[42] These include a new "Bushfire Management Overlay" applicable to areas with the highest fire risk, which triggers the need for planning permission for certain developments and requires that new development implements wildfire protection measures, such as vegetation management, to allow a "defendable space" around properties.[43]

Although general forward planning for adaptation risks is beginning to emerge in a piecemeal fashion, coastal hazard management remains at the heart of Australian adaptation regulation, with the most developed policy requirements. In several jurisdictions, coastal policies include (or did include until recently) planning benchmarks for future sea level rise drawing on international scientific assessments.[44] These planning benchmarks require a certain level of sea level rise (e.g., 0.8 meters above 1990 mean sea levels by 2100)[45] to be factored into land use and planning decisions affecting coastal areas. Some coastal planning policies have been in place for more than two decades,[46] but the majority have been developed since 2008.[47] This emergence coincided with a number of cases in state environment courts and planning tribunals directly addressing the question of whether decision makers were obliged to consider climate change impacts on proposed developments in vulnerable coastal areas under general land use planning laws.[48]

---

[42] See Clause 13.05 of the Victorian Government's State Planning Policy Framework that aims to "assist to strengthen community resilience to bushfire." This is to be achieved by prioritizing the protection of human life over other policy considerations and applying the precautionary principle when assessing bushfire risks.

[43] Ibid.

[44] The different benchmarks adopted by states are summarized in Productivity Commission, "Barriers to Effective Adaptation," at 175, Table 9.1. Some states, such as New South Wales and Queensland, had benchmarks in place but have recently suspended their operation.

[45] Vict. Coastal Council, Victorian Coastal Strategy 2008 cl. 2.1, available at www.vcc.vic.gov.au/resources/VCS2008/part2.1climatechange.htm. The Coastal Strategy is in the process of being updated, but the new draft endorses the 0.8m by 2100 benchmark of the 2008 document. See Vict. Coastal Council, Draft Victorian Coastal Strategy 2013, available at http://vcc.leadingedgehosting.com.au/assets/media/ckfinder_files/files/Draft%20VCS-2013.pdf.

[46] South Australia, for example, has had coastal planning policies in place since the early 1990s. See, further, Tim Bonyhady, "How Australia Once Led the World" (2010) 36(1) *Monash Univ. L. Rev.* 54.

[47] See Gibbs and Hill, "Coastal Climate Change Risk," 17–28.

[48] See Jacqueline Peel and Lee Godden, "Planning for Adaptation to Climate Change: Landmark Cases from Australia" (2009) vol. IX(2) *Sustainable Development L. Policy: Clim. L. Reporter* 37.

More recently, however, changes in state governments in favor of conservative political parties have resulted in a number of eastern seaboard states winding back environmental and climate change–related regulations, including planning benchmarks for sea level rise, as part of a broader campaign to reduce "green tape" and associated constraints on development.[49] The removal or watering down of these policies has tended to broaden the already wide discretion available to decision makers regarding the extent to which climate change risks are taken into account and the weight given to them in the planning process. The resulting potential for inconsistency and "de facto policy-making"[50] has opened up further opportunities for the courts to shape the regulatory process in the area of adaptation and land use planning. At the same time, these shifts and divergences have created uncertainty over the liability exposure of state and local decision makers who fail to plan for climate change, particularly in coastal areas.

4.2.3   Australian adaptation litigation

All of the adaptation litigation to date in Australia has been brought in state courts and tribunals, raising questions as to the interpretation and application of state and local laws and policies, which vary considerably from jurisdiction to jurisdiction. As in the mitigation sphere, specialist environmental and planning courts, such as the New South Wales Land and Environment Court, the Queensland Planning and Environment Court, and the Victorian Civil and Administrative Tribunal, have played a lead role in the development of this adaptation jurisprudence. Arguably, the familiarity of these courts with environmental law principles and climate science has made them a sympathetic forum for raising issues of future climate risks as compared with generalist courts (which provide the only option, in most cases, for litigation on adaptation issues in the United States), an issue explored in more depth in Chapter 6.

Australian adaptation-related case law now encompasses numerous decisions that address a range of climate change impacts,[51] from the

---

[49] For details, see Productivity Commission, "Barriers to Effective Adaptation," 175, Table 9.1. See also the discussion of specific rollbacks in New South Wales and Queensland, in what follows.

[50] Gibbs and Hill, "Coastal Climate Change Risk," 15.

[51] See Jacqueline Peel, "Australian Climate Change Litigation," Centre for Resources, Energy and Environmental Law, Melbourne Law School, web database at www.law.unimelb.edu.au/creel/research/climate-change.

likelihood of decreased rainfall in southern Australia[52] to increased fire and flood risk in other parts of the country.[53] By far, the most commonly addressed issue in the case law, however, has been sea level rise and associated coastal hazards, such as inundation, more intense storms, and erosion. The reasons for this focus are obvious given the concentration of Australia's population and infrastructure along the coast.[54] Coastal areas – favored by Australian retirees – also have rapidly growing populations that intensify land use in the coastal zone and increase human and infrastructure exposure to climate change risks.[55]

The following sections examine three key areas of Australia's adaptation jurisprudence. First, we assess the extensive Australian case law on coastal impacts. A central question in early coastal adaptation cases was the extent to which general land use and environmental laws at the state level allowed for future climate change impacts, particularly sea level rise and coastal inundation, to be taken into account in land use decisions. The subsequent development of state and local policies around planning for coastal risks has resulted in more recent case law concentrating on interpreting these requirements in assessments of the acceptability of projects in "at-risk" areas. Second, we discuss emerging case law dealing with "newer" adaptation concerns of flood and fire risk that have been highlighted by large-scale weather-related disasters such the Queensland floods and the Black Saturday Bushfires. The final section looks at how proactive adaptation-planning suits interact with litigation and concerns over liability for climate change harms. This includes the emergence of private, common law actions to recover damages as property owners and disaster victims seek to hold governments and others to account for their action or inaction in addressing disaster and associated climate change risks.

Overall, as the following sections explore in depth, the litigation around adaptation issues in Australia forms an ongoing dialogue among

---

[52] *Alanvale Pty Ltd & Another v. Southern Rural Water & Ors* (2010) 4 ARLR 9, applying the precautionary principle to refuse a groundwater extraction license given uncertainties surrounding the long-term availability of groundwater resources. The potential for reduced rainfall as a consequence of climate change was one of the matters considered by the tribunal in the case. See also *Paul v. Goulburn Murray Water Corporation & Ors* [2010] VCAT 1755.

[53] See the cases discussed in the following sections.

[54] House Standing Committee on Climate Change, "Managing Our Coasts," 1.

[55] Barbara Norman et al., *South East Coastal Adaptation: Coastal Urban Futures in SE Australia from Wollongong to Lakes Entrance* (2012, National Climate Change Adaptation Research Facility, Gold Coast).

governments, courts, private property owners, and other stakeholders over what acceptable forms of development for a climate-changed future are and where responsibility for taking protective action should lie. This dialogue potentially also provides an important example for the United States as its own adaptation litigation evolves.

4.2.3.1   Adapting to coastal impacts

Beginning in the mid 2000s, Australia witnessed several high-profile adaptation cases dealing with coastal climate change risks.[56] These decisions were regularly cited by our Australian interview participants as the most significant cases in terms of their direct and indirect influences on adaptation regulation. Overall, though, the direct regulatory change brought about by Australian climate change litigation addressing coastal impacts has been incremental and evolutionary in nature rather than transformative. Courts have not sought to assume the mantle of policy makers by specifying new planning standards such as benchmarks for future sea level rise or other adaptation risks. Instead, utilizing conventional avenues of statutory interpretation and focusing on procedural decision-making requirements, the courts, together with policy makers, have participated in a coevolutionary process that has guided the understanding of novel climate change–related regulatory provisions as well as setting important parameters for further policy development and decision making on coastal climate change risk management. The following section summarizes the principal coastal climate change cases and analyzes the ways in which they have interacted with regulatory behavior.

High-profile court decisions on coastal climate change risks began to emerge in Australia in 2007 around the same time as public concern over climate change was at its height. One of the earliest decisions was the 2007 judgment of the South Australian Environment, Resource and Development Court (ERDC) in *Northcape Properties Pty Ltd v. District Council of Yorke Peninsula*.[57] The case involved a merits review appeal of

---

[56] Seminal cases in this body of jurisprudence come from the states of New South Wales, Victoria, South Australia, and Queensland. Cases in other coastal jurisdictions, such as Western Australia, have not been as high profile. Western Australia only recently revised its sea level rise benchmark from 0.38 meters by 2100 to 0.9 meters over a one-hundred-year planning time frame to 2110. State Planning Policy No. 26, State Coastal Planning Policy under the Planning and Development Act 2005, Western Australian government, gazetted July 30, 2013, Clause 4.1.

[57] *Northcape Properties Pty Ltd v. District of Yorke Peninsula* [2007] SAERDC 50. See also Bonyhady, "How Australia Once Led the World."

the local council's decision refusing consent for the subdivision of a large parcel of land near Marion Bay on the Yorke Peninsula. The proposal was covered by a Development Plan – a planning instrument under South Australian planning legislation – that governed coastal development and sought "to encourage development that is located and designed to allow for changes in sea level rise due to natural subsidence and probable climate change during the first 100 years of the development."[58] The ERDC upheld the local government's refusal of the subdivision citing the proposal's failure "to make adequate provision for the inland retreat of the foreshore and dunes and associated native vegetation over the next 100 years."[59] Although this decision – affirmed on appeal to the South Australian Supreme Court[60] – made no explicit mention of climate change, it signaled that local planning controls making reference to sea level rise would be given serious judicial consideration and duly applied where supported by expert evidence of future coastal erosion. The rulings quickly "caught the attention" of coastal councils around the country.[61] As one of our interviewees summed up the litigation, "the judge ruled that the impact of climate change was not a possibility, it was expected, and this particular development at Marion Bay, if the projected sea level rises and other impacts were to eventuate, it would impact directly on that site."[62]

Around the same time as the *Northcape* case was being decided by the ERDC, a very similar land use challenge was under consideration by the New South Wales (NSW) Land and Environment Court in the case of *Walker v. Minister for Planning*.[63] Like the *Northcape* case, the *Walker* litigation involved a large residential development proposal located in a low-lying coastal area. The applicants sought judicial review of the government's decision to grant a "concept plan" approval for the development based on the failure of the planning minister and his department to give consideration to climate change and the potential for increased flooding risk on the site as a result of sea level rise. The legislation under which the decision was made did not mention climate change but included

---

[58] Quoted in *Northcape Properties Pty Ltd v. District of Yorke Peninsula* [2007] SAERDC 50, para. 26.

[59] *Northcape Properties Pty Ltd v. District of Yorke Peninsula* [2007] SAERDC 50, para 44.

[60] *Northcape Properties Pty Ltd v. District of Yorke Peninsula* [2007] SAERDC 50, para. 28.

[61] Skype interview, Australian Participant 10 (May 8, 2013). See also House Standing Committee on Climate Change, "Managing Our Coasts," 155–57.

[62] Skype interview, Australian Participant 10 (May 8, 2013).

[63] *Walker v. Minister for Planning* (2007) 157 LGERA 124.

an objective calling for the encouragement of ESD as well as a reference to considering the "public interest" in decision making.[64] Justice Biscoe of the NSW Land and Environment Court ruled in favor of the applicants, finding that ESD was an implied mandatory consideration for decision making and should have led to the minister evaluating the impacts of climate change for flooding on the site.[65] The judge emphasized the gravity of climate change risks, stating, "Climate change presents a risk to the survival of the human race and other species. Consequently, it is a deadly serious issue."[66]

The force of Justice Biscoe's decision in the *Walker* case was lessened by subsequent rulings of the NSW Court of Appeal that adopted a narrower construction of the planning legislation and the role of ESD principles in assessing the public interest.[67] Nonetheless, the NSW Court of Appeal did not question Justice Biscoe's characterization of climate change flood risks.[68] It also made *obiter* comments, suggesting that in the future, it was quite possible that ESD principles would be seen "as so plainly an element of the public interest" that a failure to consider them would be grounds for declaring a decision invalid.[69] In subsequent cases, these statements by the NSW Court of Appeal have provided avenues for decision makers to find that ESD principles are a relevant consideration in determining

---

[64] The encouragement of ESD is one of the objects of the Environmental Planning and Assessment Act, s 5(a). ESD is defined in the planning legislation by reference to s6(2) of the Protection of the Environment Administration Act, which elaborates the concept in terms of ESD principles such the precautionary and intergenerational equity principles.

[65] *Walker v. Minister for Planning* (2007) 157 LGERA 124, at 191–92.

[66] *Walker v. Minister for Planning* (2007) 157 LGERA 124, at 191.

[67] This was largely on the basis of the court's concern that the boundaries of judicial review needed to be carefully observed so as not to stray impermissibly into the area of merits review. Special leave to appeal to the High Court from the Court of Appeal's decision was sought and refused.

[68] The Court of Appeal agreed with the primary judge that consideration of the precautionary and intergenerational equity principles would "almost inevitably" have required a consideration of climate change flood risk. *Minister for Planning v. Walker & Ors* (2008) 161 LGERA 423, at 455.

[69] *Minister for Planning v. Walker & Ors* (2008) 161 LGERA 423, at 454–55. The Court of Appeal also remarked that it was "somewhat surprising and disturbing" that the department's report to the minister on the project did not discuss ESD principles and that the minister did not postpone his decision until he had done so. It went on to find that because the minister did not consider ESD principles at the concept approval stage, it would be necessary to address them when final development approval was sought for the project.

the public interest and for taking account of climate change risks in that context.[70]

While at the project level, the *Walker* litigation was not a success – the NSW government eventually approved the challenged coastal development after taking climate change considerations into account as mandated by the courts[71] – our interviewees nonetheless highlighted a number of broader direct and indirect influences this litigation has had on the landscape of adaptation regulation in Australia. Its principal direct impact has been the institution of a broader interpretation of statutory language calling for the encouragement of ESD and consideration of "the public interest" to cover coastal climate change risks such as sea level rise and increased flooding risk. The NSW Land and Environment Court's *Walker* decision thus has played "an important role in people taking future climate change impacts into account when they're making planning decisions";[72] the case "changed the way that these things are processed, or at least the information that is considered."[73] In addition, in 2009, the NSW state government issued a Sea Level Rise Policy Statement (since suspended) that provided specific sea level rise benchmarks to be used in identifying at-risk areas for development subject to coastal climate change hazards.[74]

---

[70] See, e.g., *Aldous v. Greater Taree City Council & Anor* (2009) 167 LGERA 13, at 26–31; *Barrington-Gloucester-Stroud Preservation Alliance v. Minister for Planning and Infrastructure* [2012] NSWLEC 197, para. 170.

[71] This result was confirmed in the subsequent decision of *Kennedy v. NSW Minister for Planning* [2010] NSWLEC 129 (Jul. 26, 2010). It illustrates the difficulties of tackling adaptation on a project-by-project basis. As one planner interviewed pointed out, "you can tackle this argument around coastal climate change block by block, you know, on the one hand, and you may well be successful in those, but on the other hand there's the planning system where the Minister for Planning can, on the same day, rezone or zone greenfields land for another 3000 blocks on the coastal edge. And that's not contestable." Telephone interview, Australian Participant 9 (May 6, 2013).

[72] In-person interview, Australian Participant 1 (Mar. 7, 2013).

[73] Skype interview, Australian Participant 14 (May 23, 2013). This interviewee also cited the example of a proposed development in a coastal area at Currawong that, post-*Walker*, was refused by the New South Wales government on the basis of the potential for unacceptable climate change impacts.

[74] This policy required coastal planning to take account of an increase above 1990 mean sea levels of 0.4 meters (1.3 feet) by 2050 and 0.9 meters (3 feet) by 2100. The Sea Level Rise Policy Statement was incorporated in 2010 into the Coastline Management Manual applicable to local government planning decisions. This manual was replaced in 2011 by the Guidelines for Preparing Coastal Management Plans under the Coastal Protection Act 1979, which incorporated the sea level rise benchmarks from the 2009 statement. As part of "stage 1" reforms to coastal management that came into effect in 2013, the New South Wales government has declared that the sea level rise benchmarks are no longer state policy,

Another case often cited as having played an influential role in the introduction of adaptation concerns to coastal development planning is the Victorian *Gippsland Coastal Board* case.[75] Like the *Northcape* case, this litigation saw a planning tribunal – in this instance, the Victorian Civil and Administrative Tribunal (VCAT)[76] – refusing consent for a coastal development on various grounds, including threats to the development posed by future sea level rise. In fact, the site involved, while certainly likely to be severely impacted by sea level rise and inundation as a result of climate change, already had marginal development value because of its low-lying nature, water-logging, and frequent flooding. The case was thus not one that on its facts necessitated a consideration of climate change risks to reach the conclusion that the proposed land was not suitable for residential development.[77] Despite this, and the lack of an express reference to climate change matters in the planning legislation,[78] VCAT extensively canvassed issues of sea level rise and coastal inundation. It found that a general requirement in the applicable planning law directing a decision maker to consider "any significant effects... which the responsible authority considers the environment may have on the use or development" was sufficiently broad to encompass the influence of climate change on the proposed development.[79]

The tribunal's decision in the *Gippsland Coastal Board* case was undergirded by the precautionary principle, which plays a central role in Australian environmental law as one of the foundational principles of ESD. Under Australian law, the precautionary principle requires that "where

leaving local governments in limbo as to the standard to apply. See NSW Environment and Heritage, SeaLevel Rise, www.environment.nsw.gov.au/climateChange/sealevel.htm.
[75] Peel and Godden, "Planning for Adaptation"; Brian J. Preston, "The Influence of Climate Change Litigation on Governments and the Private Sector" (2011) 2 *Clim. L.* 485, at 500–501.
[76] In the Victorian planning system, VCAT is empowered to conducts merits review of planning decisions. These decisions do not formally create binding precedents.
[77] In-person interview, Australian Participants 19 and 20 (Jul. 23, 2013).
[78] The applicable legislation, the *Planning and Environment Act 1987* (Vic), requires a responsible authority to consider "any significant effects... the environment might have on the use or development" (s60(e)). The relevant State Planning Policy Framework also guides decision makers to balance conflicting objectives and interests in favor of "sustainable development for the benefit of present and future generations" (Clauses 10.01 and 10.02). VCAT noted that unlike the *Northcape* cases, it had "neither the benefit of specific planning provisions or policy relating to coastal recession or sea level rise." *Gippsland Coastal Board v. South Gippsland Shire Council* [2008] VCAT 1545, at para. 36.
[79] *Gippsland Coastal Board v. South Gippsland Shire Council* [2008] VCAT 1545, at para. 37 referring to s 60(e) of the *Planning and Environment Act 1987* (Vic).

there are threats of serious or irreversible environmental damage, lack of full scientific certainty should not be used as a reason for postponing measures to prevent environmental degradation."[80] The tribunal interpreted this principle to require "a gauging of the consequences and extent of intergenerational liability arising from a development or proposal and if found to be warranted, appropriate courses of action to be adopted to manage severe or irreversible harm."[81] In this context, VCAT ruled it was "no longer sufficient to rely on what has gone before to assess what may happen again in the context of coastal processes, sea levels, or for that matter inundation from coastal or inland storm events."[82] Notwithstanding uncertainty as to the magnitude and measurability of sea level rise and other climate change impacts affecting the site, the tribunal was of the view that "rising sea levels are to be expected."[83] Its application of the precautionary principle led it to the conclusion that increasing storm severity and rising sea levels due to climate change created "a reasonably foreseeable risk of inundation of the subject land," which strengthened VCAT's overall conclusion that the land was unsuitable for development.[84]

Shortly after the *Gippsland Coastal Board* decision was handed down, the state government in Victoria released its 2008 Victorian Coastal Strategy, which establishes a general policy requirement to apply the precautionary principle as well as more specific sea level rise benchmarks for coastal development.[85] Although it does not seem that the VCAT

---

[80] This formulation of the precautionary principle is the one adopted in intergovernmental policies such as the Ecologically Sustainable Dev. Steering Comm., National Strategy for Ecologically Sustainable Development (1992) (guiding principles), and the Intergovernmental Agreement on the Environment (1992), s3.

[81] *Gippsland Coastal Board v. South Gippsland Shire Council* [2008] VCAT 1545, para. 41.

[82] *Gippsland Coastal Board v. South Gippsland Shire Council* [2008] VCAT 1545, at para. 40. This acknowledgment of the difficulties of relying on historical data and previous flood model predictions in assessing future climate change risks corresponds with calls in the literature to transcend historical forms of data analysis and associated decision making in adaptation. See Robin Kundis Craig, "'Stationarity Is Dead' – Long Live Transformation: Five Principles for Climate Change Adaptation Law" (2010) 34 *Harv. Environ. L. Rev.* 9.

[83] *Gippsland Coastal Board v. South Gippsland Shire Council* [2008] VCAT 1545, at para. 42.

[84] *Gippsland Coastal Board v. South Gippsland Shire Council* [2008] VCAT 1545, at para. 48.

[85] Victorian Coastal Strategy 2008, Clause 2.1. This strategy is directly referenced as a consideration by the Victoria Planning Provisions, State Planning Policy Framework, Clause 13.01–1, applicable to all planning schemes in the state. Amendments to Clause 13.01–1 in 2012 added a provision that "an increase of 0.2 metres over current 1 in 100 year flood levels by 2040" may be used in planning for sea level rise for urban infill development. A review of the Victorian Coastal Strategy is currently under way that is likely to adopt the same standard for infill development; for details, see www.vcc.vic.gov.au/.

decision directly led to the new policy (if it did, then, as one intervie-wee put it, "it was a damn quick reaction"[86]), there was still a very clear complementarity between the approach pursued in the case law and the evolution of regulatory requirements for coastal adaptation measures in Victoria.[87] This dialogue between VCAT and government policy makers appears to have continued over the course of subsequent cases, which have given greater clarity and substantive content to policy requirements for sea level rise planning and coastal hazard vulnerability assessment at a project level.[88] Overall, VCAT is playing a part in the regulatory process for coastal adaptation in Victoria through "regularly applying the new poli-cies and the requirement for coastal vulnerability assessments in practical terms."[89]

The mainstreaming of a consideration of coastal adaptation risks in planning decisions brought about by decisions such as those in the *North-cape*, *Walker*, and *Gippsland* cases is evident in the recent case of *Rain-bow Shores Pty Ltd v. Gympie Regional Council & Ors*, decided by the Queensland Planning and Environment Court in 2013.[90] The Queensland Planning and Environment Court is probably the most conservative of the specialist state environmental courts that have dealt with adaptation-related litigation. In previous cases, it has emphasized that the court is not

---

[86] In-person interview, Australian Participant 20 (Jul. 23, 2013).

[87] The Victorian Coastal Strategy is supported by further guidance documents issued by the Victorian Planning Minister in late 2008. Ministerial Direction No. 13, Managing Coastal Hazards and the Coastal Impacts of Climate Change and General Practice Note No. 53: Managing Coastal Hazards and the Coastal Impacts of Climate Change (rev. Jul. 2012).

[88] See *Myers v. South Gippsland Shire Council* [2009] VCAT 1022; *Myers v. South Gippsland Shire Council (No. 2)* [2009] VCAT 2414; *Ronchi v. Wellington Shire Council* [2009] VCAT 1206; *Seifert v. Coloc-Otway SC* [2009] VCAT 1453; *Owen v. Casey CC* [2009] VCAT 1946; *W & B Cabinets v. Casey CC* [2009] VCAT 2072; *Taip v. East Gippsland Shire Council* [2010] VCAT 1222; *Cadzow Enterprises Pty Ltd v. Port Phillip City Council* [2010] VCAT 634; *Bock v. Moyne SC* [2010] VCAT 1905; *Cooke & Ors v. Greater Geelong CC* [2010] VCAT 60; *D'Abate v. East Gippsland SC & Ors* [2010] VCAT 1320; *Printz v. Glenelg SC* [2010] VCAT 1975; *Stewart and Honan v. Moyne Shire Council* [2014] VCAT 360.

[89] Helen Gibson, "Climate Change and Low Lying Areas – Considerations in VCAT," paper presented at the Planning and Climate Change Conference, Monash University, October 20, 2009.

[90] [2013] QPEC 26. This decision builds on a longer history of case law in the state of Queensland that has assessed the relevance of climate change in evaluating development proposals. See *Charles Howard Pty Ltd v. Redland Shire Council* [2006] QPEC 95; (2007) 159 LGERA 349; *Daikyo (North Queensland) Pty Ltd v. Cairns City Council* [2003] QPEC 22; *Mackay Conservation Group Inc v. Mackay City Council* [2006] QPELR 209; *Copley v. Logan City Council & Anor* [2012] QPEC 39. See also Mark Baker-Jones, "Conventionalising Climate Change by Decree" (2013) 30 *Environ. Planning L. J.* 371.

a planning authority and does not have responsibility for setting design standards for development susceptible to coastal climate change risks, a matter it considers more properly a function of governments.[91] Despite the court's stance in previous cases, the relevant statutory framework applicable in Queensland contains general sustainability objectives and other language that leaves scope for the consideration of climate change matters in planning and development processes.[92]

In the *Rainbow Shores* case – which involved a proposal for a large integrated resort and residential community on the Inskip Peninsula near Rainbow Beach on the southeast Queensland coast – the court relied on this statutory language in finding that the coastal side of the peninsula was unsuitable for residential development given hazards posed by erosion, storm surge, and potential inundation in the future due to climate change.[93] Evaluating the decision, one commentator noted the evolution that has occurred in Queensland adaptation case law, remarking that the *Rainbow Shores* case "marks a critical point in planning law. It confirms that planning decision makers must take into account projections of sea level rise when assessing coastal development."[94]

In effect, courts through this series of decisions have taken a novel idea – the need to take account of future climate change impacts in coastal planning and development – and integrated it with existing statutory language

[91] *Daikyo (North Queensland) Pty Ltd v. Cairns City Council* [2003] QPEC 22, at para. 22.
[92] The Sustainable Planning Act 2009 expressly mentions climate change in several provisions, including those relating to the legislation's objective "to seek to achieve ecological sustainability" and to the conduct of decision-making processes: Sections 5(1)(a)(ii) and (c)(i); s 11(c)(iv). These references are made in terms of the effects of development for climate change, which suggests more of a mitigation focus, though this has not prevented their extension by the Court to the adaptation context. See also Judge Michael Rackemann, "Environmental Dispute Resolution – Lessons from the States" (2013) 30 *Environ. Planning L. J.* 329, at 336. This general reference was, until recently, buttressed by a State Planning Policy on Coastal Protection, which required communities and development to be protected from coastal hazards (identified in coastal hazard maps), including those stemming from climate change and projected sea level rise. Department of Environment and Resource Management, State Planning Policy 3/11: Coastal Protection (Queensland Government 2012), Part C, section 2 Coastal Hazards (in effect Feb. 3, 2012). The policy specified a sea level rise factor of 0.8 meters by 2100. The conservative state government that came to power in early 2012 suspended the operation of this policy in October 2012 and has developed a new Coastal Management Plan that deletes references to climate change in favor of "climate variability" and makes no mention of the former 0.8 meters to 2100 sea level rise benchmark. Department of Environment and Heritage Protection, Coastal Management Plan, Queensland Government, 2014, Part 2.1, Principle 1.10.
[93] *Rainbow Shores Pty Ltd v. Gympie Regional Council & Ors* [2013] QPEC 26, at para. 360.
[94] Baker-Jones, "Conventionalising Climate Change by Decree," at 372.

under state planning and environmental laws to require greater attention to adaptation issues. As one interviewee described it – speaking about the Queensland context – the process by which this has been achieved employs the normal interpretative techniques of courts:

> The law was broad enough to encompass environmental considerations, it was just that they hadn't been to the fore in people's minds. And it was a case of the court saying, well I looked at the statute, I looked at the evidence, there seems to be compelling evidence in relation to a matter of relevance under the statute, the answer is, you can't go ahead. That's a perfectly proper process and it's perfectly proper for a specialist court to develop the law in this regard. Quite often you'll see that there will be some change to the statutory contents, but the real gravity of that, the real consequence of that, isn't really realized until the court picks it up, and runs with it, and applies it. And I think that certainly the court in Queensland has quite a history of bringing down decisions from time to time which can force people to say, well, yeah, I can see now that this really does have teeth, this really does apply, et cetera.[95]

While the legislative and policy framework governing Australian coastal adaptation cases varies from state to state, some clear themes emerge from the jurisprudence that have shaped regulation in the field and provide potential pathways for other nations to follow, including the United States. These include an emphasis on the intergenerational consequences of future climate change for present development in coastal areas; endorsement of a precautionary approach to assessment of the hazards posed by sea level rise and coastal climate change risks; and recognition that general legislative requirements for ESD, or for the consideration of the public interest or significant environmental effects, can be construed to require an accounting for climate change risks without the need for a specific statutory reference to climate change.

The intervention of the courts into coastal planning decisions also seems to have injected an element of practicality into the consideration and application of rigid regulatory standards such as "0.8 meters by 2100" sea level rise benchmarks. Courts and tribunals, especially those conducting merits review, have the capacity to tailor development decisions to take account of relevant contextual factors, such as the expected life of buildings in a region, the extent of coastal hazards, and existing protective measures such as seawalls. While some have criticized the variety of decision-making outcomes reached by courts in coastal cases as evidence

---

[95] Skype interview, Australian Participant 5 (Mar. 26, 2013).

of inconsistency,[96] such diversity could also be seen as the product of more flexible and "adaptive" practices of decision making, that is, ones that are better able to accommodate and respond to the changing environmental conditions brought about by climate change.

4.2.3.2   Responding to increasing disaster risks

While adaptation litigation and regulation in Australia have been domi-nated, to date, by coastal climate change hazards, some cases have begun to address other adaptation risks, particularly flood and fire. Climate change is expected to increase both sets of risks, requiring forward think-ing adaptation planning to prepare for them in the future. However, the Australian regulatory system, in general, has been slow to draw an explicit link between emerging climate disaster risks and adaptation planning. Each new disaster is inevitably greeted with a public inquiry of some kind, but with little consideration of how climate change might exacer-bate risks in the future.[97] Political differences over mitigation policy have exacerbated this situation. For instance, at the height of the "unprece-dented" NSW fires of October 2013, Prime Minister Tony Abbott (whose government, as we discussed in Chapter 3, has repealed the national car-bon tax) dismissed claims of a link between climate change and increased wildfire risk as "complete hogwash."[98] Such political disputes overshadow the significant opportunities that exist at a regulatory level to introduce a flexible, adaptive approach to extreme flood or fire events in statutory planning frameworks by taking into consideration new levels of risk due to climate change.[99]

There are signs that litigation is beginning to bridge this gap, even though climate change is often not explicitly discussed in the judgments or

---

[96] Andrew Macintosh, "Coastal Climate Hazards and Urban Planning: How Planning Responses Can Lead to Maladaptation" (2013) 18 *Mitig. Adapt. Strat. Global Change* 1035. See also Mike Steketee, "Come Hell or High Water" *The Sydney Morning Her-ald* (online), August 9, 2013, at www.smh.com.au/business/property/come-hell-or-high-water-20130808–2rkeb.html.

[97] See Tim Bonyhady, "The Law of Disasters" in Tim Bonyhady, Andrew Macintosh, and Jan McDonald (eds.), *Adaptation to Climate Change: Law and Policy* (2010, Federation Press, Sydney), 265, for a discussion of examples.

[98] Peter Hannam, "Tony Abbott Should Never Say 'Never' about Climate Change Bushfire Link," *The Age* (Melbourne) (online), October 25, 2013, www.smh.com.au/environment/climate-change/tony-abbott-should-never-say-never-about-climate-change-bushfire-link-20131025–2w5pt.html.

[99] Alexander Zahar, Jacqueline Peel, and Lee Godden, *Australian Climate Law in Global Context* (2012, Cambridge University Press, Melbourne), at 393.

raised in the arguments of parties. For example, one interviewee explained that in the case of planning disputes considering flood risks, the notion that "what is [one in a hundred] today will not be [one in a hundred] in fifty or a hundred years' time" is a consideration that "is coming into play now in determining whether developments should be allowed to proceed."[100] Litigation over development in flood-prone areas in some jurisdictions is also starting to address the more complex question of how climate change might affect flood risk for existing development surrounding a new project, with implications for the adequacy of infrastructure provision and access to emergency services.[101] Here the issue is not that the new development itself is "getting wet" but that there is "an island, an isolated island of people... who then have problems with being cut off from services, including emergency services, in times when floodwaters combined with climate change mean that existing infrastructure and existing development will go under in the future."[102]

In the case of fire risks, stringent new planning requirements – such as the Bushfire Management Overlay (BMO) developed in the state of Victoria – are also generating litigation activity.[103] Several cases concerning interpretation and application of the BMO have come before VCAT.[104] These cases have tended to take a cautious approach to development in high–fire risk areas, with particular emphasis laid on the preeminent value of protecting human life and the consequent need to exercise caution. In the case of *Land Management Surveys v. Strathbogie Shire Council*, for instance, VCAT described the Black Saturday

---

[100] Skype interview, Australian Participant 5 (Mar. 26, 2013).

[101] See, e.g., *Arora Construction Pty Ltd & Anor v. Gold Coast City Council & Anor* [2012] QPEC 052.

[102] Skype interview, Australian Participant 5 (Mar. 26, 2013).

[103] Some of this litigation is potentially antiregulatory and parallels regulatory takings litigation in the United States. For instance, disquiet over restrictions on development in areas falling within the BMO has seen affected local governments and property owners exploring possibilities for a class action against the Victorian government on the basis of the effects on property values. See Pia Akerman, "Owners Threaten Action over Fire Plan," *The Australian* (online), August 7, 2013, www.theaustralian.com.au/national-affairs/owners-threaten-action-over-fire-plan/story-fn59niix-1226692405821#. ABC News, "Locals Threaten Legal Action over Costly Black Saturday Regulations" (Jul. 12, 2013), available at www.abc.net.au/news/2013–07–12/locals-threaten-legal-action-over-costly-black/4816492.

[104] *Robertson v. Mornington Peninsula SC* [2011] VCAT 1393; *Lester v. Yarra Ranges SC* [2012] VCAT 8; *Land Management Surveys v. Strathbogie SC* [2012] VCAT 77; *Marsden v. Macedon Ranges CC* [2012] VCAT 1038; *Kennedy v. Cardinia SC & Ors* [2012] VCAT 1676; *Adamson v. Yarra Ranges SC* [2013] VCAT 683.

Bushfires and the Royal Commission inquiry that followed as a "game-changer," ushering in a "new paradigm" in terms of future planning for wildfire risks.[105] Similarly, in *Adamson v. Yarra Ranges Shire Council*, the tribunal stressed the need for decision makers to "exercise considerable caution and to press the 'go' button only when satisfied that it is highly likely that people and property will be able to survive the worst expected conditions."[106] At the same time, the tribunal has recognized that in certain cases, it may be impossible to meet wildfire safety requirements where these require large-scale vegetation removal that would cause irreconcilable conflict with competing native vegetation and biodiversity conservation objectives.[107] In addition, the tribunal has generally adopted an approach of evaluating proposals in their broader context, refusing to grant development permits where the reduction of risk relies on others taking fire management measures, such as vegetation removal, on adjoining land.[108]

Again, this litigation around fire risks has only rarely referenced climate change explicitly. An exception is the case of *Carey & Ors v. Murrindindi Shire Council*, decided by VCAT in 2011 prior to the BMO coming into effect. This case involved an appeal of the council's decision granting a permit for the construction of a community hall on land that had been burned in the Black Saturday Bushfires.[109] Although VCAT ultimately approved the permit subject to amendments, it stressed the need for a cautious approach in evaluating the level of risk, including, for example, the closure of the community hall on extreme and catastrophic fire risk days. The deciding tribunal member remarked that he was "conscious that a prudent approach is needed and that the climate change predictions at this point suggest that Victoria will get more extreme fire danger days as time goes on, not less."[110] Comments of interviewees reinforced that even in those cases that do not expressly address the potential for fire risks to be exacerbated by climate change, there is clearly an awareness on the part of decision makers that proactive planning measures like the BMO will

---

[105] *Land Management Surveys v. Strathbogie SC* [2012] VCAT 77, at para. 58. See also *Middle Creek Properties Pty Ltd v. Wodonga CC* [2013] VCAT 258.

[106] [2013] VCAT 683, para. 46.

[107] *Robertson v. Mornington Peninsula SC* [2011] VCAT 1393; *Kennedy v. Cardinia SC & Ors* [2012] VCAT 1676. See also Naylor, "Planning to Mitigate the Impact of Bushfires in Victoria."

[108] *Lester v. Yarra Ranges SC* [2012] VCAT 8; *Adamson v. Yarra Ranges SC* [2013] VCAT 683.

[109] *Carey & Ors v. Murrindindi Shire Council* [2011] VCAT 76.

[110] *Carey & Ors v. Murrindindi Shire Council* [2011] VCAT 76, at para. 114.

also assist in dealing with more frequent wildfires under future climate change conditions.[111]

Australian adaptation litigation raising questions of fire and flood risks has not progressed to the same degree as the case law on coastal climate change hazards. There has not been a consistent or explicit recognition of the need for adaptation measures and the consideration of climate change risks in planning outside of the coastal context. However, as the VCAT wildfire decisions demonstrate, litigation is playing a role in reinforcing the heightened profile of adaptation risks, such as fire, and is starting to make the connection to the likelihood of their exacerbation with climate change. The VCAT case law interpreting the planning laws and the BMO has also laid the foundations of a precautionary approach to wildfire risk that is likely to promote adaptive outcomes over the longer term. This Australian litigation has significant implications for the US context as adapting to natural hazards emerges as an important area for US litigation. The Australian experience around litigation over climate disaster risks could provide an important model for how to link the science with policy steps.

4.2.3.3   Liability for climate change harms

As proactive planning measures to address adaptation concerns have gathered momentum in Australia, another emerging area of litigation focuses on legal liability for climate change harms and damage suffered as a result of climate-linked disasters. This litigation is developing both in the coastal context and in the aftermath of extreme weather events like wildfires and floods. The coastal cases have primarily raised questions over the liability of local governments for damage to coastal properties from erosion and storms, the effects of which are argued to be exacerbated by councils' policies or actions to deal with coastal hazards. Class actions against governments and private corporate actors have also been brought or are actively being considered to recover damages for victims of disastrous fires and floods where plaintiffs allege defendants' action or inaction contributed to the harm suffered. Climate change as an issue has remained in the background, rather than the foreground, of these cases. Nonetheless, as our interviews revealed, key stakeholders in this space – including governments, insurers, and their legal advisors – are keenly aware of the relevance of these cases for shaping future adaptation regulation.

As the following sections discuss, litigation raising liability issues – even just the fear of such litigation – is having a variety of effects on

---

[111] In-person interviews, Australian Participants 19, 20, and 21 (Jul. 25, 2013).

the regulatory landscape for adaptation in Australia, some of which are promotive and some of which are antiregulatory. This experience provides important lessons for US litigants as they also attempt to use courts to push for greater proactive action. At times liability can be a tool that helps to prompt more adaptive behaviors by government and corporate actors who take action to avoid exposure to litigation and damages claims. On other occasions, the surrounding political context in which decisions take place may mean that even positive results in the cases themselves negatively affect land use planning, at least in the near term, as decision makers favor immediate financial and political gains over long-term risk management and protecting the interests of future generations.

In the coastal context in Australia, this double-edged nature of liability was highlighted by a number of our interviewees. While most agreed that coastal adaptation cases, such as those discussed in Section 4.2.3.1, have had a pro-regulatory impact, several also observed that a side effect of the litigation, coupled with uncertainty created by key state governments revoking sea level rise policies,[112] has been heightened concerns about liability, particularly for local governments. Under Australian state liability laws, local governments have various protections from liability in relation to the decisions they make or their other actions or omissions, unless those decisions or actions can be shown to be manifestly unreasonable.[113] In a sense, then, liability concerns on the part of local governments for climate-related damage flowing from their failure to act or inadequate consideration of climate change in decision making may be more imagined than real. Nonetheless, such liability concerns are being taken seriously by local governments (and their insurers) and exerting an effect on adaptive behaviors as a consequence.

One interviewee described the "liability dilemma" facing local governments, who are the primary decision makers in most cases for coastal development, as follows:

> If they reject an application that goes before them for a development in an area that's then to be potentially vulnerable to inundation at some point, then they face the prospect of that decision being taken to an appeals tribunal or land and environment court. If they approve it, then they face the prospect in the future of winding up, you know, facing the court once

---

[112] See further Justine Bell and Mark Baker-Jones, "Retreat from Retreat – the Backward Evolution of Sea-level Rise Policy in Australia, and the Implications for Local Government" (2014) 19 *Local Govern. L. J.* 23.

[113] Baker and McKenzie, *Local Council Risk of Liability in the Face of Climate Change – Resolving Uncertainties*, a report for the Australian Local Government Association, July 22, 2011.

again, but this time in a damages claim if the property is subsequently inundated and there's damage to the property or injury to the people dwelling there.[114]

Faced with this dilemma, some local governments have continued to take a long-term view, pushing forward with proactive planning policies that safeguard local development from future climate change risks. Given the wealth of scientific information supporting the likelihood of these risks occurring, such actions by local governments would most likely be considered "reasonable" by courts and provide a defense to future liability claims. But other local governments have pursued the opposite course, opting to address short-term political risks by appeasing development applicants through the approval of proposals in vulnerable locations.

Speaking about the change in the NSW sea level rise policy – which, as the state government euphemistically characterizes it, gives councils the "flexibility to determine their own sea level rise projections to suit their local conditions"[115] – one interviewee remarked that this has "caused all sorts of grief because some coastal councils have elected to set their mark at a lower figure than previously suggested because their elected representatives may not be believers in climate change."[116] Other local government authorities have found themselves "in a very difficult position because their insurers are saying, well, the science backed up that predicted sea level rise [in the former NSW policy]; that's how you ought to be formulating your planning policies and implementing your zoning maps."[117] Matching reforms in Queensland to remove sea level rise planning benchmarks from coastal planning documents are creating similar concerns and a range of responses from local governments. Another interviewee described how a Queensland local government – the Sunshine Coast Regional Council – is attempting to indemnify itself against future liability for negligent decision making on climate risks by advising applicants that they, and not the council, bear responsibility for the adequacy and veracity of information supplied for the purpose of decision making.[118]

---

[114] Skype interview, Australian Participant 10 (May 8, 2013).

[115] NSW Environment and Heritage, "Sea Level Rise," at www.environment.nsw.gov.au/climatechange/sealevel.htm.

[116] Skype interview, Australian Participant 17 (May 30, 2013). Examples include Eurobodalla Council and Shoalhaven Council in NSW and the Gold Coast Council in Queensland, where mayors have specifically come out saying, "We don't believe in climate change": Skype interview, Australian Participant 9 (May 6, 2013).

[117] Skype interview, Australian Participant 8 (Apr. 24, 2013).

[118] Skype interview, Australian Participant 18 (Jul. 18, 2013).

The concerns of coastal local governments over how their planning and development decisions that either take account of, or disregard, coastal climate change risks may expose them to liability claims from property owners and others have been heightened by observing the ongoing litigation that has engulfed Byron Shire Council in its response to problems of erosion, storm surge, and sea level rise in Byron Bay on the NSW north coast. This litigation concerns protection of the beach at Belongil Spit, a popular holiday destination and the site of many multi-million-dollar homes. The original subdivision of the Belongil in the 1880s was a "right line" subdivision with a one-hundred-foot protecting buffer to seaward.[119] Over the past twenty to thirty years, the Belongil has experienced severe erosion such that the right line boundaries of property owners are now on the foredune or, in some places, on the beach itself.[120] Byron Shire Council has consistently refused to undertake beach protection measures or (costly) beach nourishment at Belongil. For several years, it has also had in place a policy of "planned retreat" under which development must be removed or relocated once the erosion escarpment (the landward limit of erosion) encroaches within a set distance.[121] On one view, this policy is a measure for climate change adaptation and preparedness, given that sea level rise from climate change is likely to worsen the problem of beach erosion at Belongil. However, Belongil property owners dispute this view, arguing that erosion of the beach stems from a protective seawall out from Bryon's main beach and its effects on natural sand flows.[122] Property owners have largely been prohibited by the council from constructing their own private erosion protection works to shore up their beachfront properties. This has led to litigation – some of which is still ongoing – over whether the council is required to maintain its own antierosion measures, its liability for damage caused to beachfront properties if it fails to do so, and if its planned retreat adaptation policy provides a justification for the council's actions.[123]

---

[119] A right line is a fixed line property boundary, as opposed to an ambulatory line; see, further, Bruce Thom, "Beach Protection in NSW: New Measures to Secure the Environment and Amenity of NSW Beaches" (2003) 20 *Environ. Planning L. J.* 325.

[120] Skype transcript, Australian Participant 11 (May 9, 2013).

[121] Productivity Commission, "Barriers to Effective Adaptation," at 208.

[122] Ralf Buckley, "Misperceptions of Climate Change Damage Coastal Tourism: Case Study of Byron Bay Australia" (2008) 12(1) *Tour. Rev. Int.* 71.

[123] See *Vaughan v. Byron Shire Council* [2009] NSWLEC 88; *Byron Shire Council v. Vaughan (No. 2)* [2009] NSWLEC 110; *Vaughan v. Byron Shire Council* [2012] NSWSC 75; *Ralph Lauren & Ors v. Byron Shire Council and Minister for Climate Change and the Environment* [2012] NSWLEC 274. See also Jan McDonald, "The Adaptation Imperative: Managing

Although the Byron Bay litigation has not yet resolved these questions, the lawsuits have been seen as a cautionary tale about "the challenges a local authority might face it if decides to take a highly precautionary approach to coastal climate change hazards."[124] Local government officials find the risk of being sued, no matter what they do with respect to adaptation, intimidating. If they choose to act, they may be sued by landowners whose property rights are affected. If they choose not to act, they may be sued for failing to take needed measures and for the damage resulting from their inaction. For some local governments looking on, litigation risk associated with pursuing proactive coastal adaptation measures is considered to be too high. More generally, the Bryon Bay litigation "has been instrumental in making councils generally very concerned about their potential legal liability in relation to this damage."[125] As one interviewee described it, for "most coastal councils in New South Wales," the liability issue "is the single most important issue. It is the only thing on the agenda."[126]

One response to such concerns, which may ultimately bolster the capacity of local governments to take protective coastal adaptation measures, calls for law reform to provide for greater protections from liability, including the enactment of statutory liability shields for local government decision making on coastal development that is undertaken in good faith. A statutory liability shield of this kind was introduced in the state of New South Wales in 2010.[127] An interviewee involved in the planning field in the state saw this legislative change as a direct consequence of adaptation cases, such as the *Walker* litigation, that made future climate change risk a relevant consideration in development and planning on

---

the Legal Risks of Climate Change Impacts" in Tim Bonyhady and Peter Christoff (eds.), *Climate Law in Australia* (2007, Federation Press, Sydney), 124.

[124] McDonald, "The Adaptation Imperative," at 130.

[125] Skype interview, Australian Participant 10 (May 8, 2013). Productivity Commission, "Barriers to Effective Adaptation," at 168.

[126] Skype interview, Australian Participant 17 (May 30, 2013).

[127] Section 733 of the NSW Local Government Act 1993. This exemption originally applied only to advice or actions relating to flood liable land and land in the coastal zone affected by a "coastline hazard." The effect of the 2010 legislative amendments was to extend coverage of a statutory liability exemption to local governments' provision of information relating to climate change or sea level rise and failures to upgrade flood mitigation or coastal management works in response to projected or actual impacts of climate change. Section 733(3)(f3) and (f5), Local Government Act 2003 (NSW). See also Tayanah O'Donnell and Louise Gates, "Getting the Balance Right: A Renewed Need for the Public Interest Test in Addressing Coastal Climate Change and Sea Level Rise" (2013) 30 *Environ. Planning L. J.* 220.

the coast.[128] The experience of some coastal local governments in NSW seems to be that the statutory liability shield provides the necessary security to move forward with planning policies that take account of climate change–related coastal hazards.[129] Conversely, other stakeholders have pointed to the potential for such statutory protections to produce maladaptive outcomes, because decision makers who ignore climate change risks might also escape liability.[130] In any event, even where an exemption from liability is available, it will only ever be applied after the fact, and there is no guarantee that a court will find that a government decision maker has acted in good faith (or reasonably), especially if the decision maker concerned has ignored readily available scientific information as to the extent of future climate change risks.[131]

Overall, the state of affairs at the moment is one of some confusion and uncertainty over the potential for and extent of legal liability where governments fail to take account of climate change in decision making in coastal areas. A recent report of the Productivity Commission – an independent federal government agency tasked with inquiring into a range of social and economic issues – summed up the current situation:

> Uncertainty about the circumstances in which councils are liable affects local government decisions – in particular, the extent to which adaptation considerations are incorporated into land-use planning and development practices. Several participants suggested that the prospect of legal challenge has prevented councils from acting proactively, and has resulted in the adoption of conservative approaches to development approvals.[132]

One of our interviewees described the Productivity Commission's findings on this issue as "a pretty good summary of the position facing councils."[133] At the same time, others emphasized that over the longer term, liability lawsuits are likely to drive a more positive adaptive response in the coastal adaptation sphere, particularly if Australia was to see a series of climate change–linked disasters affecting large coastal property interests or major infrastructure. As one lawyer put it,

> the risk is known, the risk is out there, you've got very credible scientists talking about this, and regardless of what governments are saying as to whether or not this is policy, it will be very hard for a respondent or

---

[128] Skype interview, Australian Participant 8 (Apr. 24, 2013).
[129] Productivity Commission, "Barriers to Effective Adaptation," 168 (citing the experience of Lake Macquarie City Council).
[130] Ibid., 169.   [131] Ibid.   [132] Ibid., 166.
[133] Skype interview, Australian Participant 10 (May 8, 2013).

defendant in those proceedings to say I was not aware of this. It would be
even harder for them to say, there's a good reason why I should not have
taken this into account. Sure the science is fuzzy around the edges and
what have you, but the courts and planning tribunals look at those types
of people and they're very mainstream, they're government funded, and
you know they're not, you know, Cassandras, they are actually just saying,
well, this is what the science is telling us. So you'd better be planning as a
consequence.[134]

Government liability for property and other damage caused by climate
change–linked weather events is also emerging as an issue in the regulatory response to other adaptation risks, particularly flood and fire. Like
the tort claims filed in the United States, which are discussed in the next
part, Australian litigation raising questions about liability for damage following weather-related disasters could potentially be a tool for addressing
maladaptive behaviors and promoting more adaptive practices. As such
litigation develops in Australia, it may see the so far dormant common
law pathway enlivened as an avenue for climate change regulation in the
nation.

For governmental actors, liability questions raised in postdisaster litigation generally relate to the adequacy of the emergency and disaster
management response, including the contribution of their actions (or
inaction) to the damage suffered. For example, in the aftermath of the
Queensland 2011 flood, which saw huge areas of the state, including the
capital city of Brisbane, under water, the law firm Maurice Blackburn
filed a class action in July 2014 against the Queensland government and
water supply authorities that operate the Wivenhoe and Somerset dams.
Large quantities of water were discharged from these dams during the
flood event, which dramatically increased downstream flooding. In 2012,
the Queensland Floods Commission Inquiry found noncompliance with
the official manual governing operation of the dams,[135] raising questions of the liability of dam operators (as well as the state government
that authorizes the manual) for any resulting damage. The class action –
which does not directly raise the issue of climate change, which, oddly,
was also excluded by the Queensland government from the Flood Commission's ambit of inquiry – alleges that the negligent operation of the
dams by water supply authorities in the lead-up to and during the 2011

---

[134] Skype interview, Australian Participant 8 (Apr. 24, 2013).
[135] Queensland Floods Commission of Inquiry, Final Report (2012), www.floodcommission.
qld.gov.au/publications/final-report.

flood significantly contributed to downstream flooding and exacerbated the resulting damage.[136] Litigation funder Bentham IMF described the litigation as playing "a critical role" in helping "to ensure better standards of behavior going forward to avoid future events."[137]

The Black Saturday Bushfire disaster has also resulted in several class actions targeting public actors, such as emergency management authorities, local governments, state government departments, and rural fire authorities. Claims against government actors in this litigation crystallized around an alleged failure to warn citizens in danger from fire threat.[138] In addition – and similarly to the situation of coastal climate change hazards – questions of public versus private responsibility for risk management are beginning to be raised in association with this litigation. For instance, is fire risk reduction entirely a state responsibility to manage (e.g., through controlled burning) or do private landholders also have an obligation to ensure proper maintenance of fire risk mitigation measures, such as vegetation clearance, around their properties?[139]

Alongside government actors who may contribute to disaster risks through inadequate adaptation planning or preventative measures, private entities have also been a target of liability claims. Following a finding of the Victorian Bushfire Royal Commission that five of the Black Saturday fires were caused by failure of electricity assets,[140] various class actions were brought seeking damages against electricity companies with responsibility for the maintenance and distribution of electricity lines. These claims have generally settled on a without-prejudice

---

[136] For details, see www.mauriceblackburn.com.au/areas-of-practice/class-actions/current-class-actions/queensland-floods-class-action.aspx. See also Peter Foley, "State Facing $1b Payout in Flood Class Action Suit," *The Queensland Times*, June 6, 2012, at www.qt.com.au/news/state-facing-1b-payout-in-flood-class-action-suit/1897029/.

[137] Maurice Blackburn Lawyers, "Stark Picture Painted as 2011 Queensland Floods Class Action Filed," July 8, 2014, at www.mauriceblackburn.com.au/about/media-centre/media-statements/2014/stark-picture-painted-as-2011-queensland-floods-class-action-filed/.

[138] E.g., *Matthews v. SPI Electricity*. This litigation was commenced in 2011 in the Victorian Supreme Court and was the largest civil class action in Victoria's history. A settlement was reached in July 2014: see Jane Lee, Richard Willingham, and Timna Jacks, "Black Saturday Victims Win $500m Settlement," *The Age*, July 15, 2014, at www.theage.com.au/victoria/black-saturday-victims-win-500m-settlement-20140715-zt7jh.html. In the class action, claims made included those against state authorities such as the Department of Sustainability and Environment, the Country Fire Authority, and the State of Victoria.

[139] Skype interview, Australian Participant 17 (May 30, 2013).

[140] 2009 Victorian Bushfires Royal Commission, *The Fires and the Fire-Related Deaths. Final Report Volume I* (2010, Victorian Government, Melbourne), Section 15.1.

basis.[141] The willingness of the defendants to settle and the size of the pay-outs agreed suggest real concerns on the part of power companies over their responsibility for fires caused by inadequately maintained power lines and aging electricity infrastructure.[142] Interestingly, exposure to litigation risk following disastrous wildfires also seems to be driving companies, such as electricity distributors, to take proactive action to climate change–proof their infrastructure to minimize the potential for costly payouts to victims of future events, connecting these liability concerns to the planning ones described earlier.[143]

To date, none of the liability claims brought in Australia following major disasters has raised arguments with respect to climate change, its potential to exacerbate disaster risk, and the consequent need for government bodies and corporate actors to take proactive measures to minimize such risks. However, as our interviewees confirmed, this issue is at the forefront of the minds of those with responsibility for risk management in this area, including government authorities, planners, private and public sector infrastructure providers, and insurers.[144] These cases thus fall in the category of cases at the "outer boundaries" of climate change litigation that we described in Chapter 1, namely, lawsuits that do not expressly raise climate change as an issue but that have clear implications for adaptation.

Inquiries following disasters, such as the Queensland Floods Commission and the Victorian Royal Bushfire Commission, although not specifically tasked to examine climate change risks, have made findings

---

[141] For instance, Powercor reached settlements for AUD$40 million in respect of the Horsham fire and AUD$10 million in respect of a fire near Pomborneit. See Cameron Houston and Michael Bachelard, "Bushfire Victims to get $40m," *The Age* (Melbourne), October 23, 2011, at www.theage.com.au/victoria/bushfire-victims-to-get-40m-20111022–1mdvq. html; AAP, "Powercor Settles Bushfire Class Action," *The Age* (Melbourne), December 19, 2012, at www.theage.com.au/victoria/powercor-settles-bushfire-class-action-20121219–2bmqn.html. SPI Electricity reached a settlement in respect of the Beechworth fire for AUD$32.85 million: see Deed of Settlement between Mercieca and Coombes, and SPI Electricity & Ors, March 5, 2012, available at www.nlgsolicitors.com.au/services?id_service_area=9. Most recently, electricity provider SPAusNet and the Victorian government reached a settlement of just less than AUD$500 million in respect of the largest fire near Kingslake: see further Lee et al., "Black Saturday Victims Win $500m Settlement."

[142] Leanne Mezrani, "Bushfires Spark Liability Debate," *Lawyers Weekly* (online), January 8, 2013, at www.lawyersweekly.com.au/news/bushfires-spark-liability-debate.

[143] Darren Gray, "Special Powerlines to Combat Bushfires," *The Age* (Nov. 29, 2013), www.theage.com.au/victoria/special-power-lines-to-combat-bushfires-20131128–2ye5h.html.

[144] Skype interview, Australian Participant 17 (May 30, 2013); Skype interview, Australian Participant 18 (Jul. 18, 2013).

that point to the role of human actors in causing or exacerbating the damage caused. The Bushfire Royal Commission, for example, found not only that the Black Saturday Bushfires were caused by electrical faults but also that the risk of power line failure increases on days of extreme fire danger. We would predict that as awareness and policy making around adaptation continue to grow, litigation will help to connect the dots between maladaptive behaviors by public and private sector actors and damage from climate change–exacerbated disasters.[145] How such litigation might then shape the regulatory response is more difficult to foresee. However, it does appear that litigation and the development of law in response to disaster risks in Australia will be an important component of its climate change adaptation efforts.[146]

4.3   Emerging adaptation litigation in the United States

The United States, like Australia, faces significant and diverse impacts from climate change, which the nation has recently begun to address more substantially through multilevel regulatory initiatives. This section explores these regulatory developments and analyzes how they interact with nascent adaptation-planning suits.

Unlike in the mitigation context, where hundreds of cases have shaped the regulatory path of the United States in significant ways, US adaptation-planning litigation is just beginning to emerge. These adaptation suits supplement a longer-standing set of cases, mentioned in the previous chapter's mitigation discussion as well, involving petitions for the listing of endangered species as threatened or endangered by climate change, and tort actions in response to disasters. This section examines the role of both these earlier cases and emerging adaptation litigation in the evolving US regulatory context. The new wave of US cases, with their focus on coastal land use planning, have much in common with the more significant Australian jurisprudence and suggest an important future pathway for the litigation's regulatory impact in the United States.

4.3.1   Climate change impacts in the United States

Like Australia, the United States faces a wide range of adaptation challenges. According to the Intergovernmental Panel on Climate Change (IPCC), these include impacts on coastal communities as a result of sea level rise, more severe storms, inundation, and shoreline erosion; the

[145] Mezrani, "Bushfires Spark Liability Debate."
[146] Zahar et al., *Australian Climate Law*, at 400.

imposition of further constraints on the country's already overallocated water resources; heat waves and increased temperatures compounding urban pollution problems and health effects; and increases in disturbances such as wildfires and insect outbreaks.[147] The third US National Climate Assessment, released in May 2014, documents the changes that have occurred in the climate since the last report in 2009 and projects further likely changes for the US climate over the next century. These concur with the IPCC assessment and include higher temperatures and more intense heat waves, a longer frost-free growing season, increased heavy downpours, intensification of strong hurricanes, sea level rise, reduced ice volume and extent, and greater ocean acidification, affecting marine ecosystems.[148]

Although the United States and Australia face many climate change impacts in common, the United States has much greater variations in geography. US coastal communities grapple with sea level rise, more severe storms, inundation, and shoreline erosion. Regions with limited water resources that are already overallocated face further constraints and difficult decisions around planning for future droughts. Heat waves and increased temperatures compound urban pollution problems and health effects. In warmer regions, temperatures are becoming more extreme, and in cooler regions, summer temperatures strain infrastructure unaccustomed to cooling needs. Many places also face increases in disturbances such as wildfires and insect outbreaks. This US geographic variation produces "an uneven distribution of likely impacts, vulnerabilities and capacities to adapt."[149] For example, although more intense droughts are predicted for the Southwest of the country as a result of climate change, the Midwest and Northeast regions are expected to receive more rainfall and experience heavier, more intense downpours and flooding.[150]

---

[147] C. B. Field et al., "North America," *Climate Change 2007: Impacts, Adaptation and Vulnerability: Contribution of Working Group II to the Fourth Assessment Report of the Intergovernmental Panel on Climate Change* (2007, Cambridge, Cambridge University Press), 617–52. See also IPCC Working Group II, "North America – Final Draft," Chapter 26, available at http://ipcc-wg2.gov/AR5/images/uploads/WGIIAR5-Chap26_FGDall.pdf.

[148] Meliillo et al., *Third National Climate Assessment.*

[149] Field et al., *Impacts, Adaptation and Vulnerability*, 619.

[150] Meliillo et al., *Third National Climate Assessment.* Spatial variability in the manifestation of impacts and the extent of adaptive capacity in the United States means that adaptation risks and responses are generally considered on a region-by-region basis. The website on "Climate Change Impacts and Adapting to Climate Change" maintained by the EPA, provides a good example. Impacts and adaptation risks are described by region as well as by sector: www.epa.gov/climatechange/impacts-adaptation/.

Significant regional variability in climate change impacts, together with the regionalized effects of extreme weather events like storms, fires, floods, and droughts, may be a factor in explaining the lower profile – at least pre– Superstorm Sandy – of adaptation in the United States compared with Australia. Whereas some events receive national attention, many more are treated as purely local disasters, which may encourage a view that they are "one-offs" rather than part of a larger national and international trend. As in Australia, however, this situation seems to be changing in conjunction with increases in the number of US weather-related events causing widespread loss and damage.

In time, 2012 may come to be seen as a turning point year. In a 2013 report on the state of the climate, the National Oceanic and Atmospheric Administration declared 2012 as the "warmest and second most extreme year on record for the contiguous US."[151] About one-third of all Americans experienced ten days or more of 100°F (37°C) heat.[152] Droughts, floods, fires, tornados, and storms affected communities across the country. And then, in November 2012, came Superstorm Sandy. Superstorm Sandy's exceptionally strong winds, heavy rain and snow, and record storm surge resulted in 131 people losing their lives and inflicted massive damage on infrastructure and property in New York and New Jersey.

Sandy has been variously described as a "Frankenstorm" and "a freakish and unprecedented monster."[153] Its severity and uncanny timing – just before the 2012 presidential election, in which climate change had not featured as an issue up to that point – catapulted climate change and adaptation issues to front-page news. Impacts from a single extreme weather event, such as Superstorm Sandy, are the most complex to connect to climate change as a scientific matter. Nonetheless, such events fit with the trend toward more extreme weather in North America that can be linked to climate change.[154] A Munich report issued two weeks prior to

---

[151] *State of the Climate in 2012* (2013) 94 Bull. Am. Meteorol. Soc. S1, available at www.ncdc. noaa.gov/news/2012-state-climate-report-released.

[152] *President Obama's Plan to Fight Climate Change*, The White House (June 25, 2013), www. whitehouse.gov/share/climate-action-plan.

[153] Elizabeth Kolbert, "Watching Sandy, Ignoring Climate Change," *New Yorker* (Oct. 29, 2012), www.newyorker.com/online/blogs/newsdesk/2012/10/watching-hurricane-sandy-ignoring-climate-change.html.

[154] Although extreme weather events and other disasters often galvanize public opinion and political action, the relationship between climate change and a particular storm is complex. Namely, the accumulation of greenhouse gases in the atmosphere leads to an increase in the frequency and severity of extreme weather events such as hurricanes,

Sandy presciently stated that North America has been the region of the world most affected by weather-related extreme events in recent decades. The study by the reinsurance group showed a nearly quintupling in the number of "weather-related loss events" in North America for the past three decades.[155] One of these events was Hurricane Katrina, affecting New Orleans in 2005, "one of the most devastating hurricanes in the history of the US." Superstorm Sandy, with its massive devastation, was not even included because of the timing of the report.

As the economic and human losses from such events have grown, there has been a gradual shift in public opinion. Surveys suggest that the general public perceives a trend toward more extreme weather in the United States. For example, a 2012 poll of US residents conducted by researchers at the Yale Project on Climate Change Communication found that respondents believed, by a margin of 2 to 1 (52 percent to 22 percent), that weather in the United States has been getting worse. The same poll found that a large majority of Americans believe that climate change has contributed to the severity of recent natural disasters.[156] This trend seems likely to continue as the United States faces more climate change–related impacts. As Chapter 6 explores in more depth, evolving public perceptions of climate change science, and of appropriate regulatory steps, are influenced by litigation and play out in arguments made in the courts. While these dynamics have occurred more in the mitigation than the adaptation sphere in the United States thus far, the emerging adaptation jurisprudence – discussed later in the chapter – may provide future possibilities for dynamic interchanges between public opinion and litigation in this context.

4.3.2   Government action to address adaptation in the United States

Most current US adaptation activity occurs at the local, state, and regional levels through mechanisms such as land use planning, protection of

---

drought, and wildfires. Specifically, scientists increasingly warn that a "changing climate leads to changes in the frequency, intensity, spatial extent, duration, and timing of extreme weather and climate events, and can result in unprecedented extreme weather and climate events." Intergovernmental Panel on Climate Change, *Managing the Risks of Extreme Events and Disasters to Advance Climate Change Adaptation*, Special Report (2012, IPCC, Geneva).

[155] Munich Reinsurance Am., *Severe Weather in North America: Perils Risks Insurance* (2012), available at www.munichreamerica.com/site/mram/get/documents_E1449378742/ mram/assetpool.mr_america/PDFs/3_Publications/ks_severe_weather_na_exec_ summary.pdf.

[156] Anthony Leiserowitz et al., *Extreme Weather, Climate and Preparedness in the American Mind* (2012, Yale Project on Climate Change Communication, New Haven).

infrastructure and ecosystems, building design regulations, and emergency preparation, response, and recovery.[157] Compared with other developed countries, the United States has been a slow mover on adaptation.[158] As noted in the introduction to this chapter, some of that slowness results from political dynamics around wanting to maintain pressure to mitigate. Professor J.B. Ruhl explains that US "neglect of national policy for climate change adaptation" is an artifact of "the policy world's fixation on achieving, or blocking, federal greenhouse gas emission legislation as part of our national strategy for climate change mitigation."[159]

However, US activity on adaptation has accelerated over the last several years. The growth of state activity exemplifies this trend. As of early 2012, thirteen states had completed adaptation plans, one state was in the process of writing its plan, and eight states had made recommendations for the creation of such plans.[160] In addition, some states had enacted legislation or created programs that address climate change vulnerabilities such as water scarcity or loss of land through sea level rise.[161] By March 2014, Georgetown's Climate Center had identified twenty-seven states and one territory as having done some form of adaptation planning.[162] This smaller-scale emphasis, however, has meant that US efforts on adaptation are highly fragmented as different smaller-scale governments use varying strategies.

At the federal level, adaptation only became a significant focus of US policy under the Obama administration. In October 2009, President Obama created an Interagency Climate Change Adaptation Taskforce to recommend ways in which federal policies and programs could better prepare for climate change. By the same Executive Order, the

---

[157] Rosina Bierbaum et al., "A Comprehensive Review of Climate Change Adaptation in the United States: More Than Before but Less Than Needed" (2012) 18(3) *Mitig. Adapt. Strat. Global Change* 361.

[158] For a review of national adaptation planning efforts in OECD countries, see M. Mullan et al., "National Adaptation Planning" (No. 54 OECD Environment Working Papers, OECD, 2013).

[159] Ruhl, "Structural Transformation," 363–66.

[160] Bierbaum et al., "A Comprehensive Review of Climate Change Adaptation."

[161] Ibid.

[162] According to the Georgetown Climate Center, states and territories that have done some form of adaptation planning include Alaska, Arizona, California, Colorado, Connecticut, Delaware, Florida, Guam, Iowa, Kentucky, Louisiana, Massachusetts, Maryland, Maine, Michigan, Minnesota, North Carolina, New Mexico, New Hampshire, New York, Oregon, Pennsylvania, South Carolina, Tennessee, Virginia, Vermont, Washington, and Wisconsin. See "State and Local Adaptation Plans," Georgetown Climate Ctr., www.georgetownclimate.org/node/3324 (last visited Mar. 5, 2014).

president directed federal agencies to "evaluate agency climate change-risks and vulnerabilities and to manage the effects of climate change on the agency's operations and mission in both the short and long term."[163]

Activity accelerated during President Obama's second term of office, with several important new developments in 2013 alone. In February 2013, federal agencies released their respective climate change adaptation plans applicable to their operations, missions, and programs. The president's Climate Action Plan issued in June 2013 set out a further series of actions by the executive government to prepare the United States for the impacts of climate change. These actions are largely directed toward removing barriers or supporting the activities of other actors at the state, local, and tribal levels that will enhance climate change "resilience." The plan also aims to build scientific capacity and identify vulnerabilities in key sectors such as agriculture, water, health, and energy.[164]

The Obama administration supplemented this plan with a further Executive Order in November 2013 that directed federal agencies to take a variety of steps on adaptation with the aim of promoting

> (1) engaged and strong partnerships and information sharing at all levels of government; (2) risk-informed decisionmaking and the tools to facilitate it; (3) adaptive learning, in which experiences serve as opportunities to inform and adjust future actions; and (4) preparedness planning.[165]

The order specifically focused on modernizing federal programs to support resilient investment; managing lands and waters for climate preparedness and resilience; providing information, data, and tools; and federal agency planning for climate-related risk. It established both a federal-level interagency Council on Climate Preparedness and Resilience and a smaller-scale focused State, Local, and Tribunal Leaders Task Force on Climate Preparedness and Resilience.

Beyond the new efforts by the Obama administration, concrete action taken by the federal government has tended to have a restricted regional focus. For instance, the Rebuilding Taskforce set up in the wake of Superstorm Sandy has required that all federally funded Sandy-related rebuilding projects meet a consistent flood risk reduction standard that takes

---

[163] Exec. Order No. 13514, 74 Fed. Reg. 52,117 (Oct. 5, 2009).
[164] White House, "President's Climate Action Plan."
[165] Exec. Order No. 13,653, Fed. Reg. 66,819 (Nov. 1, 2013).

into account increased risks from extreme weather events, sea level rise, and other climate change impacts.[166]

An important exception to that limited regional focus is the Federal Emergency Management Authority's (FEMA) efforts – now stalled – to increase premium rates as part of reforms to the National Flood Insurance Program. Such increases to reflect "true flood risk" – originally authorized under the Biggert-Waters Flood Insurance Reform and Modernization Act of 2012 – potentially would have significant national impact.[167] If implemented in a way that accurately reflects the real cost of rising sea levels and increasing coastal hazards from climate change, this regulatory action could radically reduce incentives for locating or rebuilding properties in vulnerable coastal and low-lying areas in ways that are beneficial for adaptation. However, these reforms have received a setback, with Congress passing legislation, the Homeowner Flood Insurance Affordability Act of 2014, to delay their implementation in response to growing public and political opposition to the reforms as coastal landowners digested the prospect of skyrocketing premiums.[168] Moreover, these measures raise some serious issues regarding equity, especially for low-income people who have fewer resources to respond when floods cause serious property damage.[169] These equity impacts have formed the basis for the litigation that we discuss later.

In sum, the United States has mostly responded to adaptation challenges in an incremental, ad hoc manner. While existing environmental laws – such as the Endangered Species Act, the Coastal Zone Management Act, the National Environmental Policy Act, and the Clean Water Act – may offer significant scope for crafting adaptation responses,[170] this avenue has not been extensively explored, either in regulation or

---

[166] "Federal Government Sets Uniform Flood Risk Reduction Standard for Sandy Rebuilding Projects," Hurricane Sandy Rebuilding Task Force, U.S. Dept. of Hous. and Urban Dev. (Apr. 4, 2013), http://portal.hud.gov/hudportal/HUD?src=/sandyrebuilding/FRRS.

[167] Biggert-Waters Flood Insurance Reform Act of 2012, Pub. L. No. 112-141, 126 Stat. 405 (codified as amended at 42 U.S.C. § 4001–4129, 2006).

[168] Homeowner Flood Insurance Affordability Act of 2014, Pub. L. No. 113-89.

[169] Carolyn Kousky and Howard Kunreuther, "Addressing Affordability in the National Flood Insurance Program," Wharton University of Pennsylvania, Working Paper 2013–12, December 2013, at http://opim.wharton.upenn.edu/risk/library/WP2013–12_Affordability-NFIP_CK-HK.pdf.

[170] J. Peter Bryne and Jessica Grannis, "Coastal Retreat Measures" in Michael B. Gerrard and Katrina F. Kuh (eds.), *The Law of Adaptation to Climate Change: US and International Aspects* (2012, American Bar Association, New York), 267; Dave Owen, "Climate Change and Environmental Assessment Law" (2008) 33 *Colum. J. Envtl L.* 57.

litigation. The authors of the chapter on North America in the IPCC's 2014 Working Group II report on impacts, vulnerability, and adaptation summarize the state of adaptation planning thus:

> There is increasing attention to adaptation among planners at all levels of government but particularly at the municipal level, with many jurisdictions engaging in assessment and planning processes. Yet, there are few documented examples of implementation of proactive adaptation and these are largely found in sectors with longer term decision-making, including energy and public infrastructure (**high confidence**). Adaptation efforts have revealed the significant challenges and sources of resistance facing planners at both the planning and implementation stages, particularly the adequacy of informational, institutional, financial and human resources, and lack of political will (**medium confidence**).[171]

The recent steps by the Obama administration indicate a significant shift toward more coordination and integration of adaptation concerns at a federal level. These developments, in parallel with the emerging litigation described in the next section, suggest that the United States may be at a particularly crucial moment for influencing its adaptation strategies.

4.3.3   US adaptation litigation

Just as in the policy sphere, the focus of US climate change litigants has primarily been on the big battles over mitigation action rather than adaptation. Before 2012, there had not been any adaptation litigation in the United States beyond cases under the Endangered Species Act and tort lawsuits with adaptation implications. However, this pattern has recently begun to change, with several cases that portend an emerging wave of litigation addressing the need to incorporate adaptation into government planning and land valuation decisions. While these first few cases may be an indication of future US litigation pathways – for which the extensive Australian cases described previously may be a model – they certainly have not had the impact of the mitigation cases to date.

This section reviews the US cases with significant implications for adaptation regulation. It begins with the somewhat more developed jurisprudence regarding climate-related species loss and postdisaster tort before turning to the newly emerging cases addressing coastal and disaster planning. Although the US litigation explicitly focused on litigation is nascent, the existing cases – of which six exemplar, recent cases are presented – have

---

[171] IPCC, Working Group II, "North America – Final Draft," Chapter 26, 46.

many similarities to a number of the Australian ones. Like in Australia, coastal planning issues and disaster preparedness are emerging as central issues in the US adaptation jurisprudence. The developing case law also reveals the wide-ranging impacts of climate change, with consideration of the implications for utilities and electricity infrastructure providers, water managers, and insurers.

4.3.3.1   Earlier litigation with some connection to adaptation: Endangered Species Act and natural disaster tort cases

The United States arguably already has a relatively developed line of jurisprudence on adaptation issues, focused on addressing the problems that climate change poses for species. As described in Chapter 3, petitions and associated litigation under the Endangered Species Act have resulted in the listing of several species on the grounds of climate change threats. However, the mitigation-related effects of the Endangered Species Act litigation have been thwarted by government rulemaking, such as the special 4(d) rule, that limits requiring greenhouse gas emissions reduction efforts to protect listed species.

This section builds on Chapter 3's discussion of the Endangered Species Act by focusing on two mechanisms under the Endangered Species Act that have particular relevance to adaptive action. The first is the requirement under Section 7 for all federal agencies to, "in consultation with and with the assistance of the Secretary, insure" that all actions authorized, funded, or carried out by such agencies are "not likely to jeopardize the continued existence" or "result in the destruction or adverse modification" of "critical habitat" of a listed species.[172] The second provision is Section 9, which applies to "any person," including government agencies at all levels, corporations, and individuals. Section 9 enacts a prohibition on the "taking" of any endangered species in the United States or on the high seas.[173] This taking prohibition has also been extended to threatened species via regulations issued under the act.[174]

Although the special 4(d) rule adopted by the Bush and Obama administrations has significantly limited the potential for Endangered Species Act litigation to contribute to mitigation action – at least in the context of threatened species such as the polar bear[175] – interviewees highlighted

---

[172] 16 U.S.C. § 1536(a)(2) (2012).   [173] 16 U.S.C. § 1538(a)(1) (2012).
[174] 50 C.F.R. § 17.40 (2013).
[175] The potential is greater for endangered species to which the 4(d) rule does not apply. See Brendan R. Cummings and Kassie R. Siegel, "Biodiversity, Global Warming, and the

that, as an adaptation tool, the litigation has had more substantial success and "real world impact."[176] This promotive effect on adaptation has been especially pronounced under the Obama administration, which has given agencies more latitude to take climate change into account in their planning activities. As one interviewee described it:

> the Forest Service, the Bureau of Land Management or other land management agencies used to not consider climate change at all in their land management plans. Now through litigation raising these kinds of issues – they're not doing a good job of it yet – but they are starting to at least make an effort of, like, okay, how do we maintain wildlife corridors to allow migration of species upslope or into more northernly latitudes? The same with what we're seeing with sea turtles and critical habitats under the [Endangered Species Act]. The process of recognizing the beaches in Florida that are currently critical for loggerhead sea turtles are going to be underwater and what habitat is necessary to protect the species in a changing climate.[177]

This kind of consideration likely will only continue to grow and develop as agencies continue to work to implement the Obama administration's November 2013 Executive Order.

Another area that has been a focus of proactive Endangered Species Act litigation with some emerging adaptation benefits is recovery plans for listed species. For instance, following the settlement of litigation over its failure to issue a recovery plan for two species of corals listed, in part, due to climate change threats, the National Marine Fisheries Services is currently drafting a recovery plan proposal.[178] A similar process is under way for the polar bear, albeit only prompted by the threat of litigation from groups such as the Center for Biological Diversity. The hope of advocacy groups is that these processes will set out meaningful adaptive actions for ensuring species protection in a changing climate, which may include specifying associated mitigation efforts to support such actions.

Beyond these species-related cases, tort actions seeking to impose liability on public authorities or major corporate emitters in the aftermath

United States Endangered Species Act: The Role of Domestic Wildlife Law in Addressing Greenhouse Gas Emissions" in William C. G. Burns and Hari M. Osofsky (eds.), *Adjudicating Climate Change: State, National, and International Approaches* (2009, Cambridge University Press, New York), 145.

[176] Telephone interview, US Participant 12 (Dec. 2, 2013).   [177] Ibid.

[178] Carolina Bolado, "FWS Settles with Enviro Group Over Fla. Coral Protection," Ctr. for Biological Diversity (Sep. 13, 2013), www.biologicaldiversity.org/news/center/articles/2013/law360–09–13–2013.html.

of disasters also have some connection to climate change adaptation. Suits targeting governmental actions or inaction – such as the litigation over the maintenance of flood protection measures brought against the Army Corps of Engineers in the aftermath of Hurricane Katrina[179] – often involve maladaptive behavior. These claims, like the postdisaster lawsuits that have arisen in Australia, are not explicitly framed as climate change adaptation cases. However, they may have implications for adaptation regulation because climate change is expected to increase the frequency and severity of extreme weather events and the vulnerability of coastal communities to such events.

These postdisaster tort cases' influence on adaptation could at times be promotive and at times antiregulatory, as the Australian Byron Bay example suggests. On one hand, even if not successful given the defenses that government actors, in particular, can raise to liability, these tort cases, or the potential for such litigation, can serve to make governments more likely to engage in proactive planning to avoid costly litigation and reputational damage from the filing of lawsuits against them.[180] On the other hand, these cases could augment the struggles that governmental authorities have with how to prepare and respond, especially since they often do not factor in climate change directly. In fact, some commentators have indicated that framing such cases without reference to climate change – such as in a case by the Board of Commissioners of the Southeast Louisiana Flood Protection Authority brought against oil and gas companies that focuses on dredging without mentioning sea level rise – could be maladaptive.[181]

Similarly, the small body of nuisance cases that have been brought against major corporate emitters, such as auto manufacturers and power

---

[179] *In re Katrina Canal Breaches Litig.*, 673 F.3d 381 (5th Cir. 2012) reversing earlier opinion in *In re Katrina Canal Breaches Litig.*, 673 F.3d 381 (5th Cir. 2012). In this odd decision, the same three-judge panel that had initially ruled in favor of the plaintiffs reversed itself and found the Army Corp of Engineers was completely insulated from liability by a provision of the Federal Tort Claims Act called the "discretionary-function exception." Whether similar immunity will be granted to other government defendants in future liability claims remains unclear.

[180] See Michael B. Gerrard, "Hurricane Katrina Decision Highlights Liability for Decaying Infrastructure" (2012) May 10 *N.Y. L. J.* 1.

[181] See Edward P. Richards, *The Louisiana Costal Erosion Lawsuit: Bad Science and Bad Policy*, Mineral Law Institute, commenting on *Bd. of Comm'rs of the S.E. La. Flood Prot. Auth. E. v. Tn. Gas Pipeline Co., LLC., et al.*, No. 13–6911 (D. Ct. Orleans Parish, La. Jul 24, 2013). Available at http://biotech.law.lsu.edu/blog/petition-for-damages-and-injunctive-relief .pdf) (on file with authors).

plants,[182] also has implications for the management of climate change impacts. While these lawsuits are generally thought of as mitigation cases, given their focus on attributing liability for greenhouse gas emissions, they could also have adaptation implications if they serve as a compensation mechanism for losses associated with affected communities taking adaptive action (e.g., coastal retreat).[183]

To date, these cases have not achieved any notable successes, as none has proceeded to a merits determination. Moreover, with the Supreme Court's decision in *AEP v. Connecticut* – finding that nuisance cases under federal common law are displaced by the EPA's regulatory authority under the Clean Air Act – the possibilities for these cases obtaining such relief narrowed further.[184] Nonetheless, like the Endangered Species Act cases, tort actions may serve as a vehicle for forging linkages between mitigation and adaptation by highlighting the need for strong mitigation action to avoid or minimize liability for future climate change impacts.

4.3.3.2   Emerging cases addressing adaptation planning

While the Endangered Species Act and tort cases described in the previous section have implications for US adaptation law and policy, newer cases around coastal hazards and disaster planning have a much clearer focus on government management of predicted climate change impacts. These cases share much in common with the Australian adaptation litigation described in the preceding given their focus on interpreting existing legislation, regulatory measures, and institutional responsibilities – and their capacity to extend to addressing climate change.

The first of these recent US adaptation cases – *US v. Miami-Dade County, Fla.* – considered the ways in which climate change adaptation connected to a broader land use planning dispute. The case focused on Miami-Dade County's sewage discharges into public waters in violation of the Clean Water Act and the Florida Air and Water Pollution Control Act. The 2013 filings were the latest round in long-standing litigation over these issues that resulted in consent decrees in 1994 and 1995.

---

[182] *Comer v. Murphy Oil*, 585 F.3d 855 (5th Cir. 2009); *Kivalina v. ExxonMobile Corp.*, 663 F.Supp.2d 863 (2009), *aff'd*, 969 F.3d 849 (9th Cir. 2012).

[183] Bryne and Grannis, "Coastal Retreat Measures."

[184] 131 S. Ct. 2527, 2539 (2011); see also Hari M. Osofsky, "Litigation's Role in the Path of U.S. Federal Climate Change Regulation: Implications of *AEP v. Connecticut*," (2012) 46 *Valparaiso U. L. Rev.* 447; Hari M. Osofsky, "*AEP v. Connecticut*'s Implications for the Future of Climate Change Litigation," *Yale L. J. Online* (2011).

What connected this case to climate change adaptation was an intervention by the Biscayne Bay Waterkeeper and Judi Koslen, a Key Biscayne resident, under Section 505 of the Clean Water Act. Their complaint alleged not only that the county had repeatedly violated its consent decrees but also that it was entering into a new consent degree that violated the public interest due to its failure to address climate change impacts.[185] Specifically, the June 2013 complaint in intervention focused on interpretation of the Clean Water Act, claiming that

> the proposed Consent Decree is unfair, unreasonable and contrary to the public interest because:
>
> a. The draft Consent Decree's Capital Plan will not achieve or maintain compliance with CWA, primarily because it fails to address sea level rise and climate impacts that will, if not appropriately accounted for, cause major failures in the sewage collection and treatment system during its useful life.... Over time, these failures will prevent the WASD sewage collection and treatment system from operating properly and complying with the requirements of the Clean Water Act, Florida law, and its NPDES permits.[186]

The federal district court for the Southern District of Florida ultimately denied intervenor Biscayne Bay Waterkeeper's motion to reopen the case, agreeing with the US government that the consent decree had resolved the Clean Water Act violations at issue in the case.[187] Nonetheless, the types of issues raised in this Florida-based case are not unique to Miami-Dade County. Coastal climate change impacts have been a focus of adaptation planning in many areas because they are the set of impacts for which the greatest levels of scientific certainty exist.[188] As such impacts worsen, many cities will face a wide array of core functions affected by climate change. We predict that this case is simply the first in what is likely to be a series of state-court-based disputes using a statutory interpretation pathway to challenge how localities are managing adaptation; the extensive Australian jurisprudence could serve as a model – both constructive and cautionary – for how these cases might unfold.

---

[185] Complaint in Intervention, *U.S. v. Miami-Dade County, Fla.*, No. 12-24400-FAM (S.D. Fla. June 25, 2013).

[186] Complaint in Intervention, *U.S. v. Miami-Dade County, Fla.*, No. 12-24400-FAM (S.D. Fla. June 25, 2013), at 7.

[187] *U.S. v. Miami-Dade County, Fla.*, No. 12–24400-FAM (S.D. Fla. May 8, 2014).

[188] Intergovernmental Panel on Climate Change, *Climate Change 2013: The Physical Science Basis – Summary for Policy-makers* (2013, IPCC, Geneva).

The second case example – on adaptation of energy infrastructure – began with a petition on natural hazard planning filed with the New York Public Service Commission by the Columbia University Center for Climate Change and a group of NGOs in December 2012 in the aftermath of Superstorm Sandy. The Public Service Commission, constituted through New York state legislation, serves as the primary regulator of New York's utilities, which provide power throughout the state. The petition asked the commission to "use its regulatory authority to require all utility companies within its jurisdiction to prepare and implement comprehensive natural hazard mitigation plans to address the anticipated effects of climate change."[189] Specifically, the petition raised the concern that current planning largely focuses on short-term emergency response, without adequate consideration of longer-term adaptive planning. The petition neatly illustrates how coastal management and disaster planning may intertwine in future US litigation through reinterpretation of how regulatory entities use statutorily based authority.

This case is particularly interesting because it links energy and environmental planning in its call for public utilities to plan for hazard mitigation and disaster response under conditions of increased risk from climate change. Although the petition focused in particular on New York and Superstorm Sandy, it raised issues with broader implications for utilities in areas most vulnerable to coastal and storm impacts. The petition explained:

> Extreme weather events threaten the reliable service of utilities to consumers throughout New York State. Superstorm Sandy, the most recent and devastating example in a series of storms affecting New York utilities, interrupted vital electrical, water, steam, and telecommunications services for over a million utility users throughout the state. Once interrupted, services may take weeks to reinstate, further exacerbating the human and economic costs of the storm....
>
> While the severity of Superstorm Sandy may have been unique, its destructive effect on utility service is not. In 2011, Hurricane Irene left nearly 400,000 New York City residents without power. The Public Service Commission's 2011 Electric Reliability Performance Report confirms the connection between utility outages and storm events....

[189] Letter from Anne R. Siders, Associate Director, Columbia University Center for Climate Change Law et al., to Jaclyn A. Brilling, Secretary to the New York State Public Service Commission (Dec. 12, 2012), available at http://web.law.columbia.edu/sites/default/files/microsites/climate-change/files/Publications/PSCPetitionNaturalHazard Planning_0.pdf (PSC petition).

Such outages occur at least in part because the critical infrastructure that supports New York utilities is vulnerable to storm surge and flooding.[190]

The petition was only the first step in this case. When Consolidated Edison (ConEd) – the largest utility in the state of New York – filed a petition with the commission in January 2013 for changes to its rates, the Columbia University Center for Climate Change and other NGOs formally intervened and subsequently participated in the adjudicatory hearings that followed. During the rate case litigation, a Storm Hardening and Resiliency Collaborative, including the coalition of academic centers and NGOs, formed to negotiate terms of a settlement and to implement the settlement agreement. The collaborative included four working groups, addressing (1) storm hardening design standards, (2) alternative resiliency strategies, (3) natural gas system resiliency, and (4) risk assessment/cost benefit analysis.

As a result of discussions in the design standards working group, ConEd adopted a new design standard of the latest FEMA hundred-year floodplain elevation plus three feet of freeboard ("FEMA+3") to protect its infrastructure in flood zones, which it will review every five years.[191] In its order, the commission noted that ongoing review of the standard is appropriate "in light of the rapid developments in climate science forecasts, and in federal, state and city policies."[192]

The settlement agreement reached by the collaborative was approved by the commission in February 2014. It required ConEd to implement capital programs and projects to "storm harden" and improve the resiliency of its electric, gas, and steam systems in the face of anticipated climate change and sea level rise.[193] Fundamental to the settlement agreement is the notion that capital equipment should be designed, sited, and built to withstand the climate conditions that will exist at the end of its useful life, and not just at the beginning. The commission's order also affirmed

---

[190] Ibid., at 1–2.

[191] State of N.Y. Pub. Serv. Comm'n, Order Approving Electric, Gas and Steam Rate Plans in Accord with Joint Proposal (Feb. 21, 2014), available at http://documents.dps.ny.gov/ public/Common/ViewDoc.aspx?DocRefId={1714A09D-088F-4343-BF91-8DEA3685 A614}; Consolidated Edison Co. of N.Y., Storm Hardening and Resiliency Collaborative Report (Dec. 4, 2013), available at http://documents.dps.ny.gov/public/ Common/ViewDoc.aspx?DocRefId={E6D76530–61DB-4A71-AFE2–17737A49D124} (PSC Order).

[192] PSC Order, at 67.

[193] State of N.Y. Pub. Serv. Comm'n, Joint Proposal (Dec. 31, 2013), available at http:// documents.dps.ny.gov/public/Common/ViewDoc.aspx?DocRefId={3881B193–8115– 4BA0-A01A-B8D373D59726}.

the commitment of ConEd to undertake, during 2014, a climate change vulnerability study encompassing adaptation risks such as rising heat and more severe storms. This study is intended to provide a longer-range basis for ongoing review of design standards, such as the FEMA+3 flood-proofing standard, and the commission indicated that it "expect[ed] to revisit this issue."[194]

Already, the ConEd rate case decision is being hailed as "an historic decision that will serve as a nationwide model."[195] The infrastructure concerns that were the focus of the original 2012 petition and the subsequent rate case occur in many places around the United States. Similarly the proposals developed in the work of the Collaborative and approved in the settlement agreement could apply in other states because they focus on core electricity infrastructure questions that are not specific to New York. Like the first complaint described, then, the petition and ConEd rate case decision, may become an important model for future litigation over adaptive approaches for energy infrastructure in the US context. As impacts worsen over time, public utility commissions around the country will increasingly have to grapple with how to interpret their regulatory authority to address adaptation concerns.

The third case highlighted indicates the possibility for the US takings jurisprudence to interact more directly with climate change adaptation. This jurisprudence provides one of the few direct constitutional law pathways for engaging climate change questions. The Fifth Amendment of the US Constitution requires government assertions of eminent domain authority to be for "public use" and accompanied by just compensation. An extensive jurisprudence in the US Supreme Court and other federal and state courts has interpreted this clause, at times in coastal contexts. Like some Australian cases such as the Bryon Bay litigation described earlier, some past US cases – with no explicit mention of climate change – have raised claims of regulatory takings in response to efforts by state and local authorities to restrict development in coastal areas. In both countries, the effects of regulatory takings litigation in this context has been primarily maladaptive by discouraging the adoption of proactive adaptation policies such as retreat from high-risk areas. For example, the 1992

---

[194] PSC Order, at 67.

[195] Ethan Strell, "Public Service Commission Approves Con Ed Rate Case and Climate Change Adaptation" Settlement, Climate Change Blog (Feb. 21, 2014), available at http://blogs.law.columbia.edu/climatechange/2014/02/21/public-service-commission-approves-con-ed-rate-case-and-climate-change-adaptation-settlement.

US Supreme Court case *Lucas v. South Carolina Coastal* held (under relatively specific circumstances) that a coastal protection policy preventing Lucas from building on his land constituted a per se taking.[196]

While a number of policy makers and commentators have raised concerns about this possibility for takings suits to constrain climate change adaptation efforts, a 2013 New Jersey Supreme Court opinion, *Borough of Harvey Cedars v. Karan*, suggests possibilities for climate-adaptive policies to constrain just compensation claims. The case involved a massive public works project in which the borough of Harvey Cedars

> exercised its power of eminent domain to take a portion of the beachfront property of Harvey and Phyllis Karan to construct a dune that connects with other dunes running the entire length of Long Beach Island in Ocean County. The dunes serve as a barrier-wall, protecting the homes and businesses of Long Beach Island from the destructive fury of the ocean.[197]

The parties agreed that the property has been partially taken and that under both the federal and state constitutions, just compensation is required. However, the New Jersey Supreme Court held that the protective effects of the dune must be taken into account as part of the just compensation calculation to prevent the Karans from obtaining a windfall. It accordingly reversed and remanded an earlier court decision granting the Karans US$375,000 in compensation.

This reversal by New Jersey's highest court both influenced this individual case and helped to spur additional litigation. The settlement of the case resulted in the Karans receiving US$1 instead of the US$375,000 they were set to receive before the New Jersey Supreme Court reversal. Meanwhile, New Jersey governor Chris Christie signed an executive order that directed the acting state attorney general to begin legal proceedings to obtain the more than 1000 easements required to build dunes in the communities that suffered particularly severe impacts from Superstorm Sandy.[198]

Although this case occurs in the specific context of New Jersey, like the other exemplar cases, it has broader implications. The reasoning of

---

[196] *Lucas v. South Carolina Coastal Council*, 505 U.S. 1003 (1992). For a discussion of legal tools available to facilitate retreat from at risk coastal areas, see Anne Siders, *Managed Coastal Retreat: A Legal Handbook on Shifting Development Away from Vulnerable Areas* (2013, Columbia Center for Climate Change Law, Columbia Law School, New York).

[197] *Borough of Harvey Cedars v. Karan*, 43 ELR 20149, No. A-120–11 (N.J. Jul. 8, 2013).

[198] MaryAnn Spoto, "Harvey Cedars Couple Receives $1 Settlement for Dune Blocking Ocean View," *Star Ledger* (Sep. 25, 2013), www.nj.com/ocean/index.ssf/2013/09/harvey_cedars_sand_dune_dispute_settled.html.

the state supreme court could be applied in many other takings contexts where a government is using taken land to implement measures that will protect the rest of the land from climate change impacts. The court found

> that the Appellate Division's use of the general-benefits doctrine in this case is at odds with contemporary principles of just-compensation jurisprudence. The jury was barred from hearing evidence about potentially quantifiable benefits arising from the storm-protection project that increased the value of the Karans' home. Just compensation does not entitle a landowner to a windfall from a partial taking of property. . . .

> Harvey Cedars condemned a portion of the seaside, oceanfront property of the Karans to acquire a permanent easement for the construction and maintenance of a twenty-two-foot dune to replace an existing sixteen-foot dune. The new dune was part of a much larger shore-protection project to benefit all the residents of Harvey Cedars and Long Beach Island. Unquestionably, the benefits of the dune project extended not only to the Karans but also to their neighbors further from the shoreline. Yet, clearly the properties most vulnerable to dramatic ocean surges and larger storms are frontline properties, such as the Karans.' Therefore, the Karans benefitted to a greater degree than their westward neighbors. Without the dune, the probability of serious damage or destruction to the Karans' property increased dramatically over a thirty-year period.

> A jury evidently concluded that the Karans' property decreased in value as a result of the loss of their panoramic view of the seashore due to the height of the dune. A willing purchaser of beachfront property would obviously value the view and proximity to the ocean. But it is also likely that a rational purchaser would place a value on a protective barrier that shielded his property from partial or total destruction. Whatever weight might be given that consideration, surely, it would be one part of the equation in determining fair market value.[199]

This analysis of fair market value is potentially groundbreaking for coastal adaptation regulation in the United States because it internalizes the cost of damage from climate change and the value of preventing it. Takings suits often are brought to make regulatory measures too expensive for governments to pursue. This cost internalization may significantly reduce the costs of just compensation, making adaptation-related eminent domain assertions and other measures vulnerable to regulatory taking claims more viable.

---

[199] *Borough of Harvey Cedars v. Karan*, 43 ELR 20149, No. A-120–11 (N.J. July 8, 2013); 214 N. J., at 418.

Even at this early stage, other courts have begun to follow the approach in *Karan*, reinforcing its potential influence. For example, in *Petrozzi v. City of Ocean City*, a 2013 New Jersey case also involving sand dunes and ocean views, but in a different legal context, the appellate court specifically referenced the *Karan* approach to compensation. It ordered that

> the remand judge allow further proofs of valuation, consistent... with the admonition in *Borough of Harvey Cedars v. Karan* that "the quantifiable decrease in the value of their property – loss of view – should [be] set off by any quantifiable increase in its value – storm-protection benefits."[200]

This opinion in *Petrozzi* suggests that the *Karan* reasoning may be used by courts – in New Jersey and eventually perhaps in other states as persuasive authority – in various contexts where they have to assess compensation for harms suffered from climate adaptation measures. This approach to compensation, introduced in a constitutional law context, could thus potentially have influence in statutory interpretation or common law contexts as well when damages are being calculated.

The fourth case focuses on state management of coastal waters, specifically Massachusetts's failure to address nitrogen pollution off of Cape Cod adequately. The Conservation Law Foundation and Buzzards Bay Coalition brought an action in September 2011 under the Clean Water Act to compel the EPA to address this pollution. Part of the petitioners' argument in this statutory interpretation case involved climate change. Namely, the First Amended Complaint claimed that Massachusetts's dated area plan did not adequately incorporate the ways in which climate change impacts water quality:

> 71. Since adoption of the 1978 Areawide Plan for Cape Cod, extensive scientific study developed by or available to EPA has demonstrated an ongoing and increasing trend of accelerated climate change and the impact of that change on affected embayments.
>
> 72. Federally-sponsored research has concluded that global temperatures are rising and, in turn, affect weather patterns and water quality. Climate science is unequivocal about the fact that, under the most probable future scenario, coastal ecosystems will be subjected to more strains than they would be without climate change.

---

[200] *Petrozzi v. City of Ocean City*, docket no A-1633–11T4 & A-1677–11T4 (N.J. Superior Ct. Oct. 28, 2013), http://njlaw.rutgers.edu/collections/courts/appellate/a1677–11.opn. html.

73. Climate change will impact the seasonal timing of runoff to freshwater and coastal systems. Furthermore, climate science demonstrates that climate change creates uncertainty with regard to the range of possible future impacts of such change on coastal ecosystems.

74. The 1978 Areawide Plan fails to mention climate change.

75. Defendants' failures to annually approve or to require updates of the Areawide Plan means that the impact of climate change on water quality conditions has not been evaluated in the context of Section 208.[201]

In August 2013, the case survived a motion to dismiss on one of its four counts. This count claimed that the EPA had acted arbitrarily and capriciously in approving Massachusetts's State Revolving Funds given that the plan with which the funds must be consistent had not been updated since 1978.[202] The next month, the EPA submitted a proposed plan of action and requested a stay on the basis that the Cape Cod Commission was updating the plan, which the district court approved in January 2014.[203] The EPA indicated in its submission that the commission's work plan includes "consideration of climate change, sea level rise and storm surge."[204] This case has similarities to many of the successful mitigation-focused regulatory actions discussed in the previous chapter in that the lawsuit helped to spur needed governmental action through using a broad federal environmental statute.

The final case examples – both of which were withdrawn before they proceeded to a full trial – raise questions relating to the implications of increasing climate change impacts for insurers and insureds. Although these particular lawsuits are not progressing, they may inspire similar claims in the future and so remain important examples of the potential

---

[201] First Amended Complaint, *Conservation Law Foundation v. McCarthy*, Case No. 11-cv-11657, September 10, 2012, available at www.arnoldporter.com/resources/documents/CLF%20v%20McCarthy%20amended%20complaint.pdf (last visited Mar. 6, 2014).

[202] Memorandum and Order Concerning Count IV, *Conservation Law Foundation v. McCarthy*, Case No. 11-cv-11657 (D. Mass. Aug. 23, 2013), available at www.gpo.gov/fdsys/pkg/USCOURTS-mad-1_11-cv-11657/pdf/USCOURTS-mad-1_11-cv-11657-1.pdf (last visited Mar. 6, 2014).

[203] Defendants' Report Regarding Future Proceedings, Case No. 11-cv-11657, Sep. 27, 2013, available at www.arnoldporter.com/resources/documents/CLF%20v%20McCarthy%20EPA%20proposal.pdf (last visited Mar. 6, 2014); Order, *Conservation Law Foundation v. McCarthy*, Case No. 11-cv-11657 (D. Mass. Jan. 27, 2014), available at www.arnoldporter.com/resources/documents/CLF%20v%20McCarthy%20stay%20order.pdf (last visited Mar. 6, 2014).

[204] Defendants' Report Regarding Future Proceedings, at 5.

for adaptation-related litigation to influence regulation and government behavior.

The first case involved a lawsuit filed by the Mississippi Insurance Department in the federal district court for the Southern District of Mississippi seeking to enjoin or stay rate increases introduced by FEMA for the National Flood Insurance Program.[205] As highlighted earlier, these premium rate increases – which were authorized by the Biggert-Waters Flood Insurance Reform and Modernization Act of 2012 but have since been delayed by congressional passage of the Homeowner Flood Insurance Affordability Act of 2014 – are designed to reflect the true economic cost of flood risk to property in vulnerable areas, such as on the coastline and in floodplains. It is widely recognized that the National Flood Insurance Program is not financially sustainable and that this will only be exacerbated by the occurrence of more weather-related disasters.[206] The Mississippi Insurance Department's suit – using the statutory interpretation pathway – was based on an alleged failure by FEMA to undertake required studies, including an affordability study, prior to introducing the rate increases. It sought injunctive relief along with a declaration that FEMA must undertake the required studies prior to making its rate determinations.

In response, the US government filed a motion to dismiss for lack of subject matter jurisdiction citing a lack of standing and that the Mississippi Insurance Department was not entitled to bring claims on behalf of affected Mississippi citizens. The US government also argued that an order from the court would not address the plaintiff's injuries as the relief sought is only available from Congress.[207]

In the latest development in this case, the Mississippi Insurance Department voluntarily withdrew its lawsuit following passage of the Homeowner Flood Insurance Affordability Act in early 2014. The dismissal is without prejudice, and the Mississippi Insurance Commissioner has indicated that the agency will refile the lawsuit if

---

[205] *Mississippi Insurance Department v. U.S. Department of Homeland Security* (S.D. Miss., filed. Sep. 26, 2013; first am. compl. Oct. 7, 2013). For details, see www.arnoldporter.com/public_document.cfm?id=23061&key=7B1 and www.arnoldporter.com/public_document.cfm?id=23055&key=0F3.

[206] U.S. Gov't Accountability Office, GAO-13–283, High-Risk Series: An Update (2013), available at www.gao.gov/assets/660/652133.pdf.

[207] *Mississippi Insurance Department v. U.S. Department of Homeland Security* (S.D. Miss. Nov. 18, 2013), available at www.arnoldporter.com/public_document.cfm?id=23328&key=14I0.

implementation of the flood insurance reforms does not address afford-ability concerns.[208]

The sixth case example also raised the implications of climate change for the insurance industry, as well as for local and city governments with responsibilities for maintaining infrastructure that is vulnerable to adap-tation risks. In *Illinois Famers Insurance Company v. Metropolitan Water Reclamation District of Greater Chicago*, several insurance companies sued the water reclamation district for greater Chicago and numerous other cities and local governments in Cook County, Illinois, in a class action.[209] The insurers alleged that the failure of the defendants to implement rea-sonable storm water management practices and to increase storm water capacity resulted in increased payouts to the plaintiffs' insureds follow-ing heavy rains in April 2013, which caused sewer water to flood the insureds' properties. Among other factors, the insurance companies relied on the climate change–adjusted hundred-year rainfall return frequency predicted by the 2008 Chicago Climate Change Action Plan in assert-ing claims of negligent maintenance liability, failure to remedy known dangerous conditions, and regulatory takings.[210] The pleadings stated,

> The defendant knew or should have known that climate change in Cook County has resulted in greater rainfall volume, greater rainfall intensity and greater rainfall duration than pre-1970 rainfall history evidenced, resulting in greater stormwater runoff.[211]

---

[208] *Mississippi Insurance Department v. United States Department of Homeland Security*, No. 1:13-cv-379-LG-JMR (S.D. Miss. Apr. 14, 2014), available at www.arnoldporter.com/ public_document.cfm?id=23661&key=11B1.

[209] *Illinois Farmers Insurance Co. v. Metropolitan Water Reclamation District of Greater Chicago*, No. 2014CH06608 (Ill. Cir. Ct., filed Apr. 16, 2014), available at www. arnoldporter.com/public_document.cfm?id=23667&key=18H3. See also Geoff Ziez-ulewicz, "Insurance Co. Sues Will County, 12 Towns over Flood Damage" *Chicago Tribune*, April 29, 2014, available at www.chicagotribune.com/news/local/suburbs/ bolingbrook/ct-flooding-lawsuit-bolingbrook-plainfield-tl-0501–20140429,0,4298338, full.story. A similar case is on foot in Queensland, Australia, involving damage to a resort that plaintiffs allege is the result of a poorly constructed stormwater drain installed by the local government. Part of the argument is that construction of the drain did not take into account the potential for increased rainfall as a result of changes in the climate. Skype interview, Australian Participant 18 (Jul. 18, 2013).

[210] See, further, J. Wylie Donald, "Negligent Operation of a Storm Sewer: A New The-ory of Climate Change Liability," *Climate Lawyers Blog*, May 2, 2014, available at www.climatelawyers.com/post/2014/05/02/Negligent-Operation-of-a-Storm-Sewer-A-New-Theory-of-Climate-Change-Liability.aspx.

[211] *Illinois Farmers Insurance Co. v. Metropolitan Water Reclamation District of Greater Chicago*, No. 2014CH06608 (Ill. Cir. Ct., filed Apr. 16, 2014), available at http://www. arnoldporter.com/public_document.cfm?id=23667&key=18H3.

In June 2014, Farmers Insurance filed notices of dismissal of these claims, having apparently achieved the aims sought in bringing the litigation. Announcing the withdrawal of the class action, a spokesperson for the insurance group stated,

> We believe our lawsuit brought important issues to the attention of the respective cities and counties, and that our policyholders' interests will be protected by the local governments going forward.[212]

This case neatly illustrates the kind of liability dilemma that adaptation can present for state and local authorities as they interpret their planning authority – a theme already familiar to counterparts in Australia. If the insurers' claim had progressed, the city of Chicago (ironically one of the cities with the most advanced planning for climate change) may have effectively been hoisted on the petard of its own adaptation plan. It is unclear exactly why the lawsuit was withdrawn. Some commentators have noted that the case faced numerous barriers to success with respect to liability, sovereign immunity, and public duty doctrine; for instance, the court may have granted governmental immunity, as the Fifth Circuit did in the flooding case brought by New Orleans residents against the Army Corp of Engineers following Hurricane Katrina.[213]

Regardless, lawyers, engineers, and others have noted that the lawsuit – and the potential for others like it – could have a wide range of impacts for adaptation. On one hand, the litigation risk that this suit illustrates could serve to reinforce the need for governments not only to plan for climate change impacts but also to follow through with effective implementation. This might include swifter action by municipalities to upgrade their storm water infrastructure, as well as encouraging engineers and planners to adopt forward-looking projections of climate change effects in infrastructure design standards. In this way, the Farmers Insurance suit might augment the effects of litigation like the ConEd rate case by focusing attention on the climate readiness (or lack thereof) of infrastructure. However, equally possible is that litigation of this kind drives decision-making paralysis and retreat from proactive adaptation action that has also been seen with coastal local governments in Australia. One article

---

[212] Quoted in Robert McCoppin, "Insurance Company Drops Suits over Chicago-Area Flooding," *Chicago Tribune*, June 4, 2014, at www.chicagotribune.com/news/local/breaking/chi-chicago-flooding-insurance-lawsuit-20140603,0,6767298.story. The spokesperson said the company does not intend to refile the suits.

[213] See the discussion at note 179.

on the lawsuit quotes attorney Joanne Zimolzak, a partner with law firm
McKenna Long and Aldridge, as saying,

> Municipalities looking at something like this might think, "Does it make
> better sense for me not to adopt some type of a climate action plan?" [But]
> if you had the knowledge and you failed to adopt a climate plan, then
> maybe that opens you up to a different kind of liability.[214]

If this lawsuit prompts similar cases in the future, they will help clarify
the liability of governments with respect to failures in their adaptation
planning and implementation efforts, with important flow-on effects for
adaptive responses.

4.4   Comparing adaptation litigation in Australia and the United States

The more developed Australian adaptation litigation provides a helpful
model as US litigators consider next steps. While significant differences
between the countries prevent perfect parallels, the core similarities in
their legal systems and approaches to land use planning allow for useful
comparisons to be drawn. This section suggests three main lessons offered
by Australian adaptation litigation for the nascent US litigation efforts.

The first is that litigation – in the aggregate – can help change planning
culture in ways needed for climate change adaptation. The Australian
cases have served as a useful mechanism for injecting consideration of
climate change risks into planning and infrastructure management decision making under existing regulatory frameworks. Adaptation litigation
in Australia has not involved the kind of big-splash, high-profile cases
that have characterized the US mitigation sphere, such as *Massachusetts v.
EPA*. But adaptation litigation there has been highly successful in taking
the novel (perhaps, for some, the "unthinkable")[215] idea of considering
climate change risks in current development and planning and making it
routine and workable.[216]

Cases taking sea level rise and coastal flooding into account are now
so common in Australia that they generate little fanfare.[217] The necessity

---

[214] Cited in Evan Lehmann, "Insurance Co. Sues Ill. Cities for Climate Damage," *Climate Wire*, E&E Publishing, May 14, 2014, at www.eenews.net/stories/1059999532.

[215] Christopher D. Stone, *Should Trees Have Standing? Toward Legal Rights for Natural Objects* (Kaufmann, Los Altos, 1974).

[216] Skype interview, Australian Participant 5 (Mar. 26, 2013); Skype interview, Australian Participant 17 (May 30, 2013).

[217] Skype interview, Australian Participant 7 (Apr. 11, 2013).

of assessing climate change risks as a matter of course, particularly on the coast, has seeped into the collective consciousness of those involved in the planning and development sector in Australia. The idea has taken a particularly tenacious hold in the minds of the professional staff of state and local government planning agencies, engineers and planners, and insurers. This culture change remains in place despite moves by several conservative state governments (especially in New South Wales and Queensland) and some elected local councilors in coastal regions to deny or downplay the importance of climate change risks.[218]

In the first wave of US cases, some petitioners have already succeeded in getting that kind of consideration in particular contexts. For instance, *Karan*, the takings case, illustrates the impact of including adaptation benefits in just compensation analysis, and the energy infrastructure petitions and the ConEd settlement indicate possibilities for public utility commissions to help the grid adapt. But the Australian litigation experience shows the incremental regulatory impacts that can accrue as this litigation unfolds. Once enough of these cases change individual planning decisions, planners and developers may begin to make different assumptions from the outset that are more adaptive without the necessity of stakeholders using litigation to push them. This possibility reiterates the value of continuing to bring these small-scale planning suits in the US context, even if their direct, individual impact is very local.

The second lesson that can be drawn from the Australian experience is the catalytic role played by disasters and related litigation in forwarding action on adaptation. The pre–Superstorm Sandy US climate change litigation brought in the aftermath of disasters focused primarily on tortious harms suffered by those injured. The Australian context also contains class actions aimed at recovering damages from public and private actors whose activities are alleged to have contributed to the harms suffered. But Australian lawsuits in the aftermath of major events, such as the Black Saturday Bushfires and Queensland 2011 floods, have also stimulated improved planning measures and disputes over their implementation. In both the fire and flood contexts, lawsuits have both helped push disaster planning forward and limited efforts by private property owners to oppose them. The role of this litigation provides a helpful model for US efforts moving forward.

Two of the six US adaptation-planning suits represent this type of approach, the petitions to the New York Public Commission and the

---

[218] Skype interview, Australian Participant 9 (May 6, 2013).

now-withdrawn Illinois insurance case. Both cases suggest the potential of this type of litigation in the United States. The decision by the commission in the ConEd case reflects a strong concern that infrastructure should be better prepared to deal with disasters than it was at the time of Superstorm Sandy. The lawsuit by insurers, and the threat of similar litigation in the future, signals a need for governmental authorities to match fine words in adaptation plans with on-the-ground action if they are to avoid liability. These suits – paired with the Australian experience – suggest possibilities for postdisaster lawsuits and petitions to assist needed policy change and implementation in energy and other land use areas, though as noted, this promotive impact may depend on how these cases are framed. If they do not acknowledge climate-related impacts and propose measures that do not take them into account, their results could be maladaptive as well.

A final lesson that emerges from the Australian litigation, particularly that over coastal retreat and protection measures implemented in Byron Bay, is the need to reconcile the often competing interests of public adaptation strategies and private property rights. In Australia, disputes between property owners and councils over beach protection, coupled with legal liability concerns related to local government decision making regarding coastal development, have significantly muddied the waters for proactive adaptation measures.

These Australian disputes serve as a cautionary tale about the unpredictable results of litigation and concerns over liability on behavior. They also highlight the difficulties encountered in shifting from a perspective that favors short-term private property protection to one that focuses on the longer-term approach and includes public adaptation benefits in its valuation model. This type of problem is not new to the United States. For example, US regulatory takings suits have at times served as a similar regulatory damper and have the potential in the future to constrain climate change adaptation efforts. The *Karan* case suggests, though, at least in a postdisaster context where there is a clearly recognized need for reducing vulnerability to future impacts, that private property interests may not always win out in such situations.[219] Nonetheless, the Australian experience indicates that litigation over local government planning, such as in the now-withdrawn the Illinois insurance case, is not always a useful

[219] Joseph Berger, "Complaints and Warnings about Plan to Replenish Fire Island's Dunes," *New York Times,* May 27, 2014, at www.nytimes.com/2014/05/28/nyregion/complaints-and-warnings-about-a-plan-to-replenish-fire-islands-dunes.html?hp&_r=1.

tool for driving governments toward decisions that promote proactive adaptation outcomes; the threat of litigation may equally scare them into silence and inaction or push them toward maladaptive planning.[220]

As US litigation continues to develop in this area of coastal adaptation and disaster planning, petitioners need to have an awareness of how they might prevent or mitigate such challenges. The Australian experience suggests the importance of a litigation strategy that goes beyond each individual case to situate it in the broader litigation and political context. Such a strategy may be hard in such localized cases, where those bringing suits may not be connected into national and regional networks of other potential petitioners. However, the likely consequences make it critical for those playing a leadership role in US adaptation litigation nationally and regionally to reach out to potential litigants locally and coordinate adequately.

4.5   Conclusion

As the importance and urgency of climate change adaptation have gained increasing acceptance globally, there has been a parallel attention to adaptation issues in regulation and litigation at the domestic level. Australia and the United States both face significant climate change risks and have suffered a number of extreme weather events in recent years.

To date, differences in their degree of short-term risk have likely contributed to Australia's more developed jurisprudence around adaptation. In Australia, the extensive exposure of populated centers to coastal climate change hazards, as well as the wide-ranging effects of extreme weather events for the country as a whole, seems to have propelled earlier consideration of adaptation issues by both governments and courts. Climate change impacts, to date, have not occurred to the same extent in the United States. Nonetheless, post–Superstorm Sandy, the regulatory landscape for adaptation regulation in the United States is changing rapidly, including an increasing body of cases directly focusing on planning for future climate change risks.

Whether the US adaptation litigation becomes as widespread and influential as that in Australia remains to be seen. Recent US cases suggest the

---

[220] For a similar critique in the Australian context, see Andrew Macintosh, "Coastal Climate Hazards and Urban Planning: How Planning Responses Can Lead to Maladaptation" (2013) 18 *Mitig. Adapt. Strat. Global Change* 1035.

possibilities for litigation to play an important role in local and state planning regarding land use, energy, and coastal waters and in other public and private decision making relevant to that planning, such as in the insurance context. But the sample size is still very small. In contrast to mitigation litigation, however, the capacity for adaptation cases to contribute to an overall national approach – other than through their aggregate indirect impacts on planning culture – seems more limited. The context-specific geography of climate change impacts paired with the extent of state and local authority over land use planning and public utilities means that cases likely will have greatest impact in the state in which they are located and in others with similar adaptation issues. However, as Australian litigation experience suggests, coordinating strategies are needed in the United States to maximize cumulative planning culture impacts and limit political backlash.

As to the future trajectory of adaptation litigation in both Australia and the United States, interviewees offered several interesting predictions, many of which resonate with the emerging case law to date. Several interviewees noted a potential role for litigation under environmental and planning laws (e.g., the National Environmental Policy Act [NEPA] and state equivalents such as the California Environmental Quality Act) to be a driver for incorporating climate change into strategic land use planning and development, particularly on the coasts.[221] In the United States, such litigation would mirror the Australian coastal case law brought under state environmental and land use laws, while also potentially drawing on the experience of the extensive NEPA case law seeking to integrate consideration of greenhouse gas emissions into environmental impact assessments.[222] Other interviewees saw the greater occurrence of extreme weather and natural disasters as a potential spur for litigation and associated regulatory steps. For instance, one interviewee raised increased litigation over insurance companies refusing coverage for weather-related losses as a possible stimulus for regulation to control development in vulnerable areas.[223] Another foresaw greater litigation in the aftermath of disaster against a range of actors – including architects, builders, engineers, and infrastructure providers – that might prompt a rethinking of

---

[221] Telephone interview, US Participant 12 (Dec. 2, 2013); in-person interviews with US Participants 4 (Nov. 14, 2012) and 10 (Jan. 14, 2013). The latter interviewee also discussed the link between such actions and environmental justice concerns of affected communities.

[222] See the discussion of the NEPA litigation in Chapter 3.

[223] In-person interview, US Participant 6 (Nov. 14, 2012).

design standards to ensure buildings and infrastructure are prepared for the worst climate change impacts.[224]

There is also the potential for the adaptation litigation in each country to develop in unique directions, reflecting the nuances of their respective local environmental conditions and applicable laws. An example is the case law over species listings under the Endangered Species Act, for which no true Australian parallel exists. The Endangered Species Act cases are beginning to yield results for adaptation through their recognition of the need for land and species management to take the effects of a changing climate into account. In addition, Professor Robin Kundis Craig has explored the possibility for the common law public trust doctrine – which has been used in a mitigation context – to be applied to management of coastal areas.[225] Similar ideas are being taken up by Australian scholars in thinking about how coastal property rights might be more appropriately balanced with adaptation policy needs in a climate-changed future.[226]

Inchoate in the Endangered Species Act litigation and also some of the newer planning cases in both the United States and Australia is also the question of whether litigation can play a role in fostering linkages between adaptation and mitigation efforts. This link is particularly clear in the Endangered Species Act context given that long-term survival and recovery of listed species ultimately depends on addressing the root causes of climate change. However, it has emerged in broader planning contexts. This was vividly highlighted in late 2013 by the contemporaneous timing of severe wildfires in the state of New South Wales and the introduction of legislation into the Australian Parliament by the Abbott government to repeal the national carbon pricing mechanism for reducing greenhouse pollution.[227] In response, Australian Greens Party MP Adam Bandt tweeted that "Tony Abbott's plan [to repeal the carbon tax] means more

---

[224] Telephone interview, US Participant 7 (Nov. 16, 2012).

[225] Robin Kundis Craig, "Public Trust and Public Necessity Defenses to Taking Liability for Sea-Level Rise Responses on the Gulf Coast" (2011) 26 *Land Use Environ. L.* 395.

[226] Bruce Thom, "Climate Change, Coastal Hazards and the Public Trust Doctrine" (2012) 8(2) *Macquarie J. Int. Comp. Environ. L.* 21.

[227] See, e.g., Agnes Nieuwenhuizen, "Comment, as NSW Burns, It's Time to Talk About Climate Change," *The Age* (Oct. 21, 2013), www.theage.com.au/comment/as-nsw-burns-its-time-to-talk-about-climate-change-20131021–2vwlr.html; Gerard Henderson, "Twisted Logic Links the Tragic NSW Bushfires with the Prime Minister, Climate Change and Abolishing the Carbon Tax," *The Age* (Oct. 22, 2013), www.theage.com.au/comment/twisted-logic-links-the-tragic-nsw-bushfires-with-the-prime-minister-climate-change-and-abolishing-the-carbon-tax-20131021–2vx2n.html.

bushfires for Australia."[228] The ferocious media and political response to this observation – federal Environment Minister Greg Hunt castigated Bandt for trying to politicize a "human tragedy" – illustrates just how far public and political attitudes to climate change still need to evolve in Australia to embrace linked mitigation-adaptation policies. We return to this discussion of public attitudes to climate change in Australia and the United States, and the role of litigation in shaping social norms and values, in Chapter 6, before focusing on barriers and antiregulatory litigation in Chapter 7.

As climate change impacts continue to worsen and adaptation planning becomes more imperative, linkages (and trade-offs) between mitigation and adaptation outcomes are likely to become a greater focus of regulation and litigation in the future in both countries. At times, mitigation and adaptation choices align, but not always. Adaptive measures may increase greenhouse gas emissions, and mitigation measures may be maladaptive. As the changing climate forces hard choices about our use and management of natural resources, courts will likely serve as a critical forum for resolving these dilemmas.

---

[228] David Holmes, "Is the Abbott Government Fiddling While NSW Burns?," *The Conversation* (Oct. 18, 2013), http://theconversation.com/is-the-abbott-government-fiddling-while-nsw-burns-19339.

Corporate responses to litigation

I can tell you – at the broadest level – the requirement to report the occurrence of greenhouse gas nuisance litigation to one's shareholders often is met with the question, you know, of "well, what are we doing about this?" And not even if the company is in the crosshairs of the lawsuit or the litigation. I prepare lots of 10Q disclosures . . . and you need to discuss the litigation and you need to discuss its impacts. Typically it's not just, discuss what it is and then say nothing about the company, how it's positioned. Having a credible response that would satisfy investors, particularly the more activist investors in large corporations, you would think you would want to have a response that set forth some type of strategy that indicated that you were making the right kind of investment decisions.

– US Interview Participant 5

There is a growing concern within the [coal mining] sector: we're not so much worried about the energy, like the power gen companies and things like that, but we are concerned around other mineral projects and mining projects that may be stopped on a greenhouse basis. From our perspective, it only takes one to get knocked down around greenhouse that sets a precedent. So that's where our major focus has tended to be. And part of that in terms of preparing or countering that, is to ensure that we have fairly good credentials internally in the way that we manage climate change and greenhouse issues.

– Australian Interview Participant 13

5.1   Introduction

The previous two chapters have considered litigation as a tool for improving mitigation and adaptation regulation, focusing mainly on the response of governments to climate change cases. However, corporations are equally, if not more, important actors in efforts to transition the energy economy or improve resilience.[1] Corporations in the energy sector,

---

[1] Rory Sullivan, "Introduction" in Rory Sullivan (ed.), *Corporate Responses to Climate Change: Achieving Emissions Reductions through Regulation, Self-Regulation and Economic Incentives* (2008, Greenleaf, Sheffield), 2.

particularly coal and oil and gas companies, play a crucial role in mitigation efforts; the consumption of their fuel products for electricity generation and transportation contributes nearly 70 percent of global greenhouse emissions.[2] In the adaptation sphere, corporations involved in infrastructure provision, development, and land use, as well as companies that provide property and disaster insurance, have an important part to play in helping to reduce communities' vulnerability to climate change. Other corporate actors, particularly in the financial and investment sectors, are also emerging as key players in the regulatory complex that will be necessary to move toward low-carbon societies. For example, several reports have been released on the so-called carbon bubble: the sudden loss in value of fossil fuel assets predicted to result from international constraints on carbon emissions.[3] Such developments are leading to increasing pressure on corporations to improve disclosure of climate-related risk to shareholders and investors, and on institutional investors, such as pension funds and banks, to divest themselves of fossil fuel assets.[4]

Although many corporate actors operate across national borders, very little transnational regulation of corporate activity and its environmental consequences exists.[5] Addressing corporate greenhouse gas emissions

---

[2] World Resources Institute, CAIT 2.0, WRI's Climate Data Explorer, available at http://cait2.wri.org/wri/Country%20GHG%20Emissions?indicator[]=Energy&indicator[]=Industrial%20Processes&indicator[]=Agriculture&indicator[]=Waste&indicator[]=Land%20Use%20and%20Forestry%20(Net%20Forest%20Conversion)&indicator[]=Bunker%20Fuels&year[]=2009&focus=&chartType=geo (showing energy sector figures for 2009).

[3] Carbon Tracker Initiative, *Unburnable Carbon: Are the world's financial markets carrying a carbon bubble?* (2012, Carbon Tracker Initiative, United Kingdom); Carbon Tracker Initiative and LSE Grantham Research Institute on Climate Change and the Environment, *Unburnable Carbon 2013: Wasted Capital and Stranded Assets* (2013, Carbon Tracker Initiative, London); Elaine Prior, *"Unburnable Carbon" – A Catalyst for Debate* (2013, Citigroup, Australia); Simon Redmond and Michael Wilkins, *What a Carbon-Constrained Future Could Mean for Oil Companies' Creditworthiness* (2013, Standard and Poor's Ratings Services, London); Paul Spedding, Kirtan Mehta, and Nick Robins, *Oil and Carbon Revisited: Value at Risk from "Unburnable" Reserves* (2013, HSBC Bank plc, Oil and Gas/Climate Change Europe).

[4] See, e.g., the fossil fuels divestment campaign being run by 350.org: http://gofossilfree.org/.

[5] International instruments dealing with transnational corporate environmental regulation or corporate environmental responsibility generally take the form of nonbinding guidelines and other soft law instruments with limited compliance mechanisms. See Afshin Akhtarkhavari, "The Global Compact, Environmental Principles, and Change in International Environmental Politics" (2010) 38(2) *Denver J. Int. Law Policy* 217; Elisa Morgera, "The UN and Corporate Environmental Responsibility: Between International Regulation and Partnerships" (2006) 15(1) *Rev. Eur. Commun. Int. Environ. L.* 96; Evaristus

and adaptation efforts thus remains largely the task of domestic regulatory systems. To date, the majority of climate change litigation brought in the United States and Australia to advance regulation has targeted government actors. A smaller subset of largely unsuccessful cases has sought to influence corporate behavior directly. In the United States, for example, public nuisance actions have been brought against major emitters, such as automobile manufacturers and electricity generators, in an effort to force these companies to take legal responsibility for the effects of the greenhouse gas pollution associated with their products.[6]

Even the cases focused on government regulatory behavior, however, primarily target regulation relevant to corporations. In both countries, for example, permits and licenses issued to corporations have been challenged on grounds that the development or activity concerned takes insufficient account of potential climate change impacts.[7] In the United States, litigants have sought greater regulation of corporate greenhouse gas emissions and the consequences of those emissions under major federal environmental laws. As we saw in previous chapters, this litigation, in some cases, has served as a direct pathway for new regulation that tightens procedural or substantive requirements applicable to corporations undertaking activities with climate change ramifications. Of equal, if not greater, importance than the direct regulatory effects of this litigation are its indirect consequences, which may motivate changes in corporate behavior. These indirect regulatory consequences include the role of litigation in increasing the costs associated with "dirty" energy products or maladaptive practices, whether these costs manifest as financial, reputational or other business risks.[8]

This chapter explores corporate responses to climate change litigation, drawing on interview data and case examples from the US and Australian contexts. We begin with a discussion of corporate attitudes to climate change and climate risk management and how litigation – or the risk thereof – might feed into corporate decision-making processes.

Oshionebo, "The OECD Guidelines for Multinational Enterprises as Mechanisms for Sustainable Development of Natural Resources: Real Solutions or Window Dressing?" (2013) 17(2) *Lewis and Clark L. Rev.* 545.

[6] These cases are discussed in Chapter 3.

[7] Case examples are discussed in Chapters 3 and 4.

[8] For an analysis of the importance of businesses' "social licence to operate" as a factor driving corporate compliance with environmental regulation, see Neil Gunningham, Robert A. Kagan, and Dorothy Thornton, "Social License and Environmental Protection: Why Businesses Go Beyond Compliance" (2004) 29 *L. Soc. Inquiry* 307.

We then examine the responses to climate change litigation and litigation risk in different corporate sectors, specifically the energy, land use, insurance, finance and investment, and professional advising sectors. Corporate responses to climate regulation and litigation are highly heterogeneous, varying markedly depending upon the sector involved and sometimes also among different types of companies in the one sector.[9] For example, in the energy sector, numerous coal companies have strongly opposed efforts to impose regulatory emissions reductions and have been involved in antiregulatory actions challenging clean energy measures.[10] However, other corporate actors in the fossil fuel industry, such as oil and gas companies, have been far less homogeneous in their response. In fact, some energy sector companies – such as those involved in producing low carbon fuels or power companies that have a substantial natural gas and renewables portfolio – have been strong supporters of greenhouse gas mitigation measures, intervening in support of governments in litigation brought by antiregulatory business interests.[11] In our discussion of sectoral responses to climate litigation risk, we thus highlight differences both between and within corporate sectors in the choices and behaviors companies have adopted in reaction to litigation.

5.2   Corporate climate change responses

Climate change is increasingly recognized by many corporations – particularly large businesses that operate across several jurisdictions – as an important threat that requires attention and the adoption of risk management strategies. In the World Economic Forum's "Global Risks" Report for 2014, listing the top ten global risks of highest concern in 2014, water crises ranked third; the failure of climate change mitigation and adaptation efforts ranked fifth; and a greater incidence of extreme weather events such as floods, fires, and storms ranked sixth.[12] The Global 500 Climate Change Report 2013, issued by investor group the Carbon

---

[9] Simone Pulver, "Corporate Responses" in John S. Dryzek, Richard B. Norgaard, and David Schlosberg (eds.), *Oxford Handbook of Climate Change and Society* (Oxford: Oxford University Press, 2011), 581.

[10] See the examples discussed in the following sections. Antiregulatory litigation by fossil fuel companies is discussed in Chapter 7.

[11] See the examples discussed in the following sections.

[12] World Economic Forum, *Global Risks 2014 Report* (2014, World Economic Forum, Geneva).

Disclosure Project (CDP), found similarly high levels of concern over climate change among the world's largest companies.[13] Of the 379 companies that responded to the Global 500 survey, more than one-third (37 percent) saw the physical risks of a changing climate as a real and present danger, up from 10 percent in 2011; 81 percent identified climate change risks to their business operations, supply chains, and plans, up from 71 percent in 2012.[14] In CDP's 2013 companion report for the S&P 500 that focuses on US companies, 77 percent of the 334 respondents disclosed exposure to climate change–related risks, up from 61 percent the previous year.[15] Extreme weather topped the list as the highest impact risk named by respondents.

While awareness of climate change as a threat may be growing in the corporate sector, this does not always translate into a robust response by companies. Rhetoric about opportunities often outpaces actual changes in business practices.[16] For example, a survey undertaken on behalf of KPMG's Carbon Advisory Group in 2008 found that over 80 percent of the companies surveyed had no business strategy in place to address climate change.[17] Five years on, the MIT Sloan Management Review and Boston Consulting Group (BCG) annual sustainability survey for 2013 (encompassing responses from close to 2000 business managers) found a "disconnect between thought and action" in many companies' approach to social and environmental issues, including climate change.[18] The CDP Global 500 Report 2013 also reflected this theme. The report

---

[13] CDP, *Global 500 Climate Change Report 2013* (2013, Carbon Disclosure Project, London). The "Global 500" are the largest 500 companies by market capitalization included in the FTSE Global Equity Index series as of January 1, 2013.

[14] CDP, *Global 500 Climate Change Report 2013,* Carbon Disclosure Project. See also Update, "Climate Risks Move Up Boardroom Agenda" (2012) November *Financial Management* 9.

[15] CDP, *CDP S&P 500 Climate Change Report 2013* (2013, PWC, North America), 5.

[16] Charles Jones and David Levy, "North American Business Strategies towards Climate Change" (2007) 25 *Eur. Manage. J.* 428.

[17] No author, "Climate Change Still Knocking on the Boardroom Door" (2008) 40(2) *Accountancy Ireland* 91. The KPMG survey included 209 senior UK business executives from the FTSE 350 and equivalent private companies.

[18] David Kiron et al., "Sustainability's Next Frontier," MIT Sloan Management Review, at http://sloanreview.mit.edu/projects/sustainabilitys-next-frontier/. The survey included 1,847 respondents from commercial enterprises located around the world and representing a wide variety of industries. This survey also reported that 27 percent of companies viewed climate change as a business risk but only 9 percent believed their company was prepared for climate change. See also Asset Owners Disclosure Project, *Global Climate Investment Index* (2013, AODP, Sydney).

found that across the Global 500 group, total scope 1 (direct) and scope 2 (electricity consumption), emissions had not changed significantly since 2009, with the largest fifty emitters actually increasing their emissions. In addition, limited or selective reporting of scope 3 (indirect) emissions had prevented the full impact of companies' value chains being revealed.[19] In the adaptation sphere, a survey of corporate attitudes to the business risks posed by climate change impacts among Australian companies – potentially some of the hardest hit by such impacts – showed "Australian companies appear to be struggling to move forward in responding to climate change impacts, apparently paralysed by short-term profit-first thinking, uncertain political risks and a corporate culture unused to volatility and disruption."[20] The CDP S&P 500 Report for 2013 presented a more optimistic picture for US companies that seem to be responding to the increased focus on climate issues under the Obama administration. According to the report, corporate survey responses in 2013 demonstrated "a significantly more mature level of climate management – as well as a drive to lead among peers."[21]

The following sections focus on the ways in which litigation helps to bridge this gap between awareness and action. It considers how concerns over climate change translate into action in a corporate setting. It examines both the factors that motivate companies to act and the role that litigation plays in that decision making.

5.2.1   Drivers of corporate climate action

Given the potentially transformative role of corporations as part of an effective climate change response, significant research has been devoted to the question of what drives proactive corporate climate action. Researchers have been interested both in external manifestations of corporate engagement on climate change – for example, the adoption and implementation of emissions reduction targets[22] – as well as internal

---

[19] CDP, *CDP Global 500 Report*.

[20] G. S. Johnston, D. L. Burton, and M. Baker-Jones, *Climate Change Adaptation in the Board-room*, National Climate Change Adaptation Research Facility (2013), www.nccarf.edu.au/publications/climate-change-adaptation-boardroom. See also J. M. West and David Brereton, *Climate Change Adaptation in Industry and Business: A Framework for Best Practice in Financial Risk Assessment, Governance and Disclosure* (2013, National Climate Change Adaptation Research Facility, Gold Coast).

[21] CDP, *CDP S&P 500 Report*, 4.

[22] For example, such issues are covered in the reports compiled by the CDP.

changes in corporate governance structures that demonstrate greater inte-gration of climate change considerations into management and decision-making approaches.[23] Studies of corporate responses to climate change identify several potential drivers of action by companies. These include the physical, regulatory, reputational, and liability risks posed by climate change to a business, as well as associated technological, regulatory, and reputational opportunities.[24]

Physical risks for corporations related to climate change include the potential for extreme weather and disasters to affect operations or supply chains. For example, coal mining companies in the state of Queensland in Australia suffered significant disruption to their operations in 2011 when massive floods across the state filled open pit mines with water and cut off transport routes.[25] Regulatory risks encompass those associated with compliance with future regulations, such as mandatory emissions reduc-tion requirements. Corporations operating across jurisdictions will need also to respond to diverse regulatory requirements, including subnational regulations (e.g., in California) that affect a significant proportion of the company's product market. Regulation may also present opportunities for companies to move ahead of competitors through lowering energy consumption and associated production costs, or by developing climate-friendly products. Reputational risks may manifest as customer demand for "greener" alternatives or pressure from shareholders, including green investor groups, to strengthen business responses to climate change risks and to disclose risks associated with, and divest from, fossil fuel assets. Liability or litigation risks generally concentrate on the potential for law-suits as a result of a company's failure to take mitigation or adaptation action.

The nature of these risks and opportunities, and how they are per-ceived by individual corporations, varies greatly depending on the sector concerned, the national political and social context most relevant for

---

[23] See, e.g., Caring for Climate, *Guide for Responsible Corporate Engagement in Climate Policy* (2013, United Nations Global Compact, Geneva).

[24] Pulver, "Corporate Responses." See also Foley and Lardner LLP, *The Boardroom Climate on Climate Change* (2007), at www.tacklingglobalwarming.com/docs/FoleyLardner/05_07_climatechange.pdf (when US climate legislation was still under consideration).

[25] "Lost Coal Production Tops $2b in Qld Flood," Business Day, *The Sydney Morn-ing Herald*, January 11, 2011, at www.smh.com.au/business/lost-coal-production-tops-2b-in-qld-flood-20110111-19mau.html. Extreme weather risks to projects and infras-tructure compound possible insurance increases: see Bruce Ralph and Elaine Prior, *Cli-mate Change and the ASX100: An Assessment of Risks and Opportunities* (2006, Citigroup, Australia).

the business, and firm-specific factors.[26] For example, companies in the energy sector, such as those invested in oil and gas, coal, or power production, are generally most concerned with regulatory risks and opportunities associated with proposed or existing mitigation measures. Their responses to climate change issues are thus likely to be closely attuned to, and influenced by, domestic regulatory action and litigation. By contrast, the insurance industry is most at risk from the physical impacts of climate change. It has been one of the most proactive industry sectors in addressing adaptation issues and urging governments to do so also, including via lawsuits.[27] Local insurance agencies' policies are often underwritten by multinational reinsurance companies, which take a global view of the risks posed to their business by increases in weather-related losses.[28] In general, differences in exposure to physical and regulatory risks associated with climate change, and the availability of business opportunities to respond, explain the variation in corporate responses to climate change.[29] Not surprisingly, corporations in the sectors at highest risk from climate change or from regulatory responses to it have been the most likely to address it, either as proponents or opponents.

In line with the general response of corporations to environmental and sustainability issues, some companies appear to be emerging as "leaders" in taking action to address and prepare for climate change, whereas others are "laggards," or less pejoratively, "nonleaders."[30] (The MIT Sloan Management Review and BCG survey report refers to it another way, as the difference between "walkers," who "walk the talk" of sustainability action, and those that are mere "talkers.")[31] CDP recognizes corporate leadership on climate action through the inclusion of companies on its Climate Performance Leadership Index (CPLI). A high performance score on the

---

[26] Pulver, "Corporate Responses."

[27] Sean B. Hecht, "Insurance" in Michael B. Gerrard and Katrina F. Kuh (eds), *The Law of Adaptation to Climate Change: US and International Aspects* (2012, American Bar Association, New York) 511.

[28] See, e.g., Munich Reinsurance Am., *Severe Weather in North America: Perils Risks Insurance* (2012), available at www.munichreamerica.com/site/mram/get/documents_E1449378742/mram/assetpool.mr_america/PDFs/3_Publications/ks_severe_weather_na_exec_summary.pdf.

[29] Pulver, "Corporate Responses."

[30] On the general phenomenon of environmental corporate leaders and laggards, see Neil Gunningham and Darren Sinclair, *Leaders and Laggards: Next-Generation Environmental Regulation* (2002, Greenleaf, Sheffield). The more neutral term *nonleader* is used by the CDP in its S&P 500 report.

[31] David Kiron et al., "Sustainability's Next Frontier."

CPLI "signals that a company is measuring, verifying and managing its carbon footprint, for example by setting and meeting carbon reduction targets and implementing programs to reduce emissions in both its direct operations and supply chain."[32] In its Global 500 report for 2013, CDP listed fifty-seven companies on the CPLI.[33] Another report issued by CDP in late 2013, focusing on the US context, found that twenty-nine major publicly traded companies based or operating in the United States across a variety of sectors used an internal price on carbon pollution in their business planning, ranging from US$6 to US$60 per tonne of carbon dioxide equivalent. Most companies covered by the report – including large corporations such as Walt Disney, Google, Xcel Energy, Wal-Mart, Delta, Microsoft, and PG&E Corporation – stated that they expected the eventual emergence of a regulatory approach, of some form, to address climate change. Companies establishing an internal carbon price as part of their business models viewed this "as both an evaluation of risk and a business opportunity if they take steps to limit carbon pollution before others do."[34]

The notion that leader corporations are those that perceive readiness for a climate-changed future as "a source of competitive advantage"[35] was echoed in several of our interviews. For instance, a large utility company might see benefit in increasing its renewable and natural gas portfolio in order to take advantage of business opportunities afforded by the increasing stringency of regulations for coal plants.[36] In the land use sector, another interviewee cited the example of a company that, in the aftermath of litigation, incorporated sustainability and greenhouse gas reduction measures in a large-scale urban renewal residential development to attract "green" buyers and investors.[37] These

---

[32] CDP, Global 500 Report 2013, 16.   [33] Ibid., 14.

[34] "Major U.S. Companies Disclose Internal Prices on Carbon, Cite Risk from Climate Change and Extreme Weather Business Opportunities," Carbon Disclosure Project, December 5, 2013, at https://www.cdp.net/en-US/News/CDP%20News%20Article%20 Pages/Major-US-companies-disclose-internal-prices-on-carbon.aspx (quoting Tom Carnac, president of CDP North America).

[35] Gretchen Michals, "The Boardroom's Climate Is Changing" (2009/2010) Dec/Jan *Directorship* 14.

[36] In-person interview, US Participant (Nov. 14, 2012).

[37] In-person interview, Australian Participant 3 (Mar. 8, 2013) referring to the outcome of the case of *Drake Brockman v. Minister for Planning* (2007) 158 LGERA 349. The challenge to the development on the basis of its excessive carbon footprint was unsuccessful, but the developer who later purchased the site worked with the plaintiffs and experts to come up with a more sustainable design.

examples provide indications that, at least for some companies, climate change is moving from "the organizational periphery" to be "built into corporate DNA."[38]

Liability or litigation risk is a matter often taken into account in emerging corporate climate risk management approaches.[39] However, isolating the role of liability or litigation risk as a potential factor driving corporate behavior around climate issues remains an exceptionally difficult task. Economic considerations associated with the physical and regulatory risks posed by climate change continue to be identified (and were also cited by our interviewees) as the primary driver of corporate climate-related actions. Although climate change litigation obviously cannot affect the exposure of corporations to physical climate risks, it may directly or indirectly contribute to the regulatory risks they face. Indirect effects may arise as a result of litigation making it more difficult to secure regulatory approvals for projects, which may have consequent effects for the capacity of the project to secure financing and/or for the reputation of the company with the public, shareholders, or investors. In our model for understanding litigation's regulatory impacts described in Chapter 2, we have grouped these kinds of effects under the general heading of "increasing costs and risks" for business, recognizing that these costs may be financial or reputational.

5.2.2   *Litigation risk as a component of corporate climate risk management*

Discussions of climate change litigation risk in a corporate context remain limited. However, there is some evidence of a growing understanding of litigation risk as an element of corporate climate change responses, including an appreciation of the influential role it may play, in conjunction with other factors, in shaping corporate behavior.[40] This section focuses on both direct litigation against corporations – the type of litigation that has attracted the most scholarly interest – and the more wide-reaching regulatory risks that emerge from litigation.

---

[38] CDP, S&P 500 report, 5.

[39] See, e.g., J. Lash and F. Wellington, "Competitive Advantage on a Warming Planet" (2007) 85(3) *Harv. Bus. Rev.* 94.

[40] See, e.g., Susan Shearing, "Raising the Boardroom Temperature? Climate Change and Shareholder Activism in Australia" (2012) 29 *Environ. Planning L. J.* 479; Johnson et al., *Climate Change Adaptation in the Boardroom*.

The type of litigation risk that tends to receive the most attention in analyses focused on corporations is the potential for climate change inaction (or obstruction) to give rise to liability in common law tort actions, such as negligence or public nuisance.[41] An analogy is often drawn with toxic products such as asbestos and cigarettes.[42] As with those products, the theory goes, mass tort lawsuits brought with respect to the damage caused by carbon polluting products like fossil fuels will eventually achieve success and – by imposing substantial costs on the use of such products – precipitate a new regulatory era of carbon restraints. This theory has underpinned public nuisance cases brought in the United States against major emitters such as power producers and auto manufacturers.[43]

To date, none of these cases has led to a finding on the merits in favor of the plaintiffs (although, as we discuss further in Chapter 6, the litigation may have other benefits in terms of raising the public profile of climate change issues). It appears that the lack of success in these initial cases in the United States has reduced the level of corporate concern about this avenue of climate liability, at least for the present.[44] However, particular groups, such as insurers and underwriters, clearly remain apprehensive about the potential for future lawsuits related to climate change. For example, a 2011 publication by the Geneva Association – an international insurance industry think tank – described "climate risk liability" as "a 'risk iceberg,' a real hazard of which only a minor part is visible, but the size and shape of the iceberg remain unknown."[45]

However, the types of lawsuits related to climate change faced by companies are potentially much broader than simply the possibility of tort actions against corporate emitters. Beyond the traditional sphere of pollution litigation, corporations face actions over corporate disclosure requirements and associated duties of directors and corporate officers,

---

[41] David A. Grossman, "Tort-Based Climate Litigation" in William C. G. Burns and Hari M. Osofsky (eds.), *Adjudicating Climate Change: State, National, and International Approaches* (2009, Cambridge University Press, New York), 193.

[42] Richard H. Murray, "The U.S. Supreme Court Speaks on Liability for Climate Change: But What Did It Say and Will It Have Implications Elsewhere?" in Walter R. Stahel (ed.), *Risk Management SC5: Liability Issues Related to Climate Risk* (2011, Geneva Association, Geneva).

[43] Matthew F. Pawa, "Global Warming Litigation Heats Up" (2008) April *Trial* 18. Further details of these cases are given in Chapter 3.

[44] Telephone interview, US Participant 7 (Nov. 16, 2012).

[45] Walter R. Stahel, *Liability Issues Related to Climate Risk*, Risk Management SC5, Geneva Association (2011), at https://www.genevaassociation.org/media/185056/ga2011-rmsc5.pdf.

as well as claims by shareholders and investors for greater transparency and disclosure of information relating to climate risk exposure.[46] These sorts of litigation are increasingly being actively considered and pursued as shareholder and investor groups of various types become more heavily involved in climate action. In the United States, groups such as the Ceres network[47] and the Interfaith Center on Corporate Responsibility (ICCR) have spearheaded such efforts.[48] In Australia, similar efforts have been led by the Climate Advocacy Fund,[49] and the Asset Owner's Disclosure Project (AODP).[50]

Litigation risks of this broader kind closely interact with other forms of climate business risk, such as insurance risks and reputational risks. The reputation of a corporation with its shareholders, investors, or consumers may be put in jeopardy by a perception that it is failing to meet legal obligations, statutory or otherwise, related to climate change. In addition, litigation associated with particular projects, such as coal plants or coal mines, may create uncertainty over their viability and reflect poorly on the corporation targeted, with the result that investors and financiers withdraw their support. Climate change litigation specifically addressing corporate liability and the liability of corporate officers also has the potential to affect a company's ability to obtain director and officer liability insurance.[51] Another risk is the possibility that indemnity may be denied under general commercial liability policies with respect to litigation brought against the corporation for climate change–related injuries.[52] If such denials occur, carbon-intensive industries sued for climate change damages, rather than their insurers, would be forced to foot the bill for litigation brought against them, adding further to their business costs.[53]

---

[46] Graham Erion, "The Stock Market to the Rescue? Carbon Disclosure and the Future of Securities-Related Climate Change Litigation" (2009) 18(2) *Rev. Eur. Commun. Int. Environ. L.* 164.

[47] See Ceres, "Shareholder Resolutions," at www.ceres.org/investor-network/resolutions.

[48] Interfaith Center on Corporate Responsibility, "ICCR's Shareholder Resolutions," at www .iccr.org/iccrs-shareholder-resolutions.

[49] This organization is a collaboration between Australian Ethical, an investment fund manager, and the Climate Institute, a NGO/think tank focusing on progressive climate action.

[50] The AODP focuses on the fossil fuel holdings of large superannuation and pension funds.

[51] Johnston et al., *Climate Change Adaptation in the Boardroom.*

[52] This was, in essence, the finding of the Virginia Supreme Court in the closely watched case of *AES v. Steadfast* discussed further later.

[53] Lawrence Hurley, "Va. Court Rules That Insurance Doesn't Cover Global Warming Claims," *New York Times*, September 16, 2011, at www.nytimes.com/gwire/2011/09/16/ 16greenwire-va-court-rules-that-insurance-doesnt-cover-glo-97999.html.

Although these types of suits against corporations are growing, the litigation risks that companies generally find most concerning are ones associated with regulatory change resulting from lawsuits. Despite a growing appreciation of the nature and scope of climate litigation risk, for the moment it appears that the potential for litigation associated with a company's climate change actions or inaction is at the margins of the vision of most corporate actors. One Australian interviewee, who advises clients in the land use and development sector, described climate change litigation as the furthest thing from most of his clients' minds given more immediate, short-term political and economic risks.[54] These regulatory risks are often intertwined with political dynamics, as lawsuits account for only part of why corporations face an uncertain regulatory environment. The CDP 2013 Climate Change Report for Australia and New Zealand lends support to this conclusion, with "regulatory uncertainty" associated with the Abbott government's repeal of the carbon pricing mechanism emerging as a clear preoccupation of companies.[55] Disentangling the portion of regulatory risk companies associate with litigation and how that motivates behavior is quite difficult, but the interviews suggest – as noted previously – that the risks of litigation-based regulatory change serve as a significant motivator.

Overall, then, climate change litigation has a range of direct and indirect influences on corporations. However, this big picture look only gives part of the story. Although many types of corporations – from fossil fuel to insurance to the financial – interact with these direct litigation and regulatory-related litigation risks, the dynamics vary significantly by sector and within each sector. The following section explores this variation and its implications for the regulatory role of climate change litigation in the United States and Australia.

5.3 Sectoral responses to climate litigation risk

Climate change risk differs from many other types of business risk faced by corporations because of its potential to have a widespread impact on individual companies across multiple sectors.[56] The particular climate change risks facing businesses, and their responses, thus vary considerably from sector to sector and also within sectors. Analysis of corporate

---

[54] Skype interview, Australian Participant 18 (Jul. 18, 2013).
[55] CDP, *CDP Australia and New Zealand Climate Change Report* (2013, CDP, Australia).
[56] Johnston et al., *Climate Change Adaptation in the Boardroom*.

action on, and attitudes to, climate change encompasses a wide range of economic sectors, including agriculture, energy, tourism, health care, information technology, telecommunication, insurance, and industrial manufacturing. Here we focus only on those types of corporations that have been mostly deeply involved litigation and/or affected by its consequences: companies in the energy sector; those involved in infrastructure and land use; those that provide insurance; companies in the financial and investment sector whose disclosure and decision making around climate risk associated with their investments is increasingly being targeted in lawsuits and quasi-judicial actions; and corporate law firms and other professional consultancy companies. This section considers both how these sectors interact with litigation and the variation within each sector.

5.3.1   Energy

The energy sector encompasses companies engaged in the production and supply of energy, including both extraction of sources and their uses in the secondary systems of electricity and transportation.[57] Most of the world's energy for electricity and transportation still comes from the combustion of fossil fuels – coal, oil, and gas.[58] However, the energy sector also extends to companies involved in the production and supply of energy from other sources, such as nuclear materials, renewables, and biofuels.

Many types of companies are involved with extracting, generating, transporting, and distributing energy and, as noted, the energy industry is far from monolithic in its approach to climate change. The incentives for different types of companies vary substantially, and influence how they interact with the litigation. For example, as explored in depth later, although coal, oil, and natural gas are core fossil fuel sources, the approaches of these companies to climate change regulation ranges from

---

[57] There are many different definitions of the energy sector. The Global Industry Classification Standard, for instance, separates out utilities as a distinct category. Other definitions focus on the main purpose of the sector, for example, electricity generation. The US Commerce Department uses a broader definition: US energy companies are ones that produce oil, natural gas, coal, nuclear power, renewable energy and fuels, and electricity services as well as supply energy and electricity technologies worldwide; see http://selectusa.commerce.gov/industry-snapshots/energy-industry-united-states.

[58] International Energy Agency, *World Energy Outlook 2013* (2013, OECD/IEA, Paris), noting that fossil fuels' share of the global energy mix – at 82 percent – is the same as it was twenty-five years ago.

antiregulatory to supportive of regulation in a number of situations. Coal companies, with their lower profit margins and limited investment in clean energy technology, have few incentives to support energy transition. Oil and natural gas companies are much more varied in their stances toward and interaction with the litigation, and natural gas is at times promoted as a "cleaner" transitional fuel.

The companies involved in electricity and transportation also have diverse positions that have evolved over time. Utilities, for example, do not have a strong preference for what type of fuel they use, so long as they are profitable, but have made long-term investments that constrain immediate change. The automobile industry similarly desires to profit from its vehicles, and primarily wants consistent regulation across the country to avoid the costs of differentiated standards; after some initial opposition to standards highlighted in the *Massachusetts v. EPA* case, the US automobile industry was willing to cooperate with the Obama administration and California on greenhouse gas tailpipe emissions and fuel efficiency regulations.[59] This section traces these different types of companies' positions within the energy sector and how that has influenced their relationship to climate change litigation.

In the United States, the energy sector is the country's third largest industry.[60] In 2012, over 80 percent of US total energy use was derived from burning fossil fuels.[61] The dominant position of fossil fuels in the US energy mix has changed little in the past century, but recent increases in the domestic production of oil and natural gas have prompted fuel transition (largely in favor of substituting coal-fired with natural gas–fired power generation). This trend is forecast to continue with natural gas production expected to more than double between 2012 and 2040.[62] Oil production is also booming in the United States on the back of increasing shale oil production. US oil production rose by a record 992,000 barrels per day

---

[59] See, further, the discussion in Chapter 3. Past antiregulatory litigation brought by the auto industry is discussed further in Chapter 7.

[60] SelectUSA, "The Energy Industry in the United States," at http://selectusa.commerce.gov/industry-snapshots/energy-industry-united-states.

[61] US Energy Information Administration, "What Are the Major Sources and Users of Energy in the United States?," at www.eia.gov/energy_in_brief/article/major_energy_sources_and_users.cfm (36 percent oil, 18 percent coal, 27 percent natural gas) (last updated Aug. 1, 2013).

[62] *AEO2014 Early Release Overview*, U.S. Energy Information Administration, at www.eia.gov/forecasts/aeo/er/pdf/0383er(2014).pdf.

in 2013 and is forecast to continue to grow; production has increased 46 percent overall in the past three years.[63]

By contrast, the US coal industry – faced with decreasing domestic consumption, particularly in the electric power sector[64] – has seen declining production since 2007.[65] However, recently, US coal exports have been increasing,[66] with particular growth in the Asian market (China, Japan, India, and South Korea).[67] Future growth of US coal exports to Asia (and the viability of the domestic industry) will depend on external factors, such as the pace of Asian coal demand growth and the cost of US coal exported to Asia compared to that offered by other major coal exporters (including Australia). These exports also depend on the capacity to expand US port infrastructure, especially on the West Coast. If proposed expansions go ahead, this greater access to the export market could reinvigorate the US coal industry, with top coal miners such as Peabody Energy predicting "coal's best days are ahead."[68] Environmental organizations are closely watching developments and have initiated legal challenges in an attempt to require full environmental impact assessment for coal export terminals.[69]

As noted, across the US energy sector, the response to climate change has been far from uniform and has changed over time. Companies in

---

[63] Floyd Norris, "U.S. Oil Production Keeps Rising Beyond the Forecasts," *New York Times*, January 24, 2014, at www.nytimes.com/2014/01/25/business/us-oil-production-keeps-rising-beyond-the-forecasts.html?_r=0.

[64] *Table 1. U.S. Coal Production, 2007–2013*, US Energy Information Administration, at www.eia.gov/coal/production/quarterly/pdf/t1p01p1.pdf.

[65] *Table 32. U.S. Coal Consumption by End-Use Sector, 2007–2013*, US Energy Information Administration, at www.eia.gov/coal/production/quarterly/pdf/t32p01p1.pdf.

[66] *Table 4. U.S. Coal Exports and Imports, 2007–2013*, U.S. Energy Information Administration, at www.eia.gov/coal/production/quarterly/pdf/t4p01p1.pdf.

[67] US Energy Information Administration, "25% of U.S. coal exports go to Asia, but remain a small share of Asia's total coal imports," June 21, 2013, at www.eia.gov/todayinenergy/detail.cfm?id=11791 (2 percent in 2007 to 25 percent in 2012).

[68] Source Watch, "Coal Exports from Ports on the West Coast of Canada and the United States," at www.sourcewatch.org/index.php/Coal_exports_from_ports_on_the_west_coast_of_Canada_and_the_United_States.

[69] Rob Davis, "Oil Train, Coal Export Opponent Protests Industrial Land Expansion Approved at Port Westward," *The Oregonian*, January 29, 2014, at www.oregonlive.com/environment/index.ssf/2014/01/oil_train_coal_export_opponent.html; Joel Darmstadter, "The Controversy over US Coal Exports," Resources for the Future, at www.rff.org/Publications/Resources/Pages/183-Controversy-over-US-Coal-Exports.aspx. See also Earthjustice Petition to the Army Corp of Engineers, May 22, 2013, available at www.powerpastcoal.org/wp-content/uploads/2013/05/Petition-Area-Wide-Coal-Export-EIS.pdf.

the oil industry, led by major US corporations, such as ExxonMobil, Chevron, and Texaco, were initially some of the strongest opponents of emissions reduction measures and actively participated in international antiregulatory lobbying efforts, such as the Global Climate Coalition[70] (since disbanded as prominent members left over time). However, a split later emerged in the industry, with some companies continuing their opposition to climate change regulation and others publicly supporting it.[71] Companies that maintained an adversarial stance, such as ExxonMobil, funded attacks on climate science and vigorously resisted regulation, an approach that litigation tried to challenge. For example, ExxonMobil was named as the lead defendant in the 2008 case brought by the Native Village and city of Kivalina against a range of energy producers for damages for climate-related harms. Among other claims, Kivalina accused defendants of "conspiring to mislead the public about the science of global warming."[72]

While also named in common law suits, such as the *Kivalina* case and the case of *Comer v. Murphy Oil*,[73] other multinational oil corporations like Shell have pursued a different approach on climate action, including investment in renewables, particularly wind power, and involvement in pro-regulatory lobby efforts such as the US Climate Action Partnership.[74] More recently, companies such as Chevron and ExxonMobil have also increased their emissions reduction activities and climate change programs after years of being staunchly opposed to acknowledging climate change. Their activities include creating and disclosing internal prices for carbon, presumably in anticipation of either domestic or international carbon trading schemes.[75] Nonetheless, oil and gas companies, and their industry associations, continue to take part in antiregulatory

---

[70] Seth Shulman et al., *Smoke, Mirrors & Hot Air: How ExxonMobil Uses Big Tobacco's Tactics to Manufacture Uncertainty on Climate Science* (2007, Union of Concerned Scientists, Cambridge), 9.

[71] Simone Pulver, "Making Sense of Corporate Environmentalism: An Environmental Contestation Approach to Analyzing the Causes and Consequences of the Climate Change Policy Split in the Oil Industry" (2007) 20(1) *Organiz. Environ.* 44.

[72] Environmental – Appeals Court, *Native Village of Kivalina v. ExxonMobil Corp*, Sep 24, 2012, at http://environmentalappealscourt.blogspot.com/2012_09_24_archive.html.

[73] *Comer v. Murphy Oil*, 585 F.3d 855 (5th Cir. 2009).

[74] For details, see United States Climate Action Partnership, at www.us-cap.org/.

[75] CDP, "Major U.S. Companies Disclose Internal Prices on Carbon, Cite Risk from Climate Change and Extreme Weather, Business Opportunities," CDP press release, December 5, 2013, at https://www.cdp.net/en-US/News/CDP%20News%20Article%20Pages/Major-US-companies-disclose-internal-prices-on-carbon.aspx.

lawsuits, with a particular focus on the Environmental Protection Agency's (EPA) renewable fuel standard and greenhouse gas reporting program, and measures affecting the carbon content of transportation fuels, such as California's Low Carbon Fuel Standard.[76] The Alaska Oil and Gas Association has also used the courts to fight the Endangered Species Act listing for the polar bear, fearing impacts on the capacity to expand oil exploration in the state.[77]

Compared with the oil industry, the response of coal companies to the prospect of climate change regulation has been particularly uniform. In the United States, relatively low profit margins compared to oil and lack of diversification means that the coal industry has little to gain from regulation. Coal companies have frequently participated on the antiregulatory side in climate change litigation. For instance, both Peabody Energy and the Ohio Coal Association were plaintiffs in the industry lawsuits brought against the EPA's Endangerment Finding and Tailpipe and Tailoring rules, later consolidated as the case of *Coalition for Responsible Regulation v. EPA*.[78] Peabody Energy is also reportedly behind efforts to mount challenges to state-based programs, such as California's cap-and-trade program, despite the lack of coal mining in that state. As one interviewee explained, their interest in the Californian law is because

> California's the leading edge and they don't want this program to go forward or to succeed because that only makes it that much more likely that it would succeed on a federal level. . . . So if they could stop it, they would. And what's their motivation for that? I mean this whole thing – it came out of the Romney campaign – the "War against Coal." They really believe that there's a war against coal. And, yes there is. It's dirty and unhealthy and we relied on it for most of our energy for far too long.[79]

Utilities present yet another side to the response of the corporate US energy sector to climate change. Their infrastructure investments in the fossil fuel industry have made them a key focus for litigation, but their long-term incentives are more neutral. Coal-fired power stations have been a particular target of efforts of environmental organizations, such as the Sierra Club, to stop the use of coal in the United States. Utilities across the country have found themselves embroiled in litigation and

---

[76] See, further, Chapter 7.

[77] Telephone interview, US Participant 3 (Nov. 7, 2012). See, further, Chapter 7.

[78] *Coalition for Responsible Regulation v. EPA*, 684 F.3D 102 (D.C. Cir. June 26, 2012) (No. 09–1322, 10–1092).

[79] Telephone interview, US Participant 5 (Nov. 14, 2012).

administrative appeals challenging the issue of permits for their coal-fired facilities.[80] The national scope of the anticoal campaign, of which this litigation forms one part, has been extremely effective in driving a shift away from coal-fired power in the utility sector. One interviewee explained,

> The idea is that coal is dirty and expensive and if coal plants had to internalize all of the costs – all of the environmental effects that they're causing – by installing appropriate pollution controls and by responsible mining practices, then nobody would use coal. And we're actually seeing that. Nobody is building new coal plants. And existing coal plants are shutting down because they're being forced to internalize those costs and it's not cost-effective. So, it's definitely a strategy of internalizing costs – but it's also a strategy of building public awareness that coal is a dirty fuel on so many levels that we should keep it in the ground.[81]

Some utilities (leaders) have clearly sensed the direction in which regulation is heading in this area and have played a more constructive role in litigation involving their facilities. For instance, one interviewee who acts for a large US power producer described how the company, in seeking permits for a combined cycle gas plant, worked with the EPA and major environmental groups involved in opposing the plant to agree on greenhouse gas emissions limits despite the lack of regulation on the issue at that time. The agreed upon limit was one to "establish BACT [best available control technology] from power production as something that's equivalent to gas so that there could be no more coal production." The lawyer explained,

> When we moved forward with that limit, we were working with enviros to recognize that the purpose of this is to preclude coal generation, future coal plant generation. And, subsequently EPA adopted – well, proposed right now, they haven't adopted yet – their New Source Performance standard for power plants, which is basically set at the level that can be achieved by a new combined cycle gas plant but it applies to all power plants. So you can't build a new coal plant unless you are currently, or in the future, install CCS [carbon capture and storage]. And, so we felt like they were taking a page out of our playbook. And they were to some extent.[82]

---

[80] Arnold and Porter LLP, "U.S. Climate Change Litigation Chart," at www.climateccasechart .com, provides a list of challenges against coal-fired power stations. Many more such actions do not have an explicit climate basis but are part of broader anticoal campaigns. A large number of such cases are heard before public service commissions: Telephone interview, US Participant 1 (Oct. 20, 2012).

[81] Telephone interview, US Participant 13 (Dec. 9, 2013).

[82] In-person interview, US Participant 5 (Nov. 14, 2012).

Other utilities staunchly remain in the "nonleader" category, however. Another interviewee described the industry's stance in discussions around critical questions raised in EPA rulemakings on New Source Performance Standards for coal plants, such as how to define "best available control technology," as "to try and make it as meaningless as possible":

> Industry's goal, for the most part, in those conversations, was to just say, "Well, there's really no control technology to limit CO_2 emissions, so you don't really have to do anything. But if you have to do something, the only thing you have to do is like, tweak the efficiency and make your plants a little more efficient." So you see that playing out with all of the regulations.[83]

The transportation sector's interaction with litigation has some similarities with that of the utility sector, but has evolved even more significantly over time. The motor vehicle companies are deeply tied to the fossil fuel industry, but their product does not inherently depend on producing more greenhouse gas emissions. Although they opposed regulation in the much-publicized case of *Massachusetts v. EPA* and other transportation-related cases, they for the most part have ultimately ceased to oppose the joint agency regulation they participated in crafting.[84] Moreover, motor vehicle companies have been meeting the gradually tightening standards without much difficulty.[85] Fuel companies, in contrast, have narrower interests, that vary based on the type of fuel they produce.

At times, the utility and motor vehicle sectors have interacted in litigation, with companies in one sector supporting regulation in the other sector out of a sense of their long-term strategic interest. For instance, some utility companies have intervened on the side of government in antiregulatory legal challenges brought by the auto industry. In the litigation brought by automobile manufacturers over California's "Pavley standards" that require the reduction of greenhouse gas emissions in new motor vehicles, two power companies – PG&E and Sempra – intervened in the Court of Appeal hearings in support of California and the authority of the Air Resources Board to impose the regulations pursuant to the state's Global Warming Solutions Act.[86] According to an interviewee,

---

[83] Telephone interview, US Participant 13 (Dec. 9, 2013).

[84] For details of the agreement on federal vehicle emissions standards, see Chapter 3. See the discussion of the course of this antiregulatory litigation in Chapter 7.

[85] Neela Banerjee, "2012 Autos Beat Environmental Standards, EPA Reports," *LA Times*, April 25, 2014, at http://touch.latimes.com/#section/-1/article/p2p-80019296/.

[86] *Central Valley Chrysler-Jeep v. Goldstene*, 529 F. Supp. 2d 1151 (2007).

their rationale for doing so was "if the auto manufacturers don't do it, and that is almost 40 percent of California's emissions, then there is going to be an even heavier burden that will fall on stationary sources [to reduce emissions]."[87]

More recently, PG&E, along with other clean energy corporations, also filed letters with the California Court of Appeal supporting California's Low Carbon Fuel Standard (LCFS), which other industry interests are challenging in an attempt to have it ruled invalid, either on procedural or substantive grounds.[88] In its application to file a letter brief as *amicus curiae*, PG&E urged the California Court of Appeal "to preserve the LCFS," while the Air Resources Board worked to remedy any procedural defects the court might find. The company stated,

> Like other major energy policies, the LCFS will take years to implement because of the long lead time for investments to develop new technology, the capital needed to fund investments and the permit processes. Many parties in California have been working toward creating new fuels under the LCFS and it is important to provide regulatory certainty and maintain the LCFS as a regulation. Without regulatory certainty, it is more difficult to attract capital investments and make necessary plans to enable the development [of] alternative fuels and related infrastructure. With a significant disruption to the LCFS program, it will make it less likely that California will reach its [greenhouse gas] emission reduction goals.[89]

Again "enlightened self-interest" seems to have been the motivation for PG&E's intervention, "because there is this whole market going on and there were other corporations – not the ethanol people from the Midwest that sued [California] – that actually would be harmed if there were an injunction [against the LCFS]."[90] Industry support of regulators in litigation may also have flow-on benefits, both for energy companies (who may get a more prominent seat at the table in future agency rulemakings) and for regulators who are "embolden[ed] . . . in future rulemakings to some extent because they're just so used to being beat up by highly paid

---

[87] Telephone interview, US Participant 11 (Oct. 11, 2013).

[88] *POET, LLC, et al. v. Corey, et al.* (Fresno Superior Court, Case No. 09-CE-CG-04659; plaintiffs appealed to California Court of Appeal, Fifth District, Case No. F064045; ARB petition for review, California Supreme Court, Case No. S213394).

[89] PG&E Letter to Hon. Brad R. Hill, Presiding Judge, California Fifth District Court of Appeal, available at www.edf.org/sites/default/files/PG%20and%20E%20Amicus%20Brief%20Letter%20-%202013-04-01.pdf.

[90] Telephone interview, US Participant 11 (Oct. 11, 2013).

outside counsel. When they actually have someone saying, yeah, we think you did this right and we're here to support you on it. . . . The first time that they experience it it's like, wow, we weren't expecting that. And it changes the dynamic a lot."[91]

As in the United States, fossil fuels dominate Australia's corporate energy sector. Black and brown coal supply over 75 percent of the nation's electricity demands,[92] and electricity generation from coal and natural gas represents the largest domestic source of greenhouse gas emissions, at around 33 percent of the national total.[93] The production of fossil fuels – particularly coal and liquefied natural gas – is also central to the Australian economy. Coal is Australia's largest energy export, and the country is the world's second largest coal exporter (closely following Indonesia).[94] The lion's share of Australian coal is exported to the Asian market, particularly to China, India, Japan, and Korea.[95] Over the last ten years, Australian coal exports have grown substantially and are set to continue to expand if large coal reserves in areas such as Queensland's Galilee Basin are mined.[96] This prospect has made coal mine development in the state of Queensland, and proposals for associated export-oriented infrastructure like railroads and port expansion, a focus of activism and litigation in Australia.[97]

---

[91] In-person interview, US Participant 5 (Nov. 14, 2012).

[92] Australians for Coal (formerly the Australian Coal Association), "Coal for Energy," at www.australiansforcoal.com.au/coal-4-energy.html.

[93] Australian Government, Department of Environment, Quarterly Update of Australia's National Greenhouse Gas Inventory: December 2013, Australia's National Greenhouse Accounts, Apr. 2014, at www.environment.gov.au/system/files/resources/e18788bd-2a8a-49d1-b797–307a9763c93f/files/quarterly-update-september-2013_0.pdf.

[94] Bureau of Resources and Energy Economics, Energy in Australia 2013 (Australian Government, Canberra 2013); World Energy Council, World Energy Resources: 2013 Survey (2013, World Energy Council, 23rd ed., London).

[95] Queensland, Department of Natural Resources and Mines, Quarterly Coal Report for the 3 months ended 31 December 2013, available at http://mines.industry.qld.gov.au/mining/coal-statistics.htm.

[96] See further John Rolfe, "Carmichael Mine Is a Game-Changer for Australian Coal," The Conversation, July 29, 2014, at https://theconversation.com/carmichael-mine-is-a-game-changer-for-australian-coal-29839?utm_medium=email&utm_campaign=Latest+from+The+Conversation+for+30+July+2014+-+1816&utm_content=Latest+from+The+Conversation+for+30+July+2014+-+1816+CID_8ccdf08828e10936e4064f414d0c9b01&utm_source=campaign_monitor&utm_term=writes%20John%20Rolfe.

[97] See the discussion in Chapter 3 of litigation launched against expansion of the Abbot point coal export terminal in Queensland.

Though more diversified than the US coal industry,[98] Australian coal companies likewise have little to gain from climate regulation. Mining of materials is necessarily emissions intensive – even with continuing technological advances, the problems facing mining companies are inherent in the business activity. Coal mining, oil and gas, and fossil fuel electricity generation companies attracted liabilities under the Australian carbon pricing mechanism, while it remained in place.[99] Although mining companies benefited from the issuing of free government permits under the former legislative scheme, the coal industry reportedly felt the brunt of the carbon price, with Australian coal companies paying an average of AUD$1.50 to AUD$2 per tonne of emissions and gassy mines between AUD$5 and AUD$6 per tonne.[100] Before the federal election in September 2013 that saw the Abbott government come to power on a promise to repeal the carbon tax, the investment bank UBS estimated that liabilities under the carbon pricing scheme would slice US$442 million from the 2014 earnings of big mining companies such as Glencore Xstrata, Rio Tinto, BHP Billiton, and Anglo American.[101]

Consequently, Australian mining companies have been largely antiregulatory in their stance on climate issues. Since the late 1990s, the coal industry has reportedly exerted substantial influence over government policy on climate issues.[102] The Australian coal industry is also alleged to have strong links with climate denial advocacy organizations such as the Lavoisier Group.[103] More recently, allegations have surfaced that federal withdrawal of funding from environmental groups, such as the national network of Environmental Defenders' Offices (behind many of the legal

---

[98] While some Australian coal companies, such as Yancoal and Whitehaven Coal, lack diversification and hence are very sensitive to market changes in coal prices, this is not the case for the largest companies like BHP Billiton and Glencore Xstrata.

[99] See Clean Energy Regulator, Liable Entities Public Information Database for the 2012–2013 financial year, at https://www.cleanenergyregulator.gov.au/Carbon-Pricing-Mechanism/Liable-Entities-Public-Information-Database/LEPID-for-2012–13-Financial-year/Pages/default.aspx.

[100] Madeleine Heffernan, Brian Robins, and Peter Ker, "Carbon Shift 'Not Enough,'" *Sydney Morning Herald*, July 15, 2013, at www.smh.com.au/business/carbon-shift-not-enough-20130714-2py4p.html.

[101] Ibid.

[102] Pearse et al., *Big Coal: Australia's Dirtiest Habit* (2013, UNSW Press, Sydney). See also Guy Pearse, *High and Dry* (2007, Penguin Australia, Sydney).

[103] This organization was founded in 2000 by Ray Evans, then an executive at Western Mining Corporation.

challenges to coal projects), occurred after coal mining interests lobbied the attorney general.[104]

While clearly aware of climate issues, Australian mining and energy companies have generally been slow to act to minimize the environmental impact of their business activities in relation to greenhouse gas emissions.[105] A major focus of their efforts on climate has been investment in, and piloting of, carbon capture and storage (CCS) technologies. For instance, the industry's representative organization, the Australian Coal Association, established the COAL21 fund in 2006 with the aim of raising AUD$1 billion over ten years through a voluntary levy on coal production "to support the pre-commercial demonstration of low emissions coal technologies, including carbon capture and storage."[106] Individual coal companies also have independent CCS projects, such as the Surat Basin CCS project in Queensland, which is backed by Xstrata Coal.[107] Such initiatives are regarded by coal companies as "strategic" projects:

> There's a big focus around thermal emissions from coal-fired power generation and what can be done around that so we felt that it was important to make a contribution to that effort and basically prove the concept and demonstrate that storage can . . . it's feasible – it's not commercial – but it's technically feasible to do and therefore it should be part of a suite of broader technology options to reduce emissions from fossil fuels.[108]

For companies targeted in Australian climate change litigation over coal mining projects, it seems that investment in CCS, along with other on-site emissions reduction measures (e.g., flaring or capture of mine gas), have also been motivated, in part, by the need to prepare for or counter litigation challenges. In effect, claims by environmental organizations that companies are inadequately managing their greenhouse gas emissions are met with efforts to improve the company's internal processes for

---

[104] See, further, Chapter 7. See also Christine Trenorden, "Environmental Legal Aid Slashed When Australia Needs It Most," *The Conversation*, March 11, 2014, at http://theconversation.com/environmental-legal-aid-slashed-when-australia-needs-it-most-23988.

[105] For a list of individual company actions, see Citigroup, *Climate Change and the ASX100: An Assessment of Risks and Opportunities*, 99–106.

[106] Minerals Council of Australia, "CCS Investment by the Black Coal Industry," at www.minerals.org.au/resources/coal/ccs_investment_by_the_black_coal_industry. The Australian Coal Association has recently been disbanded, a potent sign of the times for the industry in Australia.

[107] See "Surat Basin CCS Project (formerly Wandoan)," Global CCS Institute, at www.globalccsinstitute.com/project/surat-basin-ccs-project-formerly-wandoan.

[108] Skype interview, Australian Participant 13 (May 23, 2013).

managing climate change and emissions issues.[109] In addition, the prospect of having their environmental assessments prepared for projects scrutinized in court seems to have led companies to take steps to improve their internal procedures and information systems relating to emissions data on the basis that they would prefer to generate their own information rather than wait for environmental litigants "to make their own calculations." As one interviewee explained,

> if you consider that your environmental impact statement, if it does make it into a court case or a legal challenge, that tends to become a primary piece of evidence that they use to determine matters obviously. So we decided that we really needed to spend a bit of time on explaining the difference between emissions that were ours, that were direct and that happened on our operations that we could control, and emissions that were basically beyond our control and were generated either by our customers or by third parties where we really didn't have control over those.[110]

These efforts by companies are likely to continue given expectations that "every time we do a project – whether it's an expansion or a new greenfields project – the likelihood is that we are going to be legally challenged on it."[111] In other words, there is some evidence that litigation risk is prompting changes to corporate governance structures in Australian coal mining companies to be more climate-aware and proactive.

Paralleling the sectoral differences within the United States, the response of Australian energy producers and distributors to climate change has differed from that of mining companies. The main electricity producers and distributors such as AGL, Caltex, Origin, Santos, and Woodside report greenhouse gas emissions and take initiatives to reduce emissions. For instance, AGL has introduced programs to reduce emissions from its operations through flaring, sewage, and landfill generation abatement.[112] Since the mid 2000s, energy companies involved in electricity generation also have had to respond to various state-based regulatory schemes that have sought to reduce greenhouse gas emissions from power production.[113] Much of the climate-related action taken by energy

---

[109] Skype interview, Australian Participant 13 (May 23, 2013).
[110] Ibid.   [111] Ibid.
[112] Citigroup, *Climate Change and the ASX100: An Assessment of Risks and Opportunities.*
[113] For example, the GGAS scheme for electricity generators in NSW, www.greenhousegas. nsw.gov.au/, and gas emissions restrictions in Queensland (although this program closed September 30, 2014); "Queensland Gas Scheme," www.business.qld.gov. au/industry/energy/gas/queensland-gas-scheme.

producers has been driven by regulatory risk considerations related to expectations of the introduction of a national emissions trading scheme. While such risks will abate in the short-term with the Abbott government's repeal of the carbon pricing mechanism, surveys of companies suggest they still see a carbon price of some kind as likely before 2020.[114] As such, a predominant concern of Australian energy companies at present is unclear regulatory frameworks for greenhouse gas emissions reduction with the repeal of the carbon price and lack of clarity on alternative policy arrangements.[115]

The primary divergence in the regulatory influence of litigation on the US and Australian energy sectors takes place with respect to anticoal lawsuits. Evidence from our interview data suggests that climate change litigation challenging approvals for coal-fired power plants plays a more limited role in shaping corporate responses in Australia than in the United States. In contrast to the nationally coordinated campaign of the Sierra Club in the United States, Australian challenges to coal-fired power station projects can be numbered on one hand. At an individual project level, litigation may be influential in delaying a project or creating hurdles to approval that eventually see the project modified or even terminated. As discussed in Chapter 3, the early Hazelwood case in Victoria appears to have played a role in the conclusion of a Greenhouse Gas Deed between the government and the company operating the power station, which required some emissions abatement measures as part of approval of the plant's expansion.[116] The later *Dual Gas* litigation, also in Victoria – though it did not result in a refusal of the plant at issue – added sufficiently to regulatory uncertainty surrounding the project to prompt an eventual withdrawal of funding support by investors.[117] More concern within the corporate energy sector was raised by litigation mounted in 2009 against Macquarie Generation – the largest coal-fired electricity generator in the state of New South Wales.[118] This litigation challenged the scope of the company's operating license to emit greenhouse gas emissions. However,

---

[114] F. Jotzo, T. Jordan, and N. Fabian, "Policy Uncertainty about Australia's Carbon Price: Expert Survey Results and Implications for Investment" (2012) 45(4) *Austr. Econ. Rev.* 395.

[115] CDP, *CDP Australia and New Zealand Climate Change Report.*

[116] Brian J. Preston, "The Influence of Climate Change Litigation on Governments and the Private Sector" (2011) 2 *Clim. L.* 485. The Hazelwood case is discussed in Chapter 3.

[117] In-person interview, Australian Participant 1 (Mar. 7, 2013). The *Dual Gas* case is discussed in Chapter 3.

[118] Skype interview, Australian Participant 13 (May 23, 2013).

its comprehensive failure before the courts has lessened fears in Australia of a *Massachusetts v. EPA*–style lawsuit forcing the inclusion of greenhouse gas emissions limits in regulatory permits issued to power plants.[119]

5.3.2   Land use

The land use sector incorporates a diverse array of corporations, including corporate property developers and providers of infrastructure such as waste treatment plants, transportation facilities, and ports. This sector has the potential to make a significant contribution to both mitigation and adaptation or to undermine such efforts. Good urban design and strategic land use planning, for instance, can be harnessed to create more sustainable communities with reduced energy use and greenhouse gas emissions.[120] The San Bernardino County case, discussed in Chapter 3, provides a good example of the possibilities for litigation over land use planning to contribute to climate change mitigation. This suit involved the state of California suing a local county government over the failure to include greenhouse gas emissions in its general plan, rather than targeting corporations involved in land use and development directly. However, both our US and Australian interviewees identified litigation against companies, calling for greenhouse emissions to be factored into large-scale land use proposals, as a potential growth area for mitigation case law in the future.[121]

Although land use choices certainly impact mitigation, arguably land use companies interact even more significantly with adaptation planning. Buildings and infrastructure located away from high-risk areas and that are less vulnerable to climate change impacts enhance the overall climate resilience of communities.[122] These types of considerations are beginning to emerge at the level of policy in both Australia and the United States. For example, the Australian Productivity Commission's 2012 report on "Barriers to Effective Climate Change Adaptation" devotes several chapters to consideration of land use planning, building regulation, measures

---

[119] *Gray v. Macquarie Generation* [2010] NSWLEC 34; *Macquarie Generation v. Hodgson* [2011] NSWCA 424. See, further, Chapter 3.

[120] IPCC, Working Group III, Summary for Policymakers – Final Draft, at 25–26.

[121] Skype interview, Australian Participant 5 (Mar. 26, 2013); in-person interview, US Participant 4 (Nov. 14, 2012); in-person interview, US Participant 6 (Nov. 14, 2012).

[122] D. Burton, "Emerging Opportunities for Climate-Resilient Property Development," at www.climateplanning.com.au/blog/2012/4/27/emerging-opportunitiesfor-climate-resilient-property-develo.html.

to protect existing settlements and infrastructure provision.[123] The Victorian Climate Change Adaptation Plan 2013 also identifies resilience of critical infrastructure and managing climate risks to coastal settlements among its strategic priorities.[124] These themes are echoed in recent US adaptation policy at the federal level – for instance, the president's Climate Action Plan – and state-level adaptation initiatives that focus predominantly on land use planning.[125] Given the extensive litigation over these issues in Australia and emerging such litigation in the United States discussed in Chapter 4, this section focuses particularly on how adaptation litigation has influenced and has the potential to further influence land use companies.

In Australia, the response of companies involved in the land use sector to issues of climate risk has been less than overwhelming to date. In a 2013 report funded by the National Climate Change Adaptation Research Facility on "Climate Change Adaptation in the Boardroom," the authors point to "short-term industry lobbying and political fear associated with private property values" as factors resulting in "a slow uptake of climate resilient development."[126] Similarly, the report finds that "many of the infrastructure construction, maintenance and service providers to the utility sector [energy, water and communications] are not factoring climate change into asset design, construction or maintenance, with subsequent costs to shareholders."[127] Several of our interviewees pointed to the potential for this situation to change in the future as information about liability risk related to climate change disseminates throughout the sector. One interviewee thought large-scale property damage from a climate-linked event would be the probable catalyst for major tort cases raising issues over liability for climate change harms.[128]

With some exceptions, Australian property development companies have been more responsive to current regulatory requirements than to future litigation risk associated with developments that are inadequately sited or designed to withstand climate change impacts. If governments introduce new, more stringent planning standards, for example, to

[123] Productivity Commission, *Barriers to Effective Climate Change Adaptation* (2012, Productivity Commission Research Report, No. 59, Canberra), Chapters 9–12.
[124] Victorian Climate Change Adaptation Plan 2013, available at www.climatechange.vic.gov.au/adapting-to-climate-change/Victorian-Climate-Change-Adaptation-Plan.
[125] For discussion, see Chapter 4.
[126] Johnson et al., *Climate Change Adaptation in the Boardroom*, vii. See also West and Brereton, *Climate Change Adaptation in Business and Industry*.
[127] Johnson et al., *Climate Change Adaptation in the Boardroom*, viii.
[128] Skype interview, Australian Participant 8 (Apr. 24, 2013).

take account of sea level rise and coastal inundation risks, then development companies will generally follow the standards; equally though, if standards are lowered or removed by governments (as has been the case with sea level rise policies in some Australian states), then few companies appear motivated to go beyond the required standard. One interviewee related how in Queensland – a state that has wound back many of its previous environmental laws and climate change policies – a large diversified property group that had had a large climate team "got rid of them because they just don't see that there are any issues; they don't have to take into account climate change."[129] Other property development companies take the view that "because the impacts are long term, they see that they develop and get rid of the property and therefore they won't be liable for anything that happens down the road anyway."[130]

Exceptions to this pattern occur where land use and development companies take seriously the litigation risk associated with inadequate adaptation efforts. Examples provided by interviewees included one fairly large development company that no longer develops in areas that may be susceptible to the impacts of climate change.[131] Another interviewee cited the example of a property developer who proposed a condition be placed on the permit issued for a coastal development to require the properties to be relocated in the event of their being placed at risk from inundation as a result of rising sea levels.[132] Interestingly, it has often been smaller sized companies that have taken such actions in Australia. Our interviewees suggested that for the larger property development companies other economic considerations come into play:

> Very large property development companies have been involved in either taking out options on land for future development or purchasing the land outright, and in the coastal zone you're talking about land with a premium value. Now they stand to lose on a couple of different scores: one is that if those areas of land are perceived to be at risk in the future from inundation then it may affect the price that they can sell for once they are developed, but the other concern is that will they be developed, will they be permitted to be developed, if they are perceived to be in a vulnerable area?[133]

---

[129] Skype interview, Australian Participant 18 (Jul. 18, 2013).
[130] Ibid.   [131] Ibid.
[132] Skype interview, Australian Participant 10 (May 8, 2013). See also National Sea Change Taskforce, Newsletter, October 27, 2009, at http://projects.umwelt.com.au/shoalhaven-coastline/docs/SeaChangeNewsletter-Oct2009.pdf.
[133] Skype interview, Australian Participant 10 (May 8, 2013).

In the United States, the novelty of adaptation litigation, and indeed adaptation policy, has meant there are few observable effects, as yet, on this type of corporate behavior in the land use sector. One recent example, however, suggests possibilities for a greater engagement of US development and infrastructure companies with adaptation issues in the future. In Chapter 4, we discussed the ConEd rate case that followed the Columbia Climate Change Center's petition – calling for improved disaster planning and infrastructure resilience – in the aftermath of Superstorm Sandy to the New York Public Service Commission. The coalition of academic centers and nongovernmental organizations (NGOs) involved in the case noted with interest how receptive Consolidated Edison was to calls for storm hardening of its systems. Its corporate response included participation in a Storm Hardening and Resiliency Collaborative and commitments to capital works and new design standards that are intended to protect against risks from future severe storms and sea level rise.[134] Although generalizations from this single instance are difficult, the behavior of the company concerned in this case holds out the promise that similarly placed large infrastructure providers may also see the benefit in proactive adaptation actions to avoid future lawsuits. A cultural change of this kind could make a significant contribution to adaptation and resilience given the long-lived nature of many facilities installed and operated by infrastructure providers.

5.3.3   Insurance

Compared with the short-term vision of many property development and infrastructure companies, insurance companies – including those involved in the land use sector – tend to adopt much longer-term business planning horizons. Insurance companies, as a whole, are also reasonably risk averse and hence potentially more sensitive to the kinds of business risks associated with climate change. As one interviewee put it: "if there's a metaphorical race, insurers would be ahead of the judges and the judges would be ahead of the politicians. The insurers are *the* most risk averse group of people."[135] The insurance industry also has much to lose, and possibly something to gain,[136] from threats posed by

---

[134] This case is discussed in depth in Chapter 4.

[135] Skype interview, Australian Participant 8 (Apr. 24, 2013).

[136] For instance, climate change may offer opportunities to develop new sorts of products to manage climate risk and variability.

climate change. Increases in the number, cost, and variability of disaster and weather-related losses in the last decade have convinced some insurance companies, reinsurers, and their trade associations of the need to incorporate climate change into their strategic planning.[137] A robust insurance sector also has an important part to play in adaptation to climate change: "Insurance is a form of adaptive capacity for the impacts of climate change, although the sector itself must adapt in order to remain viable."[138]

While insurance companies have been active in the climate change field since the 1970s,[139] and widely acknowledge climate change as a potential business threat, the sector has still lagged in terms of preparing for the problems associated with climate change. As in other corporate sectors, there have been companies that have sought to lead by example. For instance, a major reinsurance company, the Swiss Re Group, launched a "Greenhouse Neutral Programme" in 2003 that aimed to reduce greenhouse gas emissions by 15 percent per employee by 2013 and to offset remaining emissions through the purchase of high-quality carbon credits. This emissions reduction goal was achieved six years early in 2007, and the company has since achieved greenhouse gas reductions in its operations of over 50 percent.[140]

Such programs, however, remain the exception rather than the norm.[141] A 2011 report by investor group Ceres, focusing on disclosures of climate risk by US-based insurance companies, is revealing. Climate risk disclosure by insurance companies to state regulators is mandated under a uniform standard issued by the National Association of Insurance Commissioners.[142] Examining disclosures pursuant to this standard, the Ceres report found that despite widespread recognition of the effects climate change will likely have on the frequency and severity of extreme

---

[137] Evan Mills, "Insurance in a Climate of Change" (2005) 309(5737) *Science* 1040.

[138] Mills, "Insurance in a Climate of Change."

[139] "Flood Inundation" (Munich Re, Munich Reinsurance Company, Munich, 1973). See also National Association of Insurance Commissioners, *The Potential Impact of Climate Change on Insurance Regulation* (NAIC, 2008), at www.naic.org/documents/cipr_potential_impact_climate_change.pdf.

[140] "Swiss Re," Climate Group, at www.theclimategroup.org/who-we-are/our-members/swiss-re.

[141] Kate Margolis, "Insurance Coverage Crossroads: The Insurance Industry Appears Largely Unprepared to Weather Risks of Climate Change," Bloomberg Law, July 8, 2013, at www.ceres.org/press/press-clips/insurance-coverage-crossroads-the-insurance-industry-appears-largely-unprepared-to-weather-risks-of-climate-change.

[142] NAIC, "Insurance Regulators Adopt Climate Change Risk Disclosure," News Release, March 17, 2009, San Diego, at www.naic.org/Releases/2009_docs/climate_change_risk_disclosure_adopted.htm.

events, few insurers were able to articulate a coherent plan to manage the risks and opportunities associated with climate change. In addition, the industry is focusing most of its attention on a narrow set of risks, ignoring issues like noncoastal extreme weather and climate liability, which may prove to be significant in the future. The report also found significant heterogeneity in US insurers' perceptions about and responses to climate change, suggesting the potential for significant market dislocations and potential contraction as insurers with less capacity to identify and manage climate risks experience excessive capital losses.[143]

There are potentially a variety of ways that the insurance sector may interact with litigation of relevance to climate change action. Insurers may themselves be plaintiffs in litigation designed to improve the resilience of infrastructure and hence to lower costs to their insureds and themselves incurred when extreme weather events – whether or not caused or exacerbated by climate change – cause property and other damage. As discussed in Chapter 4, one of the most interesting and potentially influential adaptation lawsuits to emerge in the United States involved a negligence claim by insurance companies against city governments in Cook County, Chicago. The claim alleged that the defendants' failure to upgrade and climate-proof storm water infrastructure contributed to damage suffered by insureds and consequent insurance payouts in respect of the April 2013 floods in the state.[144] While the case has now been withdrawn, as commentators have noted, the threat of similar suits illustrates that "in the absence of clear climate change policy, government is increasingly at risk of litigation."[145] It might seem surprising that insurance companies would be prepared to initiate such litigation given the cost and potential legal hurdles involved in bringing negligence claims against government actors. Nevertheless, the sector's concern with climate risk exposure has been growing and is being increasingly expressed.[146] In Australia,

---

[143] Sharlene Leurig, *Climate Risk Disclosure by Insurers: Evaluating Insurer Responses to the NAIC Climate Disclosure Survey* (2011, Ceres, Boston).

[144] *Illinois Farmers Insurance Co. v. Metropolitan Water Reclamation District of Greater Chicago*, No. 2014CH06608 (Ill. Cir. Ct., filed Apr. 16, 2014), available at www.arnold porter.com/public_document.cfm?id=23667&key=18H3 (subsequently withdrawn in June 2014).

[145] Mark Baker-Jones, "Responding to Litigation Risk from Climate Change – Informed Decision-making," DLA Piper Climate Change Update, May 2014.

[146] See, e.g., Lloyd's, *Catastrophic Modelling and Climate Change* (2014, Lloyds, London), at www.lloyds.com/news-and-insight/lloyds-blog/our-experts/trevor-maynard/2014/ catastrophe-modelling-and-climate-change.

insurers have not (yet) been involved in climate-related litigation as plain-tiffs. However, the executive director and CEO of the main industry body, the Insurance Council of Australia, recently called for a more prudent approach to building communities in areas exposed to extreme weather and greater attention to land use planning, signaling growing advocacy around these issues by insurance companies in Australia.[147]

More often, when insurers are involved in climate change litigation, they are on the side of defendants. For instance, insurers often stand behind primary defendants sued over their actions or inaction in dealing with climate change. In the litigation described in Chapter 4 involving Byron Bay Shire Council in Australia, where private property owners are suing the council over its "planned retreat" policy and refusal to main-tain beach antierosion measures, the council's insurers are defending the cases.[148] Insurance companies have also been involved, on the defendant's side, in class actions brought against government bodies and power com-panies in the aftermath of the devastating Black Saturday Bushfires in the state of Victoria.[149]

When a policyholder is sued for its contribution to climate change dam-age, insurance companies may seek to avoid liability under the relevant policy. This insurance industry strategy occurred in the closely watched US case of *AES Corp v. Steadfast Insurance Company*, decided by the Virginia Supreme Court in 2012. AES was one of the energy companies sued in the *Kivalina* litigation over the contribution of its greenhouse gas emissions to climate change damage to the Kivalina community. Stead-fast denied any duty to defend or indemnify AES in the *Kivalina* litigation on the basis that climate-related injuries went beyond the scope of the indemnity provided by Steadfast's general commercial liability policy. The Virginia Supreme Court affirmed an earlier trial court decision uphold-ing the insurer's claim.[150] This decision suggests that insurers will not have a duty to defend against at least some types of suits, leaving energy company insureds to meet the costs of such cases. Interestingly, Steadfast is a subsidiary of Zurich Insurance Group, a global industry giant, as is

---

[147] Insurance Council of Australia, *2013 Year in Review*, available at www.insurancecouncil. com.au/about-us/year-in-review.

[148] Skype interview, Australian Participant 17 (May 30, 2013). The Bryon Bay litigation is discussed in Chapter 4.

[149] Skype interview, Australian Participant 17 (May 30, 2013).

[150] *AES v. Steadfast* 715 S.E.2d 28 (Va. 2011) upheld by Virginia Supreme Court in its rehearing decision, Record No. 100764, Apr. 20, 2012.

Illinois Farmers' Insurance, the company that was suing Chicago municipalities over their inadequate adaptation measures.[151] Taken together,
these cases suggest a broader strategy on the part of the parent insurance
company to attempt to insulate itself both from climate-related losses and
lawsuits against its corporate policyholders that are major greenhouse gas
emitters.[152] At least in relation to the *AES v. Steadfast* decision, though,
some commentators have argued that the decision likely will have limited
effect beyond Virginia due to the narrow interpretation given by the court
to the term "occurrence" under the policy.[153]

Insurance companies may sometimes be defendants themselves in
climate-relevant cases when they have refused coverage under property
insurance policies following an extreme weather event. In the aftermath
of Superstorm Sandy, many homeowners faced the prospect of denial of
coverage by their insurance companies or companies charging very high
"hurricane deductibles" as a condition of payouts. Several New York law
firms are offering services to such clients, which may lead to a surge of
new litigation.[154] Although climate change is unlikely to be a central consideration in these cases, they may include discussions of climate science
raised by questions over the meteorological definition of the event (hurricane or storm) and the specific nature of the damage (wind or flood).[155]
There is also some emerging residential litigation, such as an action by
luxury condominium owners in New York's financial district suing the
building's management company in negligence for alleged inadequate
action to protect common areas from flooding during Superstorm Sandy
and the subsequent failure to pursue insurance claims on behalf of the
owners.[156]

The approach of some Australian insurers to managing climate-related
risks associated with an increased occurrence of weather-related losses has
been far more dramatic in the aftermath of disaster. Following successive

---

[151] Evan Lehmann, "Insurance Co. Sues Ill. Cities for Climate Damage," *Climate Wire*, E&E
Publishing, May 14, 2014, at www.eenews.net/stories/1059999532.
[152] Evan Lehmann, "Insurance Co. Sues Ill. Cities for Climate Damage."
[153] Jason Johnston, "Virginia Supreme Court Limits Insurer's Duty to Defend in Climate Change Lawsuits," The Federalist Society, Jan. 4, 2013, at www.fed-soc.org/
publications/detail/virginia-supreme-court-limits-insurers-duty-to-defend-in-climate-
change-lawsuits.
[154] See, e.g., Napoli, Bern, Ripka, Shkolnik LLP, "Superstorm Sandy Insurance Claims," at
www.napolibern.com/Superstorm-Sandy-Insurance-Claims.aspx.
[155] Burton, "Emerging Opportunities for Climate-Resilient Property Development."
[156] Barbara Ross, "Luxury condo building in Financial District hit in $35 million Hurricane
Sandy suit," *N.Y. Daily News*, Nov. 19, 2012, www.nydailynews.com/life-style/real-estate/
luxury-condo-hit-35-million-sandy-suit-article-1.1204856.

floods in the state of Queensland, some insurers announced that they would not offer insurance for particularly vulnerable areas (or only at very high premiums).[157] This type of shift in coverage may ultimately challenge mortgage viability for some locations, with potential flow-on effects for banks' mortgage portfolios.[158]

In responding to climate litigation risk, insurance companies may also play a more proactive role in climate adaptation action through promoting the adoption of risk management strategies by insureds.[159] Such approaches take account of a range of risk factors, including liability risks associated with climate litigation. As one interviewee described it, "the insurance industry as a whole is just very attentive to all of the changes that are occurring in the courts and in planning tribunals; they follow it very closely."[160] In the process, the risk-averse stance of insurers may be passed through to their policyholders. For example, local councils in New South Wales are being urged by their insurers to treat 2009 sea level rise planning benchmarks, recently abandoned by the government, as if they were still a policy requirement.[161] In the face of court cases declaring the necessity to consider climate change in planning, insurers "are not ashamed of saying: we've been trying to protect the members in the scheme from liability exposures."[162]

5.3.4 Finance and investment

The energy, land use, and insurance sectors are some of the industries at highest risk from climate change and hence have been at the leading edge of efforts to improve corporate responses to the problem. However, standing behind such frontline companies are a multitude of banks, shareholders, and investors of various kinds, who finance projects and invest in companies as part of their asset portfolios. With only modest success achieved by direct efforts to require front line companies to improve their mitigation and adaptation behaviors, there is growing interest in the

---

[157] Sophie Elsworth, "Suncorp Will Not Offer New Policies to Queensland Towns Emerald and Roma as Fallout from 2011 Floods Continues," *The Courier Mail* (Brisbane), May 7, 2012, at www.couriermail.com.au/news/queensland/suncorp-will-not-offer-new-policies-to-queensland-towns-emerald-and-roma-as-fallout-from-2011-floods-continues/story-e6freoof-1226348164193.

[158] Johnston et al., *Climate Change Adaptation in the Boardroom*; Skype interview, Australian Participant 8 (Apr. 24, 2013).

[159] Skype interview, Australian Participant 17 (May 30, 2013).

[160] Skype interview, Australian Participant 8 (Apr. 24, 2013).

[161] Skype interview, Australian Participant 17 (May 30, 2013).

[162] Ibid.

role that financiers, shareholders, and investors might play in motivating greater climate action through their investment decisions and other pressures they can bring to bear on companies in which they invest. Litigation or proposed litigation in this area has targeted a range of matters, including the investment decisions of financiers, climate risk disclosures made to investors, and the transparency of institutional investors with regard to the level of climate risk of their investment portfolios.

Large-scale energy projects generally require financing to be viable. Environmental groups have tried to affect such financing by bringing cases regarding investments in greenhouse gas–intensive projects. Several suits have targeted the lending activities of the US Export-Import Bank and the Overseas Private Investment Corporation (OPIC). While both institutions are federal agencies rather than private sector lenders (although OPIC works to mobilize private sector capital for projects), challenges to their loan practices relating to fossil fuel projects illustrate an avenue for climate change litigation that could provide a model for taking action against corporate lenders. In addition, if litigation can influence public sector lenders to be more climate-aware in their decision making, there is the potential for their new prioritization of mitigation to flow through to energy companies seeking their financing assistance.

One early lawsuit filed by several city governments and environmental organizations – *Friends of the Earth v. Spinelli* – resulted in a settlement agreement under which OPIC and the Export-Import Bank agreed to consider greenhouse gas emissions from financed projects.[163] The plaintiffs in that case argued that while harvested fossil fuels would be burned abroad, the emissions would still have impacts on the United States. More recent lawsuits filed by environmental groups in December 2012 and August 2013 have targeted loans of the Export-Import Bank for fossil fuel projects. For instance, a 2013 lawsuit alleges NEPA violations regarding the bank's approval of a US$90 million loan guarantee, which petitioners claim would enable Xcoal to broker US$1 billion in sales of coal for export to the Asian market from Appalachian coal mines.[164] An earlier December 2012 lawsuit, also involving a coalition of environmental groups, contended that the Export-Import Bank failed to undertake rigorous environmental assessments before approving US$2.95 billion in financing for an

---

[163] Formerly *Friends of the Earth v. Watson*. See Joint Motion for Dismissal with Prejudice, No. C02–4106 JSW (Feb. 6, 2009).

[164] *Chesapeake Climate Action Network v. Export-Import Bank of the United States*, No. 2013–1820 (D.D.C. 2013).

Australian liquefied natural gas project. The project encompasses drilling of up to 10,000 coal seam gas wells, installation of nearly 300 miles of gas pipeline, and construction of a processing facility and export terminal close to the Great Barrier Reef World Heritage Area in Queensland.[165] The case will test the extent to which the Endangered Species Act can be applied to federal regulatory actions outside the borders of the United States. It also creates interesting linkages between emissions reduction efforts in the United States and Australia.

These lawsuits are still pending in the courts. Nonetheless, in December 2013, the board of the Export-Import Bank adopted revised environmental procedures and guidelines governing "high-carbon intensity projects."[166] The revised guidelines require CCS to secure financing for coal-fired power plants in most countries. As environmental groups have pointed out, however, the revised guidelines still allow financing of coal-fired power plants in poor countries and permit loans for most coal mines. The policy director of Pacific Environment, one of the environmental groups involved in the lawsuits against the Export-Import Bank, commented, "It's great that the Export-Import Bank is curbing coal financing, but the loopholes appear big enough to drive a coal train through."[167]

Investors themselves may also be agents for change in the corporate sector through the pressure that they can exert on the decision making of the companies in which they invest. For example, in both the United States and Australia, groups representing investors and shareholders concerned about the risks posed by climate change to the value of their holdings have pushed for greater disclosure by companies of their climate business risks – physical and regulatory. Such information is of particular importance to institutional investors, such as banks, fund managers, and pension funds, which need to ensure long-term stability and viability of their investment portfolios.[168] As a result, institutional investors are increasingly being urged to "work toward building in, ahead of time (to the extent possible)

---

[165] Rebekah Kearn, "U.S.-Backed Project Threatens Australia's Great Barrier Reef, Environmentalists Say," *Courthouse News Service*, December 14, 2012, at www.courthousenews.com/2012/12/14/53136.htm.

[166] "Export-Import Bank Board Adopts Revised Environmental Guidelines to Reduce Greenhouse Gas Emissions, Export-Import Bank of the United States," December 12, 2013, at www.exim.gov/newsandevents/releases/2013/EXPORT-IMPORT-BANK-BOARD-ADOPTS-REVISED-ENVIRONMENTAL-GUIDELINES-TO-REDUCE-GREENHOUSE-GAS-EMISSIONS.cfm.

[167] Pacific Environment, "U.S. Government Finance Agency Curbs Coal Support," December 13, 2013, at http://pacificenvironment.org/blog/category/coal-2/.

[168] Shearing, "Raising the Boardroom Temperature?"

large-scale systemic risks, such as climate change, into risk management and strategic asset allocation decision-making processes."[169] These efforts have gained renewed importance in light of the cascade of recent reports addressing the potential "carbon bubble" caused by fossil fuel assets that will be significantly overvalued in the advent of regulatory constraints on greenhouse gas emissions.[170] One such report estimates that nearly a quarter of the value of the FTSE 100 is subject to high carbon-based companies.[171] If the carbon bubble were to occur, some 40 to 60 percent of sharemarket value could be wiped out, affecting companies and investors worldwide.[172]

An investor group in the United States that has been particularly active on climate risk disclosure issues is Ceres, a network of investors, companies, and public interest groups that advocates for sustainability leadership. Ceres leads the Investor Network on Climate Risk (INCR), which is a group of more than one hundred institutional investors representing more than US$10 trillion in assets under management.[173] In 2007, members of the ICNR, together with Ceres and the Environmental Defense Fund, filed a petition with the US Securities and Exchange Commission (SEC) asking the commission to issue an interpretive ruling clarifying that material climate-related information must be included in corporate disclosures under existing law.[174] Around the same time, then New York State attorney general, Andrew Cuomo, issued subpoena letters to five

---

[169] *Climate Change Scenarios – Implications for Strategic Asset Allocation*, Mercer (2011).

[170] See references in note 3.

[171] "Fossil Fuels Are Sub-Prime Assets, Bank of England Governor Warned," *The Guardian*, January 19, 2012 www.theguardian.com/environment/2012/jan/19/fossil-fuels-sub-prime-mervyn-king.

[172] Carbon Tracker Initiative and LSE Grantham Research Institute, *Unburnable Carbon 2013: Wasted Capital and Stranded Assets.*

[173] "Investor Network on Climate Risk (INCR)," Ceres, www.ceres.org/investor-network/incr. Members of the ICNR include prominent banks, pension funds and asset management companies such as Blackrock, Deutsche Bank, Legg Mason, New York City Employees" Retirement System, Prudential and Rockefeller Financial. "Member Directory," Ceres, www.ceres.org/investor-network/incr/member-directory.

[174] See Petition for Interpretive Guidance on Climate Risk Disclosures, File No. 4-547, 19 September 2007, www.sec.gov/rules/petitions/2007/petn4–547.pdf; Supplemental Petition, June 12, 2008, www.sec.gov/rules/petitions/2008/petn4–547-supp.pdf; Second Supplemental Petition, November 23, 2009, www.sec.gov/rules/petitions/2009/petn4–547-supp.pdf. For other petitions on point, see also Petition for Interpretive Guidance on Business Risk of Global Warming Regulation, File Number 4–549, October 22, 2007, www.sec.gov/rules/petitions/2007/petn4–549.pdf (submitted on behalf of the Free Enterprise Action Fund).

coal utility companies concerning the adequacy of climate risk disclosures made to their investors associated with plans to build new coal-fired plants.[175] The Attorney General's Office later reached settlements with three of the energy companies involved, in which they agreed to enhance their disclosures relating to climate change and greenhouse gas emissions in their annual reports filed with the SEC.[176]

In response to the Ceres and other petitions, in January 2010, the SEC issued a Commission Guidance Regarding Disclosure Related to Climate Change. The guidance clarifies the disclosure requirements associated with a number of SEC rules and regulations under the federal securities law, including Management's Discussion and Analysis of Financial Condition and Results of Operations (or MD&A) that addresses a registrant's liquidity, capital resources, and results of operations.[177] As part of the MD&A, registrants must identify and disclose known trends, events, demands, commitments, and uncertainties that are reasonably likely to have a material effect on financial conditions or operating performance.[178] The SEC guidance elaborates major areas of climate business risk that should be considered by registrants in making a disclosure of material risk, including regulatory risks – both domestic and international – associated with compliance with climate regulatory requirements, indirect effects of regulation or business trends such as decreased demand for carbon-intensive products, and physical impacts from climate change to business operations or supply chains.

Four years on from the SEC action, a report by Ceres reviewing climate disclosure by companies in their "10-K" annual reports to the SEC offers a sobering assessment of progress.[179] In the report, Ceres analyzed whether climate-related disclosures were made and the quality of those disclosures. The bar for a climate-related disclosure was set low: a climate disclosure

---

[175] "New York Subpoenas 5 Energy Companies," *New York Times*, September 16 2007, at www.nytimes.com/2007/09/16/nyregion/16greenhouse.html?_r=0.

[176] For information about the settlement agreements, see the New York Attorney General's Office press releases relating to Xcel Energy, www.oag.state.ny.us/media_center/2008/aug/ aug27a_08.html; Dynegy Inc., www.oag.state.ny.us/media_center/2008/oct/oct23a_08 .html; and AES Corporation, www.oag.state.ny.us/media_center/2009/nov/nov19a_09. html.

[177] Item 303, Regulation S-K.

[178] Elizabeth E. Hancock, "Red Dawn, Blue Thunder, Purple Rain: Corporate Risk of Liability for Global Climate Change and the SEC Disclosure Dilemma" (2004–2005) 17 *Georgetown Intl. Environ. L. Rev.* 233.

[179] Jim Coburn and Jackie Cook, *Cool Response: The SEC & Corporate Climate Change Reporting* (2014, Ceres, Boston).

was considered to be present in a particular 10-K report where just a single mention was made of climate change–related issues. Even so, on a scale running from 0 (least disclosure) to 100 (best disclosure), the average disclosure score for 10-Ks filed in 2013 was less than 5 out of 100 points for companies that disclosed climate issues. The report also found that, while more companies started making climate-related disclosures in 2010 after the SEC issued its interpretive guidance, those numbers have since flat lined and the quality of disclosures has declined. This gap between thought and action on the part of companies with respect to climate change disclosures is apparently not being addressed through strong enforcement efforts by the regulator. The Ceres report included data on SEC comment letters sent over the last four years to companies following SEC staff reviews of 10-K filings. Whereas forty-nine letters related to climate change were sent to companies and asset managers in 2010 and 2011, only three such letters were sent in 2012 and 2013.

The aptly named Ceres report – "Cool Response: The SEC and Corporate Climate Change Reporting" – suggests that regulatory change in response to NGO petitions has not been transformed into deep engagement with the issue of climate risk disclosure by either companies or the SEC. One interviewee, who was involved with efforts to strengthen the SEC rules, offered the following explanation:

> The response [to the SEC guidance] actually wasn't that great, in part because companies do have trouble figuring out what is material and it does sort of run against their grain culturally. And I think the important thing is the time horizon that corporate managers are looking at tends to be shorter than the time horizon that where you can say, you know, it's clear if we have a bunch of refineries that are located in the Gulf of Mexico that may be affected by an increase in storm intensity or rise in sea levels, that may be a grave concern. But if you are looking for something in the next two or three or four years to tell investors about it may not.[180]

Similar challenges around changing corporate culture regarding the assessment and management of long-term risks like climate change were also highlighted by Australian interviewees. Speaking about the prospect of directors' liability in the climate context, one respondent remarked,

> There is no realistic prospect in Australia of a successful action against directors for having caused or contributed to climate change. On the contrary, they are far more susceptible to an action by their disgruntled

---

[180] Telephone interview, US Participant 8 (Oct. 20, 2012).

shareholders if they disband some profitable part of their (dirty) business in the name of saving the planet. ASIC [the Australian Securities and Investments Commission] at present brings very few actions and has a ridiculously high rate of success – in other words, they like to shoot fish in a barrel. They receive hundreds of reports of alleged breaches of duty which they do not action. In my opinion, there is absolutely no way that ASIC will spend time and taxpayer money pursuing directors of filthy polluting companies who are acting legally within the scope of environmental laws, even if the science suggests that their emissions "contribute" to climate change.[181]

The US experience with legal efforts to improve climate risk disclosure by companies is salutary for those in Australia advocating changes to corporate reporting rules to incorporate climate change. Currently neither the Corporations Law nor the listing rules for the Australian Stock Exchange mandate the reporting of corporate climate change risks and management policies.[182] Paralleling the SEC regulations, however, there is some scope for climate risk disclosure provided through requirements on ASX-listed companies to make "continuous disclosure" to the market of information of which the company becomes aware that a reasonable person would expect to have a material impact on the price or value of a company's securities.[183] This provision would have extended to – at the very least – regulatory risks attendant on a company's liabilities under the now-repealed carbon pricing mechanism, although this was never tested in litigation.

Prior to introduction of the carbon price, six listed companies – Boral, Bluescope Steel, Caltex Australia, Rio Tinto, Woodside Petroleum, and Xstrata – publicly expressed concerns to the Australian government

---

[181] E-mail exchange, Australian Participant 23 (Jun. 12, 2014). The respondent further commented that such prosecutions were even less likely in the United States, which lacks a federal ASIC equivalent. The attitude is often one of "'why would anyone want to prosecute directors for business decisions?' . . . They are far more shareholder-centric and those directors with 'green' inclinations would quickly find themselves voted off boards or up before the court for breach of the fiduciary duty to make them pots of money!"

[182] Karen Bubna-Litic, "Climate Change and Corporate Social Responsibility: The Intersection of Corporate and Environmental Law" (2007) 24 *Environ. Planning L. J.* 253; Karen Bubna-Litic, Lou de Leeuw, and Imelda Williamson, "Walking the Thin Green Line: The Australian Experience of Corporate Environmental Reporting" (2001) 18(3) *Environ. Planning L. J.* 339. Reporting requirements exist for greenhouse gas emissions and energy consumption by large energy companies under the National Greenhouse and Energy Reporting Act but this information is not required to be provided to shareholders.

[183] ASX Listing Rule 3.1; Corporations Act 2001, s 674.

regarding the impact of the emissions trading scheme proposed by the government at the time on their operations, profitability, and workforce. Two environmental NGOs – the Australian Conservation Foundation and the Australian Climate Justice Program – subsequently requested a full investigation by the Australian Competition and Consumer Commission (ACCC) as to whether these statements violated competition laws by providing misleading information that contradicted information formally disclosed by the companies concerned to their investors and shareholders.[184] Although no enforcement action was brought by the ACCC in respect of the complaint, it did create some nervousness in corporate boardrooms at the time over the potential liability of directors and other executive officers who issue misleading information as to climate business risk.[185] Overall, however, the appreciation of climate risk and related disclosures remains low among Australian corporations. As one interviewee explained, "most of the corporations say, the Corporations Act doesn't require me to disclose and report on the effects of climate change so we won't and we don't."[186]

Alongside litigation designed to force regulatory change to improve corporate disclosures regarding climate risk, investor groups have investigated other potential mechanisms for influencing corporate governance and decision-making structures. In the United States, Ceres's INCR and the Interfaith Center on Corporate Responsibility have been active in initiating shareholder resolutions calling on companies to disclose how climate risk is being managed.[187] Several of these shareholder resolutions have been withdrawn after the companies involved agreed to address the concerns raised. Shareholder resolutions have been less prevalent and less successful in Australia, in part because of the greater constraints on such action under Australian Corporations Law.[188] A notable example

---

[184] Letter to ACCC, June 11, 2009; Australian Climate Justice Program, Corporate Climate Risk: Comparing Political Claims with Actual Disclosure to Shareholders (June 2009). See also Matthew Murphy, "Garnaut Calls for Emissions Inquiry," *The Age* (Melbourne), June 20, 2009, 7; Matthew Stevens, "Big Bad Six Fight ACF Stunt," *The Australian*, June 20 2009, 27.

[185] Paddy Manning, "Climate Changes for Directors," *Sydney Morning Herald*, June 20, 2009, 6.

[186] Skype interview, Australian Participant 18 (Jul. 18, 2013).

[187] Shareholder Resolutions, Ceres, www.ceres.org/investor-network/resolutions (167 climate-related resolutions as of Mar. 12, 2014, 42 withdrawn on basis that company will address). ICCR's Shareholder Resolutions, www.iccr.org/iccrs-shareholder-resolutions (2014 resolutions).

[188] Shearing, "Raising the Boardroom Temperature?"

in the Australian context was a proposed shareholder resolution put to the annual general meeting of Woodside Petroleum in 2010, calling for disclosure of the carbon price assumptions used by the company.[189] However, this attempt "fell flat" when it was opposed by institutional investors and Woodside's largest shareholder, Royal Dutch Shell.[190] As one interviewee explained, "essentially it was all just talk unless we could put pressure on the institutional investment community to back [the resolution]."[191]

The need to engage institutional investors or "asset owners" – big pension funds, insurance companies, sovereign wealth funds, foundations, and endowments – in efforts to address climate risk is the motivation behind the work of the Australian-based Asset Owners Disclosure Project (AODP).[192] Asset owners could be a potentially potent market force for changing corporate behaviors around climate change given the extent of capital they control (in excess of US$52 trillion is managed by the world's 1000 largest pension funds with less than 2 percent of this invested in low-carbon assets).[193] Consideration of litigation strategies to force greater transparency among asset owners about climate risk in their portfolios and, potentially, to enforce fiduciary obligations owed by pension funds to their members to manage climate risk appropriately remain at a nascent stage.[194] However, for those interested in the future scope of litigation to influence climate regulation and corporate behavior, this potential area for lawsuits is one that may significantly change the nature of the climate litigation landscape:

> The area where the traditional NGOs are very comfortable is stopping fossil fuel companies digging up nice parts of the world. That's where they've gone. A tree or a reef – let's go to court! And of course most of the time they lose but when they win it's champagne corks. But nothing ever changes. These companies are still looking for those opportunities and it just shifts risk to other parts of the globe. We think starving the capital – the oxygen if you like – is a much more solid strategy. And actually the company liabilities issue, when you go down to what the companies are obliged to do to manage these risks, are very real but it's not going to be a regulator to enforce them it's going to be their owners.[195]

---

[189] Ibid.   [190] Skype interview, Australian Participant 6 (Apr. 5, 2013).
[191] Skype interview, Australian Participant 12 (May 21, 2013).
[192] Asset Owners Disclosure Project, at http://aodproject.net/.
[193] Ibid., at http://aodproject.net/about/about-us.html.
[194] Skype interview, Australian Participant 12 (May 21, 2013).
[195] Ibid.

If such cases emerge over time, this approach has the potential to influence investment practices significantly in both countries.

5.3.5   *Law firms and other professional advisors*

Central to the idea that climate change litigation – of various forms – can shape corporate responses to the problem of climate change is companies having knowledge of ongoing litigation and potential liabilities, and perceiving this as posing a business risk of some kind. Unless companies are the direct (and repeated) target of climate change litigation, they may have little direct knowledge of cases going on in the courts or their findings. In this section, we focus on the sector whose business it is to provide such advice. The section considers the role of professional advisors in communicating information about climate change litigation and liability risk to corporate clients. Legal advisors, such as law firms and in-house counsel, in particular, serve as an important conduit for information about potential legal liabilities and risk avoidance strategies, which can help to motivate changes in corporate behavior. Climate change litigation and regulation in both countries have helped spur growth in this sector, as more law firms have added climate practices and more corporations have developed in-house expertise in various areas needed to respond to mitigation and adaptation concerns.

Companies rely on advisors from a range of professions to assist with their navigation of the regulatory system. For instance, companies undertaking a development project will often engage architects, builders, planners, and engineers and rely on these professionals to ensure that the project meets applicable development standards. These professionals are also often part of industry organizations that adopt best practice standards for their profession. An example from the Australian context is Adaptation Guidelines adopted by Engineers Australia, the national professional organization dedicated to the advancement of engineering and the professional development of members. The organization's Adaptation Guidelines deal with responding to the effects of climate change in coastal engineering and planning and take "a very responsible position with respect to understanding sea level rise, understanding climate change, the need to manage for the future not the status quo, the need to look out for community interest, all those sort of things."[196] Potentially, these guidelines, issued by a prominent professional organization, could

---

[196] Skype interview, Australian Participant 11 (May 9, 2013).

play a positive role in influencing engineers, and their developer clients, to improve coastal projects. As one interviewee commented, "as a professional body they will have a big impact on how things are done in terms of the responsibilities of a professional engineer to the community as well as to their client."[197]

Given the merits review nature of much adaptation-related litigation in Australia, engineers and other professional consultants often are the people called on to give evidence to the court about the extent of potential climate impacts for a proposal. Internalization of climate change norms by such professionals as part of the usual practice of assessing land use projects may thus eventually flow through to corporate developer clients. In the United States, there is also the potential for engineering companies to play a proactive role in the adaptation sphere in response to litigation. For instance, a possible indirect effect of both the ConEd rate case and Illinois insurance suit discussed in Chapter 4 is that engineers and other professional development consultancy companies will be required to uproot their existing design standards and assumptions for buildings and infrastructure; updated approaches may be based on assessments of predicted climate change impacts, a shift from the traditional industry practice focused on historical data.

The need for multifaceted advising has also led to significant growth in the climate change consulting industry, including environmental, engineering, management, and legal consulting. The *Climate Change Business Journal*, a publication formed in 2007 to "provid[e] high-value, strategic business intelligence on the Climate Change Industry," estimates that

> the climate change consulting business grew 4–6% in 2011 to revenues of $800 million for core services (GHG, energy and corporate/product life-cycle analyses; compliance and planning; emissions inventories and trading; strategy and policy development) in the United States. This was dramatically slower than the 20–30% growth recorded in 2008, but considering the severity of the economic downturn and the failure of Congress to pass federal climate change legislation, it demonstrates that the imperative to manage GHGs and climate change risks has not gone away.
>
> Environmental consulting & engineering (C&E) firms such as CH2 M Hill, ERM and Environ lead the $800 million US climate change consulting market with 23% share of total revenues in core services, according to CCBJ's research. Management consultancies like McKinsey and Boston Consulting Group follow with 18% marketshare; and law firms such as Mintz Levin and Hogan Lovells rank third with 15% of the market. The

---

[197] Skype interview, Australian Participant 11 (May 9, 2013).

balance of the market is served by assurance firms, energy consulting firms and specialist climate change or sustainability firms.[198]

Although many types of advisors play a role, lawyers arguably are the professional group most closely engaged with regulatory developments, litigation, and liability risks. Climate change litigation has played a significant role in encouraging the development of this practice area in both countries, though to a greater extent in the United States than in Australia, where the number of cases is not as large. Many firms now have dedicated climate change practice groups, and some firms have emerged with that as a core focus. Climate change is also becoming an issue more integrated into general environmental law practices, an effect that seems to have arisen to some extent as a result of litigation seeking to extend environmental laws to cover climate concerns. For instance, a number of our US interviewees did not self-identify as climate lawyers but nonetheless had extensive experience in NEPA, CEQA, Clean Air Act, or Endangered Species Act litigation in which climate change was raised as a major issue.

Moreover, most large corporate law firms issue regular newsletters and updates on major climate cases relevant for clients as well as undertaking analyses of business risks for clients. Firms specializing in employee placement have recognized this trend. For example, US-based Roth Staffing Companies identifies environmental law as one of the seven hottest legal practice areas, with a description that emphasizes climate change and energy transition:

> A rising awareness of environmental issues, such as the use of clean technology, renewable energy, managing carbon assets and keeping green house gas inventories, has created work for environmental law attorneys. As going green becomes a global priority, lawyers who can advise clients on green initiatives and sustainability issues are in demand. Experts predict that greenhouse gas, climate change, global warming and other environmental legislation will increase the legal work for environmental lawyers in coming years.[199]

Lawyers as a whole tend to be risk averse and, through their advice to clients, can be effective communicators of the extent of climate litigation and other legal risks faced by companies. The legal sector may thus serve

---

[198] Environmental Business International, Professional Services in Climate Change Consulting, Climate Change Business Journal, February 2012, www.climatechangebusiness.com/Professional_Services_in_Climate_Change_Consulting.

[199] Roth Staffing Companies LLP, "The 7 Hottest Law Practice Areas," February 14, 2013, www.rothstaffing.com/candidate/?p=448.

an important role in driving climate change adaptation and mitigation responses in the broader private corporate sector. One interviewee, an Australian lawyer who has worked at leading national law firms, gave a sense of how this might occur:

> I certainly think that the evolution of climate change litigation is informing advice that lawyers give clients where those clients' activities or proposed activities may have some connection with climate change or the impacts of climate change. A good example might be where a lawyer says to a client who's about to undertake a development which is out on the sea level in Sydney, have you thought about the predicted increase in sea levels over the next fifty to one hundred years, and if you haven't thought about that then it's more likely than not that your insurers have thought about that and that maybe a factor which you are going to need to take into account in financing this project or getting insurance for some of the physical assets. And I know from personal experience that I put that to somebody about three or four years ago whilst standing at the end of a very underdeveloped industrial area in Sydney that is about to be turned into something that is very big. That was not an issue that they had thought of, but they went away and they did think about it and whilst I don't think it's changed the physical characteristics of the development it did have an impact on some costings that they did and some contingent liabilities that they did.[200]

Like the companies they advise, however, it seems most lawyers have some way to travel in order to serve as effective communicators of climate litigation risk to their clients. They will need to be more informed about the scope of climate litigation risk and to take a proactive approach. In this respect, "proactive, early consideration of legal obligations and duties, and compliance with evolving regulatory requirements" will be preferable to an approach in which attention to climate legal risk only comes about "in reaction to legal claims, insurance losses and recovery of reputation."[201] Litigation will likely continue to play an important role in spurring the development of that knowledge.

5.4 Conclusion

Although the potential for corporate action to contribute positively to addressing climate change is immense, the evidence of change so far, and the role of climate change litigation in initiating such change, is modest. Both reports dealing with corporate responses to climate change and

---

[200] Skype interview, Australian Participant 8 (Apr. 24, 2013).
[201] Johnston et al., *Climate Change Adaptation in the Boardroom*, 11.

data obtained in our interviews suggest there are indeed some companies taking active steps to improve their efforts on mitigation and adaptation and their consequent exposure to litigation risk. At the other end of the spectrum, many companies – particularly in the energy sector – are actively engaged in opposing regulatory advances through litigation. The vast majority of companies seem to sit somewhere in the middle between these two groups. Surveys of corporate attitudes to climate change across multiple sectors suggest these "nonleaders" are aware of the potential business risks posed by climate change, including liability and litigation risks, but have been slow to change business practices or internal corporate decision making and management structures in response. One explanation may be that current legal structures applicable to corporations still overwhelmingly reward short-term, profit-making activities that benefit shareholders rather than the adoption of practices for the serious consideration and management of longer-term risks, such as those posed by climate change.

The chapter has focused on companies in those sectors – energy, land use, insurance, and finance and investment – that potentially have the most to lose from climate change and that also stand to make the greatest contribution to addressing the problem. In addition, it has examined the sector that advises these other key corporate groupings. Litigation has played a part in efforts to influence corporate actors in each sector to improve the actions they take to mitigate greenhouse gas emissions and prepare for climate change impacts. Our prediction is that the area of litigation involving corporate responses to climate change is one that will continue to grow across time in both the United States and Australia. Moreover, as actions against the US Export-Import Bank and contemplated lawsuits targeting asset owners illustrate, climate litigation focused on corporations has the capacity to transcend national boundaries and exert a truly global impact. It also seems increasingly likely that, in terms of transformative action, companies from other sectors may often lead those from the energy sector. In particular, the insurance, financial, and investment communities' response to climate change litigation and the business risks that it poses ultimately may prove the most crucial in tipping the balance toward a cleaner energy future.

Litigation's role in shaping social norms

I would say for every socially important issue of an era the courts always play a critical role that in part is very real and in part is a symbolic battleground. So the civil rights movement was mostly people marching in the streets but there was a huge role of court decisions on desegregation and other aspects of civil rights that were critical to that campaign. But those court decisions probably would never have occurred if people weren't marching in the streets. We've recently seen that with gay marriage in the United States where court cases have been a center point of that effort, but it's really about a social movement that's created the political pressure so that battle's now seemingly almost won. So I would say the climate context is similar. There will be important court cases – *Massachusetts v. EPA* is far and above the most important of all on it so far – and they help motivate the issue, they help steer the direction of the movement and development of policy. But what really matters is a broader civil society movement that shifts public opinion, including the opinion of judges, and legislators who draft the law that we then litigate based upon.

– US Interview Participant 12

Litigation can be an important opportunity for the community to participate in and have their views heard in a decision-making forum. It provides an event that the community can organize and rally around, focus on and use as a basis for fund-raising. From the point of view of a public interest litigator, the most successful litigation (i.e., that which has the most impact) is litigation that forms part of a good community campaign.

– Australian Interview Participant 1

6.1 Introduction

Litigation on important social issues, such as climate change, is often initiated not just to advance regulation but also with the goal of influencing the public debate. Indeed, raising the public profile of climate change and influencing social perceptions of the risk are seen as "key to meaningful governmental and private action on climate change."[1] Surveys of public opinion on climate change in the United States and Australia demonstrate the pivotal role politics and media reporting (as opposed to climate scientific information) play in shaping public attitudes.[2] In an effort to influence the public and political debate, both pro-regulatory and antiregulatory groups have sought to garner favorable media and new media attention for their positions by a variety of means, including through initiating litigation.[3]

In our interviews with US and Australian participants engaged in pro-regulatory climate change litigation, interviewees frequently cited the capacity of litigation to shift social perceptions, influence the public debate, endorse the findings of climate science, and place or maintain the climate issue on the regulatory agenda as significant benefits of the lawsuits. Through their decisions on climate change issues, courts can help give legitimacy and authority to the view that climate change is an urgent, major problem that requires regulatory action. Even when a positive judgment with regulatory implementation is unlikely, such as

---

[1] Robert J. Brulle, Jason Carmichael and J. Craig Jenkins, "Shifting public opinion on climate change: an empirical assessment of factors influencing concern over climate change in the U.S., 2002–2010" (2012) 114(2) *Climatic Change* 169. See also Rob Verchick, "Climate, Culture and Cognition: October 30, 2014, SSRN, http://papers.ssrn.com/sol3/papers.cfm?abstract_id=2516887 (discussing the need for climate action to resonate with people's values and cultural world views in order to achieve progress).

[2] Hans von Storch and Werner Krauss, "Culture Contributes to Perceptions of Climate Change," Nieman Reports, Winter 2005, at www.nieman.harvard.edu/reports/article/100600/Culture-Contributes-to-Perceptions-of-Climate-Change.aspx; James Painter, *Climate Change in the Media: Reporting Risk and Uncertainty* (London: IB. Tauris, 2013); Boykoff, Maxwell, *Who Speaks for the Climate: Making Sense on Media Reporting on Climate Change* (New York: Cambridge University Press, 2011); Maxwell T. Boykoff and Jules M. Boykoff, "Balance as bias: global warming and the US prestige press" (2004) 14 *Global Environmental Change* 125; Adriana Bailey, "How Grammatical Choice Shapes Media Representations of Climate (Un)certainty" (2014) 8(2) *Environmental Communication* 197.

[3] In this chapter our focus is primarily on pro-regulatory litigation. However, we acknowledge that litigation can be, and has been, used by antiregulatory interests for opposite ends, including to highlight the economic costs associated with regulation and to cast doubt on the veracity of climate change science. We discuss this antiregulatory litigation in more depth in Chapter 7. In addition to industry lawsuits opposing regulatory action on climate change – which are often a forum for anti-regulatory interests to advance sceptical views of climate science, to raise uncertainties or highlight business impacts – there is also a growing body of cases, mostly in the United States, targeting climate protestors and climate scientists. The motivation for these cases largely seems to be to question the integrity of the protestors and scientists concerned. For further details of these cases, see Arnold and Porter LLP, "U.S. Climate Change Litigation Chart," at www.climatecasechart.com.

in the case of the petition that the Inuit brought to the Inter-American Commission on Human Rights, the cases can help raise awareness of the problems that climate change is causing. Climate change litigation – whether successful or not – thus has important indirect influences on the regulatory landscape through the role it plays in shaping social norms, including public perceptions of climate change, accepted understandings of climate science, and views on the appropriate regulatory response.

However, the deeply partisan environment in both countries somewhat mutes these indirect influences on social norms. So many key stakeholders have entrenched views on climate change, which litigation is unlikely to alter significantly.[4] This partisanship influences the ways in which regulators respond to lawsuits, and reactions to their responses, as this chapter also explores. How agencies and legislators interact with climate change decisions will be modulated by prevailing public attitudes and by their own views on climate change. Whereas some may remain hostile to regulation even in the face of public support for climate action (thereby providing a focal point for public opposition and activism), others will be emboldened by positive court rulings and supportive public opinion to push harder in their climate regulatory initiatives. When public opinion on climate change is more ambivalent or divided, regulators may derive comfort from judgments that mandate action that would otherwise be politically difficult to undertake.

Moreover, these indirect influences involve multidirectional interactions rather than a unidirectional one. Courts themselves can be influenced by shifts in public opinion regarding climate change, and their decisions can at times reveal changing perceptions of the science. For example, the US Supreme Court expressed much more skepticism about its ability to engage climate change science in *AEP v. Connecticut* than in *Massachusetts v. EPA*, paralleling and perhaps reflecting the shift in public opinion in the period between those two cases. The political environment also shapes which cases are brought in the first place; such decisions determine the spectrum of issues and potential framings of those issues that courts have before them to adjudicate. Understanding the relationship between litigation, social norms, and regulatory change thus requires consideration both of how cases shape norms and political responses, and how evolving norms and politics shape cases over time.

This chapter examines these dynamics through its consideration of (1) how litigation shapes public opinion and political behavior, and, as

---

[4] Dan Kahan, "Why we are poles apart on climate change," (2012) 488 *Nature* 255 (Aug. 16, 2012).

a consequence, regulatory choices and (2) how public debates over science and regulation manifest in cases. Section 6.2 begins by assessing the influence of climate change cases on public views in the United States in Australia and the role of the litigation in bolstering the public interest climate campaigns of environmental nongovernmental organizations (NGOs) and activists. This section also examines the ways in which partisanship has impacted both regulators' responses to these cases and public and political perceptions of and reactions to those regulators' responses. The next section then explores how perceptions of climate change play out in the cases themselves, with a particular focus on the ways in which understandings of science are used to argue for the appropriateness or inappropriateness of regulatory action at different scales.

6.2   Litigation and public perceptions of climate change

This section begins our examination of the multidirectional dynamics around litigation and social norms by considering public attitudes toward climate change in the United States and Australia and the effects of litigation on those attitudes. Political conflict and negative reporting about climate change by conservative media outlets have helped to shape the public debate on climate change in both countries, often in ways that have impeded ambitious climate action. Against this backdrop, climate change litigation has played three main roles in helping to shape (or reshape) public perceptions in a proactive fashion: (1) making the political culture and public debate more climate-informed; (2) supporting and galvanizing grassroots climate campaigns; and (3) translating abstract scientific concepts into tangible impacts that the general public can understand and relate to better.

In playing these roles, however, climate change litigation has been unable to escape the partisan environment that motivates it and that it influences. Regulatory responses to litigation and reactions to those responses continue to be shaped by the deep divides in the United States and Australia over climate change. The final part of this section explores these complex dynamics in both countries and the ways in which partisanship influences regulatory responses to climate change.

6.2.1   Public attitudes to climate change: United States and Australia

Compared with the citizens of many other developed nations, particularly Europeans, people in the United States and Australia exhibit fairly low levels of concern about climate change as a threat and a greater ambivalence about climate change science.[5] In the United States, for example, although 63 percent of participants in a 2013 poll thought climate change was real, less than 50 percent of them believed that it is caused by humans and viewed it as a cause for concern.[6] Gallup's 2014 poll measuring how much people in the United States worry about climate change compared with other environmental problems found that only 34 percent worried "a great deal," essentially the same number as in 1989.[7] In addition to seeing climate change as a lower priority threat than other environmental issues like pollution of drinking water, people in the United States tend to view climate change as something threatening to "others" and as having impacts that happen "away" rather than affecting them "at home."[8]

In contrast to their US counterparts, Australians are more likely to believe that climate change is happening (more than 80 percent in agreement) and to see human activity as a significant contributing cause.[9] Moreover, a greater occurrence of extreme weather events in Australia seems to have prompted concern about local climate change effects. Even so, this has not translated directly into environmental concerns rising up the hierarchy of the *general* concerns of the Australian public. In recent

---

[5] Irene Lorenzoni and Nick F. Pidgeon, "Public Views on Climate Change: European and USA Perspectives" (2006) 77 *Clim. Change* 73.

[6] Anthony Leiserowitz et al., *Climate Change in the American Mind: Americans" Global Warming Beliefs and Attitudes in November 2013* (2014, Yale Project on Climate Change Communication and George Mason University Center for Climate Change Communication, New Haven, CT), available at www.environment.yale.edu/climate-communication/files/Climate-Beliefs-November-2013.pdf. See also Julie Ray and Anita Pugliese, "Worldwide, Blame for Climate Change Falls on Humans: Americans among Least Likely to Attribute to Human Causes," Gallup, 22 April 2011; Allison Kopicki, "Is Global Warming Real? Most Americans Say Yes," *New York Times*, June 1, 2014, The Upshot. How the poll question is phrased can be influential; for example, people in the United States tend to see "global warming" as more of a concern (because of the association with extreme weather events) than "climate change" (which suggests more climate variability): see Allison Kopicki, "Americans More Worried about 'Warming' Than 'Climate Change,'" *New York Times*, May 29, 2014, at www.nytimes.com/2014/05/30/upshot/climate-change-or-global-warming-tough-choice-for-pollsters.html?emc=edit_tnt_20140529&nlid=52930963&tntemail0=y&_r=0.

[7] www.gallup.com/poll/168236/americans-show-low-levels-concern-global-warming.aspx.

[8] Cass R. Sunstein, "On the Divergent American Reactions to Terrorism and Climate Change" (2007) 107 *Columbia L. Rev.* 503.

[9] Zoe Leviston et al., *Fourth Annual Survey of Australian Attitudes to Climate Change: Interim Report*, January 2014 (CSIRO, Canberra), available at www.csiro.au/Outcomes/Climate/Adapting/Annual-Survey-of-Australian-Attitudes-to-Climate-Change.aspx.

surveys, Australians consistently rank climate change as lower in importance than other general concerns, including the economy and other environmental issues.[10]

Strong political divides over the existence of, and appropriate responses to, human-induced climate change appear to have been an influential factor in shaping public attitudes to climate change in both countries. During US President George W. Bush's administration, the executive branch often opposed climate change mitigation policies, with industry lobbying efforts allegedly being highly influential in shaping the administration's position on the issue.[11] There were also several reports of political pressure being placed on agency scientists to suppress discussion of climate change.[12] However, the Bush administration's approach was not the only one pursued by US governmental entities during that period. Many politicians at federal, state, and local levels pushed back against the Bush administration, which is part of what led to multimedia efforts like those surrounding Al Gore's *Inconvenient Truth* and to influential cases such as *Massachusetts v. EPA*. That case, for example, was decided in the same year – 2007 – as Al Gore and the Intergovernmental Panel on Climate Change (IPCC) won the Nobel Peace Prize.[13]

Moreover, Bush administration political attitudes toward climate change were somewhat at odds with broader public attitudes at this time, which exhibited a general willingness to engage in some level of climate change mitigation despite continuing questions over the degree of scientific uncertainty regarding climate change.[14] Gallup recorded its highest

---

[10] Ibid. Respondents ranked climate change as the fourteenth most important concern among sixteen general concerns, and seventh out of eight environmental concerns.

[11] John Vidal, "Revealed: How Oil Giant Influenced Bush," *The Guardian*, June 8, 2005, at www.theguardian.com/news/2005/jun/08/usnews.climatechange; Tim Dickinson, "Six Years of Deceit Inside the Bush Administration's Secret Campaign to Deny Global Warming and Let Polluters Shape America's Climate Policy," *Rolling Stone*, June 28, 2007, at www.rollingstone.com/politics/news/six-years-of-deceit-20070628.

[12] See, e.g., "Written Testimony of Francesca T. Grifo, Ph.D. Senior Scientist with the Union of Concerned Scientists Scientific Integrity Program Before the Committee on Oversight and Government Reform U.S. House of Representatives," www.ucsusa.org/assets/documents/scientific_integrity/ftg-written-testimony.pdf. See also Holly Doremus, "Science Plays Defense: Natural Resource Management in the Bush Administration" (2005) 32 *Ecol. L. Q.* 249.

[13] The Nobel Peace Prize 2007, at http://nobelprize.org/nobel_prizes/peace/laureates/2007/.

[14] *Americans on Climate Change: 2005 Questionnaire*, Program of International Public Attitudes Poll, at www.pipa.org/OnlineReports/ClimateChange/ClimateChange05_Jul05/ClimateChange05_Jul05_quaire.pdf. See also Matthew C. Nisbet and Teresa Myers, "Twenty Years of Public Opinion about Global Warming" (2007) 71 *Public Opinion*

levels of public concern about climate change in March 2007 (41 percent worrying "a great deal').[15] Nonetheless, the US public often appeared to believe that climate change was more likely to affect people who were geographically "distant."[16] This depersonalization of climate change as a problem may help to explain how the public generally perceived climate change as a real and present issue but one that sat at the lower end of public issues, particularly when compared to personal and social issues, such as the economy.[17]

With the election of President Obama in 2008, political attitudes to climate change initially shifted in favor of action,[18] corresponding with increased public belief in the need for, and acceptance of, climate mitigation policies.[19] However, the failure to pass emissions reduction legislation through the US Congress, coupled with the 2009 Copenhagen summit's weak outcomes for international action on climate change, led to a considerable cooling of the administration's public ardor for addressing climate change's "urgent dangers."[20] During 2011 and 2012, the phrase "climate

Q. 444, at http://climateshiftproject.org/wp-content/uploads/2013/01/NisbetMyers2007_20yrsGWOpinion_POQ.pdf; W. Kip Viscusi and Richard J. Zeckhauser, "The Perception and Valuation of Risks of Climate Change: A Rational and Behavioural Blend," Harvard Law School, John M. Olin Center for Law, Economics and Business, Discussion Paper Series (2005), 2.

[15] Frank Newport, "Americans Show Low Levels of Concern on Global Warming," *Climate Change: Americans' Views in 2014*, April 4, 2014, Gallup Politics, at www.gallup.com/poll/168236/americans-show-low-levels-concern-global-warming.aspx.

[16] Anthony A. Leiserowitz, "American Risk Perceptions: Is Climate Change Dangerous?" (2005) 25(6) *Risk Anal.* 1433.

[17] Lorenzoni and Pidgeon, "Public Views on Climate Change," 86–87. See also Jan C. Semenza et al., "Public Perception of Climate Change: Voluntary Mitigation and Barriers to Behavior Change" (2008) 35 *Am. J. Preventative Med.* 479.

[18] "Obama's Speech on Climate Change," *New York Times*, September 22, 2009, at www.nytimes.com/2009/09/23/us/politics/23obama.text.html?pagewanted=all&_r=0; Suzanne Goldenberg, "Barack Obama Pleads with Congress to Pass Historic Climate Change Bill," *The Guardian*, June 25, 2009, at www.theguardian.com/environment/2009/jun/25/barack-obama-climate-change-bill; "Obama Announces Climate Change Deal with China, Other Nations," December 19, 2009, at http://edition.cnn.com/2009/POLITICS/12/18/obama.copenhagen/.

[19] Brett W. Pelham, Awareness, "Opinions about Global Warming Vary Worldwide: Many Unaware, Do Not Necessarily Blame Human Activities," Gallup, April 22, 2009, www.gallup.com/poll/117772/awareness-opinions-global-warming-vary-worldwide.aspx; Anita Pugliese and Julie Ray, "Awareness of Climate Change and Threat Vary by Region: Adults in Americas, Europe Most Likely to Be Aware, Perceive Threat," Gallup, December 11, 2009, www.gallup.com/poll/124652/awareness-climate-change-threat-vary-region.aspx.

[20] Richard J. Lazarus, "Presidential Combat Against Climate Change" (2013) 126 *Harv. L. Rev. F.* 152.

change" was barely uttered by the president. According to Richard Lazarus, it was as if "climate change had become the political equivalent of Harry Potter's Lord Voldemort: the crisis that dared not be named."[21]

When Superstorm Sandy hit the East Coast in late 2012, political and public attitudes to climate change in the United States shifted once more. The Obama administration has since taken a "do whatever it takes" attitude to addressing climate change during the president's second term, using executive powers to advance mitigation and adaptation regulation in the face of congressional intransigence on the issue.[22] Over this time, successive polls of the US public have showed gradually increasing levels of public concern about climate change.[23] There also appears to be growing support among the US public for mitigation measures to reduce carbon emissions, even if such measures would add to energy costs.[24] Nevertheless, President Obama is generally viewed as being further out in front on this issue than either the public or other parts of the political machine.[25]

In Australia, the ten-year period of the government of Prime Minister John Howard saw the emergence of a very similar political stance on climate change to that of the Bush administration, particularly from 2001 onward. Like President Bush's administration, the Howard government rejected the Kyoto Protocol and resisted the introduction of domestic mitigation measures, under heavy lobbying from the coal mining industry.[26] This approach generated similar public and political dissent to that seen

---

[21] Lazarus, "Presidential Combat," at http://harvardlawreview.org/2013/03/presidential-combat-against-climate-change/.

[22] For discussion of the administration's actions in this regard, see Chapters 3 and 4.

[23] Frank Newport, "Americans' Worries About Global Warming Up Slightly," Gallup, March 30, 2012, at www.gallup.com/poll/153653/americans-worries-global-warming-slightly.aspx; Lydia Saad, "Americans' Concerns About Global Warming on the Rise," Gallup, April 8, 2013, at www.gallup.com/poll/161645/americans-concerns-global-warming-rise.aspx; Lydia Saad, "Republican Skepticism toward Global Warming Eases," Gallup, April 9, 2013, at www.gallup.com/poll/161714/republican-skepticism-global-warming-eases.aspx.

[24] Lisa Lerer, "Americans by 2 to 1 Would Pay More to Curb Climate Change," *Bloomberg News*, June 11, 2014.

[25] Bruce Stokes, "Obama Ahead of U.S. Public on Climate Change," Pew Research Center, June 26, 2013, at www.pewglobal.org/2013/06/26/obama-ahead-of-u-s-public-on-climate-change/; and "Climate Change: Key Data Points from Pew Research," www.pewresearch.org/key-data-points/climate-change-key-data-points-from-pew-research/.

[26] Guy Pearse, *High and Dry: John Howard, Climate Change and the Selling of Australia's Future* (2007, Penguin, Camberwell).

in the United States, with the Labor state governments of the day pursuing proactive climate policies and working toward an interstate emissions trading scheme.[27] Dissatisfaction with the Howard government's approach to climate change and an increasing public belief in the need for action – bolstered, as in the United States, by the *Inconvenient Truth* film and the IPCC's *Fourth Assessment Report* – contributed to the victory of Kevin Rudd and the Labor Party at the 2007 federal election.

Paralleling developments in the United States, the year 2007 was a particularly high point for Australian public awareness and concern regarding climate change.[28] However, over the next four years, there was a general shift "down" in the Australian public's attitude toward the threat of climate change.[29] As in the United States, the failure of the Rudd government to pass emissions reduction legislation (the predecessor of the eventual carbon pricing mechanism)[30] and uncertainty over the nature of international action in the wake of the Copenhagen summit were apparently contributing factors.[31] Having come to power declaring climate change to be "the greatest moral challenge of our time," Prime Minister Rudd's failure to pass emissions trading legislation shredded his popularity and led to his dramatic replacement by Julia Gillard just months before the 2010 federal election.[32] During the election campaign, Prime Minister Gillard

---

[27] For discussion of state initiatives and the proposed interstate emissions trading scheme (which was shelved when Kevin Rudd was elected prime minister), see Alexander Zahar, Jacqueline Peel, and Lee Godden, *Australian Climate Law in Global Context* (2013, Cambridge University Press, Melbourne), 151–57.

[28] The Climate Institute, *Climate of the Nation: Australians attitudes to climate change and its solutions* (March 2007), at www.climateinstitute.org.au/verve/_resources/climatenation_2007.pdf; Natalie Collins, "What Do Australians Say about Climate Change?," Policy and Governance Discussion Paper 09-01 (2009, Crawford School of Economics and Government, Australian National University, Canberra), at https://crawford.anu.edu.au/degrees/pogo/discussion_papers/PDP09–01.pdf.

[29] Anita Pugliese and Linda Lyons, "Australians' Views Shift on Climate Change," Gallup, August 6, 2010, www.gallup.com/poll/141782/australians-views-shift-climate-change.aspx.

[30] This was the Carbon Pollution Reduction Scheme legislation that was blocked in the Senate in 2009 and 2010.

[31] Australians support for tackling climate change decreased over the period of the Rudd government from a high of 75 percent in 2007 to just 46 percent support in 2011. Fergus Hanson, "The 2011 Lowy Institute Poll," June 20, 2011, at www.lowyinstitute.org/publications/2011-lowy-institute-poll.

[32] Miranda Devine, "Greatest Moral Challenge Turns Out to Be Rudd's Dearest Folly," *Sydney Morning Herald*, April 29, 2010, at www.smh.com.au/federal-politics/political-opinion/greatest-moral-challenge-turns-out-to-be-rudds-dearest-folly-20100428-tscw.html.

insisted that there would be no carbon tax introduced by any government she led. However, following her narrow win at the election, she was only able to form government through a coalition with the Australian Greens Party and independents. As part of this process, the Gillard government committed to establishing a new national carbon policy.[33]

The proposed carbon pricing mechanism that eventually emerged from negotiations between the Gillard government and the Greens (see, further, Chapter 3) proved highly unpopular with the electorate. A very effective campaign conducted by then opposition leader Tony Abbott against Prime Minister Gillard's "broken promise" not to introduce a carbon tax was an important contributing factor in this shift. Although many Australians continued to believe that climate change was real, a declining number of them saw this change as being a result of human activity.[34] A strong correlation also emerged between political preference and belief in and attitudes toward climate change.[35] For instance, a Morgan telephone poll conducted in July 2011 (when the Clean Energy Act was being debated in the federal parliament) found that 37 percent of respondents asked for their view of global warming believed "concerns are exaggerated," and 58 percent opposed the proposed carbon pricing mechanism.[36]

In the September 2013 election, Tony Abbott took the Australian prime ministership, with the promise to "axe the carbon tax" forming a central plank of the Coalition Party's campaign. The Abbott government has since implemented the government's plans to repeal the Clean Energy Act and to dismantle other parts of the climate change/clean energy bureaucracy, including agencies focused on providing climate information to the public such as the Climate Commission.[37] The attitude of the federal government and conservative state governments around the country (which

[33] Alison Rourke, "Australian PM Julia Gillard Signs Pact with Greens," *The Guardian*, September 1, 2010, www.theguardian.com/world/2010/sep/01/julia-gillard-australia-greens-deal.

[34] Zoe Leviston et al., *Australians' Views of Climate Change* (2011), CSIRO Report, at www.garnautreview.org.au/update-2011/commissioned-work/australians-view-of-climate-change.pdf.

[35] Ibid.

[36] Roy Morgan Research, "Only 37% of Australians Support the Gillard Government's Carbon Tax While Clear Majority (58% – Up 5%) Do Not," July 15, 2011, at www.roymorgan.com/findings/finding-4686-201302150110.

[37] Tom Arup, "Abbott Shuts Down Climate Commission," *Sydney Morning Herald*, September 19, 2013, at www.smh.com.au/federal-politics/political-news/abbott-shuts-down-climate-commission-20130919-2u185.html.

hold power in four of Australia's six states) seems to be one of strong skepticism with respect to the human contribution to climate change.[38] Specific climate measures are either being repealed or placed under review,[39] and general environmental controls are being wound back on the premise that they place undue regulatory burdens on business.[40] The federal government has also signaled less enthusiasm for action on adaptation.[41] Despite raging bushfires around Sydney, drought in Queensland, and heat waves in the southeast during the summer of 2013–14, Prime Minister Tony Abbott made numerous statements denying any link between such events and climate change.[42] The Abbott government's adverse political stance on climate change ironically appears to be bolstering previously flagging public attitudes toward the issue. For instance, the Climate of the Nation poll conducted by JWS Research in June 2014 found that 70 percent of respondents supported the mainstream science regarding climate change (up by 10 percent from 2012)

[38] See, e.g., Rick Feneley, "Abbott's Warriors Place Their Trust in an Ancient Virtue," *Sydney Morning Herald*, December 12, 2009, at www.smh.com.au/environment/climate-change/abbotts-warriors-place-their-trust-in-an-ancient-virtue-20091211-kokj.html; Lenore Taylor, "Climate Sceptic to Lead Review of Australia's Renewable Energy Target," *The Guardian*, February 17, 2014.

[39] Besides the now-repealed carbon tax, the list of measures slated for repeal at the federal level includes the Clean Energy Finance Corporation (CEFC), the Australian Renewable Energy Agency (ARENA), and the Energy Efficiency Opportunities Act. The Renewable Energy Target is currently undergoing review with the expectation that recommendations will be made to remove or scale back this program. Ongoing negotiations with parties that hold the balance of power in the Senate may see certain clean energy measures – such as the Renewable Energy Target, ARENA, and the CEFC – saved. The Abbott government's alternative climate policy, known as "Direct Action," has been widely criticized by economists and others for its vagueness and potential to cost significantly more than a carbon price to reduce greenhouse gas emissions by the same amount.

[40] For instance, the federal government is also proposing reforms to the Environment Protection and Biodiversity Conservation Act that would see federal decision-making powers under the act delegated to state governments.

[41] That said, the Abbott government has restated funding for the National Climate Change Adaptation Research Facility after it was cut by the previous government.

[42] See, e.g., Rod McGuirk, "Australia PM Tony Abbott: Climate Change-Wildfire Connection Is 'Complete Hogwash,'" *Huffington Post*, October 25, 2013, at www.huffingtonpost.com/2013/10/25/tony-abbott-climate-change-wildfire_n_4162828.html; Judith Ireland, "UN Official 'Talking through Her Hat' on Bushfires and Climate Change, Says Tony Abbott," *Sydney Morning Herald*, October 23, 2013, at www.smh.com.au/federal-politics/political-news/un-official-talking-through-her-hat-on-bushfires-and-climate-change-says-tony-abbott-20131023-2w0mz.html.

and 85 percent said the effects of climate change were already evident in Australia.[43]

Although their influence in the public sphere has varied over time, skeptical views of climate change and the role of human activities as a cause have received a significant boost in Australia and the United States from politically conservative sections of the media, even as more liberal media outlets continue to portray climate change as a growing crisis. For example, the prominent media company News Corp – owned by Australian entrepreneur Rupert Murdoch – has consistently conveyed a negative stance on climate change action at the domestic and international levels through the outlets it controls. In the United States, these outlets include Fox News and the *Wall Street Journal*, both known for their extensive coverage of climate change science as suspect and of regulatory efforts as misguided.[44] In Australia, the Murdoch-controlled media includes *The Australian* newspaper and numerous other state-based and local newspaper publications. These newspapers have spearheaded attacks on climate change science and government and NGO efforts to address climate change.[45] Negative press coverage of climate change in the United States and Australia appears to be feeding into public opinion. For

---

[43] Oliver Millman, "Australians Unhappy over Coalition's Response to Climate Change," *The Guardian*, June 22, 2014, at www.theguardian.com/environment/2014/jun/22/australian-unhappy-coalitions-response-climate.

[44] See, e.g., Chris Mooney, "CHARTS: Nearly 70 Percent of Fox Climate Pundits Doubt Global Warming," *Mother Jones*, October 10, 2013, at www.motherjones.com/bluemarble/2013/10/climate-denial-fox-media-matters; Richard McNider and John Christy, "Why Kerry Is Flat Wrong on Climate Change," *Wall Street Journal*, February 19, 2014, at http://online.wsj.com/news/articles/SB10001424052702303945704579391611041331266.

[45] See, e.g., Andrew Bolt, "Fighting the Global Warming Religion," *Herald Sun*, November 1, 2013, at http://blogs.news.com.au/heraldsun/andrewbolt/index.php/heraldsun/comments/fighting_the_global_warming_religion/; David Holmes, "Scientists Confess? The Attack on the IPCC That Went Terribly Wrong," *The Conversation*, September 22, 2013, at http://theconversation.com/scientists-confess-the-attack-on-the-ipcc-that-went-terribly-wrong-18496 (discussing allegations of *The Australian* newspaper against the 2012 IPCC report); Graham Lloyd, "Doubts over IPCC's Global Warming Rates," *The Australian*, September 16, 2013, at www.theaustralian.com.au/news/health-science/we-got-it-wrong-on-warming-says-ipcc/comments-e6frg8y6–1226719672318; Oliver Milman, "One Third of Australia's Media Coverage Rejects Climate Science, Study Finds," *The Guardian*, October 30, 2013, at www.theguardian.com/environment/2013/oct/30/one-third-of-australias-media-coverage-rejects-climate-science-study-finds; Wendy Bacon, *Sceptical Climate Part 2: Climate Science in Australian Newspapers*, October 2013, Australian Centre for Independent Journalism, http://sceptical-climate.investigate.org.au/part-2/.

example, a study in the United States found that the more time people spend consuming conservative media, the more skeptical they become of climate change science and the less certainty they have that climate change is happening.[46]

6.2.2 Role of litigation in shaping public perceptions of climate change

In this contentious sociopolitical environment that often constrains regulatory action on climate change, pro-regulatory climate change litigation has played a variety of roles in seeking to shape public views on the issue. This section explores the ways in which it has raised public and political awareness, bolstered grassroots climate change campaigns, and helped make climate change more relatable in both countries.

During the years of the Bush administration in the United States and the Howard government in Australia, a major concern of environmental groups was to get some public acknowledgment and acceptance of climate change by political leaders and government institutions. In the United States, important early cases in this vein included not only the most high-profile case, *Massachusetts v. EPA*, but also *Center for Biological Diversity v. Brennan* (seeking the Bush administration's release of a suppressed scientific assessment of climate change required under the Global Change Research Act 1990),[47] the lower court decisions in *AEP v. Connecticut* and other public nuisance cases,[48] the first round of cases brought under the Endangered Species Act seeking listing for species threatened by climate change, *Friends of the Earth v. Spinelli* (challenging the failure of the Overseas Private Investment Corporation and the Export-Import Bank of the United States to produce environmental impact assessments addressing the substantial greenhouse emissions of overseas projects they approved),[49] and, at a larger scale, the Inuits' petition to the Inter-American Commission on Human Rights (claiming that the US failure to take sufficient steps to mitigate climate change violated

---

[46] Jay D. Hmielowski et al., "An Attack on Science? Media Use, Trust in Scientists, and Perceptions of Global Warming," *Public Understanding of Science*, published online April 3, 2013, doi:10.1177/0963662513480091.

[47] 571 F.Supp.2d 1105 (N.D. Cal. 2007).

[48] The 2005 district court opinion in *AEP v. Connecticut*, for example, describes these political dynamics in detail as part of its discussion of the political question doctrine. *Connecticut v. AEP*, 406 F. Supp. 2d. 265 (S.D.N.Y. 2005) (overruled by *AEP v. Connecticut*, 131 S. Ct. 2527, 2539 (2011)).

[49] See Brendan R. Cummings and Kassie R. Siegel, "Biodiversity, Global Warming, and the United States Endangered Species Act: The Role of Domestic Wildlife Law in Addressing

their human rights).[50] Interviewees described these kinds of cases as "critical" in helping to force the US government "to accept and acknowledge and treat climate change as something they could not ignore... even if [the cases] didn't directly lead to greenhouse reductions, they shifted – helped shift – agency culture to be climate-informed."[51]

The results of similar profile-raising litigation efforts in Australia over this same period had more mixed results. For example, while the Hazelwood decision in Victoria and the Anvil Hill case in New South Wales saw important acknowledgments by the courts of the need to take climate change into account in environmental assessment of greenhouse gas–intensive projects,[52] challenges at the federal level, such as the Wildlife Whitsunday case, tended to reinforce hostile political attitudes to domestic climate change action. In the Wildlife Whitsunday case – which argued for greenhouse gas emissions and the impacts of climate change on the Great Barrier Reef to be included in assessments of new coal mine proposals – Justice Dowsett of the Federal Court concluded his judgment dismissing the applicant's case against the mines with the comment that the challenge was "really based upon the assertion that greenhouse gas emission is bad, and that the Australian government should do whatever it can to stop it including, one assumes, banning new coal mines in Australia."[53]

However, though the Wildlife Whitsunday case certainly did not achieve the outcomes hoped for by the applicants,[54] it did contribute to efforts by NGOs to raise the public profile of environmental damage to the Great Barrier Reef and the contribution of indirect coal emissions and climate change to that harm. These efforts have gathered momentum in the last few years, with greater public attention and opposition to mining-related development along the Queensland coastline adjacent to the reef[55] and heightened international scrutiny of Australia's actions to

Greenhouse Gas Emissions" in William C. G. Burns and Hari M. Osofsky (eds.), *Adjudicating Climate Change: State, National, and International Approaches* (2009, Cambridge University Press, New York), 145.

[50] Hari M. Osofsky, "The Inuit Petition as a Bridge? Beyond Dialectics of Climate Change and Indigenous Peoples' Rights" (2007) 31(2) *Am. Ind. L. Rev.* 675.

[51] Telephone interview, US Participant 12 (Dec. 2, 2013). See also in-person interview, US Participant 2 (Oct. 22, 2012).

[52] See the discussion of these cases in Chapter 3.

[53] *Wildlife Preservation Society of Queensland Prosperine/Whitsunday Branch Inc v. Minister for Environment and Heritage* (2006) 232 ALR 510, 524.

[54] Skype interview, Australian Participant 4 (Mar. 20, 2013).

[55] See, e.g., Senate Environment and Communications Legislation Committee, Inquiry into the Environment Protection and Biodiversity Conservation Amendment (Great Barrier

protect this World Heritage listed area.[56] In an illustration of how shifting social norms and corporate attitudes to climate change can combine, two of the world's largest banks – HSBC and Deutsche Bank – announced that they will not provide finance for coal export terminals near the reef, which put this ecosystem in danger.[57]

Although interviewees cited raising awareness as a significant outcome of the first wave of climate litigation, they generally acknowledged that the attention garnered by these cases was, in most instances, inadequate to stimulate meaningful regulatory action. One interviewee described it as "an Alcoholics Anonymous kind of thing – the early battle was to get them to admit there was a problem. Now they all admit that there is a problem but they're still not doing anything about it."[58] The major exception to this rule was *Massachusetts v. EPA*, which not only had substantial direct regulatory impacts but also greatly influenced public perceptions of climate change. Interviewees variously described this case as "a game-changer,"[59] the "bedrock" of US climate law,[60] and "the foundation of everything" that has been done in the climate regulatory space.[61] The case is also well known in Australia.[62]

One of *Massachusetts v. EPA*'s principal contributions has been to change the nature of the public debate so that a profession of climate change skepticism is often treated as a political choice rather than as an objective dispute with the science of climate change. These effects have flowed, at least in part, from the respect and deference accorded to courts, particularly the Supreme Court:

> In this country, as much as we sometimes ridicule and complain about them, we do tend to have high regard for courts, especially federal courts and most especially the Supreme Court, notwithstanding all the hits that

Reef) Bill 2013, Australian Government, Canberra, June 2013, para. 3.120, recommendation 1. See also the new cases brought by the Mackay Conservation Group and NQCC over the Abbot Point coal terminal expansion discussed in Chapter 3.

[56] In 2015 the World Heritage Committee will consider whether the Reef should be placed on the list of world heritage "in danger." See, further, Chapter 3.

[57] Ellen Fanning, "Global Financial Campaign against Abbot Point Gains Momentum," *ABC News, Radio National*, May 26, 2014, at www.abc.net.au/radionational/programs/breakfast/global-financial-campaign-against-abbot-point-gains-momentum/5476816.

[58] Telephone interview, US Participant 12 (Dec. 2, 2013).

[59] In-person interview, US Participant 4 (Nov. 14, 2012).

[60] Telephone interview, US Participant 5 (Nov. 14, 2012).

[61] Telephone interview, US Participant 7 (Nov. 16, 2012).

[62] For instance, the case was cited by Justice Biscoe in *Walker v. Minister for Planning* as authority for the proposition that there is scientific support for a link between a rise in global temperatures and an increase in the atmospheric concentration of greenhouse gases resulting from human activities.

it has taken, from right and left. And there is this degree to which having court decisions that take this problem seriously really is a . . . it causes everybody to perk up and take notice. So, at least in the deliberations and corporate boardrooms, they say we can't completely dismiss this anymore and when it's something like *Massachusetts v. EPA* that not only constituted an affirmation of the seriousness of the science but it also said that this entire, elaborate regulatory apparatus that we have in the Clean Air Act, at least the threshold requirements for applicability are met.[63]

Alongside highlighting *Massachusetts v. EPA*, several interviewees identified tort cases brought in the United States against corporate emitters as having played an important role in influencing public perceptions of the climate change problem. These cases have not been a success in legal terms, but the litigation is seen to have "moved forward on having companies and others have to confront these issues."[64]

Australian cases generally have not had as high a public profile as some of the cases in the United States. However, particular decisions of the New South Wales (NSW) Land and Environment Court, such as those in the Anvil Hill and Warkworth mine cases, have attracted significant media and publicity[65] and were also identified by interviewees as cases "that really resonate in the minds of politicians and ultimately will resonate in the minds of business leaders."[66]

While high-profile cases, especially in the US Supreme Court, have tended to have the most significant national impact on the public debate over climate change, lower-profile cases have also been important both at a smaller, more localized scale and at a larger scale through their aggregate impact in the two countries. At a grassroots level, several interviewees spoke of the important role litigation can play in galvanizing a campaign by providing "an event that the community can organize and rally around, focus on and use as a basis for fundraising."[67] A number of successful campaigns have built community support for climate action from the ground up utilizing a mix of tools, but with litigation often serving as a

---

[63] Telephone interview, US Participant 8 (Nov. 26, 2012).

[64] In-person interview, US Participant 6 (Nov. 14, 2012).

[65] See, e.g., Sarah-Jane Tasker, "Workers Plead for Rio Extension to Keep Warkworth Mine Open," *The Australian*, June 1, 2013, at www.theaustralian.com.au/archive/business/workers-plead-for-rio-extension-to-keep-warkworth-mine-open/story-e6frg9e6–1226654812233; David Farrier, "The Limits of Judicial Review: Anvil Hill in the Land and Environment Court" in Tim Bonyhady and Peter Christoff (eds.), *Climate Law in Australia* (2007, Federation Press, Sydney), 189, 205.

[66] Skype interview, Australian Participant 8 (Apr. 24, 2013).

[67] In-person interview, Australian Participant 1 (Mar. 7, 2013).

focal point for local efforts. For example, the Sierra Club's Beyond Coal campaign, which has resulted in the retirement of numerous coal-fired power plants across the United States, involves a coordinated effort by Sierra Club chapters working together with local groups to publicize the environmental and health effects of coal combustion by various means (media, rallies, lobbying, etc.).[68] A key aspect of the campaign, however, has been the group's involvement in administrative hearings and other cases that arise whenever a targeted coal-fired plant seeks a modification or renewal of its operating permit or goes before a public service commission requesting a rates increase. Greenhouse gas emissions produced by coal is often raised as an issue in these cases and the broader public campaign of which they are part.[69]

Respondents from public interest organizations repeatedly emphasized that litigation alone is rarely effective as a tool for addressing climate change in the absence of a broader community campaign.[70] Others noted, though, that within a campaign, litigation may offer more benefits to a group in garnering public and media attention to their cause than other available strategies. As one interviewee put it, "if [environmental groups] drop a banner from the side of the bridge or something, it doesn't really have that same sort of effect."[71]

A final way that litigation has contributed to public perceptions of climate risk is in framing issues of causation and impacts in concrete ways that are readily understood by lay people and which resonate with their experience.[72] Studies around the public communication of climate science have repeatedly demonstrated that the lay public struggles to grasp many of the complexities of the scientific data and have difficulty relating to the rather abstract global-scale effects from climate change discussed

---

[68] Sierra Club, Beyond Coal, at http://content.sierraclub.org/coal/.

[69] Telephone interview, US Participant 1 (Oct. 20, 2012); Telephone interview, US Participant 13 (Dec. 9, 2013).

[70] In-person interview, Australian Participant 1 (Mar. 7, 2013); in-person interview, Australian Participant 3 (Mar. 8, 2013); in-person interview, US Participant 2 (Oct. 22, 2012); telephone interview, US Participant 11 (Oct. 10, 2013).

[71] In-person interview, Australian Participant 2 (Mar. 8, 2013).

[72] Elizabeth Fisher, "Climate Change Litigation, Obsession and Expertise: Reflecting on the Scholarly Response to *Massachusetts v. EPA*" (2013) 35(3) *L. Policy* 236. Frames are "interpretative storylines that set a specific train of thought in motion, communicating why an issue might be a problem, who or what might be responsible for it, and what should be done about it." Matthew C. Nisbet, "Communicating Climate Change: Why Frames Matter for Public Engagement" (2009) 51(2) *Environment* 12, 15.

in the scientific literature.[73] In a courtroom setting, however, there is the need to communicate information about climate change and its impacts in a way that fits with prevailing legal and social norms.

Some climate change litigation has done this very successfully. For instance, the litigation around the Endangered Species Act listing for the polar bear is credited with having "very much helped make the polar bear an icon for climate change, and made it understandable in a very simple way to millions of people."[74] Australian interviewees involved in litigation over scope 3 emissions from coal mining, such as the Wandoan and Alpha mine cases discussed further later in this chapter, related how the cases helped generate new ways of representing the climate impact of the mines' exported emissions that more effectively demonstrated the links between a particular project and global climate change effects. Speaking about *Xstrata Coal Qld v. Friends of the Earth Brisbane* (the Wandoan case), one interviewee commented,

> Running the case did create a lot of knowledge and networks that have helped community groups in other campaigns. Certainly, the knowledge that we gained we've also been using to help clients in their submissions to government on projects and in their negotiations with government. We're able to use particularly some of the stuff... which really had not been done before, the project-level stuff. So now they can point to those things and say it is having a measurable impact whether you take it into account or not.[75]

US cases raising the application of the public trust doctrine in the context of climate change are another category of cases that have presented a novel, and potentially very powerful, framing of the climate change problem. Although some courts have shown an initial receptiveness to this framing, these cases have thus far had a relatively limited direct regulatory effect.[76] However, they help to associate action on climate change in the public

---

[73] See, e.g., Nisbet, "Communicating Climate Change"; see also Nick Pidgeon and Baruch Fischhoff, "The Role of Social and Decision Sciences in Communicating Uncertain Climate Risks" (2011) 1 *Nat. Clim. Change* 35; Richard C. J. Somerville and Susan Joy Hassol, "Communicating the Science of Climate Change" (2011) *Phys. Today* 48.

[74] Telephone interview, US Participant 12 (Dec. 2, 2013).

[75] In-person interview, Australian Participant 2 (Mar. 8, 2013).

[76] E.g., *Svitak v. Washington*, No. 69710-2-I (Wash Ct. App. Dec. 16, 2013); *Bonser-Lain v. Texas Commission on Environmental Quality* (Dist. Ct. of Travis City, Tex. Aug. 2, 2012); *Sanders-Redd v. Martinez* 42 ELR 20159, No. D-101-CV-2011–01514, (D.N.M., 07/14/2012). The latter decision was overruled on appeal, *Sanders-Redd v. Martinez*, (D.N.M., Order on Summary Judgment, June 26, 2013). For full details of these lawsuits, see Arnold and Porter LLP, "U.S. Climate Change Litigation Chart" (Common Law Claims – Public Trust Doctrine Lawsuits).

mind with ideas of protecting shared community resources and acting responsibly in the interests of "our children and our children's children."[77]

The breadth of the climate change issue lends itself to multiple framings of what the public interest in addressing the problem might be. Litigation efforts by different pro-regulatory groups offer varying visions of the public interest served through climate change action that may be complementary, but also potentially come into conflict. In the United States, for example, groups advocating for environmental justice for low-income communities and communities of color have sometimes found themselves opposing mainstream environmental groups in court when arguing for greater attention to the burdens placed on communities by polluting facilities in their neighborhood.[78] Through the cases they have chosen to bring, environmental justice groups have also tried to draw greater attention to the impacts of climate change on already-vulnerable communities, an issue that they feel is often neglected by the major environmental organizations.[79] According to one interviewee,

> The sooner that the broader environmental movement starts to realize that people of color are becoming a significant part of the electorate and the sooner that they realize that global warming is much more than the plight of polar bears and other animals or just some abstract warming of the planet or ocean acidification. The sooner that they come to Jesus and realize that the people are being harmed right now and will be increasingly harmed, that's a much better way to advocate for climate change policy than arguing for protections for the polar bear. So if Leonardo Dicaprio wanted to be a bigger player on global warming he should step up and advocate for people instead of polar bears.[80]

---

[77] In-person interview, Australian Participant 1 (Mar. 7, 2013).

[78] See, e.g., *Association of Irritated Residents v. California Air Resources Board*, 42 ELR 20127, No. A132165, (Cal. App. 1st Dist., 06/19/2012).

[79] The Sierra Club and Natural Resources Defense Council (NRDC) in the United States have major campaigns around climate change mitigation but only address adaptation as an aspect of other areas such as species conservation. An exception is the recent ConEd rate case (see Chapter 4), addressing disaster planning and power infrastructure resilience in New York, in which the NRDC and Environmental Defense Fund took part. Even so, the aspects of the settlement order these groups emphasized in subsequent media releases were its potential "to increase the flexibility of the energy system, while reducing its climate pollution impact" and recognition of "the important role of Consolidated Edison and other utilities in setting rates that encourage the smart charging of electric vehicles." "Con Edison to Take New Measures to Protect Against the Effects of Climate Change," Environmental Defense Fund, February 20, 2014, www.edf.org/media/con-edison-take-new-measures-protect-against-effects-climate-change.

[80] In-person interview, US Participant 10 (Jan. 14, 2013).

However, another interviewee described such "polar bear envy" as setting up an illusory competition between climate activists working on different aspects of the larger problem:

> So this sense of competitiveness with the polar bear rather than, you know, my experience is a significant chunk of the world loves polar bears and we shouldn't feel, climate activists more broadly, shouldn't feel competitive with polar bears, that polar bears are getting attention that rightly belongs in impoverished communities or low-lying Pacific Islands or you know all the literally hundreds of millions of people who are already suffering from climate change. There's this sense that polar bears are getting undue attention. And I think it's the opposite. I think it's we should be celebrating all the attention polar bears are getting because as much attention as we can get to climate change is a good thing. At the same time we shouldn't pretend that polar bears are the only thing threatened by climate change. And so whenever I talk about polar bears I always want to add on, if we do what's necessary to save the polar bear we also do what's necessary to avert the worst impacts of climate change for everyone else, for ourselves, and Florida, and future generations.[81]

These different viewpoints expressed by those deeply involved in the litigation reinforce the complexity of assessing the public interest in this context and gaining consensus on appropriate pro-regulatory action.

In Australia, different understandings of the climate issue are also beginning to emerge that are likely to play out in litigation. To date, all the Australian climate change litigation has been brought by mainstream NGOs, community groups, and activists; environmental protection and anticoal framings have been dominant in these efforts.[82] However, campaigns targeting investors, led by groups such as the Asset Owner's Disclosure Project and the Climate Institute, construct the need for climate action very differently. Taking more of "a greedy capitalist" approach, the focus is on protecting shareholder/member value by encouraging companies and investors to better disclose climate business risk and to avoid risky asset holdings.[83] This approach accords with broader trends in the development of public communication strategies on climate change that

---

[81] Telephone interview, US Participant 12 (Dec. 2, 2013).

[82] Leading Australian environmental groups such as the Australian Conservation Foundation, Greenpeace Australia Pacific and the Wilderness Society have a focus in their climate change activities on fossil fuels and clean energy.

[83] Skype interview, Australian Participant 12 (May 21, 2013).

are increasingly framed around such "personalized" messaging and could become the basis for future litigation.[84]

6.2.3 Partisan politics and regulatory responses to climate change litigation

As the preceding discussion illuminates, one way of viewing climate change litigation and its influences on public perceptions of the climate issue is as a court-mediated "dialogue between civil society and government."[85] As one interviewee described it, regardless of whether the litigation brings about direct legal change, "the litigation still has huge importance, I think, in the context that it maintains the public dialogue and debate, and puts political pressure on the administration to do more."[86] However, how legislators and agencies respond to that external pressure will be in part determined by those regulators' own policy stance with respect to change climate, which may itself be shaped by ever-shifting prevailing social norms.

This section describes the ways in which partisan politics shape the interacting influences of court decisions, public opinion, and regulatory attitudes on regulatory pathways. It traces how the iterative relationship between litigation and public opinion can provide political reinforcement to proactive regulators, put public pressure on reluctant ones, and reshape regulatory approaches.[87] As these examples illustrate, because of the complexities of partisan politics and entrenched viewpoints, litigation and the public reaction to it are not always enough to bolster a proactive regulator or force action by a reluctant one. Those who oppose regulation are unlikely to accept justifications based on litigation, and hostile regulators sometimes resist decisions requiring them to act. This section uses examples from the two countries to trace the complicated relationship among partisan politics, litigation, public opinion, and regulators.

---

[84] Heather Smith, "Want Everyone Else to Buy into Environmentalism? Never Say 'Earth,'" *Grist*, March 12, 2014, at http://grist.org/climate-energy/want-everyone-else-to-buy-into-environmentalism-never-say-earth/.

[85] Telephone interview, US Participant 12 (Dec. 2, 2013).   [86] Ibid.

[87] Adapted from Bradley C. Canon, "Studying Bureaucratic Implementation of Judicial Policies in the United States: Conceptual and Methodological Approaches" in Marc Hertogh and Simon Halliday (eds.), *Judicial Review and Bureaucratic Impact: International and Interdisciplinary Perspectives* (2004, Cambridge University Press, Cambridge), 76.

For regulators who are proactive in addressing climate change, litigation brought by industry or other challengers can often act as a restraint on regulatory initiatives or at least slow down the process of regulatory development, as we discuss further in the next chapter. On occasion, however, proactive regulators also use climate change cases as a justification for and legitimation of a policy approach the administration or agency wants to undertake, particularly when this course carries political risks due to the public debate over climate change.[88] Court decisions can confer legitimacy for action by allowing regulators to represent to the public that their actions are founded on a legal base and are mandated by the courts.[89] In effect, litigation can provide "cover" for regulators who are willing to act but feel concerned about the political consequences.

Regulators in both the United States and Australia at times have used litigation in this way, but the intense politics surrounding climate change in both countries have often made these efforts fraught. In the US context, for example, the Obama administration, despite failing to pass comprehensive climate change legislation,[90] proceeded with direct climate regulatory measures under the Clean Air Act by relying on the Supreme Court's *Massachusetts v. EPA* decision. When President Obama charged the secretary of transportation and administrator of the National Highway and Traffic Safety Administration with updating fuel economy standards – a charge that ultimately helped lead to the greenhouse gas motor vehicle regulations that the agency promulgated jointly with the EPA – he explicitly mentioned the case: "in adopting the final rules in paragraphs (a) and (b) above, you consider . . . the Supreme Court's decision in *Massachusetts v. EPA* and other relevant provisions of law and the policies underlying them."[91]

In the years since, politicians have debated the extent to which the Supreme Court decision mandated President Obama's action, with many Democrats claiming that he was required to act and Republicans saying

---

[88] Canon, "Studying Bureaucratic Implementation of Judicial Policies in the United States: Conceptual and Methodological Approaches," 80.

[89] Maurice Sunkin, "Conceptual Issues in Researching the Impact of Judicial Review on Government Bureaucracies" in Marc Hertogh and Simon Halliday (eds.), *Judicial Review and Bureaucratic Impact: International and Interdisciplinary Perspectives* (2004, Cambridge University Press, Cambridge), 43.

[90] American Clean Energy and Security Act of 2009, H.R. 2454.

[91] Memorandum from President Barack Obama to the Secretary of Transportation and the Administrator of the National Highway Traffic Safety Administration, (Jan. 26, 2009), available at http://www.whitehouse.gov/the_press_office/Presidential_Memorandum_fuel_economy/.

that he was not.[92] For instance, in the congressional context, Democratic senator Diane Feinstein claimed, "I believe EPA has to act under the Massachusetts case."[93] In contrast, Republican Senator John Barrasso, who authored the unsuccessful legislation trying to strip the EPA of its regulatory authority, stated, "The Supreme Court gave EPA permission to act, but it did not mandate it to act. I think EPA is overstepping what it should be doing in terms of impacting Americans' ability to compete globally."[94] While the opinion thus gave President Obama a way to justify his actions both legally and politically, those opposed to his proactive actions tried to undermine that use of the litigation.

Litigation has continued to interact with this political debate, most notably in the June 2014 Supreme Court decision in *Utility Air Regulatory Group v. EPA*, the US Supreme Court's third decision directly addressing climate change.[95] As described in depth in Chapter 3, the Court in this case partially upheld and partially struck down the EPA's approach to regulating greenhouse gas emissions from stationary sources under the Clean Air Act. In an opinion authored by Scalia, the Court used strong language to describe the EPA's overstepping of its authority with respect to the regulatory approach the Court deemed as neither mandated nor within EPA's discretion. For example, the opinion stated,

> [I]n EPA's assertion of that authority, we confront a singular situation: an agency laying claim to extravagant statutory power over the national economy while at the same time strenuously asserting that the authority claimed would render the statute "unrecognizable to the Congress that designed" it. Since, as we hold above, the statute does not compel EPA's interpretation, it would be patently unreasonable – not to say outrageous – for EPA to insist on seizing expansive power that it admits the statute is not designed to grant.[96]

Although the Court went on to uphold the EPA's other approach, which in practical terms allows the EPA to regulate the vast majority of stationary sources it was aiming to regulate, this language parallels that expressed by those in Congress opposing President Obama's approach.

---

[92] Lawrence Hurely and Elana Schor, "Congress Emits Half-Truths in Spin War Over *Mass. v. EPA*," *New York Times*, March 17, 2011, at www.nytimes.com/gwire/2011/03/17/17greenwire-congress-emits-half-truths-in-spin-war-over-im-12380.html?pagewanted=all.

[93] Hurely and Schor, "Congress Emits Half-Truths in Spin War Over *Mass. v. EPA*."

[94] Ibid.   [95] *Utility Air Regulatory Group v. EPA*, 134 S.Ct. 2427 (June 23, 2014).

[96] *Utility Air Regulatory Group v. EPA* at 2444 (citations omitted).

Moreover, the contentious partisan interchanges in Congress over proposed EPA regulation of power plant greenhouse gas emissions continued in the weeks following the opinion as part of the lead-up to the fall 2014 mid-term elections. Democratic Senator Barbara Boxer of California cited an ABC News poll indicating that 70 percent of the public supports limiting carbon emissions from power plants even if costs rise and stated, "This is what the American people want, and anyone who tries to undermine the president here is going against the will of the people."[97] Senator Boxer also connected debates over climate change science directly with electoral politics: "Right now, the first thing we have to do is make sure we have people who believe in science and not deniers elected to the Senate, whatever party they're in."[98] In response, Republican Senator Mitch McConnell of Kentucky described the EPA's comment process as a "sham listening session" while talking about President Obama's attack on coal.[99] Democratic Senator Chris Murphy of Connecticut, in contrast, spoke directly to the Republican portrayal of President Obama's regulation of coal, saying, "This is not a war on coal. This is a war on ignorance and negligence."[100] These exchanges through dueling press conferences in July 2014 – only one set of exchanges among many – reinforce the deeply divergent views of regulation pursuant to *Massachusetts v. EPA* that continue to dominate US dialogue and court decisions' limited ability to mediate these disputes.

In Australia, the path to national climate change regulation was equally contentious, with climate change dubbed the "killing fields" of federal politics given the number of leaders from both political parties who lost their jobs after either opposing or trying to advance policies to deal with the issue.[101] Although politicians have not attempted to use federal climate litigation to provide cover for regulatory action in the same way as President Obama did with the *Massachusetts v. EPA* decision in the United States, the cases have helped to foster public debate around the best ways to deal with climate change at the national level, which was needed at different times to allow pro-regulatory government efforts to move forward.

For instance, a 2009 government review of the Environment Protection Biodiversity Conservation Act – the principal federal environmental

---

[97] Edward Felker, "Lawmakers Take Partisan Swipes Over EPA Carbon Rule," *Energy Guardian*, July 30, 2014.

[98] Ibid.   [99] Ibid.   [100] Ibid.

[101] For discussion, see Jacqueline Peel, "The Australian Carbon Pricing Mechanism: Promise and Pitfalls on the Pathway to a Clean Energy Future" (2014) 15(1) *Minn. J. L. Sci. Technol.* 429.

law – gave extensive consideration to the question of whether the statute should cover greenhouse gas emissions in response to submissions that emphasized the gaps revealed in litigation such as the Wildlife Whitsunday case.[102] The review recommended that statutory reforms include a new environmental assessment requirement for projects emitting more than 500,000 tonnes of greenhouse gas emissions annually and encouraged "consideration of options to capture both direct and indirect emissions" to the extent possible.[103] As a national emissions trading scheme was under consideration by the Rudd government at the time, a greenhouse trigger was recommended as an interim measure only.[104] Although the Rudd government ultimately rejected the recommendation for an interim greenhouse trigger, the review report helped to strengthen the government's case that an emissions trading scheme was the best regulatory option for addressing industrial and stationary source emissions.[105]

While willing regulators may treat a climate change decision issued by the courts as legitimizing, justifying, or enabling regulatory action, a different reaction can be observed on the part of administrations that take a policy stance hostile to the idea of effective action to address climate change. Antiregulatory officials are likely to find judicial decisions in favor of climate regulation unwelcome and may seek to minimize compliance or forgo it altogether.[106] Although they cannot ignore direct edicts from courts to act where this is required by law, they can delay their response or choose courses of action that ultimately mute the impact of the court

---

[102] See particularly Hawke Review Interim Report, Comment 3: Mr. Matthew Dickie.

[103] A. Hawke et al., *The Australian Environment Act: Report of the Independent Review of the Environment Protection and Biodiversity Conservation Act 1999*, October 30, 2009 (Department of Environment, Australian Government), para. 4.102, p. 113. Ultimately, however, the review "did not support using the proposed trigger to capture coal exports because companies engaged in the mining of coal have limited capacity to reduce emissions produced overseas substantially." Hawke Review, para. 4.103, p. 113. The review also did not support other proposed solutions such as the use of offsets for offshore emissions.

[104] This legislation was for the Carbon Pollution Reduction Scheme (CPRS), which ultimately failed to secure Senate support. The government rejected the interim trigger recommendation on the basis that it expected to legislate and implement the CPRS. When that legislation failed to pass again in 2010, the trigger idea was not revived.

[105] Department of Sustainability, Environment, Water, Population and Communities, "Australian Government Response to the Report of the Independent Review of the Environment Protection and Biodiversity Conservation Act 1999," August 20, 2011, at www.environment.gov.au/legislation/environment-protection-and-biodiversity-conservation-act/epbc-review-2008.

[106] Canon, "Studying Bureaucratic Implementation of Judicial Policies in the United States: Conceptual and Methodological Approaches."

decision on government and societal behavior. Even so, court decisions in such circumstances can serve to highlight alternative views about the science and the appropriateness of regulation and provide a site for public activism and resistance to administration policy.

Under the administration of President George W. Bush, for example, the EPA was actively discouraged from taking action to address greenhouse gas emissions or supporting proactive regulatory action by states. The *Massachusetts v. EPA* case, as well as other litigation of this period, forced the Bush administration to articulate and expose to public scrutiny the reasons for its refusal to introduce national regulatory measures for climate change. The arguments put forward by the EPA in the *Massachusetts* case to justify its decision not to act included that regulating greenhouse gas emissions would be "unwise" in light of residual scientific uncertainty over the causal link between such emissions and climate change, that motor vehicle regulations would amount to a "piecemeal approach" to climate change in conflict with the president's "comprehensive" approach involving a range of nonregulatory measures, and that unilateral US regulation might jeopardize negotiations with key developing countries to reduce their greenhouse gas emissions.[107] The majority's dismissal of these policy concerns reinforced the alternative view that national regulation of greenhouse pollution was appropriate and authorized under federal law.

The Bush administration's regulatory response to this opinion was limited, despite public claims of compliance, reflecting its continued hostility to this federal regulatory approach. Only when the pro-regulatory Obama administration came in several months later did the EPA start significant consideration of the question of whether greenhouse gases endangered public health and welfare, as well as parallel reconsideration of the Bush administration's denial of California's request for a waiver under the Clean Air Act to regulate motor vehicle greenhouse gas emissions. As one interviewee pointed out, when the Supreme Court's judgment first came down, there was a divergence between "the career staff" at the EPA, who favored using the Clean Air Act to address greenhouse pollution, and "the political staff," who were Bush administration appointees, who had the opposite reaction, stressing the need for congressional rather than agency action.[108] Ultimately, it was only the alignment in the political and professional personnel brought about through the installation of the Obama administration that allowed EPA action to go ahead.[109]

---

[107] *Massachusetts v. EPA*, 549 U.S. 497 (2007), 498.
[108] Telephone interview, US Participant 9 (Dec. 3, 2012).   [109] Ibid.

In Australia, the hostile regulator response has been evident at both the federal and state levels over time. A recent illustration comes from the state of New South Wales, which was the setting for the Warkworth mine decision issued by Chief Justice Preston of the NSW Land and Environment Court. As discussed in Chapter 3, this case is one of only a handful of Australian court decisions that have refused coal mines. The Warkworth decision generated a swift and substantial antiregulatory backlash from the pro-mining NSW government, which is described further in the Chapter 7. However, the Warkworth litigation – in the Land and Environment Court and subsequently in the NSW Court of Appeal that upheld Chief Justice Preston's decision – has equally facilitated a prominent public discussion about the social and environmental impacts of coal mining and the extent to which they are justified by economic benefits such as local employment and revenue. It is this kind of discussion that will be necessary if social attitudes that have supported coal mining are to shift substantially in Australia.

The role of courts in fostering public debates over climate regulation looks set to become even more important in Australia as the country enters a new period of political hostility toward the issue of climate change at the federal level. Activists and lawyers bringing climate change cases in such circumstances recognize that the chances of proactive outcomes from the litigation are slim.[110] Rather, "it's very much the purpose of incrementally changing and, well, improving the law." In addition, as one public interest lawyer put it,

> I think that it's also important to "speak truth to power" and to be running these cases. . . . They [governments and coal mining companies] would much prefer it if we didn't raise these issues so they didn't have to address them and they could just slip it through quietly. . . . So I think it's important that they don't just get through scot-free without being challenged on these issues and forced to recognize them.[111]

Even in a hostile regulatory environment, then, climate change litigation can be a way of maintaining the climate issue in the public eye and on the political agenda. That may not lead to immediate, direct regulatory change but may be influential in other ways, including through

---

[110] Interviewees felt that governments were likely to ignore judicial recommendations to refuse permits or will simply legislate to reverse the effect of any court decision they do not like. Examples are considered further in the following chapter on anti-regulatory backlash against litigation.

[111] Skype interview, Australian Participant 4 (Mar. 20, 2013).

promoting NGO campaigns, swaying public opinion, and altering the choices of corporate actors.

Finally, as the previously discussed Wildlife Whitsunday case illustrates in the Australian context, court judgments can also shape the public debate around the best regulatory strategy a proactive regulator should employ in implementing a climate change mandate. In the United States, lawsuits brought by community groups on environmental justice grounds against the California Air Resources Board's Scoping Plan for AB32 and the cap-and-trade program further demonstrate this dynamic.[112] In *Association of Irritated Residents (AIR) v. CARB*, environmental justice advocates challenged the Scoping Plan alleging that it failed to minimize greenhouse gas emissions and protect vulnerable communities as required by AB32. The plaintiffs' concerns primarily related to the cap-and-trade program:

> [The] contention [was] that the Air Resources Board was engaging in a single-minded march towards cap-and-trade and had authority to initiate other policy options, besides cap-and-trade, to deal with carbon. And the environmental justice community in California is very united in its position that cap-and-trade is itself a discriminatory policy. That it has a disparate and adverse impact on communities of color.[113]

An initial judgment issued in the case by a California Supreme Court trial judge found violations of the California Environmental Quality Act and imposed an injunction preventing the Air Resources Board from implementing the Scoping Plan until it undertook an adequate environmental analysis.[114] According to one interviewee, this litigation

> change[d] the public debate about cap-and-trade in California. There was a lot of media coverage about [the] case. And so instead of the media being, oh cap-and-trade is great, it's going to reduce emissions, as the NRDC or EDF want to see, the stories were about low-income communities of color who made cap-and-trade an issue in the justice context.[115]

Subsequently, the Air Resources Board issued an environmental analysis to support the Scoping Plan, which was approved by the California Supreme Court, paving the way for implementation of the Scoping Plan

---

[112] See also *Citizens Climate Lobby v. California Air Resources Board*, 43 ELR 20024, No. CGC-12–5195544 (Cal. Super. Ct., Jan. 25, 2013).

[113] In-person interview, US Participant 10 (Jan. 14, 2013).

[114] *Ass'n of Irritated Residents v. Cal. Air Res. Bd.*, 206 Cal. App. 4th 1487, 1493 (2012).

[115] In-person interview, US Participant 10 (Jan. 14, 2013).

and associated measures such as the cap-and-trade program.[116] However, in response to the litigation, the agency also adopted an Adaptive Management Plan to accompany the cap-and-trade regulation. This latter plan encompasses a program of continuous monitoring and review of air quality impacts from the cap-and-trade regulation on low-income communities.[117] Although stakeholders have varying views regarding the value of this plan, the dynamics around this litigation illustrate the ways in which cases can create dialogue among those who may agree on the value of regulating climate change but disagree on methods.[118]

These partisan dynamics around climate change do not simply manifest in disputes over how regulators should respond to cases. Rather, the courtrooms in which these cases are litigated become important public stages for debates over the science and impacts of climate change. For example, pro- and antiregulatory claimants, and the judges adjudicating their claims, have repeatedly entered the public dialogue over climate change science. This role of courts in conveying different understandings of science and the associated need for regulation has been particularly important in both countries in cases involving questions of multilevel governance. Namely, litigants use arguments about the nature of climate change to make claims about the appropriate level of government at which to regulate it. The next section turns to these cases in more depth as examples of the multidimensional dynamics between litigation and social norms.

6.3 Courts as sites for public debates over science and regulatory scale

A major battleground in the public opinion war over climate change has concerned the validity of climate change science. Despite empirical assessments showing an overwhelming scientific consensus about the

---

[116] *Ass'n of Irritated Residents v. Cal. Air Res. Bd.*, 2011 WL 8897315 (Cal. Super. May 20, 2011).

[117] California Air Resources Board, "Adaptive Management," at www.arb.ca.gov/cc/capandtrade/adaptivemanagement/adaptivemanagement.htm.

[118] For discussion of the litigation, see Penni Takade, "*Association of Irritated Residents v. California Air Resources Board*: Climate Change and Environmental Justice" (2013) 40 *Ecol. L. Q.* 573. Not all view the ARB's program positively. U.S. interview participant 10 described the plan as "worth a cup of warm spit basically!" In-person interview, US Participant 10 (Jan. 14, 2013).

reality and causes of climate change,[119] political debate and media reporting in countries such as the United States and Australia have contributed to public impressions of scientific disagreement and uncertainty.[120] These debates about climate change science are not simply over its validity but also over the scale of the problem and appropriate regulatory solutions. Those opposed to action cast the contribution of local activities to climate change as a mere "drop in the ocean"[121] or alternatively argue that the climate problem is "too big" to be regulated at smaller scales, placing the onus on securing a global agreement in order to address the problem.[122] Proponents of regulation, conversely, stress evidence of local level impacts already occurring. This helps to "scale down" the problem in ways that make it amenable to taking regulatory steps at smaller scales.[123]

Courtrooms have served, and continue to serve, as a key public forum for these debates. They both influence and are influenced by the public dialogue over climate change science and regulation. On one hand, briefings, oral argument, and opinions can indirectly support greater regulation by affirming mainstream climate science and presenting scientific and scalar information on impacts in a way that is readily comprehended by lay judges and members of public. On the other hand, at times of greater public skepticism, courts may be more hesitant to make positive statements about climate change science, which in turn can reinforce public concerns. In the US context, the evolution of the Supreme Court's discussion of science is instructive.

---

[119] W. R. L. Anderegg, "Expert Credibility in Climate Change" (2010) 107(27) *Proc. Natl. Acad. Sci.* 12107; P. T. Doran and M. K. Zimmerman, "Examining the Scientific Consensus on Climate Change" (2009) 90(3) *Eos Trans. AGU* 22; N. Oreskes, "Beyond the Ivory Tower: The Scientific Consensus on Climate Change" 306(5702) *Science* 1686.

[120] Boykoff and Boykoff, "Balance as Bias."

[121] Jacqueline Peel, "Issues in Climate Change Litigation" (2011) 5(1) *Carbon Clim. L. Rev.* 15.

[122] For an example of this kind of "too big" argument, see Laurence H. Tribe, "Too Hot for Courts to Handle: Fuel Temperatures, Global Warming, and the Political Question Doctrine" (Washington Legal Foundation, 2010). As one interviewee summarized it, "if you work on climate, everywhere you turn [is] the notion that climate is a global problem. So from standing all the way up to the broadest political level of this is a challenge we face. And I don't think it's insurmountable. I mean we had cumulative impacts law develop very well because courts understood that that this is not an excuse to ignore a problem. It's an imperative to focus on it even more strongly because so many of our environmental problems are cumulative problems and climate change is the ultimate." In-person interview, US Participant 2 (Oct. 22, 2012).

[123] Hari Osofsky, "Diagonal Federalism and Climate Change: Implications for the Obama Administration" (2011) 62 *Alabama L. Rev.* 237.

In the following sections, we review prominent examples of the treatment of intersecting issues of science and regulatory scale in climate litigation from the two countries: (1) the US Supreme Court's decision in *Massachusetts v. EPA* and its subsequent climate change ruling in *AEP v. Connecticut* and (2) Australian cases considering the relevance of scope 3 emissions in environmental assessments of coal mines. These cases illustrate the ways in which courts can shape social norms regarding climate science and themselves be influenced by public opinion regarding science and the most appropriate regulatory responses. We conclude with observations regarding some of the differences between the US and Australian courts deciding these issues in climate cases that may affect the extent to which they can play a pro-regulatory role.

6.3.1 Science, scale, and law in the climate decisions of the US Supreme Court

The Supreme Court's decision in *Massachusetts v. EPA* was important for US climate law in a multitude of ways, as has been described in earlier chapters. The case is also a good example of the legitimating role that courts can play with respect to climate science, as well as the ways in which judicial treatment of the scientific evidence implicates questions about the most appropriate scale of climate regulatory activity.[124] In the arguments presented to the Supreme Court, litigants employed different framings of the relevant science – combined with different scaling of climate change impacts – to advance their particular litigation goals. Respondents stressed the large scale of climate change, and the resulting scientific uncertainties about subnational contributions to it, in an attempt to block regulation. By contrast, the petitioners asserted the appropriateness of national-level regulation and the high level of scientific certainty around subnational contributions and effects to try to push for action by the EPA.

In its decision, a majority of the Supreme Court sided with the petitioners on the question of standing and on their substantive claims regarding whether greenhouse gas emissions from motor vehicles were an air pollutant that the EPA had the authority to regulate under Section 202(a)(1) of

---

[124] Hari M. Osofsky, "The Intersection of Scale, Science, and Law in *Massachusetts v. EPA*" (2007) 9 *Oregon Rev. Intl. L.* 233. See also Hari M. Osofsky, "The Intersection of Scale, Science, and Law in *Massachusetts v. EPA*" in William C. G. Burns and Hari M. Osofsky (eds.), *Adjudicating Climate Change: State, National, and International Approaches* (2009, Cambridge University Press, New York), 129.

the Clean Air Act. In the process, the majority delivered a powerful reinforcement of scientific evidence regarding the impacts of climate change
on the United States and of the argument that this evidence justified
national-scale regulation to mitigate the problem.

On the question of standing, that is, whether the petitioners had a
sufficient interest to bring a claim in court – an issue discussed in more
depth in Chapter 7 – the respondents' briefs wove together scientific
uncertainty over future climate change impacts with an argument that
climate change was a global-scale problem to dispute the appropriateness
of the petitioners being allowed to be before the Supreme Court.[125] By
contrast, the petitioners' reply sought to rescale the issue back to the state
and local levels and emphasized currently occurring impacts such as rising
sea levels and coastal erosion, exacerbation of air pollution problems with
rising temperatures, and glacial melt.[126] The Supreme Court sided with
the petitioners and indicated that the "widely shared" character of climate
change risks did not prevent Massachusetts from having an interest in the
case's outcome.[127] It concluded the standing analysis:

> In sum – at least according to petitioners' uncontested affidavits – the rise
> in sea levels associated with global warming has already harmed and will
> continue to harm Massachusetts. The risk of catastrophic harm, though
> remote, is nevertheless real. That risk would be reduced to some extent if
> petitioners received the relief they seek. We therefore hold that petitioners
> have standing to challenge the EPA's denial of their rulemaking petition.[128]

Although the Court's holding on standing narrowly focused on the interests of state parties, its approach scaled down the problem of climate
change and its regulation and highlighted the risks faced by states as a
result of this "global" phenomenon. The dissenters, who sided with the
respondents, took the opposite approach to the majority on the question of scale. Chief Roberts's dissent, for example, articulated his concern
about whether the occurrence of emissions around the world made the
impact of US national-level regulatory behavior less clear at a subnational scale.[129] At the core of this battle over standing in *Massachusetts* lay
scientific data. Importantly – and as has become increasingly common

---

[125] Brief for Federal Respondent, *Massachusetts v. EPA*, 549 U.S. 497 (No. 05–1120), 2006
WL 3044970, at 13. Brief for Respondents Alliance of Auto Mfrs, Engine Mfrs Ass'n, Nat'l
Auto. Dealers Ass'n, Truck Mfrs. Ass'n, *Massachusetts v. EPA*, 549 U.S. 497 (No. 05–1120),
2006 WL 3023028 at 13.
[126] Reply, *Massachusetts v. EPA*, 549 U.S. 497 (No. 05–1120), 2006 WL 3367871, at 2–3.
[127] *Massachusetts v. EPA*, 549 U.S. 497, 522 (2007).
[128] *Massachusetts v. EPA*, 549 U.S. 497, 526 (2007).   [129] Ibid., 546.

in climate change litigation – both sides acknowledged the problem of climate change. However, they parted ways in their views on how the scientific information, and its uncertainties, should be mapped onto the existing legal structures.

With respect to the substantive claims, respondents pursued a theme of scientific uncertainty intertwined with a claim that regulatory measures implemented at the state level would fail to match the global nature of the climate change problem. For instance, the brief of respondent CO_2 litigation group argued,

> Since the projected effect of greenhouse gas emissions is a function of changes in the global atmosphere, rather than local or regional air quality, and it is the aggregate contribution of all greenhouse gas emissions around the world to global atmospheric greenhouse gas contributions that is believed by many to cause global climate change, notions of attaining or not attaining an ambient air quality standard within a state or an air quality control region are inapplicable.[130]

As with the standing argument, respondents portrayed climate change as something occurring at a supranational level and over a long time period and highlighted substantial deficits in prevailing understandings of how anthropogenic greenhouse gas emissions should fit into that model. The petitioners' argument, by contrast, relied on the various levels at which the Clean Air Act provides regulatory authority. They emphasized that "Section 202 *does* provide a perfectly feasible mechanism for regulating emission of these pollutants from motor vehicles: the establishment of the same sort of limits on these pollutants that EPA has already imposed on pollutants such as carbon monoxide and hydrocarbons."[131]

The majority of the Court sided with the petitioners over a vigorous dissent.[132] It held that Clean Air Act Section 202(a)(1), read together with the act's broad definition of "air pollutant," gives the EPA statutory authority to regulate greenhouse gas emissions from motor vehicles.[133] Moreover, the Court rejected the EPA's alternative argument that even if it had statutory authority, it should not exercise it.[134] In so doing, the opinion noted that the agency could not avoid its regulatory responsibilities

---

[130] Brief for Respondent CO_2 Litigation Group, *Massachusetts v. EPA*, 549 U.S. 497 (No. 05–1120), 2006 WL 3043971, at 20.

[131] Brief for Petitioners, *Massachusetts v. EPA*, 549 U.S. 497 (No. 05–1120), 2006 WL 2563378, at 29 (emphasis in original).

[132] *Massachusetts v. EPA*, 549 U.S. 497, 549–560 (2007) (Justice Scalia joined by 3 other dissenting judges).

[133] *Massachusetts v. EPA*, 549 U.S. 497, 527–32 (2007).

[134] *Massachusetts v. EPA*, 549 U.S. 497, 532–35 (2007).

simply by invoking scientific uncertainty. Rather the EPA was required to address the statutory question of whether "sufficient information exists to make an endangerment finding."[135]

The Supreme Court's *Massachusetts* decision reinforces the important role that litigation can play in constructing the appropriate scale of climate regulatory activity and endorsing an associated view of scientific data. Through its approach to these issues, the Court not only "legitimizes concerns" over climate change[136] but also lends its authority to a particular view of what the facts are.[137] Although the Court did not rule on climate change science, the decision has been seen as endorsing the reality of climate change. The "massive public and professional attention" drawn by the case[138] has been a conduit for the reverberation of this view throughout the subsequent public and political debate on climate change.

However, as influential as *Massachusetts* was and continues to be, one strong opinion – even a landmark US Supreme Court one – is limited in its ability to reshape public perceptions. Each opinion is issued in a broader context in which many other political, media, new media, and even judicial statements also matter. And courts are not immune to the societies in which they live. The shift in how the Supreme Court treats science in *AEP v. Connecticut* a mere four years later – which mirrors the changes in US public opinion over that time period, as described earlier – provides an important reminder that these conversations remain evolutionary. Professor Maxine Burkett explains:

> The *AEP* Court takes time in its relatively slender decision to inject doubt about elements of climate science. Abandoning the confidence demonstrated in *Massachusetts v. EPA*, the Court cites to a magazine article expressing doubt about climate change impacts as a counterweight to the voluminous peer-reviewed articles on which the EPA based its findings. Further, the Court pauses again to make a facile indictment of all breathing, sentient beings. In an instant, it dismisses the relative excess with which some have burned carbon for luxury and profit versus those who have for food and shelter.[139]

---

[135] *Massachusetts v. EPA*, 549 U.S. 497, 534 (2007).
[136] David Markell and J.B. Ruhl, "An Empirical Assessment of Climate Change in the Courts: A New Jurisprudence or Business as Usual" (2012) 64 *Fla. L. Rev.* 15, 20.
[137] Fisher, "Obsession and Expertise," 242.
[138] Jody Freeman and Adrian Vermule, "Massachusetts v EPA: From Politics to Expertise" (2007) *Supreme Court Review* 51.
[139] See Maxine Burkett, "*Climate Justice and the Elusive Climate Tort*" (2011) 121 *Yale L.J. Online* 115, www.yalelawjournal.org/forum/climate-justice-and-the-elusive-climate-tort.

Whether or not this shift in how the Supreme Court treated science in *AEP* was influenced by shifts in public attitudes to climate change since *Massachusetts*, the way in which it discussed science evolved in parallel with those attitudes.

AEP did not focus simply on the substance of climate science but also on the appropriateness of courts as arbiters of the scientific debates. The opinion explicitly claimed that the EPA is better situated than courts to assess climate change science. The Court explained that "federal judges lack the scientific, economic, and technological resources an agency can utilize in coping with issues of this order" and then elaborated on specific mechanisms that agencies have, but courts lack.[140] This point is not a new one. This statement, for example, parallels the concerns that Justice Scalia raised during the *Massachusetts* oral argument: "I told you before I'm not a scientist. That's why I don't want to deal with global warming, to tell you the truth."[141] But the combination of more skepticism about the science itself and about the court's role in examining in it in the *AEP* decision constitutes a substantial step back from *Massachusetts*.

Overall, these two cases reinforce the multidirectional interactions around public opinion and social norms that take place through climate change litigation. The US Supreme Court has served as a forum in which pro- and antiregulatory forces can make public claims about science and regulation. Briefs, oral arguments, and opinions are well publicized and function as vehicles for high-profile public debate over these issues. The articulation of views on climate science and regulation by this respected body influences public views and norms, but those views and norms in turn come through in the documents filed with and opinions articulated by this court.

6.3.2 Scaling "local" in Australian cases on scope 3 emissions

As a general rule, Australian climate change litigation has strongly endorsed mainstream climate science views and thereby helped to foster a more informed public debate on the issue.[142] However, on the difficult policy issue of scope 3 emissions – in effect whether Australian fossil fuel projects should account for the greenhouse gas pollution to which they

---

[140] *Am. Elec. Power Co. v. Connecticut*, 131 S. Ct. at 2539–40.
[141] Transcript of Oral Argument, *Massachusetts v. EPA*, 549 U.S. 497 (2007), 2006 WL 3431932, at 12–13; see also Osofsky, "The Intersection of Scale, Science, and Law in *Massachusetts v. EPA*."
[142] Skype interview, Australian Participant 8 (Apr. 24, 2013).

contribute through their indirect emissions – there has been more divergence among courts over science and the appropriate regulatory scale for dealing with this issue. Scope 3 greenhouse gas emissions are those that do not result directly from an operation's activities or its energy consumption but rather are downstream consequences of those activities. For instance, scope 3 emissions for coal mining include the emissions produced when the harvested coal is burned.

Three of these cases over scope 3 emissions are highlighted in this section, all of which have arisen in the coal mining state of Queensland where public and political attitudes to climate change regulation have been among the most hostile in the country.[143] Like the *Massachusetts* decision, the scope 3 emissions cases illustrate the ways in which climate science is used in the courtroom to make arguments about where the regulation of climate change should take place. They also demonstrate how courts themselves are social actors whose stance on scientific issues can influence evolving perceptions of the climate change problem.

One of the earliest cases in which the scope 3 emissions issue was raised was *Re Xstrata Coal*, heard by the Queensland Land and Resources Tribunal. The application before the tribunal concerned Xstrata Coal's proposed expansion of an existing coal mining lease to facilitate development of a new open-cut coal mine that would produce an average of 1.9 megatonnes of coal per annum over its fifteen-year lifetime. NGO objectors to the application argued that approval should only be granted subject to conditions that would "avoid, reduce or offset the emissions of greenhouse gases that are likely to result from the mining, transport and use of the coal from the mine."[144] In its decision on the application, the Land and Resources Tribunal not only dismissed the existence of a "demonstrated causal link between [the] mine's [greenhouse gas] emissions and any discernible harm – let alone any 'serious environmental degradation' – caused by global warming and climate change"[145] but also endorsed skeptical views of climate science. This included the president of the tribunal

---

[143] Mark Solomon, "QCoal's James Mackay Developing Environmental Policy for Newman Government in Queensland," ABC News, May 5, 2014, www.abc.net.au/ news/2014–05–05/qcoals-james-mackay-developing-environmental-policy-for-lnp/ 5431008; "'We're in the Coal Business': Campbell Newman Slams UNESCO Great Barrier Reef Warning," June 2, 2012, www.news.com.au/national/unesco-slams-great-barrier-reef-management-youve-got-eight-months-to-fix-it/story-e6frfkw0–1226 381188474.

[144] *Re Xstrata Coal Queensland Pty Ltd & Ors* [2007] QLRT 33.

[145] *Re Xstrata Coal Queensland Pty Ltd & Ors* [2007] QLRT 33 at para. 21.

citing scientific papers that criticized the widely respected Stern Review on the Economics of Climate Change as "biased, selective and unbalanced" and as a "scientifically flawed... vehicle for speculative alarmism."[146] The president also conducted his own review of the scientific evidence in the IPCC's *Fourth Assessment Report*, finding its conclusions to be unconvincing. The tribunal's decision was later overturned by the Queensland Court of Appeal, although on grounds of a denial of natural justice rather than any substantive fault with the analysis of the tribunal.[147]

Additional Queensland lawsuits on scope 3 emissions from coal mining since the *Xstrata* litigation have not expressed skeptical views of climate science but also have rejected the view that indirect emissions occurring outside of Queensland should be considered in environmental assessments under state laws. One such case, heard by the Queensland Land Court (the successor to the Land and Resources Tribunal), concerned the Wandoan mine, an open-cut coal mine proposed by Xstrata to operate for in excess of thirty years in the coal-rich Surat Basin in northwest Queensland.[148] The mine's thermal coal deposits are estimated at over 1.2 billion tonnes, with expected production of around 30 million tonnes of coal per annum. Consultants for the mining company prepared an environmental impact statement in support of the proposal that calculated that over the life of the mine, the mining and use of the coal would produce 1.3 billion tonnes of greenhouse gases with 99 percent of these emissions coming from the combustion of the coal. In the Land Court's judgment, the total emissions from the mine were compared with global emissions and were found to represent 0.17 percent of annual global emissions.[149]

Similarly to the first *Xstrata* case, the environmental group objecting to approval of the mine under Queensland's environmental and mining

[146] *Re Xstrata Coal Queensland Pty Ltd & Ors* [2007] QLRT 33 at para. 16. The Stern Review was commissioned by the UK government and has been extensively relied on by policymakers as evidence of the high economic costs of delaying action to address climate change.

[147] *Queensland Conservation Council Inc v. Xstrata Coal Queensland P/L & Ors* [2007] QCA 338.

[148] *Xstrata Coal Qld Pty Ltd & Ors v. Friends of the Earth Brisbane and Department of Environment and Resource Management* [2012] QLC 013.

[149] *Xstrata Coal Qld Pty Ltd & Ors v. Friends of the Earth Brisbane and Department of Environment and Resource Management* [2012] QLC 013 at para 501. This equates to more than double Australia's annual emissions for 2013, which were 542.1 Mt CO_2 equivalent: www.environment.gov.au/system/files/resources/e18788bd-2a8a-49d1-b797–307a9763c93f/files/quartlery-update-september-2013_1.pdf.

legislation argued that the "adverse environmental impact caused by [the mine's] operations" extended beyond the effects of on-site greenhouse gas emissions to include "indirect downstream impacts" such as the impacts of emissions produced through transport and use of the coal. In response, Xstrata sought to downplay the scope 3 emissions problem by arguing that the mining and burning of coal from the Wandoan mine would have a negligible or no separate impact on climate change and ocean acidification. The company also contended that stopping the project would not affect the level of greenhouse gases in the atmosphere, as the coal would simply be mined elsewhere, leading to equivalent or higher emissions.[150]

To support their argument that the indirect effects of coal mining at the Wandoan mine would constitute an "adverse environmental impact" relevant to the subnational scale of the Queensland legislation, the objectors presented scientific evidence that tried to scale down climate change from the global to the local level. A key part of the evidence was a report on "Contribution of the Wandoan Coal Mine to Climate Change and Ocean Acidification" prepared by Dr. Malte Meinhausen, a respected German climate scientist whose work has been relied on in reports of the IPCC. Dr. Meinhausen's report sought to present the scientific evidence in a variety of ways to inform the court about the contribution that the mine operations would make to climate change and to local environmental harm. Its analysis included an assessment of the available carbon budget to 2050 (how much carbon could be released by 2050 if avoiding dangerous anthropogenic warming), the percentage of that budget that would be used up by greenhouse gas emissions from the mining operations, and the climatic effects of the estimated 1.3 billion tonnes of emissions from the mine in terms of their role in increasing global average temperatures, raising sea levels, and exacerbating coastal flooding risks.[151]

The deciding judge of the Queensland Land Court – although not denying climate change was a problem – expressed significant skepticism about the report's approach. President MacDonald noted that "Dr Meinhausen purported to calculate the effect of the project's greenhouse gas emissions by calculating the temperature increase attributable to burning the amount of coal from the project and estimated that 23,000 people would be inundated by the consequent rise in sea levels." Her Honor

---

[150] These submissions are outlined in the Land Court's judgment at para 515.
[151] A copy of the report is available from Environmental Law Publishing, www.envlaw.com. au/.

dismissed this "attempted quantification of the specific impacts of this project" as "unconvincing."[152] In her judgment, President MacDonald ruled that the mining operations to be considered by the Court were confined to the physical activities associated with winning and extracting coal from the mine's locality and did not extend to transport of coal and burning at overseas locations or associated emissions.[153] Furthermore, the judge ruled that – even if such emissions could be considered – "it is difficult to see from the evidence that this project will cause any relevant impact on the environment,"[154] placing weight on the applicant's arguments that if the project were refused, the coal would simply be sourced from elsewhere.[155]

Following this judgment, the Alpha coal mine litigation (discussed in Chapter 3) was an attempt by a subgroup of claimants involved in the Wandoan case to revisit the outcome in this case "to have the scope 3 emissions taken into account."[156] The litigants' predictions that the Alpha coal mine case would "likely be decided the same way by the Land Court, that is that scope 3 emissions are irrelevant"[157] proved correct, and the group involved has now sought judicial review in an attempt to reverse the climate-related aspects of the judgment.[158] In the Alpha mine case, however, the Queensland Land Court (with a different member presiding) showed much greater sympathy for the climate change arguments advanced and a more deferential approach to the scientific evidence. For instance, the judge refuted the mining company's submission that the combined scope 1, 2, and 3 emissions at 0.16 percent of global greenhouse gas emissions were "negligible." His Honor noted that,

> expressed another way, a percentage of 0.16 equates to a ratio of 1 as to 625. In my view, particularly considering the possible local, State and global consequences which may flow from increased [greenhouse gas] emissions,

---

[152] *Xstrata Coal Qld Pty Ltd & Ors v. Friends of the Earth Brisbane and Department of Environment and Resource Management* [2012] QLC 013 at para 552.

[153] Ibid. at para 528.   [154] Ibid. at para 559.

[155] Similar rulings were used to dismiss arguments under the state environmental legislation regarding the issue of an environmental authority: at para. 605.

[156] In-person interview, Australian Participant 2 (Mar. 8, 2013). See also *Hancock Coal Pty Ltd v. Kelly & Ors and Department of Environment and Heritage Protection (No. 4)* [2014] QLC 12, para 201.

[157] In-person interview, Australian Participant 2 (Mar. 8, 2013).

[158] *Coast and Country Association of Queensland v. Smith and Hancock Coal Pty Ltd*, Application for a Statutory Order of Review, Supreme Court of Queensland, Brisbane Registry, No. 4249/14, May 6, 2014 (copy on file with authors).

a factor of 1 as to 625 is both real and of concern. It cannot be dismissed as negligible.[159]

Ultimately, however, the judge agreed with the mining company that stopping the mine would not affect climate change, as "the coal will simply be sourced from somewhere else."[160] His Honor concluded,

> I can sympathise with the position of the objectors who see [greenhouse gas] emissions rising, and the likely adverse climate change consequences that will flow should nothing be done to alter the course that the world is heading down. I have no reason to doubt the eminent expert evidence that was presented in this case to that effect. However, I must on the evidence of this case determine that it is the demand for coal-fired electricity, and not the supply of coal from coal mines, which is at the heart of the problem. Clearly, the possibility of dire consequences from climate change is a matter which falls to be addressed by the international community and the Federal Government.[161]

The cases suggest that an evolution of sorts has occurred in judicial views of the science and associated scalar issues over the seven-year period between the original *Xstrata* decision in 2007 and the Alpha coal mining judgment issued in 2014. While the shift in judicial attitudes may not seem substantial, it has to be judged against its sociopolitical context, namely, the state of Queensland, which has some of the strongest anti–climate change rhetoric in Australia, regularly voiced by state politicians. The cases thus highlight the ongoing, and iterative, dynamics between public perceptions of science and regulation and the way in which these issues are treated in courts. As the jurisprudence continues to develop and public views continue to evolve, courts will likely remain a focal point for debating what regulation by which governmental entity or entities appropriately flows from current understandings of the science.

6.3.3   How US and Australian courts compare as forums for consideration of science

The *Massachusetts* and Queensland coal mining cases discussed in the previous sections illustrate opposite ends of the spectrum in terms of

---

[159] *Hancock Coal Pty Ltd v. Kelly & Ors and Department of Environment and Heritage Protection (No. 4)* [2014] QLC 12, para. 209.

[160] Ibid. at para. 229.

[161] *Hancock Coal Pty Ltd v. Kelly & Ors and Department of Environment and Heritage Protection (No. 4)* [2014] QLC 12, paras. 230, 231.

how courts may take part in the construction of issues of science and scale in their climate change decisions. In *Massachusetts v. EPA*, the majority's acceptance of the scientific evidence regarding subnational impacts – despite its generality and uncertainties – undergirded a parallel acceptance of the appropriateness of national-scale regulatory action. In the Queensland coal mining cases, although judicial attitudes appear to be shifting as the litigation continues, there has been resistance to claimants' attempts to scale down the climate change problem to demonstrate local impacts and the appropriateness of state-level regulatory action. Both sets of cases also illustrate how judges' familiarity with and trust in climate science can shape their consideration of that evidence. For instance, the judge in the Wandoan case expressed significant skepticism about an assessment by a leading climate scientist. In *Massachusetts v. EPA*, while the majority appeared to be comfortable with accepting the science, Justice Scalia – who dissented – expressed concerns about his level of scientific knowledge in his earlier quoted comments during oral argument.

However, while these two case studies illustrate interesting variations in the treatment of scale and science in this context, they are unrepresentative of the comparative treatment of science and scale issues across the two jurisdictions despite each coming from one of the countries. In fact, as the *AEP* case a mere four years after *Massachusetts* indicates, even the same court may evolve in its treatment of these issues over time as public attitudes, the Court's composition, and the matters before it change.

Looking beyond these two case studies across the breadth of climate change litigation in the United States and Australia, some general comparative differences emerge in the approach of courts to climate science and related issues of scale. By and large, Australian climate change cases – unlike those in the United States – have been heard by state-level courts and administrative tribunals that have some level of specialty in the areas of environment, planning, and land use. Members of these courts and tribunals are usually a mix of judges (drawn from specialist practice or academia) and nonjudicial members who are experts in areas such as planning, urban design, environmental science, or land valuation. Many cases are conducted on the basis of merits review in which the court takes on the role of the original decision maker and remakes the decision after a full hearing of the factual material and legal arguments. These features may help to explain why – with the exception of cases at the extremes, like the 2007 *Xstrata* decision – Australian climate change litigation has been marked by a close and serious consideration of scientific arguments about climate change.

Australian interviewees also expressed their general confidence in courts as an independent, less politicized, forum for consideration of climate change issues:

> Judges can't leave their personalities at home when they go and sit on the bench. And, you know, jurimetrics will tell you that. But, on the whole, what judges do that politicians don't do is that they actually listen to both sides of the argument, they weigh it up, the rules of evidence apply, a lot of stuff that's irrelevant gets swept to one side and you tend to get in those cases where hard issues are involved and perhaps a lot of money is involved, you do get some reasonably good experts giving their opinions. So it's a little bit like a Senate hearing as opposed to people just spitting at each other across the floor of the House of Representatives where a lot of law gets made, not always good! There's a lot of compromise. So I certainly don't say that the courts should be doing everything here, but what they do bring is they bring a discipline and a rigor and oftentimes they'll bring with them the benefit of a lot of thoughtful expert testimony to some of the decisions that they make.[162]

Perhaps because generalist judges vary more in their level of scientific training, environmental knowledge, and willingness to engage complex scientific and technical issues than those serving on specialized environmental and land use tribunals,[163] US interviewees noted much more variable experience with judges. On one hand, US interviewees pointed to some examples of judges and courts that were very engaged with the detail of the scientific evidence in climate change cases and gave careful consideration to how that evidence was relevant in the interpretation of legal issues.[164] On the other hand, they also identified examples where judges seemed reluctant to embrace a new, and potentially difficult, area. These judges often focused on standing and the political question doctrine and never reached the merits of a climate case.[165]

---

[162] Skype interview, Australian Participant 8 (Apr. 24, 2013).

[163] Justice Brian J. Preston, "Operating an Environmental Court: The Experience of the Land and Environment Court of New South Wales" (2008) 25 *Environ. Planning L. J.* 385; Justice N. R. Bignold, "NSW Land and Environment Court – Its Contribution to Australia's Development of Environmental Law" (2001) 18(2) *Environ. Planning L. J.* 256.

[164] Examples cited by interviewees included Judge Sessions", opinion in *Green Mountain Chrysler Plymouth Dodge Jeep v. Crombie,* 508 F. Supp. 2d 295 (D.Vt 2007); Judge Garland's opinion in *In Re: Polar Bear Endangered Species Act Listing,* case No. 11–5219, U.S. Court of Appeals for the District of Columbia Circuit; Judge Fletcher's opinion in *CBD v. NHTSA,* 538 F.3d 1172 (9th Cir. 2008); and Judge Hall's opinion in *Connecticut v. AEP,* 582 F. 3d 309 (2nd Cir. 2009).

[165] This was a particular complaint in tort cases such as the *Kivalina* litigation and *California v. General Motors, et al.,* 2007 U.S. Dist. LEXIS 68547 (N.D. Cal. 2007).

When we posed questions to US interviewees about the competence of courts in dealing with climate change science and assessing arguments relating to climate change regulation, the response was similarly mixed. Overall, respondents felt "it depends a lot who the judges are."[166] One interviewee involved in pro-regulatory litigation commented,

> There's such an element of Russian roulette when you file a case. There's only so much you can do in terms of being strategic in where you bring your case because there are judges that are very hostile to environmental law everywhere and there are judges that really understand it and take it very seriously. And wherever you are you're rolling the dice every time you bring a case.[167]

Equally, some involved on the industry side of lawsuits felt that a lack of scientific expertise on the part of courts was leading to "inadvertent uber-extra deference to the agencies" in assessing the scientific evidence and arguments put forward in support of regulation.[168]

Moreover, the strongly politicized treatment of climate change science and regulation in the United States, together with the current partisan politics surrounding its judicial appointment system, seemed to interviewees to be reflected in variations among judges. Interviewees often saw the political orientation of the administration that appointed federal judges as an important determining factor in how they approach climate change science:

> I've yet to encounter an Obama appointed or a Clinton appointed judge who doesn't understand that climate change is real. They very well may not appreciate the severity of it, they may think that the appropriate role of the courts is very narrow and that it is a question for the Congress and the president, not the courts to deal with, but they are clearly aware of the problem. Versus there is still a large subset of the American judiciary that either actually or at least ideologically takes a position that climate change is not real or not established or uncertain or otherwise not something to be dealt with. And those judges are not particularly friendly to climate litigation.[169]

---

[166] In-person interview, US Participant 6 (Nov. 14, 2012), noting "... that's not specific to climate change, it's just the way it is." Also telephone interview, US Participant 11 (Oct. 10, 2013).

[167] In-person interview, US Participant 2 (Oct. 22, 2012).

[168] Telephone interview, US Participant 3 (Nov. 7 2012); telephone interview, US Participant 9 (Dec. 3, 2012).

[169] Telephone interview, US Participant 12 (Jan. 14, 2013).

Overall, the differences between the judicial treatment of climate change in the two countries seem to relate more to the nature of tribunal involved than to core differences between the jurisdictions' judiciaries. The types of observations interviewees had regarding US judicial attitudes and capacity with respect to climate science and regulation were paralleled by the experiences of litigants and lawyers in Australia who were appearing before (generalist) federal courts or state courts of appeal. Similarly, the experience of US respondents mostly involved in administrative adjudications, such as rate cases before public service commissions or locally based land use disputes, more closely tracked that of Australian litigants bringing cases in specialist state courts. These findings stress that in evaluating judicial treatment of climate science and its influence on public perceptions of climate risk, courts cannot be lumped together as a monolithic entity. At the same time, the findings suggest that certain kinds of judicial or quasi-judicial forums – specialist rather than generalist; administrative rather than judicial review – may be more receptive to adjudicating and communicating arguments about scientific data and how they relate to the appropriate scale of and approaches to climate change regulation.

6.4   Conclusion

Beyond the direct regulatory changes that climate change cases induce through interpreting constitutional provisions, statutes, or the common law, they also exercise a significant indirect influence over climate change regulation. This chapter has focused on the second type of indirect influence highlighted in our model: the roles courts play in shaping social norms and public attitudes with respect to climate change. Its analysis reinforces that these influences are complex and multidimensional and that these interactions take place not only in the media and on the Internet but also in the courtrooms and regulatory agencies themselves.

Part of the way in which climate change cases have helped to shape the framing of the climate change problem is through endorsing particular understandings of scientific data and deciding the scale at which climate change should be addressed through regulation. But these cases, in turn, appear to be shaped by evolving public perceptions of science and regulation, as the shift in US Supreme Court discussions of climate change science over time reflects. Moreover, our interviews in both countries reinforced that tribunal type may influence substantially interactions with scientific issues, with more specialized, administrative tribunals less likely to hesitate to address science or to be influenced by the partisan politics over climate change.

Political factors and media reporting remain important forces molding public – and sometimes judicial, executive, and legislative – opinion on climate issues, especially in countries such as the United States and Australia. However, as the chapter has outlined, both high- and low-profile climate change cases, as well as coverage of them in traditional and new media, can contribute to developing social norms by putting climate change on the agenda of politicians and agencies, galvanizing community campaigns, and framing climate change science and impacts in ways that resonate with lay experience. Moreover, these cases appear to influence regulators in various ways, whether they are proactive, reluctant, or hostile to action on climate change. Cases have served promotive roles by reinforcing and providing political cover for proactive regulators and by putting pressure on reluctant ones. But, as the chapter explores, this influence has been muted by the deeply partisan environment in both countries.

Throughout this chapter, we have focused on primarily pro-regulatory litigation and the positive role it can play in influencing social norms. However, we also have examined some of the political barriers to this litigation being more influential. The next chapter turns to this issue of barriers in more depth, examining constraints on access to justice, antiregulatory litigation, and backlash against lawsuits.

Barriers to progress through litigation

Well, are courts the appropriate forum to be addressing climate change regulatory requirements? By and large, no, to the extent you are looking to them to organically address or develop comprehensive regulatory programs. I don't think the courts should necessarily be stepping in where there's a lack of will or activity from the executive or legislative branches of government. But on the other hand, if there is existing law and an existing framework under which these factors should be considered... then is it appropriate for the courts to act in their limited role.... I think that is both permissible, it's traditional and historically what the courts have always done and it's necessary because otherwise the law would just be frozen and environmental law would be frozen. You'd never have a way to adapt to new circumstances, new knowledge, new issues unless it was done legislatively or administratively through the agencies' regulatory and rulemaking authority. So you need – I mean in our three-branch system – you need to have some check and some role and that's what the courts are doing.

– US Interview Participant 3

I think at the moment though, especially in Queensland and New South Wales... there will be a determined effort to wind back the opportunities of courts and tribunals to become involved. But there is no doubt that in this country the courts and tribunals in this area are our greatest hope because they can – freed of policy influences – look at the principles which are now universal, or global should I say, sustainability principles, and there's no hesitation for them to be applied.

– Australian Interview Participant 15

7.1 Introduction

Most of this book focuses on the possibility for litigation to spur greater climate change regulation. However, litigation as a tool for direct and indirect regulatory change has its limits. At times, petitioners face barriers to judicial resolution of climate change claims. Courts are not always the appropriate place to address problems and disagreements. The separation of powers among the executive, legislative, and judicial branches confines the circumstances in which courts have the power to act and undergirds doctrines of judicial restraint. These constitutional constraints and broader doctrines of legislative deference have at times had a dampening effect in the US context, where standing, political question doctrine, and displacement have been raised to try to prevent federal courts from reaching the merits in important climate change cases. However, access barriers go beyond just these questions of appropriateness and deference. Some pro-regulatory stakeholders – especially in Australia, because of its approach to costs – choose not to bring potentially legitimate claims because the risks of prohibitive expenses are simply too high.

These access issues are not the only constraint on the ability of litigation to promote regulatory change. The "warfare" between pro- and antiregulatory interests[1] – which takes place not just in courtrooms but also more broadly in society and politics – significantly complicates the task of assessing the overall regulatory impact of climate change litigation. As noted in many places throughout this book, sometimes pro-regulatory petitioners lose, and not all lawsuits brought attempt to advance climate change regulation. Indeed, although climate change litigation may have originated as actions by pro-regulatory interests to pressure governments to introduce measures for emissions reduction and adaptation, today's landscape of climate change litigation embraces a much greater diversity of interests. Especially in the United States, petitioners bring lawsuits to block or limit regulatory initiatives by the legislative and executive branches; a particular feature of the post–*Massachusetts v. EPA* period has thus been the emergence of numerous additional antiregulatory climate change cases.[2] Moreover, empirical assessments of the US climate case law suggest that this body of antiregulatory litigation – although not yet making up the majority of cases – is steadily growing.[3] These suits have

---

[1] David Markell and J.B. Ruhl, "An Empirical Assessment of Climate Change in the Courts: A New Jurisprudence or Business as Usual" (2012) 64 *Fla. L. Rev.* 15, 65.

[2] David Markell and J.B. Ruhl, "An Empirical Survey of Climate Change Litigation in the United States" (2010) 40(7) *Environ. L. Reporter* 10644, 10650.

[3] In their 2010 assessment of the US climate change case law, Markell and Ruhl found pro-regulatory litigation remained the dominant thrust, with only 15 percent of cases being antiregulatory in their motivations and effects. Two years later, however, the proportion of antiregulatory cases had risen steadily to close to 20 percent of the cases surveyed. See Markell and Ruhl, "An Empirical Survey," 25; Markell and Ruhl, "A New Jurisprudence or

challenged vehicle and stationary source emissions reduction under the
Clean Air Act, as well as a host of other federal and state regulatory action
designed to reduce greenhouse gas emissions or transition from coal to
cleaner energy sources.[4]

Even when petitioners gain access and obtain a positive verdict, the
response to the opinion may end up having an antiregulatory effect. This
has often been the experience in Australia, even though there has not
been the same trend in the initiation of antiregulatory climate change
litigation as there has been in the United States.[5] In part, this dearth
may be a consequence of more limited Australian federal environmental
statutes and the accompanying administrative law actions under them
that have provided the basis for some of the challenged regulations in the
United States. Furthermore, Australia has a more fertile environment for
industry to influence antiregulatory legislative action. Those seeking to
advance projects that produce significant greenhouse gases or to block
restrictions on emissions can generally find a friendly ear for their concerns in state or federal governments, which then enact legislation to clear
away roadblocks to a particular proposal or otherwise to limit the capacity
for proactive climate change litigation. Australian antiregulatory interests
therefore tend to focus more on responding to lawsuits in the public policy
arena – and on advancing their own legislative agenda there – an approach
that would be much less effective in the US federal context, where the
Congress remains largely deadlocked on both pro- and antiregulatory
matters.

This chapter surveys these various barriers to achieving progress
through climate change litigation. It begins in Section 7.2 by examining access barriers, considering both separation of powers and financial barriers. The chapter next examines antiregulatory litigation and its
effectiveness in "suppress[ing] climate change as a factor in regulation
and liability decision-making."[6] Finally, the chapter considers situations

Business as Usual," 66. As of October 2012, Columbia Climate Change Law Center's graph
of filed cases organized by type listed a staggering 172 claims (or 33 percent of all cases
filed) in the category of industry lawsuits. See Arnold and Porter LLP, "Types of Climate
Cases Filed," October 3, 2012, at www.climatecasechart.com/.

[4] Arnold and Porter LLP, "U.S. Climate Change Litigation Case Chart," at www.
climatecasechart.com (Industry lawsuits).

[5] Hari M. Osofsky and Jacqueline Peel, "The Role of Litigation in Multilevel Climate Change
Governance: Possibilities for a Lower Carbon Future" (2013) 30(4) *Environ. Planning L. J.*
303.

[6] This is how Markell and Ruhl, "A New Jurisprudence of Business as Usual," 15 describe the
aims of antiregulatory litigation in the United States.

in which proactive litigation fails to achieve its desired effect due to a negative outcome in the case itself, or the ensuing public and legislative response.

7.2   Barriers to court access

In this section, we review barriers to pro-regulatory petitioners accessing courts to address climate change concerns. These include constraints stemming from the limited judicial role in systems that adhere to separation-of-powers doctrines, and other barriers posed by the cost of litigation, particularly for nongovernmental claimants.

In the United States, the most significant barriers to merits consideration have involved courts deciding either not to allow a petitioner to bring the claim or not to reach the claims due to prior legislative action. First, while *Massachusetts v. EPA* cleared away standing hurdles for state petitioners in a climate context, that decision did not resolve when nonstate petitioners have standing, an issue that *AEP v. Connecticut* also failed to resolve. Lower courts have since split on this issue. In the jurisdictions denying standing, their stance serves as a significant barrier for some pro-regulatory climate change litigants. Second, political question doctrine arguments – and particularly the issue of whether there have been initial legislative determinations that make judicial action inappropriate – have been raised and even succeeded in lower courts in the public nuisance context. However, the Supreme Court in *AEP v. Connecticut* did not treat political question as a barrier, making it less of a concern than standing. Finally, though not a threshold access issue in the same way as standing and political question doctrine, displacement also involves interbranch deference and has served as a barrier to pro-regulatory petitioners in the context of common law public nuisance claims.

In Australia, standing and other separation-of-powers barriers have been far less of an issue in climate cases. Open or relaxed standing provisions apply in the specialist courts where most of the litigation takes place and also under the federal environmental assessment law.[7] Moreover, though some administrative decisions can only be challenged through judicial review (where similar concerns arise around the appropriateness of judicial intervention as in the US context), a substantial number of decisions of relevance for climate change can be reviewed by courts or

---

[7] See, e.g., Environment Protection and Biodiversity Conservation Act 1999 (Cth), ss 475, 489.

tribunals on their merits.[8] A far more critical issue for litigants has been rules around the award of costs. As most Australian climate change claimants on the pro-regulatory side are impecunious environmental groups or communities, the potential for an adverse ruling on costs can mean the difference between bringing a case to raise climate change issues in court and forgoing litigation all together. The US approach (which also applies in some jurisdictions in Australia),[9] in which each party generally pays its own costs, may also raise these concerns, but US litigants do not seem to view cost as a particular hurdle to bringing pro-regulatory claims. In the final section, we thus focus on the costs issue as a key barrier for court access in the Australian context.

7.2.1   Separation-of-powers barriers

The respective legal systems of the United States and Australia place significant weight on the importance of the separation of powers as a guarantee of democratic government. A formal interpretation of the separation-of-powers doctrine limits courts' role to the interpretation and application of laws and regulations issued by the other branches.[10] This section examines the barriers that US separation-of-powers doctrines create and the more limited ways in which these issues have arisen in Australia.

Three doctrines involving the relationships among branches serve as potential or actual constraints on US climate change litigation. As one US interviewee described it, the "separation-of-powers issue...comes up in different guises whether you call it a political question doctrine or displacement or standing.... It's, well, what is the role of the courts and what is the role of the Congress and the executive...It all comes

---

[8] As discussed in Chapter 2, merits review is a form of administrative review in Australia where courts or tribunals remake the original decision after consideration of all relevant facts and legal issues. Merits review is available for many types of decisions under state planning and environmental laws. See Philippa England, "The Legal Basis for Australian Environmental Planning and Governance" in Jason Byrne, Neil Sipe, and Jago Dodson (eds.), *Australian Environmental Planning: Challenges and Future Prospects* (2014, Abingdon, Routledge), 39.

[9] For example, the Victorian Civil and Administrative Tribunal is generally a "no costs" jurisdiction for planning and land use cases: s 109, *Victorian Civil and Administrative Tribunal Act 1998* (Vic).

[10] Jack M. Beerman, "Common Law and Statute Law in US Administrative Law" in Linda Pearson et al. (eds.), *Administrative Law in a Changing State: Essays in Honour of Mark Aronson* (2008, Hart Publishing, UK), 45.

down to the same issue of what branch or what government has what power."[11]

First, standing is a core threshold issue that determines whether a litigant can access US courts to make a claim about climate change. The standing doctrine involves constitutional separation of powers, even though it focuses only on the judicial branch, because it emerges from the limited powers given to the federal judiciary under Article III. Despite the fact that the Supreme Court has twice found standing in the context of climate change, those cases – with their state government petitioners – did not resolve broader issues about who can bring which kinds of climate change–related claims. Professor Daniel Farber explains why standing determinations involve so much uncertainty, especially in this highly politicized context:

> Article III standing has three seemingly simple components: (1) the plaintiffs must suffer an actual injury, (2) the injury must be caused by the defendant, and (3) the courts must be able to provide a remedy for that injury.…
>
> The unpredictability and ideological nature of standing law seems inherent in the three-part test, whose terms seem to serve as a kind of Rorschach ink-blot allowing each Justice to project her own worldview onto each case. The Court has never defined what constitutes an "injury" for purposes of standing, leaving it to each Justice to decide what kinds of grievances should be considered cognizable injuries. The second element is a mirror in which the judge can perceive her own preferences – when an injury is "fairly traceable" is simply a question of what a judge regards as fair. The third element replicates the problems of the first one, since the Court must decide whether the benefits sought by the plaintiff through the remedy should count for constitutional purposes. One need only look at *Massachusetts*, where the conservatives were certain that the case failed all three prongs of the test whereas the liberals were equally certain that it passed the hurdles. From what can be gleaned from the Court's cryptic comment in *AEP*, the dissenters in *Massachusetts* held their ground in *AEP*.[12]

The unpredictability that Professor Farber discusses is compounded by the narrow holding regarding standing in *Massachusetts*. The following language from the opinion makes it plain that the Supreme Court's

---

[11] Telephone interview, US Participant 7 (Nov. 16, 2012).

[12] Daniel A. Farber, "Standing on Hot Air: American Electric Power and the Bankruptcy of Standing Doctrine" (2011) 121 *Yale L. J. Online* 121, 121–22, www.yalelawjournal.org/pdf/1003_115a7rfi.pdf.

standing analysis only applies clearly to states and possibly other governmental entities:

> Only one of the petitioners needs to have standing to permit us to consider
> the petition for review. We stress here, as did Judge Tatel below, the special
> position and interest of Massachusetts. It is of considerable relevance that
> the party seeking review here is a sovereign State and not, as it was in
> Lujan, a private individual. . . .
>
> When a State enters the Union, it surrenders certain sovereign prerog-
> atives. . . .
>
> These sovereign prerogatives are now lodged in the Federal Government,
> and Congress has ordered EPA to protect Massachusetts (among others)
> by prescribing standards applicable to the "emission of any air pollutant
> from any class or classes of new motor vehicle engines, which in [the
> Administrator's] judgment cause, or contribute to, air pollution which may
> reasonably be anticipated to endanger public health or welfare." 42 U.S.C.
> § 7521(a)(1). Congress has moreover recognized a concomitant procedural
> right to challenge the rejection of its rulemaking petition as arbitrary and
> capricious. § 7607(b)(1). Given that procedural right and Massachusetts'
> stake in protecting its quasi-sovereign interests, the Commonwealth is
> entitled to special solicitude in our standing analysis.[13]

Because of this language about the "relevance" of Massachusetts being
a "sovereign State" and its entitlement to "special solicitude," the decision in *Massachusetts* left open the question of standing for nonstate
petitioners.

The second climate change Supreme Court case, *AEP v. Connecticut*, did not resolve this uncertainty. Although, as discussed Chapter 6,
the Supreme Court treats science more skeptically in *AEP* than in *Massachusetts*, its approach to standing flows directly from its approach in
Massachusetts. A four-justice plurality in *AEP* found standing based on
Massachusetts's reasoning, while four justices opposed standing.[14] Assum-
ing that Justice Sotomayor, who did not participate in *AEP* because she
had heard the case while sitting on the Second Circuit, either joins the
group supporting standing or abstains from the issue – which seems far
more likely than her joining the group in opposition – *AEP* reinforces
that the Court will continue to view US state petitioners as having the
particularized interest necessary to make regulatory challenges.

However, the plurality's affirmation of *Massachusetts*'s approach to
standing, which focuses heavily on the governmental status of some of

---

[13] *Massachusetts v. EPA*, 549 U.S. 497, 518–20.

[14] For analysis of these standing issues, see Farber, "Standing on Hot Air."

the petitioners, still does not resolve the question of whether it would find standing in a suit with only nongovernmental petitioners. This issue is currently being litigated in challenges to projects that have a large carbon footprint, such as coal-fired power plants. Some of these cases involve federal law, and in the years following the *AEP* decision, the lower courts have split on whether to grant standing to nongovernmental petitioners. For example, the US District Court for the District of New Mexico found that six citizen environmental groups lacked standing in a challenge to oil and gas leases based on climate change,[15] while the US District Court for the District of Colorado held that the nongovernmental organization (NGO) WildEarth Guardians had standing to challenge leases that allow the venting of methane from a coal mine, including on climate change grounds.[16] Although these district courts' opinions only have precedential weight within their own districts, they will influence the ongoing dialogue about whether standing is appropriate in cases without governmental petitioners, cases that currently serve as one of the few ways in which citizens can attempt to shape the energy choices of major corporations.

Second, reflecting separation-of-powers constraints, courts are often reluctant to rule on climate change issues that they view as straying into the policy domain of the legislative and executive branches. This restraint is most clearly expressed in the United States through the political question doctrine – courts deem issues as non-justiciable because they raise political issues best decided by other branches. However, thus far this doctrine has had a limited impact. For instance, in the public nuisance context, some lower courts found political question barriers, but the US Supreme Court disagreed; a plurality of the Supreme Court held in *AEP v. Connecticut* that no threshold barriers (including political question) prevented the dispute.[17] This ruling will likely constrain political question as a significant argument in future US cases.

A third important constraint in the US context, which was recognized by the Court in *AEP*, is the displacement doctrine: powers given statutorily to other branches "displace" the judiciary's power to consider other pathways. So, for example, the *AEP* decision found that the EPA's authority to regulate greenhouse gases – even if the EPA chose not to assert that

---

[15] *Amigos Bravos v. U.S. Bureau of Land Mgmt.*, 2011 WL 3924489 (D.N.M. Aug. 3, 2011). For examples of similar cases, see Arnold and Porter LLP, "U.S. Climate Change Litigation Case Chart," www.climatecasechart.com/.

[16] *WildEarth Guardians v. U.S. Forest Service*, 828 F.Supp.2d 1223 (D.Colo. 2011), appeal dismissed (10th Circ. 12–1005, 12–1023) (Mar. 7, 2012).

[17] This case is discussed further in Chapter 3. See 131 S. Ct. 2527 (2011).

authority – displaced the possibility for a claim under common law public nuisance. The opinion explained that if the EPA acted inadequately, it should be challenged through an administrative lawsuit under the Clean Air Act rather than through nuisance claims. Federal courts have followed this approach in other public nuisance cases since the *AEP* decision. For example, commenting on the court's decision in *Kivalina* that the federal common law claim of public nuisance for climate change damage was similarly displaced, Circuit Judge Sidney R. Thomas stated,

> Our conclusion obviously does not aid Kivalina, which itself is being displaced by the rising sea. But the solution to Kivalina's dire circumstance must rest in the hands of the legislative and executive branches of our government, not the federal common law.[18]

The displacement doctrine as articulated in these public nuisance cases thus reflects an impulse to keep climate change regulation on a statutorily based track when other branches have acted.[19]

In theory, standing, political question, and displacement pose potentially formidable barriers to petitioners trying to access the US courts regarding climate change. To date, however their applicability has been limited. Barring another clarifying Supreme Court ruling, standing likely will only be a barrier for nongovernmental petitioners in jurisdictions that are issuing such denials; pairing with governmental petitioners will help address the issue even in those places. Political question similarly appears to be less of a concern than lower court public nuisance case rulings made it initially seem; after *AEP*, this doctrine seems unlikely to pose a major barrier. Displacement has been used as a block for common law claims in the context of public nuisance, but does not pose a barrier for the statutory claims that form the vast majority of US climate change litigation. *AEP* made it clear that the statutory administrative law challenges remained appropriate. So, thus far these doctrines have mostly acted to constrain certain types of petitioners and claims, rather than serving as a blanket barrier to climate litigation.

However, the relatively narrow judicial interpretation of these doctrines with respect to court access does not represent the only way in which separation of powers can serve in an antiregulatory role in this context. Separation-of-powers arguments have also been used by the

---

[18] *Native Village of Kivalina v. ExxonMobil Corp.*, 696 F.3d 849 (9th Cir. 2012).

[19] Hari M. Osofsky, "Litigation's Role in the Path of U.S. Federal Climate Change Regulation: Implications of AEP v Connecticut" (2012) 46 *Valparaiso Univ. L. Rev.* 447.

Supreme Court to limit executive branch action, specifically EPA's regulatory authority over climate change. For example, in its June 2014 opinion in *Utility Air Regulatory Group v. EPA*, the Court mentioned separation of powers as one of the reasons the "Tailoring Rule" was inappropriate:

> Were we to recognize the authority claimed by EPA in the Tailoring Rule, we would deal a severe blow to the Constitution's separation of powers. Under our system of government, Congress makes laws and the President, acting at times through agencies like EPA, "faithfully execute[s]" them. The power of executing the laws necessarily includes both authority and responsibility to resolve some questions left open by Congress that arise during the law's administration. But it does not include a power to revise clear statutory terms that turn out not to work in practice.[20]

This approach in *Utility Air Regulatory Group* reinforces that even if plaintiffs are able to overcome separation-of-powers constraints on court access and on the issues courts will reach, constitutional limits on the roles of the three branches, as interpreted by US courts, may still stymie efforts at climate change regulation.

In Australia also, separation-of-powers constraints and standing have not posed significant barriers to accessing courts in climate cases, although courts may still be hesitant to extend too far into the perceived policy realm of the other branches. In the case of standing, most Australian environmental and planning laws – which have formed the basis for the majority of the litigation to date – contain specific statutory provisions on standing that facilitate access to the courts. For example, Section 123 of the New South Wales (NSW) Environmental Planning and Assessment Act 1979 confers "open standing," permitting any claimant to bring a matter before the court regardless of their personal interest in the outcome of the case.[21] However, if climate litigants were to pursue common law claims, such as public nuisance, they would likely face more substantial standing barriers due to the necessity of satisfying the Australian common law standing test requiring proof of a "special interest."[22]

---

[20] *Utility Air Regulatory Group v. EPA*, 134 S.Ct. 2427, 2446 (Jun. 23, 2014) (citations omitted).

[21] The section provides: "Any person may bring proceedings in the [NSW Land and Environment] Court for an order to remedy or restrain a breach of this Act, whether or not any right of that person has been or may be infringed by or as a consequence of that breach."

[22] E.g., *Australian Conservation Foundation v. Commonwealth* (1990) 146 CLR 493. See, further, Michael Barker, "Standing to Sue in Public Interest Environmental Litigation: From ACF v Commonwealth to Tasmanian Conservation Trust v Minister for Resources" (1996) 13 *Environ. Planning L. J.* 186.

There are no formal equivalents in Australian law to the political question and displacement doctrines that apply in the United States. Instead there is a rather inchoate notion of non-justiciability that shares some similarities with political question in that it may be invoked by courts as a reason for declining to review complex policy or politically sensitive decisions of the executive branch.[23] In most administrative decision-making review, and certainly that which occurs in climate cases, the concept of non-justiciability is most clearly given effect in the distinction drawn between review of the legalities of a decision (termed judicial review) and review of the merits. Concern on the part of courts that a substantive consideration of climate-related arguments may stray into the area of merits review has been evident in several climate cases involving judicial review of government decision making,[24] and was viewed as a constraint on climate litigation by some interviewees. One interviewee described the limitations of judicial review actions for advancing climate regulation as follows:

> Judicial review has particular categories of grounds for review. We are told that that those categories are not closed but the reality is that they have not been opened up for years and it's very easy for government, Ministerial decisions, to simply make sure, and they do.... They go through, they get a lawyer and they go, right, here's the legislation, what are all the mandatory considerations I need to take into account as a result of the legislation, have I taken those into account, yes, tick, tick, tick, is there anything in there that I have placed too much weight on in a way that would breach traditional, administrative grounds of review, no, is it unreasonable, no, has procedural fairness been afforded if I must do that, yes. It's too easy, in effect, to ensure that you comply with all of those grounds of review. And we are told time and time again ... that you just cannot delve into the merits and you must be very careful not to delve into the merits.... So it makes it difficult for a trial judge in a judicial review decision beyond looking at the decision, looking at the material that the minister or decision-maker took in account, have they satisfied all the requisite demands of that material and [that] the legislation places on them, if so, that's it. End of the case.[25]

Even in a merits review setting – where judges have greater freedom to examine the legal and factual issues in dispute – Australian courts remain

---

[23] Chris Finn, "The Justiciability of Administrative Decisions: A Redundant Concept?" (2002) 30 *Fed. L. Rev.* 239.

[24] A prominent example is the adaptation case of *Walker v. Minister for Planning; Minister for Planning v. Walker* discussed in Chapter 4.

[25] Skype interview, Australian Participant 16 (May 30, 2013). See also Kirsty Ruddock, "Has Judicial Review Killed ESD?" (2013) 28(6) *Austr. Environ. Rev.* 625.

cognizant of their limited role, especially where questions of regulatory policy arise. For instance, in *Hunter Environmental Lobby v. Minister for Planning*, the NSW Land and Environment Court examined whether it was appropriate for the Court to impose conditions on an approval for a coal mine expansion that would require the mine to offset its direct greenhouse gas emissions through the purchase of carbon credits. The NSW Minister for Planning argued that "development approval conditions are unsuitable for implementing a regulatory regime to require proponents to offset some or all of the [greenhouse gas] emissions of their projects," citing concerns about the effectiveness, efficiency, and equity of such an approach.[26] Initially, however, Justice Pain ruled that it would be appropriate to include an offsetting condition for direct (scope 1) emissions from the mine and invited parties' further submissions on the wording of the condition.[27] Her Honor noted,

> The minister considered that a carbon pricing scheme was a preferable means from a policy and economic perspective to drive reductions in [greenhouse gas] emissions but no such system is yet [*sic*] to operate in Australia or NSW and this approval is sought now.[28]

In the intervening period between the initial judgment of the Court and the new hearing to consider submissions on the wording of the offset condition, the Australian government passed the Clean Energy Act to establish a national carbon pricing mechanism.[29] Given these developments and the Court's conclusion that that the new scheme met "at a practical level the purpose of imposing a condition requiring the offsetting of Scope 1 [greenhouse gas] emissions," Justice Pain ruled the offset condition was no longer warranted.[30] In a similar fashion to US decisions foreclosing federal common law pathways for climate change regulation, this decision – albeit on a smaller scale – signaled deference to national, uniform legislative approaches for mitigation where such approaches are in existence.

This general awareness of the need for a balance between judicial intervention and legislative and executive action to deal with climate

---

[26] *Hunter Environmental Lobby v. Minister for Planning*, [2011] NSWLEC 221, para. 60.
[27] Ibid., paras 92–94.   [28] Ibid. para. 101.
[29] Clean Energy Act 2011 (Cth) (repealed). This case is discussed further in Chapter 3.
[30] *Hunter Environment Lobby Inc v. Minister for Planning (No 2)* [2012] NSWLEC 40, para. 17.

change was also a common motif in the interviews we conducted with climate litigation participants – some of whom included judges who have decided such cases. Even among those interviewees who called for a greater "robustness" on the part of courts considering climate cases, there was a recognition that "judges have to deal with the cases that are brought before them and run, I have to also say, by the lawyers in a particular way."[31] Another interviewee described the process courts were engaged in as "trying to walk the line and not legislate climate change regulation or controls but also recognize where climate changes issues or considerations need to be undertaken or evaluated under the present framework."[32] Unsurprisingly, our judicial participants were among the most sensitive to this need for a balanced approach. As one commented, "I believe strongly in the Court and what we do but we are *part* of a big picture, we are not *the* big picture."[33] Another Australian interviewee summarized the sentiment thus:

> I think that it is incredibly dangerous for a . . . court to either be or be seen to be using its jurisdiction to ensure a particular agenda if that agenda is more of a policy one than one that is based on any proper statutory and objective basis. My approach to those sort of cases is to sit there as a judge and to say, well, my job is to work out what the law is and apply that. Now, if I look at the Act and it talks about climate change and I look at the regulations under the Act, that's fine. But if what I am really being asked to do is to rewrite government policy because it'll give me a warm inner glow, that's not something I have a great deal of time for.[34]

Across the two countries, then, the core similarity with respect to separation-of-powers constraints is that courts at times defer to legislatures or the executive branch as occupying the field or as the more appropriate actor. However, in part because the United States has more cases under federal environmental statutes and has common law actions, these doctrines have arisen as a more significant barrier in that jurisdiction. As the types of cases brought in each country continue to evolve, these types of constraints may become more important or, alternatively, may be revealed by the developing case law to be less of a barrier than initially thought.

[31] Skype interview, Australian Participant 14 (May 23, 2013).
[32] Telephone interview, US Participant 3 (Nov. 7, 2012).
[33] Skype interview, Australian Participant 22 (Sep. 13, 2013).
[34] Skype interview, Australian Participant 5 (Mar. 26, 2013).

7.2.2 Cost barriers

Although separation-of-powers constraints are evident in both countries to a greater or lesser degree, Australia and the United States diverge in the extent to which cost poses a barrier to proactive climate change litigation. In sum, costs associated with bringing climate cases before the courts pose a significant hurdle to such litigation in Australia but do not appear to create the same issues in the United States. In this section, we review the reasons why litigation costs may stymie otherwise worthy Australian climate claims, and the efforts of courts to lessen this access barrier, before explaining the different considerations that apply in the US context.

In Australia, many climate change legal battles pit poorly resourced environmental NGOs and community groups against powerful corporate actors and governments. This feature of the litigation has made who pays for litigation costs a central issue for access to justice.[35] Environmental and community groups involved in litigation try to limit their own costs by seeking legal aid funding; utilizing the services of low-cost community legal centers, such as the national network of Environmental Defenders Offices; and requesting the appearances of counsel and experts on a pro bono basis, where possible.[36] Some of the state-level specialist environmental and planning courts and tribunals in which climate change cases are brought are "no costs" jurisdictions; in other words, parties generally bear their own costs.[37] However, in other jurisdictions, there are provisions for the award of "adverse costs orders,"[38] and in some courts – such as the NSW Land and Environment Court and the Planning and Environment Court in Queensland – the award of costs is in the discretion of the court.[39] The "usual rule" in Australia with respect to costs is that costs follow the event – that is, the losing party is responsible for payment of both sides' costs[40] – and an order seeking costs will often be pursued by the winning party.

---

[35] See, e.g., Anne Kallies and Lee Godden, "What Price Democracy? Blue Wedges and the Hurdles to Public Interest Environmental Litigation" (2008) 33(4) *Alt. L. J.* 194.

[36] This practice can create its own issues – with the lack of availability of pro bono advocates, "compassion fatigue" can arise on the part of experts and legal counsel.

[37] For example, planning appeals in the Victorian Civil and Administrative Tribunal or for merits appeals in the NSW Land and Environment Court.

[38] Adverse cost orders are provided for under s 74(2)(b) of the *Victorian Civil and Administrative Tribunal Act 1998* (Vic) and s 29 of the *South Australian Environment, Resources and Development Court Act 1993* (SA).

[39] See s 98 *Civil Procedure Act 2005* (NSW), s 457 *Sustainable Planning Act 2009* (Qld).

[40] Part 42 r 42.1, *Uniform Civil Procedure Rules 2005*.

For individuals or impecunious environmental groups, even the risk of an order requiring payment of the other side's costs (often substantial where government and corporate defendants are involved) can dissuade them from bringing a case.[41] One interviewee described how a meritorious climate case ultimately did not go ahead because of the risk posed by a possible costs order against the individual considering the litigation. Not only would the litigant's livelihood have been on the line, but also due to the costs risk, it was impossible to secure an indemnity from other larger environmental groups to underwrite the litigation.[42] This was a common story related to us in our Australian interviews.

Courts, such as the NSW Land and Environment Court, that hear a lot of environmental and public interest cases have sought to develop rules that would minimize the access barriers posed by costs orders. Although such cases do not directly change the law relating to climate change, they make it easier for environmental NGOs and other public interest litigants to continue legal challenges without fear of having to bear enormous financial burdens in doing so. For instance, the NSW Land and Environment Court has adopted a specific rule allowing the grant of an exemption from the usual costs rule in environmental planning and protection cases where it is "satisfied that the proceedings have been brought in the public interest."[43] A three-part test is used by the Court to make this determination: (1) can the litigation be characterized as having been brought in the public interest; (2) if so, is there "something more" than the mere characterization of the litigation as having been brought in the public interest; and (3) are there any countervailing circumstances, including conduct of the applicant, that speak against departure from the usual costs rule?[44]

The Court has found this public interest test to be satisfied in several climate change cases. For instance, in the case of *Kennedy v. NSW Minister for Planning* – a continuation of the *Walker* litigation concerning the climate flood risk for a low-lying coastal site discussed in Chapter 4 – the judge noted that "there is a particularly strong element of public interest in the climate change/flooding issue in relation to this

---

[41] Skype interview, Australian Participant 22 (Sep. 13, 2013).

[42] In-person interview, Australian Participant 2 (Mar. 8, 2013).

[43] Rule 4.2(1) Land and Environment Court Rules 2007, which applies to class 4 proceedings – environmental planning and protection. The rule does not apply to class 8 proceedings, which are those involving mining matters.

[44] *Caroona Coal Action Group Inc v. Coal Mines Australia Pty Limited and Minister for Mineral Resources (No 3)* (2010) 173 LGERA 280.

development site."[45] In the case of *Gray v. Macquarie Generation*, which involved a novel but unsuccessful argument by applicants that the license for a large power station did not permit the unconstrained emission of carbon dioxide, the Court also ruled that the public interest exemption to the usual costs rule applied. Justice Pain found that the litigation should be characterized as public interest litigation and that each party should therefore pay its own costs. In making this ruling, Her Honor noted that the litigation was "broadly concerned with the impact of emissions of carbon dioxide from coal-fired power stations on climate change" and the applicants' motivation in pursuing the litigation was "based on their concerns about the environmental impacts of climate change."[46] Moreover, the respondent company was "a substantial emitter of carbon dioxide which is an essential part of its electricity generating functions as a coal-fired power station" and the applicants' case was "directed to addressing those substantial emissions which focus of concern is reflective of local, national and international concern about the adverse impacts of climate change resulting from carbon dioxide emissions from development such as coal-fired power stations."[47]

While this jurisprudence has been welcomed by environmental claimants, as interviewees pointed out, the availability of a public interest exemption from costs may provide little comfort to litigants who have no certainty that the exemption will be applied when they commence a case.[48] In addition, as one lawyer interviewed commented, efforts by courts to clarify how the test applies may "just mak[e] it more and more technical in terms of advising your clients."[49]

Potentially more significant are rules the NSW Land and Environment Court has developed around maximum or protective costs orders for public interest litigants. A protective costs order can be sought by a public

---

[45] [2010] NSWLEC 164, at para. 10. Ultimately the Court upheld the minister's request for costs on this issue as, despite the strong public interest in raising it, "the Minister responded positively to the Court of Appeal majority view in the *Walker* litigation that potential climate change flooding effect had to be taken into account when approval of the development was sought and, largely in consequence of that response, the flooding/climate change ground failed" in the *Kennedy* case.

[46] *Gray v. Macquarie Generation (No 2)* [2010] NSWLEC 82, para. 15.

[47] Ibid. para. 17. The Court also noted that the argument pursued by the applicants, albeit dismissed, was novel and did "raise a potentially significant legal issue . . . if the matter had proceeded to final hearing"; para. 21.

[48] Ordinarily costs are determined at the conclusion of proceedings once the result in the case is known.

[49] Skype interview, Australian Participant 14 (May 23, 2013).

interest litigant at an early stage in the proceedings as a way of capping costs liability and reducing uncertainty over costs exposure that may otherwise serve as a barrier to litigation.[50] The NSW Land and Environment Court made its first protective costs order in 2009 in a case involving an environmental NGO suing over river pollution from the activities of a power generator. The parties' costs were capped at AUD$20,000 by the Court, a decision upheld on appeal to the NSW Court of Appeal.[51] Although no such orders have been issued so far in climate change cases, interviewees noted that it is likely "you'll see more of those kinds of applications now."[52] For the environmental group concerned, the order "meant that the group, even before they got very far at all – it was shortly after they filed their commencing procedure – they sought an order from [the Court] limiting the costs in the proceeding even if they lost. So they knew they were only ever up for x thousand dollars."[53]

Because costs are structured differently in the United States,[54] this issue has not arisen in a parallel way in US climate litigation. As one of our US interviewees explained,

> The "American Rule" (in fact followed in America) is that each side typically bears its own costs. A court can issue sanctions and order a party to pay the other side's costs for especially frivolous or outrageous conduct, but that is extremely rare.... The federal Equal Access to Justice Act requires the federal government to pay the other side's fees if they win, and some states have similar laws, but it doesn't go in the other direction. Losing plaintiffs may have to pay defendant's fees if they have brought a SLAPP [strategic lawsuit against public participation] suit, but that too is rare. I do not believe that climate change litigation in the US has been inhibited at all by fear of having to pay the other side's fees, and it hasn't been inhibited much by inability to find pro bono lawyers. In fact I am approached with some frequency by lawyers who want to do pro bono climate change work but can't find cases.[55]

---

[50] Hon. Justice Nicola Pain and Sonali Seneviratne, "Protective Costs Orders: Increasing Access to Courts by Capping Costs" (2011) *Austr. Environ. Rev.* 276. These orders are also available in federal courts, though they have mainly been awarded in less complex private commercial cases.

[51] *Blue Mountains Conservation Society Inc v. Delta Electricity; Delta Electricity v. Blue Mountains Conservation Society Inc* (2009) 170 LGERA 1.

[52] Skype interview, Australian Participant 22 (Sep. 13, 2013).   [53] Ibid.

[54] Chris Tollefson, "Costs in Public Interest Litigation Revisited" (2011) 39 *The Advocates' Q.* 197.

[55] Telephone interview and e-mail exchange, US Participant 7 (Nov. 16, 2012, and May 19, 2014).

These differences between the two countries – in both the cost rules and how they affect potential petitioners – highlight the importance of this issue. The extent to which petitioners fear major financial repercussions of filing appears to impact whether potentially meritorious suits are brought and who is able to influence the debate over climate change through the courts.

7.3 Antiregulatory litigation

Access to courts and the inability to get decisions on the merits are not the only, or even the most significant, barriers that climate change litigation faces in promoting progress. Litigation is sometimes antiregulatory in its focus or consequences. Opponents of regulation turn to the courts to try to overturn proactive regulation, some of which has emerged in response to litigation. Even when proactive climate change litigation succeeds in courts, it may not always have pro-regulatory effects. Backlash against the outcome may prevent the mitigation or adaptation outcomes the case sought to induce. And the pro-regulatory side does not always win. At times, when pro-regulatory petitioners lose, especially in Australia, those opposing regulation bolster that outcome with legislation, as has occurred following a number of the cases opposing coal mines. Due to the differences in how opponents to regulation primarily interact with litigation in the two countries, this section considers antiregulatory litigation with a focus on the United States. We do not discuss Australia directly in this section, because no antiregulatory litigation equivalent to that in the United States has been filed there.[56] Instead, the Australian experience is the focus of Section 7.4, which analyzes antiregulatory consequences of litigation.

Increasingly, in assessing the overall regulatory impact of climate change litigation in the United States, the role of case law challenges brought by antiregulatory interests needs to be taken into account. Like Newton's third law of motion, it seems that for every advance brought about by pro-regulatory cases, there is an equal and opposite reaction through antiregulatory litigation. Antiregulatory climate litigation has not been confined to the United States,[57] but it has been far more

---

[56] If it had proceeded, the writ filed against provisions of the now repealed Clean Energy Act 2011 (Cth) by mining entrepreneur and Member of Parliament, Clive Palmer, would have been the first such case. This writ was discussed in Chapter 2 as an example of a constitutional claim.

[57] There have been a number of such cases in the European Union, including the challenge by American airlines against aviation emissions rules under the EU Emissions Trading

extensive there than in other countries. This comports with the general tradition in US environmental law of regulation being shaped significantly by proactive litigation and opposing industry lawsuits.[58]

Many antiregulatory lawsuits in the United States have raised questions about the appropriate interpretation of particular statutes or roles of different levels of government that feed into larger debates around how US climate regulation should proceed. These include whether general environmental laws like the Clean Air Act or the Endangered Species Act are the best tools for regulating greenhouse gas pollution and the appropriate scope of independent state regulation of climate change within a federal system of governance. Other cases seem to have had little other purpose than to delay, frustrate, or create uncertainty over regulation[59] or to intimidate and dissuade climate scientists and activists from pressing their cause.[60]

Not all US lawsuits contesting climate regulation have been brought by industry,[61] but the majority of the cases involve business claimants who will be directly impacted by the regulatory measure being challenged. In such cases, some antiregulatory litigants appear to be reviving the same strategies used in past battles over health and environmental regulation for products such as asbestos, cigarettes, and toxic chemicals. In litigation challenging state climate regulatory measures, for example, one interviewee explained that antiregulatory petitioners

> had two kind of themes (a) that it wasn't happening... climate change wasn't happening and... [(b)] the amount of reductions you get from these regulations is insignificant because it's a global problem and look what China and India are doing so we shouldn't... don't make us do this.[62]

In this section, we examine the main types of US antiregulatory cases and the effects they are having on climate change regulation. The bulk of US

Scheme. For discussion see Sanja Bogojević, "EU Climate Change Litigation, the Role of the European Courts and the Importance of Legal Culture" (2013) 35(3) *L. Policy* 184.

[58] Thomas McGarity, "EPA at Helm's Deep: Surviving the Fourth Attack on Environmental Law" (2013) 24 *Fordham Environ. L. Rev.* 205.

[59] Interviewees cited as an example the lawsuit brought by the California Chamber of Commerce to challenge auction provisions under the state's cap-and-trade program.

[60] For details of these cases, see Arnold and Porter LLP, "U.S. Climate Change Litigation Chart" (Climate Protesters and Scientists), at www.climatecasechart.com.

[61] For instance, there have been a number of cases brought challenging regulatory measures on environmental justice grounds. For an example, see the case of *Association of Irritated Residents v. CARB* discussed in Chapter 6.

[62] Telephone interview, US Participant 11 (Oct. 10, 2013).

antiregulatory litigation has focused on federal regulation, including EPA motor vehicle and stationary source regulation under the Clean Air Act pursuant to the US Supreme Court's mandate in *Massachusetts v. EPA*[63] and listing of species under the Endangered Species Act. Another significant focus of antiregulatory litigation has been challenging proactive state regulatory initiatives in the climate field. Cases in this category have attempted to limit or eliminate state and municipal vehicle standards, as well as state regulatory programs seeking to reduce greenhouse gas emissions or to foster a transition from fossil fuels to cleaner energy sources. A number of the more recent state-level cases claim that state efforts violate the dormant Commerce Clause of the US Constitution, with divergent outcomes in the district courts considering them.

7.3.1 Challenges to federal regulatory action

Once it became apparent that the Obama administration was prepared to regulate greenhouse gas emissions under the Clean Air Act pursuant to *Massachusetts v. EPA*, antiregulatory litigation swiftly followed. In the suite of cases opposing EPA's rulemaking efforts – which were consolidated as *Coalition for Responsible Regulation v. EPA* – various states and industry groups argued that the EPA's actions (the Endangerment Finding, the tailpipe rule for vehicles, and timing and tailoring rules for power plants) were based on an improper construction of the Clean Air Act and were arbitrary and capricious. These challenges were comprehensively dismissed by the DC Circuit in an opinion that was partially reversed in June 2014 by the Supreme Court in *Utility Air Regulatory Group v. EPA*. The DC Circuit opinion held that

> 1) the Endangerment Finding and Tailpipe Rule are neither arbitrary nor capricious; 2) EPA's interpretation of the governing [Clean Air Act] provisions is unambiguously correct; and 3) no petitioner has standing to challenge the Timing and Tailoring Rules.[64]

As discussed in depth in Chapter 3, the Supreme Court's partial reversal focused very narrowly on a small subset of the issues that the DC Circuit addressed. Its certiorari grant was limited to the question of "whether EPA permissibly determined that its regulation of greenhouse gas emissions

---

[63] It is not only these EPA rules that have been challenged. Essentially any step taken by the EPA has attracted antiregulatory claims.

[64] *Coalition for Responsible Regulation v. EPA*, 684 F.3d 102 (D.C. Cir. June 26, 2012).

from new motor vehicles triggered permitting requirements under the Clean Air Act for stationary sources that emit greenhouse gases."[65] It did not reconsider the DC Circuit's upholding of the Endangerment Finding or tailpipe rule. With respect to the EPA's stationary sources regulation, it partially reversed and partially upheld the DC Circuit, with the result that the EPA can still regulate the vast majority of the stationary sources that it planned to address but cannot use some of its particular planned pathways under the Clean Air Act to do so.

Interviewees analyzing the DC Circuit opinion prior to Supreme Court's partial reversal viewed this earlier decision as an important milestone in the ongoing litigation and regulation to address greenhouse gas emissions at the national level. According to them, the DC Circuit not only "affirmed regulatory authority" on the part of the EPA[66] but also helped to "creat[e] some momentum and some credibility for the direction the agency had taken."[67] As one interviewee explained, the decision

> signified a strong endorsement of EPA's use of the Clean Air Act as a regulatory tool and as a direct progeny of *Massachusetts v. EPA*. The Court basically said, look, *Massachusetts v. EPA* required this, we're not going back. So that was a very important step. And also it was just incredibly important for the regulatory terrain over the next few years because we don't anticipate that anything's going to happen at the federal level legislatively.[68]

Interviewees also highlighted the DC Circuit opinion's indirect consequences for the public debate over climate regulation in the period following the opinion. By normalizing the regulatory measures being taken by the EPA as the next logical step in the process begun by the Supreme Court decision in *Massachusetts*, the case helped to take the heat out of allegations by the Chamber of Commerce, other industry groups, and a number of states that the EPA was "going off the rails and doing something crazy."[69]

Moreover, the DC Circuit's decision contained a strong endorsement of climate science that has been seen as helpful in combating climate skepticism raised in political contexts and in the media. The court reiterated the

---

[65] *Certiorari granted in part and denied in part, Utility Air Regulatory Group v. EPA*, 2013 WL 1155428, 81 USLW 3560 (U.S.Dist.Col. Oct 15, 2013) (NO. 12–1146).

[66] Telephone interview, US Participant 9 (Dec. 3, 2012).

[67] Telephone interview, US Participant 8 (Nov. 26, 2012).

[68] In-person interview, US Participant 5 (Nov. 14, 2012).

[69] Telephone interview, US Participant 8 (Nov. 26, 2012).

Supreme Court's finding that "in recent decades [a] well-documented rise in global temperatures has coincided with a significant increase in the concentration of [greenhouse gases] in the atmosphere."[70] It also upheld the EPA's finding that greenhouse gases endanger the public health, describing the scientific record relied on by the agency as "substantial."[71] The court noted that

> EPA's scientific evidence of record included support for the proposition that greenhouse gases trap heat on earth that would otherwise dissipate into space; that this "greenhouse effect" warms the climate; that human activity is contributing to increased atmospheric levels of greenhouse gases; and that the climate system is warming.[72]

The mixed result in the Supreme Court's subsequent decision in *Utility Air Regulatory Group v. EPA* has led to both sides claiming victory. Immediately following the decision, Liz Purchia said on behalf of the EPA that the opinion "largely upheld" the EPA's approach and would allow its power plant rules to go forward: "We are pleased that the Court's decision is consistent with our approach to focus on other Clean Air Act tools like the Clean Power Plan to limit carbon pollution, as part of the President's Climate Action Plan."[73] In contrast, US Chamber of Commerce president Thomas Donohue, who opposed the EPA regulation, characterized the opinion as follows: "EPA is now on notice that it does not have unlimited authority to impose massive costs on the U.S. economy and mandate a fundamental redesign of America's electricity system."[74] Harry Ng, general counsel for the American Petroleum Institute, similarly described the opinion as "a stark reminder that the EPA's power is not unlimited."[75]

Some of the pro-regulatory effects of the DC Circuit's ruling in *Coalition for Responsible Regulation* are likely to persist notwithstanding the Supreme Court's decision to partially reverse it. Arguably, the Supreme Court's decision to decline review of the EPA's Endangerment Finding, its underlying science, and the vehicle emission standards promulgated by the EPA may be taken as an implicit affirmation of much of the federal agency's authority to address climate change through greenhouse gas regulation under the Clean Air Act, even as the Court partially struck

---

[70] *Coalition for Responsible Regulation v. EPA*, 684 F.3d 102 (D.C. Cir. June 26, 2012), citing *Massachusetts v. EPA* at 504–5.
[71] Ibid., 22.   [72] Ibid., 28–29.
[73] Edward Felker, "EPA, Industry See Gains in Supreme Court Carbon Ruling," *Energy Guardian*, June 23, 2014.
[74] Felker, "EPA, Industry See Gains in Supreme Court Carbon Ruling."   [75] Ibid.

down the EPA's approach to stationary sources.[76] Although it is too soon
to know what the long-term direct and indirect effects of this case will be,
the Supreme Court appears to accept EPA regulation of greenhouse gas
emissions for both motor vehicles and stationary sources under the Clean
Air Act with some constraints on which regulatory pathways it uses. This
acceptance of EPA regulation, within limits, under broad environmental
statutes – which echoes the approach of the Court in *Massachusetts v. EPA*
and *AEP v. Connecticut* – may end up having more pro- than antiregulatory consequences. The outcome of this litigation, the most significant
antiregulatory litigation to date, thus reinforces a theme throughout the
book: whether litigation is filed with promotive or constraining goals, the
outcome of the case could have an opposite regulatory effect.

Although the Clean Air Act challenges are the only ones that have
reached the Supreme Court, antiregulatory litigation challenging federal
action has not been limited to the field of air pollution. Federal government actions with respect to climate-imperiled species listed under the
Endangered Species Act have also attracted a number of antiregulatory
suits. Originally, as discussed in Chapters 3 and 4, it was federal agencies
under the Bush administration that were being sued to act on petitions
for listing of species, including the polar bear. Once that listing occurred,
however, it was challenged by the state of Alaska and oil and gas companies concerned about the economic impacts of listing of the bear and
federal actions to designate and safeguard the bear's critical habitat in the
Arctic. At the same time, separate litigation brought by pro-regulatory
petitioners challenged the special 4(d) rule and the exemptions it grants
for greenhouse gas–emitting activities that may have an adverse impact
on listed threatened species or their habitats.[77]

Antiregulatory suits in the Endangered Species Act context have focused
particularly on questions of the adequacy of the science relied on by the
federal government in listing climate-imperiled species and the meaning
of statutory language requiring that a species be "in danger of extinction"

---

[76] Meredith Wilensky, "FAQs on the Supreme Court's Grant of Cert on EPA's Regulation
of Greenhouse Gas Emissions," *Climate Law Blog*, Columbia Center for Climate Change
Law, October 21, 2013, at http://blogs.law.columbia.edu/climatechange/2013/10/21/faqs-
on-supreme-courts-cert-grant-on-epas-regulation-of-greenhouse-gas-emissions/.

[77] *In re Polar Bear Endangered Species Act Listing & § 4(d) Rule Litig.*, 2011 U.S. Dist. LEXIS
119476 (D.D.C., Oct. 17, 2011); *In re Polar Bear Endangered Species Act Listing & § 4(d) Rule
Litig.*, 2011 U.S. Dist. LEXIS 70172 (D.D.C., June 30, 2011); *In re Polar Bear Endangered
Species Act Listing & § 4(d) Rule Litig.*, No. 11–5219 (U.S. Court of Appeals, D.C. Cir., Mar.
30, 2013).

or "likely to become endangered within the foreseeable future" in the context of a long-term problem such as climate change.[78] Even more so than in the Clean Air Act context, where the Supreme Court partially struck down the EPA's approach, as discussed previously, courts have so far been supportive of agencies' rulemaking efforts and deferential to agencies' interpretations of both the applicable science and the statutory language of the Endangered Species Act. Courts have affirmed agency listing decisions as well as promulgation of the 4(d) rule (following the issue of a new environmental review by the Obama administration). Dismissing an appeal by the state of Alaska and oil industry groups against the decision of Judge Sullivan upholding the polar bear listing, the DC Circuit Court of Appeals explained,

> The appellate court's task in a case such as this is a "narrow" one. *Motor Vehicle Mfrs. Ass'n of U.S., Inc. v. State Farm Mut. Auto. Ins. Co.*, 463 U.S. 29, 43 (1983). Our principal responsibility here is to determine, in light of the record considered by the agency, whether the Listing Rule is a product of reasoned decision making. It is significant that Appellants have neither pointed to mistakes in the agency's reasoning nor adduced any data or studies that the agency overlooked. In addition, Appellants challenge neither the agency's findings on climate science nor on polar bear biology. Rather, the principal claim advanced by Appellants is that [the Fish and Wildlife Service] misinterpreted and misapplied the record before it. We disagree.[79]

As noted in Chapters 3 and 4, these rulings by the courts largely upholding federal regulatory action under environmental statutes – in response to challenges – stand in strong contrast to decisions in federal common law cases that have attempted to attribute responsibility for climate change harms directly to emitters. They thus reinforce the statutory pathways the US government is currently pursuing to regulate climate change from greenhouse gas emissions. As one interviewee explained in reference to these statutory cases, "the courts are trying to find a balance, I think, between allowing agencies to interpret the mandate of *Massachusetts v. EPA* but not allowing agencies to overreach at the same time."[80] The Supreme Court's decision in *Utility Air Regulatory Group*, with its partial affirmation and partial reversal after granting certiorari on narrow

---

[78] Telephone interview, US Participant 3 (Nov. 7, 2012).
[79] *In re Polar Bear Endangered Species Act Listing & § 4(d) Rule Litig.*, No. 11–5219 (U.S. Court of Appeals, D.C. Cir., Mar. 30, 2013), 3.
[80] Telephone interview, US Participant 9 (Dec. 3, 2012).

grounds, only reinforces this role that courts are playing with respect to the executive branch. This delicate dance by the courts is likely to continue as federal regulatory efforts progress and attract further litigation challenges.

7.3.2   Challenges to state regulatory action

Antiregulatory climate litigation in the United States predates the previously discussed challenges to EPA's regulatory efforts under broad environmental laws. The first antiregulatory cases – brought during the presidency of George W. Bush – did not focus on federal climate action, which was very limited at the time. Rather, they challenged action by proactive states that sought to fill the void left by a lack of federal climate legislation and of progressive climate regulatory efforts at the national level. Although the federal government has become more active under the Obama administration, several leader states, especially California, still constitute the front edge of climate change regulation and related clean energy initiatives, and challenges to their efforts have continued. The most significant recent challenges claim that these states are overstepping their authority to regulate interstate commerce and therefore violating the US Constitution's dormant Commerce Clause. This section considers the early cases, these more recent constitutional challenges, and the implications of challenges to state action for progress on climate change regulation.

The majority of the early antiregulatory suits against states were brought by auto manufacturers targeting California's attempts to introduce greenhouse gas emissions standards for vehicles, known as the Pavley standards. Under the Clean Air Act, California has the authority to enforce its own standards for air pollution from vehicles subject to getting a waiver from the EPA. Although such waivers have generally been granted as a matter of course, the Bush administration denied California's waiver request with respect to greenhouse gas emissions. This denial led to litigation that was ultimately resolved, as discussed in Chapter 3, by the Obama administration granting the waiver.[81] If the waiver is granted, other states can choose whether to follow any applicable national standard or to adopt Californian standards as their own. As of December 2007, fourteen additional states had opted to follow California's vehicle emissions standards, and another four were considering it; fifteen of those states intervened

---

[81] Clean Air Act, 42 U.S. Code § 7543 – State standards.

in the litigation that California brought when the EPA denied its waiver request.[82]

Before the final Pavley standards had even been adopted by the California Air Resources Board, the state was sued by various auto manufacturers. The auto companies also initiated lawsuits in three other states: Vermont, Rhode Island, and New Mexico. As one interviewee described it, this "strategy" ensured the cases would be heard in four different US Court of Appeals districts, maximizing the chances of a favorable decision and stretching the resources of state attorney generals' offices.[83] Ultimately, however, the auto companies were not successful in their challenges to the Pavley standards.[84] Moreover, with the advent of the Rose Garden agreement, by which the Obama administration granted California's waiver and agreed to harmonize national and California standards over time,[85] the auto companies laid down their arms: "once the waiver came in the auto industry has gone, oh, if I have to build these cars in thirteen states, if I get more time then I will do it for fifty states. So the litigation was I think fundamental for getting that process moving on the vehicle side."[86]

A key theme of the cases brought by auto companies in the Pavley litigation was that state-level regulation was ill-suited to the scale of the

---

[82] These states that had adopted California standards included Arizona, Connecticut, Florida, Maine, Maryland, Massachusetts, New Jersey, New Mexico, New York, Oregon, Pennsylvania, Rhode Island, Vermont, and Washington, which represent approximately one-quarter of the US vehicle fleet and vehicle miles traveled. The four states considering adoption were Colorado, Delaware, Illinois, and Utah. See States That Have Adopted California Motor Vehicle Greenhouse Gas Emission Standards (as of Dec. 20, 2007), www.epw.senate.gov/public/index.cfm?FuseAction=Files.View&FileStore_id=6913a8db-b9f2–4ae0–8491-e452d4a50cec (citing Congressional Research Service and Pew Center on Global Climate Change, NGA, 2007); Environmental Defense Fund, "13 States Adopting California Clean Car Standards Would Reap Significant Economic and Environmental Benefits," press release, June 30, 2009, www.edf.org/news/13-states-adopting-california-clean-car-standards-would-reap-significant-economic-and-environme.

[83] Telephone interview, US Participant 11 (Oct. 10, 2013): "And if you look at what states the autos picked they picked two factors the way I see it: one is circuit and then also small attorney general offices. So when the New York Attorney General's Office tried to intervene in the Vermont case because they are in the same U.S. Court of Appeal, the auto manufacturers opposed that so they had to fight their way into the case."

[84] *Green Mountain Chrysler Plymouth Dodge Jeep v. Crombie*, 508 F. Supp. 2d 295, 301 (D.Vt. 2007); *Central Valley Chrysler-Jeep, Inc. v. Witherspoon*, 37 ELR 20023, No. No. 04–6663, (E.D. Cal., Jan. 16, 2007).

[85] The White House, Remarks by the President on national fuel efficiency standards, Rose Garden, May 19, 2009 (Office of the Press Sec., Washington D.C.), at www.whitehouse.gov/the-press-office/remarks-president-national-fuel-efficiency-standards.

[86] Telephone interview, US Participant 11 (Oct. 10, 2013).

global greenhouse gas problem. As California and numerous other states have moved forward with regulatory programs for reducing greenhouse gas emissions and promoting renewable energy in their jurisdictions, this argument has reemerged in a new round of state-level antiregulatory challenges arguing that these programs violate the US Constitution's dormant Commerce Clause. While the explicit language of the Commerce Clause provides Congress with authority to regulate interstate commerce, the Supreme Court has interpreted that power as also including a dormant restriction on states; they cannot pass laws that interfere with interstate commerce. The dormant Commerce Clause jurisprudence prohibits laws that discriminate against out-of-state business, provide burdens on interstate commerce that outweigh benefits, or regulate extraterritorially.[87]

The lawsuits brought against California's Low Carbon Fuel Standard (LCFS), Colorado's Renewable Energy Standard, and the Minnesota Next Generation Energy Act have significant implications for states' ability to address climate change. In all three cases, industry litigants are raising constitutional arguments under the dormant Commerce Clause in an effort to have the state laws declared invalid. Whereas the California legal provisions challenged focus most directly on climate change, the other two states' laws address the transition away from coal and to renewable energy, a shift crucial for mitigating climate change. To date, the pro-regulatory side has won in California and Colorado, and the antiregulatory side has won in Minnesota, but these results may change on appeal.

As interviewees explained, the underlying agenda of this antiregulatory litigation against proactive state measures seems to be to limit existing efforts and stop their spread to other states, thereby halting momentum for a clean energy transition. These challenges against California, Minnesota, and Colorado laws – which involve a constitutionally based variation on the "too big" arguments discussed in Chapter 6 – raise questions about the limits of state regulatory authority in this space and have created some uncertainty. Even the partial success of dormant Commerce Clause arguments so far is forcing climate change lawyers to reevaluate the vulnerability of state-level climate programs: "the whole dormant Commerce Clause – which is something we all thought was dead, didn't

---

[87] For an analysis of the dormant Commerce Clause in this context, see Alexandra B. Klass and Elizabeth Henley, "Energy Policy, Extraterritoriality, and the Dormant Commerce Clause," *San. Diego J. Clim. Energy L.* (forthcoming).

even exist when we were in Law School – you know, all of a sudden this [litigation] has affirmed that this is a viable argument."[88] Thus, as Judge Ronald M. Gould of the Ninth Circuit Court of Appeals held in the latest iteration of industry lawsuits in federal court against California's LCFS, "what states may do of their own accord to deter or slow global warming"[89] remains an unsettled issue.

The ongoing federal LCFS lawsuits against California illustrate the various tensions raised in this latest strand of antiregulatory climate change litigation against states. In the LCFS lawsuits, industry groups – primarily representing Midwest ethanol producers – are suing California on the basis that the LCFS's approach to assessing carbon intensity of transportation fuels unlawfully discriminates against out-of-state businesses. The LCFS adopts a life cycle analysis in its assessment – that is, it takes into account the greenhouse gas emissions involved in the production and transportation of fuels. The plaintiffs argue that this regulation favors Californian producers over other producers who have higher costs associated with transporting their product to California. In September 2013, the Ninth Circuit Court of Appeals issued a decision strongly supporting the LCFS and overturning a lower court decision that the LCFS violated the dormant Commerce Clause by discriminating against out-of-state fuels. The Court ruled,

> The Fuel Standard performs lifecycle analysis to measure the carbon intensity of all fuel pathways. When it is relevant to that measurement, the Fuel Standard considers location, but only to the extent that location affects the actual [greenhouse gas] emissions attributable to a default pathway. Under Dormant Commerce Clause precedent, if an out-of-state ethanol pathway does impose higher costs on California by virtue of its greater [greenhouse gas] emissions, there is a nondiscriminatory reason for its higher carbon intensity value. Stated another way, if producers of out-of-state ethanol actually cause more [greenhouse gas] emissions for each unit produced, because they use dirtier electricity or less efficient plants, [the California Air Resources Board] can base its regulatory treatment on these emissions. If California is to successfully promote low carbon intensity fuels, countering a trend towards increased [greenhouse gas] output and rising world temperatures, it cannot ignore the real factors behind [greenhouse gas] emissions.[90]

---

[88] In-person interview, US Participant 5 (Nov. 14, 2012).
[89] *Rocky Mountain Farmers Union, et al. v. Corey*, No. 12–15131 (9th Cir. Jan. 22, 2014) (denying rehearing en banc).
[90] *Rocky Mountain Farmers Union v. Corey*, 730 F.3d 1070 (2013), 36.

As Professor Ann Carlson notes, this decision represented "a ringing endorsement for California's attempt to capture all of the carbon emissions generated through producing, refining and transporting fuel."[91] Moreover, the decision provided strong support for smaller levels of government to take action to address climate change despite the "global" nature of the problem, provided such local approaches are well thought-through and scientifically based. Indeed, the Ninth Circuit emphasized the importance of such subnational (and subglobal) efforts in dealing with climate change:

> California should be encouraged to continue and to expand its efforts to find a workable solution to lower carbon emissions, or to slow their rise. If no such solution is found, California residents and people worldwide will suffer great harm. We will not at the outset block California from developing this innovative, nondiscriminatory regulation to impede global warming. If the Fuel Standard works, encouraging the development of alternative fuels by those who would like to reach the California market, it will help ease California's climate risks and inform other states as they attempt to confront similar challenges.[92]

The Ninth Circuit's approach to the dormant Commerce Clause has been allowed to stand on appeal. Early in 2014, the Ninth Circuit denied en banc review, and the Supreme Court in June 2014 also denied petition for review of the case. The Supreme Court's denial of review puts to rest questions over whether the LCFS violates the dormant Commerce Clause on its face. However, the litigation over the LCFS continues. Questions as to whether the regulation is discriminatory in purpose or effect remain, with the Ninth Circuit remanding this issue to the lower court for determination.

The Colorado and Minnesota cases focus on different aspects of those states' renewable energy laws and have had opposite outcomes at this stage, though, as noted, appeals may change the ultimate outcomes. *Energy and Environmental Legal Institute v. Epel* involves a challenge by a pro-coal nonprofit and one of its members to the Colorado Renewable Energy Statute. The antiregulatory "plaintiffs seek a declaration that the provision requiring that Colorado utility companies obtain an increasing

---

[91] Ann Carlson, "Ninth Circuit Upholds California's Low Carbon Fuel Standard," Legal Planet Blog, September 18, 2013, at http://legal-planet.org/2013/09/18/breaking-news-ninth-circuit-upholds-californias-low-carbon-fuel-standard/.

[92] *Rocky Mountain Farmers Union v. Corey*, 730 F.3d 1070 (2013), 70.

proportion of their electricity from renewable sources violates the Commerce Clause of the United States Constitution."[93] More specifically, they claim that its requirement that Colorado electricity providers meet a "Renewables Quota" constitutes constitutionally forbidden extraterritorial regulation of out-of-state businesses. The district court rejected their argument on the grounds that the law only regulates Colorado electricity generators, even if it has an impact on out-of-state businesses:

> First, the Renewables Quota does not impact transactions between out-of-state business entities. If a Wyoming coal company generates electricity and sells it to a South Dakota business, the Colorado Renewables Quota does not impact that transaction in any way. The Renewables Quota only regulates Colorado energy generators and the companies that do business with Colorado energy generators.
>
> Moreover, the Renewables Quota does not mandate that an out-of-state energy generator do business in any particular manner. Colorado energy companies are free to buy and sell electricity from any in-state or out-of-state generator. The RES does not limit these transactions, set minimum standards for out-of-state generators that wish to do business in Colorado, or attempt to control pricing of the electricity. Rather, the RES comes into play only with regard to whether energy purchased by a Colorado utility from an out-of-state electricity generator will count towards the Colorado utility's Renewables Quota. As such, the RES does not impose conditions on the importation of electricity into Colorado.
>
> The Court agrees with Plaintiffs that the RES may influence the way out-of-state electricity generators do business because the Renewables Quota provides Colorado utilities an incentive to purchase electricity that can be credited towards their Renewables Quota. However, the fact that this incentive structure may negatively impact the profits of out-of-state generators whose electricity cannot be used to fulfil the Quota does not make the Renewables Quota invalid. The dormant Commerce Clause neither protects the profits of any particular business, nor the right to do business in any particular manner.[94]

The court also reached the other two prongs of the dormant Commerce Clause, including extensive discussion of burdens issues similar to the ones that the LCFS case addressed. After finding that the law has simply shifted the type of electricity being used in Colorado rather than decreasing the amount of electricity being purchased from in-state or out-of-state sources, the Colorado district court focused on the political will behind the act and made a separation-of-powers argument. It noted, "Fifty-four

---

[93] ___ F.Supp.2d ___, 2014 WL 1874977 (D. Colo., May 9, 2014).   [94] Ibid.

percent of Colorado voters voted to approve renewable energy standards for the state in 2004. . . . The Supreme Court has frequently admonished that courts should not "second-guess the empirical judgments of lawmakers concerning the utility of legislation."[95] The Colorado opinion, like the California one, thus shows considerable deference to the legislative branch and a tendency to interpret the law's burden relatively narrowly.

However, despite these judgments upholding Californian and Colorado states' laws, the Minnesota case provides a cautionary tale of the potential antiregulatory impacts that dormant Commerce Clause lawsuits could have. *North Dakota v. Heydinger* involved a challenge by North Dakota, lignite coal industry representatives and multistate electric cooperatives to a provision of Minnesota's Next Generation Energy Act – a broader law that sets Minnesota's renewable energy goals – that requires carbon dioxide offsets for importation from new out-of-state coal-fired power plants. The district court ruled in favor of the antiregulatory petitioners on the grounds that interstate electricity industry's participation in the Midcontinental Independent System Operator (MISO) gives the regulation extraterritorial effect:

> MISO is the RTO [Regional Transmission Organization] responsible for operating and controlling the transmission of electricity in and among several states, including Minnesota. Like the transmission of information over the internet, the transmission of electricity over the MISO grid does not recognize state boundaries. Therefore, when a non-Minnesota entity injects electricity into the grid to satisfy its obligations to a non-Minnesota member, it cannot ensure that the electricity will not travel to and be removed in – in other words, be imported to and contribute to statewide power sector carbon dioxide emissions in – Minnesota.
>
> Likewise, non-Minnesota entities that enter into long-term power purchase agreements for capacity to satisfy their non-Minnesota load cannot ensure that the electricity, when bid into the MISO market and dispatched, will not travel to and be removed in – in other words, increase statewide power sector carbon dioxide emissions in – Minnesota.
>
> Therefore, a North Dakota generation-and-transmission cooperative cannot ensure that the coal-generated electricity that it injects into the MISO grid is used only to serve its North Dakota members and not its Minnesota members. Consequentially, in order to ensure compliance with Minn. Stat. § 216 H.03, subd. 3(2)–(3), out-of-state parties must conduct their out-of-state business according to Minnesota's terms – i.e., engaging in no transactions involving power or capacity that would contribute to or increase Minnesota's statewide power sector carbon dioxide emissions.

[95] Ibid.

As noted by the Environmental Group Amici, this is the "paradigm" of extraterritorial legislation.[96]

This reasoning by the district court provides an interesting contrast to the approach taken by the courts in the California and Colorado cases. Though certainly part of the issue in the Minnesota case is the particular provision and its potential to be applied broadly – an issue that could be addressed by a state interpretive entity making clear that it will be interpreted more narrowly, as it has been in practice – the district court used the physical interconnectedness of electricity markets to find an extraterritoriality problem. Its reasoning has potential implications for the future as RTOs play an ever-more important role in electricity markets and in addressing interstate energy issues. Consider, for example, the district court's analysis of the problems with Minnesota's regulatory process later in the opinion:

> In addition to regulating wholly out-of-state transactions, which is itself a violation of the extraterritoriality doctrine, Minn. Stat. § 216 H.03, subd. 3(2)–(3), also improperly requires non-Minnesota merchants to seek regulatory approval before undertaking transactions with other non-Minnesota entities. Minn. Stat. § 216 H.03, subd. 4, provides an exemption from the prohibitions in § 216 H.03, subd. 3, if an entity can demonstrate to the MPUC's satisfaction that it will offset the prohibited carbon dioxide emissions. Thus, only by undertaking a "carbon dioxide reduction project" approved by a Minnesota agency can, for example, a North Dakota generation-and-transmission cooperative inject coal-generated electricity into the MISO grid to serve its North Dakota members.
>
> If any or every state were to adopt similar legislation (e.g., prohibiting the use of electricity generated by different fuels or requiring compliance with unique, statutorily-mandated exemption programs subject to state approval), the current marketplace for electricity would come to a grinding halt. In an interconnected system like MISO, entities involved at each step of the process – generation, transmission, and distribution of electricity – would potentially be subject to multiple state laws regardless of whether they were transacting commerce outside of their home state. Such a scenario is "just the kind of competing and interlocking local economic regulation that the Commerce Clause was meant to preclude." Healy, 491 U.S. at 337.

Although many of the particular concerns in this case involve the specific language of the Minnesota law at issue, this reasoning raises interesting questions about how the changing nature of electricity governance in the

---

[96] *North Dakota v. Heydinger*, ___ F. Supp. 2d___, 2014 WL 1612331 (D. Minn. Apr. 18, 2014).

United States – with hybrid regional entities helping to address interstate energy transition concerns[97] – might interact with litigation's regulatory influence on climate change over time. Beyond how these cases contribute to Commerce Clause jurisprudence and its application to climate change and clean energy regulatory measures, the litigation is also likely to be important in shaping the evolving dialogue in the United States over the appropriate balance between federal and state authority in addressing climate change as regional entities become ever more important in that dialogue.

As discussed earlier in the context of challenges to federal regulation, the effects of antiregulatory litigation can be mixed. Certainly cases in which antiregulatory parties prevail can serve as a significant barrier to progress. Even when unsuccessful, the barrage of antiregulatory litigation accompanying every attempt at climate regulation – state or federal – often has the effect of slowing regulation down. It may also at times encourage agencies to go for less ambitious options in order to make them less easily challenged by litigation. But, as noted, litigation brought against proactive regulators can have variety of effects, not all of which undermine regulatory efforts. For instance, this litigation may promote more transparent regulatory processes and efforts to engage stakeholders in the design of regulation. It also can bolster the regulators when they prevail.

Interviewees describing California's experience of antiregulatory litigation reflected this complexity in their responses. Given its proactive stance on climate change mitigation, litigation involving California has generally seen the state in the role of defendant, seeking to fend off litigation challenges to its regulatory measures from (primarily) industry and business organizations.[98] For Californian regulators, "the effort to move forward on these [regulatory] efforts is really, from a litigation standpoint, it's a defensive one."[99] Asked how antiregulatory litigation has shaped regulatory efforts to deal with climate change, one interview participant responded,

> Well, obviously if we lose, it will have some effect. But the main effect is that it takes resources and it can slow progress. But in terms of have we seen litigation that is going to make us change how we're going to do

[97] See Hari M. Osofsky and Hannah J. Wiseman, "Hybrid Energy Governance" (2014) *Ill. L. Rev.* 1.
[98] Telephone interview, US Participant 11 (Oct. 10, 2013).
[99] In-person interview, US Participant 6 (Nov. 14, 2012).

the regulations? Not really other than we're making a large effort to try to make things litigation-proof even though we know we're going to get sued.

[*Interviewer asked what sorts of ways might antiregulatory litigation impact regulations*]

Well, let me talk about – a little more generically – about the impact of litigation on regulations, and then we can talk about it in the climate change context. So do you know who Robert Reich is? He was the head of the Department of Labor under Clinton.... He, long ago, long before he was at the Department of Labor, he wrote an article called "How Nit-Picking Regulations Got That Way." And I think that he's exactly right with what he wrote. And he said the regulator writes a regulation, fairly straightforward. The lawyer for the regulated entity comes in and says, ah, there's ambiguity here, here and here, doesn't apply to my client. Regulator goes back, addresses each of the ambiguities, triples the size of the regulation and says OK, now we have a regulation, you're covered. Ah, no, here are five more ambiguities, on and on. And I think that that is absolutely how our regulations – which is, of course, what those who are covered by them complain about, oh, they're too complex, they're too difficult – part of the reason for that is because of the endless litigation by those who are regulated....

So I think that's true in the climate change arena. So I think that has an effect on how regulations are written from the outset. And as there are attacks and challenges that feeds into some of the changes that regulations go through.[100]

Not all agencies respond in the same way to litigation attacks on their climate-related regulations. Describing the reaction of California's Air Resources Board to antiregulatory litigation, another interviewee commented, "They do not shy away from any kind of regulatory effort whatsoever because they are going to get sued. That is not in their DNA."[101] A more likely response was that the agency would take great care in drafting the regulation to eliminate the possibility of successful legal challenges.[102] The same interviewee noted another possible link between litigation challenges to the Air Resources Board's (ARB) regulatory efforts and moves by regulators to improve the transparency of the regulatory process:

> ARB is noted amongst [Californian] state agencies for having a very transparent process. And they have lots of workshops before they decide what they are going to do. So if you go back and look at the Scoping Plan –

---

[100] In-person interview, US Participant 6 (Nov. 14, 2012).
[101] Telephone interview, US Participant 11 (Oct. 10, 2013).   [102] Ibid.

that was in 2008–9 through that period – I think they had over 200 work-shops before that Scoping Plan draft was even released. If you look at the cap-and-trade regulation there was probably over a hundred workshops on what the design could be before they did a regulation. And I think that is just kind of ARB's approach and philosophy about making things very open, let's have a discussion about what the options are and what are the pros and cons and they do that very much in the public eye through these workshops. They also have lots of individual meetings with people. And I – this is just a conjecture on my part – but I would say that part of that is the more public discussion about what the technologies can deliver and the more that's out there in the public then it actually does kind of get a groundswell of, well, of course we should regulate landfills because it is doable, or of course we should regulate transportation fuels since it is just such a significant part of our carbon load basically that we have to address. So I think – I hadn't thought about that before – but I think because ARB has been sued on virtually all of its major regulations since 1970 when it started, I think that probably, it could be one of the reasons why it has a dramatically more public, transparent workshop process than a lot of the other state agencies do.[103]

Overall, courts have generally been supportive of governmental regulatory efforts, limiting the chilling effect of antiregulatory litigation. As one interviewee explained in the federal context, "virtually every good thing the EPA has done has been upheld. They've been baby, tentative steps but they've been upheld. I mean agencies are very difficult to overturn their decisions."[104] However, the antiregulatory litigation – like the barriers to access – can undermine efforts at progress on climate change by making them more expensive and time consuming, and at times, such as in *Utility Air Regulatory Group v. EPA*, close particular regulatory pathways.

7.4   Resistance to and backlash against litigation

Unlike the United States, Australia has not had a deluge of antiregula-tory climate change litigation in response to proactive regulation. Such litigation might have been expected had the Australian carbon pricing mechanism continued to operate but is no longer necessary given the Abbott government's repeal of the Clean Energy Act. As noted in the introduction, industries opposed to climate regulation in Australia have not needed to use the judicial process to challenge new requirements intro-duced by the courts or adverse decisions on individual projects. Instead, industry has frequently been able to turn to supportive governments at

---

[103] Telephone interview, US Participant 11 (Oct. 10, 2013).
[104] In-person interview, US Participant 2 (Oct. 22, 2013).

the state or federal level for assistance in combating business threats posed by climate change cases. This battle has been played out particularly in the sphere of mitigation. As one interviewee noted, this seems to reflect a fear on the part of Australian governments that "litigation would take that issue of energy management out of their hands."[105]

In this section, we review examples of antiregulatory responses to climate change litigation in Australia. We first look at reactions to cases dealing with issues of greenhouse emissions reduction and climate change mitigation where case law development potentially affects the implementation of large-scale coal power or coal mining projects. These responses have included legislation to overturn the effects of a case, repeal of progressive climate or other environmental legislative provisions, and government support for industry legal challenges to court decisions. In addition to these responses, some proactive cases have generated a substantial backlash from governments that has included the removal or institution of restrictions on legal aid and public interest environmental funding. The effects of this backlash augment the access barriers around costs faced by nongovernmental petitioners that were described in Section 7.2.

As highlighted in Chapter 3, Australian cases challenging greenhouse gas–intensive energy projects have not had a high success rate in terms of stopping such projects from going ahead. Where decisions are handed down rejecting a coal project – such as the Warkworth mine decision issued by Chief Justice Preston of the NSW Land and Environment Court in 2013 – they tend to attract a lot of attention in the media, government, and industry, much of it negative.[106] Interviewees we spoke to about the lack of success in mitigation cases in Australia were often philosophical, seeing the cases as still important to run to keep a public spotlight on the climate issue.[107] However, several noted with concern a new trend of strong adverse reactions to cases – even unsuccessful ones – that may ultimately negate some of the positive advances achieved by earlier litigation.

In the coal-rich state of Queensland, antiregulatory responses to high-profile litigation seeking the consideration of the full climate change impact of coal mining activities have been the most direct and comprehensive. These cases were considered in Chapter 6 as an example of evolving judicial attitudes to climate science and regulation. In the earliest

---

[105] Skype interview, Australian Participant 15 (May 30, 2013).

[106] See, e.g., Sarah-Jane Tasker, "Workers Plead for Rio Extension to Keep Warkworth Mine Open," *The Australian*, June 1, 2013, at www.theaustralian.com.au/business/mining-energy/workers-p%E2%80%A6ension-to-keep-warkworth-mine-open/story-e6frg9e6–1226654812233.

[107] Skype interview, Australian Participant 4 (Mar. 20, 2013).

of these cases – the *Xstrata* case (2007) – the environmental NGOs object-ing to the proposed extension lost at first instance before the Queensland Land and Resources Tribunal but were successful in overturning the tri-bunal's decision on appeal to the Queensland Court of Appeal.[108] The Court of Appeal's decision did not specifically address the greenhouse gas emissions issue raised by the objectors but found that the tribunal had not accorded natural justice (due process) to the objectors when, subsequent to the hearing, it considered and relied on climate skeptic material adverse to their case without affording them the opportunity to respond.[109] On the same day as the Court of Appeal judgment was delivered, overturning the tribunal's decision and requiring the matter to be reheard, the Queensland government announced that it would amend the state mining and environmental legislation to authorize the mine extension and avoid delay to the project. A media release issued by the government declared, "This action comes in response to today's court ruling that, on a legal technicality, could have stalled the mine's further development." The media release quoted the Queensland Premier:

> We will protect the mine's 190 jobs and the investment in the mine. . . . The coal industry is central to the Queensland economy and we will not allow a technicality to threaten its development and jobs. . . . To let the court decision stand would risk our biggest export industry and the government is not prepared to take that risk. There is no doubt the coal industry needs to combat greenhouse gas emissions and that is why the government and industry are investing heavily in clean coal technology.[110]

Four days later, legislative amendments were passed by the Queensland Parliament to validate approvals for the mine's extension.[111] As one interviewee described it, "the approach of the government was effectively saying, we are happy for you to appeal to the court and have independent

---

[108] *Re Xstrata Coal Queensland Pty Ltd & Ors* [2007] QLRT 33 (Queensland Land and Resources Tribunal); *Queensland Conservation Council Inc v. Xstrata Coal Queensland P/L & Ors* [2007] QCA 338 (Queensland Court of Appeal).

[109] *Queensland Conservation Council Inc v. Xstrata Coal Queensland P/L & Ors* [2007] QCA 338.

[110] Joint Statement, The Hon Anna Bligh (Premier) and The Hon Geoff Wilson (Minister for Mines and Energy), "Government to legislate to ensure mine's future," 12 October 2007, available at http://statements.qld.gov.au/Statement/Id/54462.

[111] Mining and Other Legislation Amendment Act 2007 (Qld) inserting s 418AA (validation of inclusion of additional surface area No. 2 in mining lease 4761) into the Mineral Resources Act 1989 and s 579A (validation of amendment of environmental authority MIM800098402) into the Environmental Protection Act 1994.

third-party review but if we don't like the answer we'll just change the law to validate the approval anyway."[112]

Another challenge to a Queensland coal mine in the Wandoan case also seems to have generated an antiregulatory response even though the pro-regulatory petitioners lost the case. The case was brought by Friends of the Earth Brisbane, which argued that the mine's scope 3 emissions associated with burning of harvested coal should have been taken into account in issuing approvals for the mine. As Chapter 6 discussed, this argument failed before the Queensland Land Court.[113] Even so, an antiregulatory legislative response followed swiftly on the heels of the decision.

Shortly after the judgment was issued, the Queensland government released a "Greentape Reduction" Bill proposing various amendments to the state's environmental and planning legislation to "streamline" deci-sion making.[114] One amendment to the "standard criteria" for decision making on environmental approvals included removing references to principles of ecologically sustainable development (ESD) as set out in the National Strategy for Ecologically Sustainable Development (NSESD) and substituting a reference to the subset of ESD principles listed under the Intergovernmental Agreement on the Environment.[115] The effect of this amendment has been that Queensland government decision makers determining whether to issue an environmental approval are no longer required to take account of the NSESD principle that "the global dimen-sion of environmental impacts of actions... should be recognised and considered."[116]

---

[112] In-person interview, Australian Participant 2 (Mar. 8, 2013). See also *Queensland Con-servation Council Inc v. Xstrata Coal Queensland Pty Ltd & Ors* [2007] QLC 0128 where the Land Court (the successor of the former Queensland Land and Resources Tribunal) confirmed that the effect of the legislative amendment was to validate the mining lease and environmental approvals for the mine extension and to remove the opportunity of the Queensland Conservation Council to have its objections on the greenhouse issue reconsidered.

[113] See *Xstrata Coal Qld Pty Ltd & Ors v. Friends of the Earth Brisbane and Department of Environment and Resource Management* [2012] QLC 013 (27 March 2012) (Wandoan mine case).

[114] See Environmental Protection (Greentape Reduction) and Other Legislation Amendment Bill 2012. The Bill was enacted and came into force in March 2013.

[115] These are non-binding intergovernmental policies on government cooperation and responsibilities in the environmental field. They underpin environmental laws in every state and territory in Australia.

[116] ESD Steering Committee, National Strategy for Ecologically Sustainable Development (1992). This principle does not appear in the Inter-governmental Agreement on the Environment (1992).

The coincidence in timing between the Wandoan judgment and the release of the amending bill suggested a desire on the part of the Queensland government to prevent questions of the global emissions impact of coal mines being raised in future disputes.[117] At a practical level, the precedent set by the Wandoan case also had negative impacts as "it confirmed what the [Environment] Department was already doing most of the time which was disregarding scope 3 emissions."[118] Since the Wandoan case, litigators have noticed a trend whereby "all the environmental impact statements have been saying now we don't need to tell you the scope 3 emissions because they are irrelevant because of the [Wandoan] decision."[119]

Antiregulatory responses to climate change litigation in other Australian states have generally not been as robust and obvious as in Queensland. However, interviewees suggested that links could nonetheless be drawn between particular cases and subsequent regulatory developments to decrease the stringency of climate-related or environmental laws. For example, in Victoria, the early case involving Hazelwood power station in 2004 held that greenhouse gas emissions needed to be taken into account in assessing a planning application for extension of the life of the plant. Ultimately, this decision did not prevent the Victorian government granting the authorizing permits.[120] Moreover, the case seemed to be taken as a "forewarning" of the potential for courts to place constraints on the freedom of government decision making on energy issues. As one interviewee related, subsequently, "the development of [Victorian climate] policy was somewhat reluctant, halfhearted. The departments were certainly given the slow push rather than a proactive one."[121]

A more pronounced antiregulatory reaction accompanied the 2012 decision of the Victorian Civil and Administrative Tribunal (VCAT) in the *Dual Gas* case.[122] As we highlighted in Chapter 3, in this case VCAT subjected the approval of a new 600MWe power station employing a coal gasification technology to a condition preventing the project

[117] In-person interview, Australian Participant 2 (Mar. 8, 2013).
[118] Ibid.   [119] Ibid.
[120] Charles Berger, "Hazelwood: A New Lease on Life for a Greenhouse Dinosaur" in Tim Bonyhady and Peter Christoff (eds.), *Climate Law in Australia* (2007, Federation Press, Sydney), 161.
[121] Skype interview, Australian Participant 15 (May 30, 2013).
[122] *Dual Gas Pty Ltd & Ors v. Environment Protection Authority* [2012] VCAT 308 (29 March 2012).

commencing until the retirement of an equivalent amount of more green-house gas–intensive electricity generation capacity in Victoria. The case was the first to test the provisions of the state's climate law – the Climate Change Act 2010 – including the effect of its legislated greenhouse gas emissions reduction target.[123] Days before hearings in the case commenced, the Victorian government announced an independent review of the Climate Change Act. The report of the review, and the government's response to it, were tabled in the Victorian Parliament by the Minister for Environment and Climate Change on March 27, 2012,[124] two days before VCAT handed down its *Dual Gas* decision. In its response to the review, the government accepted recommendations to remove the emissions reduction target in the Climate Change Act and indicated it would not proceed with the introduction of a state-based greenhouse emissions intensity standard for power generators – two issues that had been the subject of extensive argument before VCAT. One of our interviewees saw these developments as a clear reaction to the *Dual Gas* case and the potential for similar litigation against energy projects: "it's that litigation effectively, and the outcome of it, that have had a negative impact on this state government acting responsibly, in my view, and [it] has wound back the policies for fear that such litigation might occur again."[125]

In New South Wales (NSW), where much of the Australian mitigation-related litigation has been brought, the current conservative state government also appears to be pursuing an antiregulatory path in response to a succession of challenges by environmental NGOs and activists to coal projects, including those taken on climate change grounds. While early NSW climate change cases, such as Anvil Hill, saw the government engaging in pro-regulatory action in response to the litigation,[126] more recent decisions, such as the Warkworth mine case,[127] have prompted a very different reaction. In May 2013, the NSW Planning Minister took the unusual step of joining the mining company behind the Warkworth mine extension proposal in its (ultimately unsuccessful) appeal of the Land

---

[123] Former s 5 of the act provided that the Victorian government must ensure an emissions reduction of 20 percent below 2000 levels by 2020.

[124] For details, see State Government Victoria, "Review of the Climate Change Act," www.climatechange.vic.gov.au/home/review-of-climate-change-act.

[125] Skype interview, Australian Participant 15 (May 30, 2013).

[126] See Chapter 3 for a discussion of this case and its aftermath.

[127] *Bulga Milbrodale Progress Assoc Inc v. Minister for Planning and Infrastructure and Warkworth Mining Limited* [2013] NSWLEC 48.

and Environment Court's refusal decision.[128] Around the same time, the NSW government proposed, and subsequently finalized, amendments to the State Environmental Planning Policy governing mining activities that were reported in the press as being designed to limit the grounds for future refusals of mining permit applications.[129] Interviewees also saw these regulatory changes as a direct response to the Warkworth case.[130] Under the new policy requirements, which commenced in November 2013, the "principal consideration" of decision makers evaluating a mining proposal is to be the "significance of the resource" including its economic benefits; "any other matter for consideration," such as the environmental effects of the proposal, must only be given weight "proportionate to the importance of that other matter in comparison with the significance of the resource."[131]

Just as the pro-regulatory impacts of climate change litigation can be direct or indirect, so antiregulatory responses may take a direct or more indirect path. Some of the responses to mitigation-related litigation identified by our Australian interviewees seem to fit into this indirect category. While in the cases described previously, those opposing regulation introduced direct legal or policy change to maintain the status quo of greenhouse gas–intensive development and resource use, in other instances, governments responded by taking actions that reduce the capacity of objectors to air climate change concerns before the courts. Examples include the decision of Legal Aid New South Wales (a state government agency) to cut all legal aid funding for public interest environmental matters, effective July 1, 2013,[132] and proposed changes to the planning law system in New South Wales that may restrict the kinds of development proposals that can be appealed to the Land and Environment Court.[133]

---

[128] *Warkworth Mining Limited v. Bulga Milbrodale Progress Association Inc* [2014] NSWCA 105.

[129] Ben Hagemann, "Rio Pushes Again for Mt Thorley Warkworth Expansion," Australian Mining, March 20, 2014, at www.miningaustralia.com.au/news/rio-pushes-again-for-mt-thorley-warkworth-expansio.

[130] Skype interviews, Australian Participants 16 and 22 (May 30 and Sep. 13, 2013).

[131] State Environmental Protection Policy (Mining, Petroleum Production and Extractive Industries) Amendment (Resource Significance) 2013, Clause 12AA.

[132] See Legal Aid NSW, Legal Aid News, May 2013, http://news.legalaid.nsw.gov.au/link/id/zzzz51899e6423536090/page.html. This change is particularly detrimental for impecunious environmental or community groups wishing to challenge coal projects as if they cannot access legal aid they may not be able to bring the case and if they still go ahead they do not enjoy the protection from costs liability afforded legal aid funded litigants.

[133] NSW Government, Planning and Environment, *White Paper, a New Planning System for New South Wales* (April 2013).

These kinds of indirect antiregulatory responses have taken place at a federal level as well, with funding cuts for community legal assistance in environmental matters provided by the Australian Network of Environmental Defenders Offices (EDO).[134] The EDO offices in New South Wales, Queensland, and Victoria have been involved in advising and assisting many of the groups involved in climate change cases and related litigation on coal mines and coal seam gas proposals. During 2012–13, EDO New South Wales came under sustained media attack for its "anticoal" legal challenges from commentators writing in the Murdoch-controlled press.[135] In December 2013, the federal government announced that it would be cutting all Commonwealth funding to EDOs,[136] a decision that seems to have been driven, to a large extent, by concern over EDOs' role in litigating large coal resource and coal power projects. The chief executive officer of the New South Wales EDO, Jeffrey Smith, said the mining industry would be "breaking out the champagne" at news of the federal funding cuts. In an interview with *Guardian Australia*, he stated, "The mining industry has been lobbying against us for some time because we help community groups take on big developments, we help the Davids take on the Goliaths. I don't think there's any coincidence they've singled out EDOs across Australia. We are what stands between the community and unsustainable development."[137]

Together, these antiregulatory developments across Australia in the key areas of mitigation and energy policy and projects underscore the inadequacy of simply examining positive judgments when evaluating the extent of litigation's promotive impact. Although at times litigation

---

[134] In-person interview, Australian Participant 3 (Mar. 3, 2013) speaking about funding cuts to EDO NSW. In July 2012, the Queensland government also withdrew all state funding from both Queensland EDO offices.

[135] Among many examples, see Imre Salusinszky, "Public Funds Used to 'Enable Activists to Break Law,'" *The Australian*, January 17, 2013, at www.theaustralian.com.au/national-affairs/state-politics/public-funds-used-to-enable-activists-to-break-law/story-e6frgczx-1226555416133; Chris Merrett, "Boost for Anti-Coal Body Shows Labor Knows How to Alienate Its Heartland," *The Australian*, July 5, 2013, www.theaustralian.com.au/business/opinion/boost-for-anti-coal-body-shows-labor-knows-how-to-alienate-its-heartland/story-e6frg9uf-1226674521628#.

[136] Oliver Millman, "Coalition Cuts All Government Funding to Environmental Legal Aid Centres," *The Guardian*, December 18, 2013, at www.theguardian.com/environment/2013/dec/18/coalition-cuts-all-government-funding-to-environmental-legal-aid-centres. This includes revocation of the funding of AUD$10 million over four years promised by the previous Gillard government and the AUD$100,000 annual grant to each EDO provided for the last twenty years.

[137] Quoted in Millman, "Coalition Cuts All Government Funding."

spurs regulatory developments that would not have happened otherwise, backlash against positive decisions or against even the ability for future such cases to be brought can serve as an important barrier to progress.

7.5 Conclusion

This chapter has explored the barriers to climate change litigation serving as a tool for regulatory progress, considering both concerns over access to justice and over litigation and its aftermath serving antiregulatory ends. More so than in some of the other chapters, notable differences between the two jurisdictions emerge at every turn. Separation-of-powers issues are a more significant barrier in the United States, whereas cost concerns arise more in Australia. US antiregulatory interests bring increasing numbers of cases, while Australian ones mostly use legislative methods. In comparative research, the existence of these kinds of differences – particularly in how technical legal rules operate and the influence of the prevailing political context – is unsurprising and does not, in itself, undermine the value of comparison. Moreover, despite the differences in how particular barriers manifest in the United States and Australia, a core similarity remains; in both countries, litigation's effect is not always promotive. Understanding these barriers and thinking about ways they might be overcome or circumvented in future cases is thus critical to those seeking to achieve progress through litigation.

Professors Markell and Ruhl's assessment that the contestation between pro- and antiregulatory interests in the United States is leading to "an increasingly robust and complex litigation landscape but with mixed results for both sides" is certainly borne out by the tug-of-war between environmental groups and industry over regulatory measures in both countries.[138] In terms of case outcomes, it seems that pro-regulatory interests currently have the edge over antiregulatory challengers in the United States. In this respect, pro-regulatory interests have received a significant boost from the presence of willing regulators at the federal level and in some states. In addition to cases designed to force (more or better) government action on climate change, an increasing number of cases involving pro-regulatory interests, such as environmental groups, see them in the role of interveners supporting government defendants in suits brought by industry to challenge regulatory action. This trend is likely to continue for the remainder of the Obama administration; beyond that, it

---

[138] Markell and Ruhl, "A New Jurisprudence or Business as Usual," 15.

is difficult to anticipate how the pro-regulatory–antiregulatory battle will play out. Clearly some business interests in the United States are prepared to fight to the death on the issue of climate change regulation, both through the political process and in the courts. However, an interesting development in some recent cases, as discussed in Chapter 5, has been the intervention of other businesses, such as clean energy producers, on the side of government regulators in antiregulatory lawsuits. In addition, some oil and gas companies have increasingly positioned themselves as part of an energy transition away from coal, with the result that this part of the fossil fuel energy sector has become far less monolithic in its regulatory opposition.

The Australian picture is more complex, ironically due in part to its more functional legislative process. While litigation has produced some important pro-regulatory outcomes in the mitigation sphere, as described in Chapter 3, the antiregulatory responses to it have undercut these gains significantly. This tendency for positive judgments to lead to backlash poses an important challenge for those framing pro-regulatory litigation in Australia. Potential petitioners need to consider not only the likely outcome of that case in the courts but also the overall political environment in which it is taking place and ways to limit the possible negative responses.

Despite these barriers, our overall assessment of the constructive regulatory impact of this litigation remains positive. As explored in depth in our concluding chapter, litigation has had important effects in improving regulatory outcomes in both jurisdictions and likely will continue to create pressure for future regulatory decision making to be more responsive to climate change.

The future of climate change litigation

I mean to me when you say "is litigation effective or not," well, no one thing is effective in a vacuum. We could have all the grassroots organizing and social movements we want. That won't be effective if we don't have laws change and court decisions. And good court decisions won't be effective unless you have the other pieces coming along. . . . But I wouldn't really call that a defect of litigation so much as just that we need all the pieces to work together.

– US Interview Participant 2

I don't have a vision of some shining light in the distance that we will reach and it will be Nirvana and coal companies will all just lay down their arms and we'll all just get along and chart a sustainable future. I only see a future of running a lot of these cases within the current paradigms to win what we can and save what we can.

– Australian Interview Participant 4

8.1   Introduction

When we began this book, our interest was in how climate change litigation affects regulation and what part it plays in multilevel climate change governance. The picture revealed in previous chapters is a complex one. The story of climate change litigation in countries like the United States and Australia extends well beyond high-profile, iconic cases like the US Supreme Court's decision in *Massachusetts v. EPA* to iterative interactions among smaller-scale cases, pro- and antiregulatory advocates, and legislative and executive decision making. Litigation focuses not only on greenhouse gas emissions and clean energy transition but also, increasingly, on adaptation and disaster planning. The effects of litigation on the climate regulatory landscape are both direct and indirect, with some of its most important influences – on corporate behavior and social norms – often the least easy to delineate precisely. Moreover, legal and behavioral

change brought about by proactive climate change litigation needs to be
balanced against the effects of a growing body of antiregulatory litigation,
coupled with other barriers to progress, such as access to justice limitations, separation-of-powers constraints, and legislative backlash following
litigation.

It seems unlikely that litigation raising climate change issues will cease
any time soon. Indeed, our interviewees in both the United States and
Australia suggested that it would increase – in the United States largely as
a response to federal regulatory efforts and also with growing attention to
issues of adaptation; in Australia as a way of maintaining political pressure
and the public profile of climate change in the face of the antiregulatory
agenda of the present federal and several state governments.

In this final chapter, we build from the previous chapter's discussion
of barriers to take stock of the overall impact of these cases on regulatory
progress. Although antiregulatory cases and responses to them certainly
are significant, pro-regulatory cases still comprise the majority of lawsuits
brought raising climate change issues in the United States and Australia.[1]
Drawing on insights from interviews, we seek to answer the question
posed at the start of this book, namely, how litigation on climate change
issues has and will influence US and Australian regulatory pathways to a
cleaner energy future. We also asked our interviewees for their thoughts
on the ways in which climate change litigation is likely to develop in
coming years. In the concluding section of the chapter, we present their
views and ours on the future of climate change litigation in the United
States and Australia, and beyond.

8.2   What has been achieved by pro-regulatory climate change litigation

Although the antiregulatory effects of climate change litigation have
become more prominent in recent years, the contributions of proactive
litigation to climate change regulation in both the United States and
Australia remain substantial. In the case of the United States, litigation such as the *Massachusetts v. EPA* decision and associated case law
has played a pivotal role in the development of federal climate change

---

[1] David Markell and J.B. Ruhl, "An Empirical Survey of Climate Change Litigation in the
United States" (2010) 40(7) *Environ. Law Reporter* 10644, 10650; Jacqueline Peel, "Australian Climate Change Litigation," Melbourne Law School Centre for Resources, Energy
and Environmental Law, at www.law.unimelb.edu.au/creel/research/climate-change.

regulation under major environmental laws like the Clean Air Act. In Australia, the achievements of pro-regulatory climate change litigation have been less striking but have nonetheless brought about a quiet transformation of environmental decision-making processes to be more climate aware. In this section, we review the principal contributions of litigation to climate change regulation in each country, across both mitigation and adaptation, and through direct and indirect pathways. We also summarize insights from the comparative analysis that help to illuminate differences in the regulatory pathways pursued through litigation in the United States and Australia.

8.2.1   Contribution of US climate change litigation

Perhaps not surprisingly, when we asked our US interviewees which cases had had the most significant positive impact on climate regulation in the country, most named *Massachusetts v. EPA*.[2] Nearly a decade on, the case still stands as an important milestone on the path to climate change regulation in the United States, although subsequent cases, including the Supreme Court's other climate decisions in *AEP v. Connecticut* and *Utility Air Regulatory Group v. EPA*, have added considerable nuance since then.[3] As one interviewee explained, "the *Massachusetts* case armed the federal government with the power to proceed and as soon as Obama took office, EPA began using that. So I think that was enabling, powerfully enabling."[4] Another described the case as one "where a court really told the executive branch to reverse course, and effectively forced them to do so, and at the same time legitimized a whole set of actions that would have been either impossible or subject to powerful challenges, [or] all kinds of delay otherwise."[5] The same interviewee expressed the opinion that the litigation played an important gap-filling role: "it's very hard to make an argument that we would have comprehensive federal climate legislation were it not for *Massachusetts v. EPA* or some other piece of litigation."

Interviewees recognized that there were a range of factors shaping the EPA's eventual regulatory actions to address greenhouse gas emissions from vehicles and power plants. However, they saw the *Massachusetts v. EPA* litigation, and opinions that followed it, such as the DC Circuit's

---

[2] *Massachusetts v. EPA*, 549 U.S. 497 (2007).
[3] *American Electric Power v. Connecticut*, 131 S. Ct. 2527 (2011); *Utility Air Regulatory Group v. EPA*, 134 S. Ct. 2427, 2449 (June 23, 2014).
[4] Telephone interview, US Participant 7 (Nov. 16, 2012).
[5] Telephone interview, US Participant 8 (Nov. 26, 2012).

upholding of that regulation in *Coalition for Responsible Regulation*[6] (which was largely left alone by the Supreme Court on appeal), as "critical."[7] One interviewee summed up the situation as follows:

> I think the litigation played a huge role. I really can't say whether [EPA was] going to do it anyway. I would like to think that President Obama would've done it whether or not the Supreme Court told him to. But, the *Massachusetts v. EPA* case was quite – it was an order to the EPA to determine whether or not greenhouse gases endanger public health and welfare. And EPA had to do that. . . . And everything that the EPA has done since then on greenhouse gases arises out of that original case.[8]

Massachusetts v. EPA was far from the only case cited by interviewees as having had important pro-regulatory effects. Giving an overview of the most significant cases, one interviewee commented,

> Well, unquestionably *Massachusetts v. EPA* is number 1, far ahead of anything else. I would say that *Center for Biological Diversity v. NHTSA* together with the two cases against the Surface Transportation Board about the rail lines – I think those were significant in terms of NEPA analysis. I think the *Friends of the Earth v. Watson* [*Spinelli*] was significant in terms of NEPA's involvement in foreign investment decisions. I think that the informational subpoenas that [New York] Attorney General Andrew Cuomo issued against electric utilities helped spark SEC action. I think that some of the polar bear listing litigation has been significant.[9]

Beyond individual cases, several interviewees also identified how the case law in particular areas – such as under the National Environmental Policy Act (NEPA) or the Endangered Species Act – has had cumulative pro-regulatory impacts. This has been particularly evident in the raft of litigation and administrative proceedings brought against coal-fired power plants, which have had a net effect of "forcing coal plants to account for some of their unrealized externalities."[10] There have also been impacts

---

[6] *Coalition for Responsible Regulation, Inc v. EPA*, 684 F.3d 102 (D.C. Cir. June 26, 2012) (No. 09–1322, 10–1092).

[7] Telephone interview, US Participant 11 (Oct. 10, 2013).

[8] Telephone interview, US Participant 13 (Dec. 9, 2013).

[9] Telephone interview, US Participant 7 (Nov. 16, 2012). Cases involving the Surface Transportation Board have included *Mid States Coalition for Progress v. Surface Transportation Board*, 345 F. 3d 520 (8th Cir. 2003), *Mayo Foundation v. Surface Transportation Board* (8th Cir., 2006), *In re Tongue River Railroad* (Surface Trans. Board, 2010) and *Northern Plains Resources Council v. Surface Transportation Board* (9th Cir., Dec. 2011). All were NEPA cases challenging approvals for rail infrastructure necessary to transport coal.

[10] Telephone interview, US Participant 1 (Oct. 20, 2012).

on project development more broadly, as one experienced environmental and natural resources lawyer explained:

> In terms of how you advise clients [climate change is] certainly on the list now of issues you need to consider. So if you're coming up with a checklist or you want to say, well, here's a top ten list to make sure your environmental impact assessment covers these areas, then certainly climate change effects is going to be on that list. So it's changed it that way. And it's probably – I don't know if "change" is the right word – but I think you're seeing an evolution in the thinking of project proponents in terms of trying to pursue carbon-neutral practices and trying to account for both – from a quantitative or qualitative level in terms of impact assessment – accounting for it that way but also I think accounting for it in a social, and sustainability and perceptive way of their carbon impacts and trying to – not in a pejorative way – but trying to establish a green or green-consistent basis for their project, whether it's a mining project or a railroad development or a power plant or what have you.... But I think it's definitely on project developers' radar screen, both from the existing regulatory framework – like how do you address it under NEPA and the Endangered Species Act – but also just in terms of what we might say is, you know, the social framework, and what companies think is expected of them and what they want to do to gain social acceptance and support for their projects.[11]

Litigation in this sense has been influential in the "long game" by "start[ing] to institutionalize the notion of climate change as part of decision making at a local government level" – an effect that, "in some ways, may end up being the bigger success."[12] As one interviewee pointed out, "no matter what kind of global scheme would have come out of Copenhagen, hopefully will come out of Paris, it is implemented at the very, very local level and so it's these land use issues often where the real gains in climate are happening. That's been, I would say, other than the Clean Air Act, the realm of climate litigation that has the most real-world impact on atmospheric carbon dioxide levels."[13]

Given the nascent state of US adaptation case law, most of our interviewees focused on this kind of incremental effect in the mitigation context, discussed in depth in Chapter 3. However, a few also predicted that the adaptation lawsuits explored in Chapter 4 would follow a similar course and perhaps even support mitigation efforts. One interviewee said, for

---

[11] Telephone interview, US Participant 3 (Nov. 7, 2012).

[12] In-person interview, US Participant 6 (Nov. 14, 2012).

[13] Telephone interview, US Participant 12 (Dec. 2, 2013).

example, that the emerging adaptation litigation "will hopefully be transformative and improve our planning, and you know, force decisions about infrastructure and development that are not just more resilient to climate change but also ideally are closer to being carbon neutral that get to the mitigation side as well."[14] This kind of interweaving of adaptation and mitigation, which has begun in a specific context through the Endangered Species Act litigation, could go a long way toward ensuring that efforts to build a cleaner energy future go hand in hand with those designed to ensure safe, livable communities that are resilient in the face of a changing climate.[15]

In addition to the direct regulatory consequences of climate cases, interviewees also identified a number of positive indirect effects from the litigation. They most often mentioned the capacity of litigation to generate publicity and public profile for climate issues, a topic explored in depth in Chapter 6. For example, one interviewee speaking about the *Kivalina* litigation – which did not achieve any formal legal victories with respect to the claims of nuisance and conspiracy it raised[16] – noted that the case nonetheless "garnered a lot of attention."[17] Another described *Massachusetts v. EPA* as "a watershed moment" that "was a huge wake-up call (I think) to industry; and same with states that were not wanting to regulate greenhouse gases."[18] The case, along with others affirming climate change science, helped "in making the problem concrete and more serious and taking it less out of the realm of 'is this real,' do we do anything about it, is this a problem that's so big that we all agree the only first step can be a comprehensive international treaty where every nation on earth, poor and rich, signs on to something."[19] Courts' responses to the question of whether national or state regulation should be deferred until an international climate solution is reached has generally been "no": "courts have been receptive to the argument that that is not how real-world problems are solved and so taking a step here and there is [appropriate]."[20]

---

[14] Telephone interview, US Participant 12 (Dec. 2, 2013).
[15] Mary Nichols, Chairman, California Air Resources Board, "AB32 and California's Energy Future," *Energy and Climate Change* (conference), Berkeley Law School, Nov. 14, 2013, Environmental Law Section of the State Bar of California.
[16] *Native Village of Kivalina v. ExxonMobil Corp.*, 696 F.3d 849 (9th Cir. 2012).
[17] In-person interview, US Participant 10 (Jan. 14, 2013).
[18] Telephone interview, US Participant 13 (Dec. 9, 2013).
[19] Telephone interview, US Participant 8 (Nov. 26, 2012).   [20] Ibid.

Other indirect effects on corporate behavior stemming from the litigation, the subject of Chapter 5, were identified by interviewees. One commented, "I think, the course of the decisions is that this is ever more clearly a serious problem with serious hazards and costs, not only in the remote term, but even in the medium term and maybe the short term. And I think the effect of those is . . . people are risk averse, they don't want to get in trouble, they don't want to be accused of sweeping things under the rug."[21] Another interviewee was more hesitant on the specific links between the case law and corporate action but still saw the litigation as having been influential for positive behavioral change:

> With private entities I would say the . . . it's clearly elevated their rhetoric. So most of them now talk better talk, other than the coal industry per se but certainly power companies and utilities. I would say a lot of . . . if you tease it out . . . a lot of the things we are seeing from utilities are, you know, some portion of it is climate driven. You know, the end result is climate driven, the motivation is climate driven. . . . So climate is driving the litigation and that litigation is forcing the utilities, the power companies, to respond. And the smart ones realize their best response is shifting to less carbon-intensive generation packages.[22]

Even so, of the participants we interviewed who represented or worked for pro-regulatory groups, most were dissatisfied with the gains achieved by litigation in terms of outcomes for emissions reduction or improving adaptation, reinforcing the concerns raised in Chapter 7. As one put it, "there's a huge disconnect between what we need to achieve and what we're doing."[23] For some, this problem lay partly with the institutional role of courts in both countries, which "are often not the fastest to embrace a new thing" and have also been constrained by "a perception . . . that this was public policy more than legal issue, and that the courts were not the appropriate place for establishing public policy."[24]

Problems with the underlying legal framework and the political will to enforce existing environmental measures were also cited repeatedly as barriers to faster progress. An environmental justice lawyer explained that "the problem with using courts" is "that you are stuck with the law and the law is often not written in a way that protects low-income communities of color; it's written in a way that protects polluters and the interests

---

[21] Telephone interview, US Participant 8 (Nov. 26, 2012).
[22] Telephone interview, US Participant 12 (Dec. 2, 2013).
[23] In-person interview, US Participant 2 (Oct. 22, 2012).
[24] In-person interview, US Participant 6 (Nov. 14, 2012).

of polluters."[25] Another interviewee was more positive about the scope offered by existing law to achieve climate outcomes but dissatisfied with what had been achieved thus far by citizen enforcement efforts under that law:

> I think that – I mean that it won't be probably that surprising of an opinion for me to hold – that environmental law's a really important piece of the picture and I think citizen enforcement is a really important piece of the picture. But, of course, you know I can't sit here with emissions going through the roof and the seas rising all around us and say, yes, it's been effective, it's been as effective as I want. And we are where we want to be. No we're not. But that's not . . . I mean I guess I would hate it if the message people took from that is, oh, environmental law is a waste of time or it's not where we should be putting our effort. 'Cause we should be putting more effort into it. I mean it has a constructive role to play. We're just facing a really big problem.[26]

In sum, US climate change litigation has significantly shaped the regulatory path of the nation through both direct and indirect means. While most attention has rightly been directed to *Massachusetts v. EPA* and the EPA rulemaking that has followed, other cases – especially under NEPA and the Endangered Species Act and through the campaign to limit the use of coal – have also influenced regulatory efforts, corporate behavior, and social norms in important ways. Moreover, under the existing environmental law framework at the federal level, the pathway endorsed by the Supreme Court in *AEP v. Connecticut*, "the potential is incredible" to make further gains in climate regulation through litigation if the federal administration in power is willing to respond to the cases with strong executive enforcement action.[27]

8.2.2 Contribution of Australian climate change litigation

Compared with the transformational role played by litigation in shaping climate change regulation in the United States, the achievements of pro-regulatory litigation in Australia seem modest. Many of our Australian interviewees expressed their disappointment that climate change cases have not had a more significant impact. As one interviewee put it, "at the moment, neither the environmental impact assessments, nor the courts,

---

[25] In-person interview, US Participant 10 (Jan. 14, 2013).
[26] In-person interview, US Participant 2 (Oct. 22, 2012).   [27] Ibid.

nor the politicians are really making it clear that in terms of mitigation you can't allow any more coal power plants, you can't allow us to open any more coal mines, you can't allow us to export any more coal, because the international consequences are too great and it's not in Australia's public interest."[28]

To some extent, our interviewees' pessimism over the effectiveness of Australian climate change litigation reflects high expectations of its capacity to transform the regulatory landscape in response to the urgency of combating climate change emphasized by the available science. Nonetheless, when we asked interviewees to reflect critically on the regulatory effects of the case law, direct and indirect, and across both mitigation and adaptation spheres, most identified a significant positive change – as compared with five to ten years ago – in how climate change is considered and factored into project-based and planning decisions.

Like their US counterparts, Australian interviewees most consistently identified pro-regulatory cases' proactive role as raising the level of "consciousness" of climate change in the minds of decision makers, energy sector corporations, and development applicants.[29] One interviewee summarized the impact of lawsuits, such as *Walker v. Minister for Planning*,[30] the *Gippsland Coastal Board* decision, and the Anvil Hill case,[31] as helping to make climate change "something now that is assessed rather than being ignored or considered in a superficial way," albeit "it hasn't got to the stage where development proposals regularly get rejected by regulators because they will result in large greenhouse gas emissions."[32] This effect has been brought about through direct statutory interpretation pathways when courts and tribunals have construed legislative expressions of ecologically sustainable development (ESD) principles in environmental laws to encompass climate change.[33] The role the courts have tended to play in such cases is "basically saying, 'Is this a relevant consideration or not in your decision-making process under these regulatory frameworks?'"[34]

---

[28] Skype interview, Australian Participant 14 (May 23, 2013).

[29] In-person interview, Australian Participant 1 (Mar. 7, 2013). This effect was also noted by other Australian interview participants (nos. 3, 4, 5, 8, 9, 10, 14, 15, 18, and 22).

[30] (2007) 157 LGERA 124. For discussion of this case, see Chapter 4.

[31] *Gippsland Coastal Board v. South Gippsland Shire Council & Ors* [2008] VCAT 1545. For discussion of this case, see Chapter 4.

[32] In-person interview, Australian Participant 1 (Mar. 7, 2013).

[33] Brian J. Preston, "The Influence of Climate Change Litigation on Governments and the Private Sector" (2011) 2 *Clim. L.* 485.

[34] In-person interview, Australian Participant 20 (Jul. 25, 2013).

In terms of outcomes at the project level, however, interviewees identified a salient difference between mitigation-related cases against greenhouse gas–intensive developments, such as power plants and coal mines, and adaptation-related cases seeking the refusal of projects on the basis of their potential long-term climate change vulnerability. Interviewees generally felt that "the cases about adaptation have had more success . . . than the cases about mitigation."[35] Part of the reason may lie in the fact "that mitigation requires individual proponents, as well as the government, to take action," whereas the cases on adaptation have had a more procedural focus aiming to "change the baseline, in which case governments and instrumentalities can say, well, that's the new norm."[36]

Another theme that emerged clearly from the Australian interviews was that the climate change litigation there – as in the United States – has had a range of indirect regulatory effects beyond any direct legal change. Interviewees from the public interest sector cited the beneficial role of litigation in galvanizing campaigns and community organizing around the issue of climate change. While views in that sector clearly remain divided over the relative benefits of litigation as opposed to other forms of climate change campaigning,[37] there are many who regard litigation as "a good tool to precipitate media, politics and all those other sorts of things" and as an effective way of "having these issues put into the public space."[38] Others pointed to the delaying effect of litigation on projects that have a significant carbon footprint, delays that may make a project less attractive to potential funders.[39] Concerns over the economic cost of delay associated with court rulings have also been cited by industry actors as a factor pushing uncertainty over investing in coal projects to "unacceptable" levels.[40] Overall, there was a sense that litigation risk and potential delays due to litigation could lead to decisions to defer greenhouse gas–intensive projects, or compromise the finances otherwise available, so that companies "go for some other kind of energy project that doesn't have those risks, those protest risks."[41]

---

[35] In-person interview, Australian Participant 1 (Mar. 7, 2013).

[36] Skype interview, Australian Participant 14 (May 23, 2013).

[37] See also Mark Diesendorf, *Climate Action: A Campaign Manual for Greenhouse Solutions* (2009, UNSW Press, Sydney).

[38] In-person interview, Australian Participant 2 (Mar. 8, 2013).

[39] In-person interview, Australian Participant 2 (Mar. 8, 2013); Skype interview, Australian Participant 4 (Mar. 20, 2013).

[40] Sarah-Jane Tasker, "Workers Plead for Rio Extension to Keep Warkworth Mine Open" *The Australian*, June 1, 2013, at www.theaustralian.com.au/business/mining-energy/workers-p...ension-to-keep-warkworth-mine-open/story-e6frg9e6–1226654812233.

[41] In-person interview, Australian Participant 2 (Mar. 8, 2013).

As Chapter 3 illustrated, mitigation-focused climate change cases in Australia have not had a high success rate in directly stopping coal and other greenhouse gas–intensive energy projects. Indeed, some intervie-wees characterized the impact of the case law as "disastrous" when mea-sured against the standard of effectiveness in reducing greenhouse gas emissions.[42] Others took a more optimistic view, noting that "losing a case can be a really effective way of showing that the law is not protecting the environment and needs to be amended."[43]

However, successive cases, even ones that were unsuccessful in achiev-ing their primary aims, do seem to have served more indirectly as a site for learning, particularly about ways of presenting the scientific evi-dence to demonstrate the associated climate change impacts of large energy projects. Cases such as the Xstrata[44] and Wandoan coal mine litigation[45] – which failed in their respective attempts to have mining and environmental permits for huge Queensland coal mines refused – nonetheless have generated methodologies and studies that have proved useful in subsequent cases and campaigns against other coal mines. One lawyer commented, "The first case, the Xstrata case, it was really just about learning how to calculate scope 3 emissions. We didn't know how to do that when the case started."[46] This experience and expertise developed through the litigation has allowed environmental groups objecting to pro-posals to make a better case for measurable impacts from the development proposed, helping overcome the persistent argument of coal companies that there is no specific link between their activities and environmental impacts from global climate change.[47]

Beyond the public interest sector, our interview data suggested that climate change litigation is also having some indirect regulatory effects on the behavior of corporate actors. Like US attorneys, Australian legal practitioners advising corporate clients pointed to how "the evolution of climate change litigation is informing advice that lawyers give clients where those clients' activities or proposed activities may have some con-nection with climate change or the impacts of climate change."[48] For

---

[42] Skype interview, Australian Participant 14 (May 23, 2013).
[43] In-person interview, Australian Participant 1 (Mar. 7, 2013).
[44] Re Xstrata Coal Queensland Pty Ltd & Ors [2007] QLRT 33.
[45] Xstrata Coal Qld Pty Ltd & Ors v. Friends of the Earth Brisbane and Department of Envi-ronment and Resource Management [2012] QLC 013 (Wandoan mine case).
[46] Skype interview, Australian Participant 4 (Mar. 20, 2013).
[47] Jacqueline Peel, "Issues in Climate Change Litigation" (2011) 5(1) Carbon Clim. L. Rev. 15.
[48] Skype interview, Australian Participant 8 (Apr. 24, 2013).

instance, a lawyer would be far more likely now to raise with a client who is proposing a large coastal development the potential impacts of sea level rise and the consequent need to take that into account in financing the project and insuring the physical assets.[49] Another interviewee expressed the view that companies "take [the cases] a lot more seriously now... because the courts take them seriously."[50]

Corporations targeted in climate change litigation also seem to be making an effort "to ensure that we have fairly good credentials internally in the way that we manage climate change and greenhouse issues" to resist litigation challenges to projects.[51] These efforts might involve, for example, greater consideration of climate change and carbon issues in business planning processes, in the environmental impact assessments prepared in support of projects, in on-site measures for mitigating emissions, and in longer-term investment decisions regarding potential mitigation technologies like carbon capture and storage.[52]

Overall, however, interviewees expressed a sense that climate change litigation remains at an earlier stage in its development and impact in Australia than in the United States. For some corporate clients, one lawyer commented, climate change is not even on the radar.[53] This may be a function of the lower volume of climate case law in Australia compared with the United States (which has seen more than eight times the number of claims filed). Some predicted, though, that this lack of attention to climate change may change over time with continuing litigation: "I guess what will happen is there will be a handful of really important cases – Anvil Hill was a good example – where judges say things that really resonate in the minds of politicians and ultimately will resonate in the minds of business leaders."[54]

8.2.3 Explaining divergences between the US and Australian litigation experiences

The comparative analysis conducted in this book helps to shed some light on why climate change litigation has not had an equivalent influence in Australia as in the United States. For instance, strong US federal environmental laws have offered litigants opportunities to press for

---

[49] Skype interview, Australian Participant 8 (Apr. 24, 2013).
[50] Skype interview, Australian Participant 16 (May 30, 2013).
[51] Skype interview, Australian Participant 13 (May 23, 2013).   [52] Ibid.
[53] Skype interview, Australian Participant 18 (July 18, 2013).
[54] Skype interview, Australian Participant 8 (Apr. 24, 2013).

substantive climate regulatory mandates, an option not available to Australian litigants under the country's narrower federal environmental law framework.[55] This difference has resulted in Australian climate change litigation concentrated at the state level and focused primarily on pathways of procedural statutory interpretation.

On one hand, this smaller-scale emphasis has meant most of the Australian cases have been brought before state-level specialist environmental courts. As discussed in Chapters 6 and 7, these courts do not present significant access to justice barriers from standing rules and other separation-of-power constraints (though costs may still be a significant hurdle to proactive litigation).[56] They also arguably are more favorable forums than the generalist courts of the US judicial system for the consideration of complex questions of climate science and regulation.[57] These tribunals have made a number of progressive decisions at the state level on questions of both mitigation and adaptation. On the other hand, the "bottom-up" nature of Australia's climate case law has had consequences for its broader regulatory influence. It is difficult for individual state-level decisions to achieve the resonance of a *Massachusetts v. EPA*. Moreover, if judges in state specialist environmental courts were to issue "really strident judicial decisions that make it quite clear that it's gone on long enough, that government has to actually take action," they might well find their decisions overturned by higher-level courts or facing a backlash from legislators.[58]

Analysis of the case law from each country also revealed important differences in who brings climate change litigation, which is influential in determining the volume of litigation as well as the legal avenues pursued. For instance, in the United States, many pro-regulatory litigants are nongovernmental organizations (NGOs), but numerous states have also brought suits. Courts may be more responsive to actions brought by governments asserting rights to defend the public interest than similar cases taken by environmental NGOs; in the standing context, for example, as discussed in Chapter 7, the Supreme Court was willing to show "special solitude" to Massachusetts. Moreover, the sheer number and diversity of environmental groups in the United States – who do not face the same potential for adverse cost orders as do Australian litigants – coupled with the abundance of lawyers willing and able to take on pro bono case work

[55] See, particularly, the discussion of Australian mitigation case law in Chapter 3.
[56] See, further, Chapter 7.   [57] See, further, Chapter 6.
[58] Skype interview, Australian Participant 14 (May 23, 2013).

has fostered a burgeoning US climate case law pursuing a wide variety of legal strategies.

By contrast, in Australia, climate change litigation inevitably has had a "David versus Goliath" dynamic, with poorly resourced environmental NGOs taking on governments and powerful corporate actors in lawsuits. Not only can it be more difficult for environmental plaintiffs to succeed in such circumstances, but cost rules that create a risk of significant financial responsibility in the case of losses also pose a substantial hurdle to litigants getting before the courts. This cost structure additionally limits the potential for pro-regulatory groups to mount a focused campaign of impact litigation targeted to improving outcomes on mitigation or adaptation, as one Australian interviewee noted:

> Litigation, particularly from the community sector, is really messy. It's almost like stars have to align to have the right legal argument, the right factual scenario, the right people to run the right legal argument and factual scenario, the right client who's willing either to put their livelihood on the line or has enough money to bear the costs risks. With a community group, the client often needs support from other community groups, particularly in relation to costs but also in relation to campaigning and support. And it's really hard to bring all those things together.[59]

The bottom-up, locally focused nature of Australia's climate change litigation experience, however, may be a key factor explaining its more developed case law on adaptation issues compared with the United States. Adaptation measures are, by their nature, locally or regionally focused and deeply connected to decision making around land use, planning, and environmental management.[60] In both countries, these issues are primarily dealt with under state and local regulatory frameworks.[61] The availability of easily accessible specialist environmental courts in Australian states where questions of climate change adaptation can be raised – initially in test cases but now far more regularly in mainstream planning litigation – may help to explain Australia's more developed jurisprudence around adaptation. Earlier exposure to climate change impacts in Australia would also appear to be playing a role. US petitioners potentially have much to learn from this experience, including the value of numerous

---

[59] In-person interview, Australian Participant 2 (Mar. 8, 2013).
[60] E. Lisa F. Schipper and Ian Burton, "Understanding Adaptation: Origins, Concepts, Practice and Policy" in E. Lisa F. Schipper and Ian Burton (eds.), *The Earthscan Reader on Adaptation to Climate Change* (2009, Earthscan, London), 1.
[61] Michael Gerrard and Katrina Fischer Kuh (eds.), *The Law of Adaptation to Climate Change: United States and International Aspects* (2012, American Bar Association, Chicago).

smaller-scale decisions in building a planning culture more aware of and proactive about adaptation risks.

In both countries, substantial work remains to be done to forge better connections between mitigation and adaptation policies to ensure measures in each area function synergistically.[62] In the United States, the emerging adaptation litigation addressing coastal planning issues – especially in the context of public utilities commissions' electricity infrastructure planning – suggests useful possibilities, as do the more developed efforts under the Endangered Species Act. In Australia, class actions brought by victims of extreme weather events and proactive lawsuits focused on disaster risk reduction are also likely to play an important role in creating more effective mitigation–adaptation policy linkages.[63]

8.3   Future pathways for climate change litigation

Predicting how climate change litigation will develop in the future is not an easy exercise given the many uncertainties that pervade the climate regulatory space. In our interviews with US and Australian participants, we posed this question about the future of climate change litigation at the end of the interviews as an exercise in crystal ball gazing. The following sections summarize the responses of interviewees to this question, as well as our own assessment based on their responses and our broader research. We found that the interviewees – who are leading experts and active participants in the litigation – offered many useful perspectives regarding how climate change litigation might continue to unfold in both the United States and Australia in coming years.

8.3.1   United States

No country has embraced litigation as a tool of climate change governance to a greater extent than the United States. Litigation has been used in a variety of ways to address climate change concerns: to force governments to act, to stop governments from acting, to regulate private behavior, to attack government regulatory measures, to sue corporate emitters, to

---

[62] R. Klein et al., "Challenges in Integrating Mitigation and Adaptation as Responses to Climate Change" (2007) 12 *Mitig. Adapt. Strat. Global Chang* 639; S. Moser, "Adaptation, Mitigation and Their Disharmonious Discontents: An Essay" (2012) 111 *Climatic Change* 165; J.B. Ruhl, "Climate Change Adaptation and the Structural Transformation of Environmental Law" (2010) 40 *Environ. L.* 343.

[63] Jacqueline Peel and Hari M. Osofsky, "Sue to Adapt?," (2014) *Minn. L. Rev.* (forthcoming).

challenge climate science, and to promote or support adaptive behavior.[64] An overwhelming message from our US interviews was that litigation is likely to continue to play a significant role in shaping the US regulatory landscape in coming years. As one interviewee put it: "I see enormous litigation going on for the foreseeable future."[65]

Interviewees engaged in proactive climate change litigation do not generally view litigation as the only tool able to produce social or legal change or even necessarily the most effective option. Instead, "a lot of this stuff is born of, less of the sense that litigation is the optimal strategy, and more of the sense that at least courtroom doors are open and if you think you can put together some good arguments you can get a court to do something whereas a legislature, this Congress, is difficult."[66] The general attitude of interviewees toward the prospect of comprehensive federal climate legislation, at least in the near term, was pessimistic. One interviewee described the situation as follows:

> At the federal level, I'd be shocked if there was federal climate change legislation for the foreseeable future. It's just too difficult an issue. And not just the Republicans fitting about it. If the Republicans weren't screaming about . . . there are a lot of Democrats that take cover under the Republicans screaming about it; Democrats from coal states and things like that. OK, so, I just think that there's a lot of opposition out there. I don't see that changing anytime soon.[67]

For some, the limited likelihood of new federal climate legislation was not a particular concern given the possibilities for pursuing regulatory action under other environmental laws:

> We have the strongest domestic environmental laws in the world! . . . We have the Endangered Species Act for imperiled plants and animals, we have the Clean Air Act – an incredibly successful law – we have the Clean Water Act which can address ocean acidification. I mean these laws are tried and true. And, you know, where they've not done as well as they should it is not an inherent – well, of course, there's a whole scholarship talking about how inefficient our environmental laws are and how they could be made better – but I really don't think they failed due to any inherent flaws in the laws, just political pressure.[68]

---

[64] Arnold and Porter LLP, "U.S. Climate Change Litigation Chart," available at www.climatecasechart.com/.
[65] Telephone interview, US Participant 11 (Oct. 10, 2013).
[66] Telephone interview, US Participant 8 (Nov. 26, 2012).
[67] In-person interview, US Participant 4 (Nov. 14, 2012).
[68] In-person interview, US Participant 2 (Oct. 22, 2012).

However, as discussed in depth in Chapter 6, the Obama administration's greenhouse gas regulation under the Clean Air Act, particularly with respect to stationary sources, remains controversial, with divides in the reaction of Democrats and Republicans in whether they think the regulation was mandated by *Massachusetts v. EPA*. In fact, even some Democrats facing reelection in states with substantial coal industries have attacked the power plant regulations. Allison Lundergan Grimes, a Democratic challenger to Senator McConnell in Kentucky in the 2014 midterm elections, stated that she would "fiercely oppose the president's attack on Kentucky's coal industry."[69] Similarly, West Virginia secretary of state Natalie Tennant, a Democrat who ran for the Senate in 2014, said she would "stand up to President Obama, Gina McCarthy, and anyone else who tries to undermine our coal jobs."[70]

Whether or not interviewees saw the federal regulatory program emerging under existing laws like the Clean Air Act and the Endangered Species Act as a good thing, most expected that such regulatory efforts would continue to be the focus of substantial US climate litigation in coming years. This litigation was expected to take place "on both sides, coming both from challenges to whatever steps government does take and efforts to force them to do more."[71] On the pro-regulatory side, the expectation was that plaintiffs would "try to continue to shoehorn climate change into the existing regulatory schemes and try to get as much benefit out of them as possible, absent any major federal policy."[72] One interviewee involved in proactive climate litigation predicted that in the next stage of the litigation, there would be more diversity among groups as to how hard to push governments on improving regulation (something that would also vary depending on the political orientation of the national administration):[73]

> I think you'll probably see less unanimity amongst environmental groups in terms of whether particular governmental actions are adequate or whether other ones should be forced.... You know I think this first round [of litigation] there was a sense that this is progress, it may be inadequate, it may not have been perfect, but it's progress and who wants to be against. Looking at the massive fusillade the agency is taking for doing even this,

---

[69] Edward Felker, "Obama, Opponents Square Off Over Power Plant Rule," *Energy Guardian*, June 2, 2014.
[70] Ibid.   [71] Telephone interview, US Participant 8 (Nov. 26, 2012).
[72] In-person interview, US Participant 10 (Jan. 14, 2013).
[73] In-person interview, US Participant 5 (Nov. 14, 2012).

who wants to be on the other side? I think we've gotten past that, apparently. I think there will be less certainty about what the proper next steps are.[74]

For many pro-regulatory groups, litigation will involve more of "what's going on now,"[75] with "constant litigation over the regulatory scheme under the Clean Air Act":[76]

> Basically, following up on EPA regulation and defending EPA regulation when industry challenges it; suing EPA if they end up not issuing the rules. That will all continue . . . with the Carbon Pollution Standard – as that gets implemented, that has the potential for spawning litigation in every state, either to get the state to act – to get EPA to force the state to act depending on what the next administration looks like – or industry challenging state implementation plans, whatever the state plans are that implement the Carbon Pollution Standard for that state. You'll see, I'm fairly certain, lots of industry litigation challenging that.[77]

As one interviewee noted, whether pro-regulatory groups pursue suits over government climate change regulation or inaction on their own or in support of state government plaintiffs will be affected by the kinds of barriers to progress discussed in Chapter 7, including developments in the standing jurisprudence:

> So if the standing case law holds, or continues to develop in a way narrowing it to states, whether or not there's significant climate litigation based on emissions will really depend on what's happening at the state level and what kind of politics a given state's attorney-general or governor feels and how committed they are to taking action. So it will move directly from citizen litigation to government litigation. But that will, of course, be spurred on by civil society activism pressuring the state governments to bring such litigation.[78]

Others anticipated that the focus of antiregulatory litigation involving the federal government would expand with the EPA's growing regulatory activity in the climate change field:

> I think [future litigation is] going to be focused on EPA now trying to regulate specific sectors of the economy. We've seen them address the coal utility sector through New Source Performance Standards which have

---

[74] Telephone interview, US Participant 8 (Nov. 26, 2012).
[75] Telephone interview, US Participant 13 (Dec. 9, 2013).
[76] Telephone interview, US Participant 12 (Dec. 2, 2013).
[77] Telephone interview, US Participant 13 (Dec. 9, 2013).
[78] Telephone interview, US Participant 12 (Dec. 2, 2013).

said "no new coal plants can be built." That's going to be litigated and finalized. But I think that is also going to be expanded to other sectors like refining and chemical manufacturing where we're going to see EPA impose greenhouse gas standards that are going to effectively control the energy efficiency of manufacturing facilities. I think that's going to be one of the big developments in the next five years. I think another one is going to be with fuel. EPA is also requiring increased CAFE or mile per gallon standards in automobiles. That's going to have a big effect on reducing greenhouse gases, as well as renewable fuel standards. So we're going to see increased pressure on increasing fuel efficiency and increased renewable fuels. . . . I think [the litigation is] going to come up more on the renewable fuels side as EPA continues to increase the stringency of renewable fuel requirements. I think we're going to see that more and more with people arguing there is not enough renewable fuel to meet the requirements of what EPA is requiring.[79]

Beyond litigation around federal climate regulation – brought both by proponents and opponents of the regulation – the other major area of litigation activity anticipated by our interviewees concerned actions involving states, particularly antiregulatory suits targeting their proactive efforts: "obviously in the next few years, state actions on climate and related energy, renewable energy policies are going to be the subject of litigation, continued litigation."[80] Some interviewees focused in particular on the expansion of the dormant Commerce Clause challenges discussed in Chapter 7:

There's this Colorado lawsuit challenging the Colorado renewable portfolio standards – is just one example of that. There's been the Minnesota Next Generation Energy Act – [that] has been challenged. I would not be surprised to see challenges against similar statutes in California, Oregon, and Washington. As states decide that they want to move forward with regulating greenhouse gases, I think we'll see challenges to that.[81]

In this area of litigation, beyond the constitutional issues of how far states can go in regulation, questions regarding the competence of states to address the large-scale causes and effects of climate change are likely to loom large. As one interviewee put it: "I think the big question is, given that the federal government won't likely step out in front and do anything

---

[79] Telephone interview, US Participant 9 (Dec. 3, 2012).
[80] Telephone interview, US Participant 8 (Nov. 26, 2012). Also telephone interview, US Participant 9 (Dec. 3, 2012).
[81] Telephone interview, US Participant 13 (Dec. 9, 2013).

in the near term that amounts to a carbon price, can states do this on their own?"[82]

Compared with their confidence in the likelihood of continuing litigation over federal and state climate regulatory measures, our interviewees saw little prospect for an immediate resurgence of private tort lawsuits and other common law actions like the public trust cases in the face of recent losses.[83] In this area, most expected a "lull" in activity given the Supreme Court's approach to displacement in *AEP v. Connecticut*, although "as the science of attribution gets better, and, you know, there's increasing studies of *x* number of companies are responsible for *y* percentage of emissions, that there may be more, there may be resuscitation of those kinds of cases in a more tailored way that are less about injunction but more about damages."[84]

Climate change litigation in the United States has always pursued a diverse range of legal theories, and this pattern is likely to continue as litigants consider creative ways to prompt further regulatory action. For example, federal common law nuisance suits against greenhouse polluters may have been foreclosed by the Supreme Court's decision in *AEP v. Connecticut*, but lawyers continue to explore the possibilities for such cases under state nuisance laws.[85] Tort suits might also emerge in a more localized context to address community environmental justice concerns with respect to high-emitting projects or infrastructure in sectors like transportation.[86] Other federal agencies, beyond the EPA, may also find

---

[82] In-person interview, US Participant 5 (Nov. 14, 2012).

[83] Telephone interview, US Participant 7 (Nov. 16, 2012).

[84] Telephone interview, US Participant 12 (Dec. 2, 2013). Also in-person interview, US Participant 6 (Nov. 14, 2012).

[85] Thomas E. Fennell and Deborah Story Simmons, *The Rising Tide of Public Nuisance Claims*, Jones Day, available at www.jonesday.com/files/Publication/abcfc4a2–3776–41f2–9af1-ef122d7c7e5e/Presentation/PublicationAttachment/90e54d1b-16ea-4c20-b6ad-f8b09efeac2c/RisingTide.pdf; Tracy Hester, "A New Front Blowing In: State Law and the Future of Climate Change Public Nuisance Litigation" (2012) 31(1) *Stanford Environ. L. J.* 49; Jeffrey N. Stedman, "Climate Change and Public Nuisance Law: AEP v Connecticut and its Implications for State Common Law Actions" (2012) 36(3) *William and Mary Environ. L. Policy Rev.* 865; J. Wylie Donald, "No En Banc Appeal in Kivalina. So What's Next for Climate Change Litigation?" *Climate Lawyers Blog*, December 8, 2012, www.climatelawyers.com/post/2012/12/08/No-En-Banc-Appeal-in-Kivalina3b-So-Whats-Next.aspx.

[86] See, for example, cases being brought by Communities for a Better Environment together with other NGOs over the adverse health impacts of vehicle pollutants like carbon monoxide that also contribute to global warming: Communities for a Better Environment, "Current Cases and Campaigns," www.cbecal.org/legal/current-cases-2/.

themselves the subject of lawsuits as pro-regulatory litigants look more closely at the implications of their policies and regulations for energy strategy and greenhouse gas emissions. In this respect, a recent action against the Federal Housing Finance Agency, challenging a directive issued by the agency preventing Fannie Mae (the Federal National Mortgage Association) and Freddie Mac (the Federal Home Loan Mortgage Corporation) from purchasing mortgages for properties encumbered by liens under local government programs designed to promote renewable energy, may be a forerunner of future lawsuits.[87]

As the preceding discussion demonstrates, US climate change litigation is likely to continue its dominant focus on mitigation issues, particularly regulations concerned with reducing greenhouse gas emissions from major sources. Beyond the conventional targeting of coal projects and regulatory measures for coal-fired power plants, there is evidence of a broadening focus on other fossil fuels and "unconventional" energy sources. For instance, alongside its Beyond Coal campaign, the Sierra Club now runs a Beyond Natural Gas campaign in recognition of the climate and environmental effects associated with the current explosion – aided by new technological developments in hydraulic fracturing – in exploration for and development of natural gas as a power source in the United States.[88] Along similar lines, other pro-regulatory groups are extending their climate campaigns and associated litigation to encompass unconventional energy sources like shale gas. As one interviewee described it:

> I mean we didn't know a couple of years ago how much the new fracking methods would change – I mean just overnight! I mean it's really been stunning to watch the impact on the energy sector over the last few years. Who knew these new methods would allow companies to target the Monterey shale? Or that we'd see the kind of boom we've seen in Texas or North Dakota in terms of shale oil. So I think we're going to be continuing to fight those extreme fossil fuel proposals as an important part of – you know when you have a new fossil fuel gold rush like that it really undercuts policies to decarbonize – so that's an important part of it, continuing to push the programs we already have under existing laws. But we have to be nimble.[89]

Actions targeting corporate disclosure requirements and the investment decisions of agencies like the Overseas Private Investment Corporation

---

[87] *County of Sonoma v. FHFA*, 9th Cir. March 19, 2013.
[88] Sierra Club, "Beyond Natural Gas," http://content.sierraclub.org/naturalgas/.
[89] In-person interview, US Participant 2 (Oct. 22, 2012).

and the US Export-Import Bank likewise show a broader concern with US energy policy and how this feeds into national and global possibilities for climate change mitigation. As the United States continues to shift away from burning coal domestically, and as hydraulic fracturing and deepwater drilling open new supplies of oil and natural gas, lawsuits around exports of these fossil fuels likely will continue to grow.

As we saw in Chapter 4, there is also a greater focus in recent US case law on issues of climate change adaptation and damage from extreme weather events, although this jurisprudence is far less developed than the comparable body of case law in Australia. Several of our interviewees saw adaptation litigation as a growth area in the United States, especially in association with damaging severe weather. One interviewee commented, "I think there is now – especially after Hurricane Sandy – more attention to [adaptation] and more attention to constraining development on the coastline. That will inevitably lead to litigation."[90] Others saw a range of litigation possibilities emerging in association with adaptation and climate damage concerns:

> I think, over time, what you're going to – just as a guess here obviously – what I think is you're going to see a lot more litigation over property impacts and storm damage and things like that. Because, you know, the constant statement is always, you can't attribute a particular storm to climate change, well, in fact that's not quite true and it's changing pretty fast.... And again I think the other piece of litigation you'll start to see more of is probably related to insurance. Insurance companies will try to escape coverage and I think there will be litigation over causation and what the coverage is. I think that will be more interesting in some ways because if insurance companies won't write insurance for floodplains, you know, that changes policy.[91]

Overall, then, we expect to see US litigation's continued growth and development around both mitigation and adaptation issues in the coming years. With respect to mitigation, we expect to see litigation continue to expand, dominated by pro- and antiregulatory suits, focused on regulation pursuant to existing federal and state environmental statutes and new state climate change and clean energy statutes. We anticipate a continued focus on domestic coal but also increasing litigation about natural gas and oil as well as exports of fossil fuels. Regarding adaptation, we think that the recent cases are just the beginning of a new wave of litigation

---

[90] Telephone interview, US Participant 7 (Nov. 16, 2012). Also telephone interview, US Participant 12 (Dec. 2, 2013).

[91] In-person interview, US Participant 6 (Nov. 14, 2012).

and that more local land use planning, state public utility planning, and takings suits will be brought in the coming years.

8.3.2 Australia

It has often been remarked that the area of climate change law "is not for the faint of heart."[92] This was borne out by our interviews with those involved in climate change litigation in Australia. In public and political forums, climate policy – including the climate change science underlying it – remains heavily contested.[93] Antiregulatory actions taken by governments, climate skepticism fueled by politicians and the conservative media, a powerful mining lobby, and drastic funding cuts for environmental advocacy groups mean that the environment for climate change litigation to influence regulation proactively is as hostile now in Australia as it ever was in the heyday of the conservative Howard government, when such litigation first began to take hold. As discussed in depth in Chapter 7, because legislation is easier to pass in Australia than in the United States, this hostile environment poses more of a barrier for litigation in Australia than it would in the US context. At the federal level, the repeal of the carbon tax and continuing efforts by the Abbott government to water down or remove other clean energy programs has cast a significant pall over the country's future climate policy. In addition, in many states, "the language of climate change is barely mentioned at all" by governments, making it "very hard for policymakers to give frank and fearless advice on the issue."[94]

Against such a backdrop, the views of our interviewees as to what the future holds for climate change litigation in Australia, and what it might achieve, were understandably cautious in comparison to the United States. Some were quite pessimistic about the future opportunities for court-led change:

> I think I am a great believer in legal strategies being very important to any public interest campaign. But I'm concerned that the options for achieving any more policy change on climate change won't be through the courts. And probably because the court system, certainly in Australia,

---

[92] Jutta Brunnée, "Climate Change and Compliance and Enforcement Processes" in Rosemary Rayfuse and Shirley V. Scott (eds.), *International Law in the Era of Climate Change* (2012, Edward Elgar, Cheltenham), 290, 290.

[93] On public attitudes to climate change in Australia and the role of the conservative media in fostering climate scepticism, see, further, Chapter 6.

[94] Skype interview, Australian Participant 9 (May 6, 2013).

has quite robustly identified problems that have then been picked up by the bureaucracy and the assessment processes. But at the moment it is the political wheel and process that is simply resisting any further change, both for adaptation and mitigation.[95]

Others took a more optimistic stance, although still anticipating fierce battles:

> I don't think there is any responsible and informed environmental lawyer, or tort lawyer in fact, that will not say that the longer-term scenario is an increased and more inventive use of courts and tribunals to bring about the necessary reforms to respond to climate change. And I think that will be largely driven by the growth of liability law in the tortious area and insurance and those litigators will lead the opportunity and take the law forward. Now, that's inevitable. So there will be lots and lots of different ways by which people will try. Many of those cases will be lost along the way but the law will evolve. In the short term, short to medium term, I think that we will have determined efforts on behalf of conservative governments in just about all jurisdictions in Australia and overseas to try to resist that inevitable trend. And I think that the next two, three, four, five years will probably be the grimmest tussle between the executive arm of government and the independent arm of government in the form of the judiciary. I think it's inevitable we are going to see more and more energy cases fought out. It's inevitable that governments will resist the outcomes which the courts will provide. It's inevitable that they will be appealed on. But the response as far as getting government change and community support will be very much a negative in the next three, four, five, hopefully not, but may well be, longer period of years.[96]

Overall, however, like their US counterparts, our Australian interviewees believed that climate change litigation would continue in Australia and play a role in shaping regulation and behavior. As one interviewee put it,

> I think, on the whole, that climate change litigation is here to stay. I think the sort of people who are involved in prosecuting these sorts of cases are both committed and also quite clever and I think some of the tribunals in which these arguments are being run are sympathetic fora for arguments of that kind. And I suspect that the law is going to develop further.[97]

The increasingly hostile political environment for climate action in Australia may in fact be a spur for further litigation "because I think climate change litigation – particularly for the bigger, more sophisticated

---

[95] Skype interview, Australian Participant 14 (May 23, 2013).
[96] Skype interview, Australian Participant 16 (May 30, 2013).
[97] Skype interview, Australian Participant 8 (Apr. 24, 2013).

campaign groups with more to lose – litigation becomes more appealing when you're not getting any traction with the decision-makers."[98] Although the capacity of environmental groups to bring such litigation will undoubtedly be hindered by government funding cuts to legal assistance organizations such as the Environmental Defenders Office, there is the potential that overseas funding, particularly from US-based groups, may help to fill the gap. As one interviewee related to us, the perception is that the anticoal campaign is progressing well in the United States but that Australia still represents somewhat of a wild frontier on this issue, which is of concern given the country's massive coal resources and Asian fossil fuel export markets.[99] This difference may prompt more assistance to flow into Australia.

As to what kinds of cases might be taken in coming years in Australia, the feeling among many interviewees was that pro-regulatory groups would continue to pursue a range of options, along the lines of the current approach. One interviewee remarked,

> I don't see a silver bullet and I agree with Al Gore that we don't have silver bullets we have silver buckshot. I take the view that we have to do many things. There's no single, one case that will win or produce a dramatic change overnight. I don't think that is reality. So I don't see a massive change in the future. I think it's about running the cases we have, with the tools we have now, as well as we can.[100]

This view was shared by participants on the other side of the litigation fence, with climate change being one of the arrows in the quiver of litigants' armory in any case:

> I think definitely there is going to be more case law in this area. I think every new coal project that comes up – whether it be an expansion or a greenfields project – will be subject to a legal challenge and certainly greenhouse will form part of that. I think that there are three big areas. So there's obviously climate change and greenhouse and the scope 3 emissions, basically trying to create an argument around that that's adding to global emissions and therefore shouldn't be allowed. I think water and biodiversity are the other two. I think there's a convergence between the water one, in particular, and climate change.... So climate change I think, rather than being the sole focus, is being also used as a vehicle for other issues as well. So we will continue to see litigation where climate change is thrown in as a cause for why a project should not go ahead. It's becoming a bit like – and I

[98] In-person interview, Australian Participant 1 (Mar. 7, 2013).
[99] In-person interview, Australian Participant 3 (Mar. 8, 2013).
[100] Skype interview, Australian Participant 4 (Mar. 20, 2013).

hesitate to use this – coal, in particular, I think is becoming like tobacco, big tobacco.[101]

In effect, climate change seems likely to become more of a mainstream issue in litigation and risk management associated with development projects and planning – "business as usual," as Professors Markell and Ruhl have called it in the US context – rather than an issue that transforms the litigation and regulatory landscape. Speaking about the adaptation case law, one interviewee offered affirmation for this view:

> The thing I am finding doing adaptation and looking at this is that . . . some people have looked at it as being the big new thing that is going to change the world but I don't think it is going to be the only big thing. I think generally it will *add* to everything we do everyday with our practice; it will be another thing we take into account.[102]

Another, focusing particularly on coastal and adaptation risk planning efforts in the state of Victoria, commented,

> I get the sense that litigation, or the threat of litigation, is one of a multitude of factors that influence policy development in relation to these issues. And the policy actually influences the policy development far more directly – as it should! – rather than litigation risk. It's there in the background. It's almost used as a way of ventilating the policy issues and having the policy debate, particularly because most of our litigation is merits review. It's not civil litigation, it's not about money. It's about whether these projects are a good idea and it's about balancing the various interests that need to be considered. Litigation in Victoria tends to be a complement rather than a driver of policy development.[103]

Clearly, as a result of how the case law and regulation have developed so far, some legal avenues are considered unlikely to be used or further developed in Australian climate litigation. A common view, for example, was that "judicial review is dying as a vehicle to engage in environmental litigation or climate change litigation."[104] None of our interviewees anticipated that the repeal of the Clean Energy Act that established the carbon pricing mechanism would generate significant litigation. Indeed, if anything, the view was that removal of the carbon price might encourage courts to be more adventurous in their decisions on climate issues.[105] While many

---

[101] Skype interview, Australian Participant 13 (May 23, 2013).
[102] Skype interview, Australian Participant 18 (Jul. 18, 2013).
[103] In-person interview, Australian Participant 20 (Jul. 25, 2013).
[104] Skype interview, Australian Participant 16 (May 30, 2013).
[105] In-person interview, Australian Participant 3 (Mar. 8, 2013).

Australian pro-regulatory groups were inspired by US litigation such as the *Massachusetts v. EPA* and *AEP v. Connecticut* cases, attempts to mount similar cases have been unsuccessful, and there is little enthusiasm for pursuing further lawsuits based on air pollution or tortious causes of action. Several interviewees remarked on the limited prospects for private tort actions against large emitters under Australian law. As one put it,

> Nobody's really tried that in Australia and I don't think it would succeed for a while yet. So I think that's quite a big difference in the context of Australia and the United States because in Australia companies aren't really looking at having that kind of individual liability attributed back to them at this stage whether by litigation or by anything else.[106]

Another commented,

> Courts in Australia are nervous about never-ending economic loss. And that would be part of the difficulty I think so you would have to have some sort of quite tangible direct effect which I think would be predicated upon an incident. Not just, well we have companies, they emit, that causes a nuisance, we'd like damages thanks as a national collective of people. I think that would have no chance at all of succeeding in Australia.[107]

Even so, it is clear that a creative spirit remains alive among pro-regulatory groups involved in climate change campaigns and litigation. Various possibilities for future litigation were canvassed by interviewees, including interest in exploring public trust avenues, climate justice cases focused on securing resources for adaptation, and negligence cases against state governments for climate damage associated with their wind-back of adaptation programs.[108] As one interviewee explained, in part the litigation "has a life of its own, which you can't really pick up from necessarily the judgments" and which influences the kind of cases brought:

> There's an influence between cases as well. Some cases become faddish and they run with that and others don't. . . . So there is an element of popularity and I think that's because people talk to one another, barristers talk to one another, it's who is on the bench at the time. And one action inspires someone else's action. Oh, that was a point that was run, that got some mileage, let's try it in this one. And so it does feed off itself in an informal way. And that's very hard to document but it's undoubtedly true.[109]

---

[106] In-person interview, Australian Participant 1 (Mar. 7, 2013).

[107] Skype interview, Australian Participant 16 (May 30, 2013).

[108] In-person interview, Australian Participant 1 (Mar. 7, 2013); in-person interview, Australian Participant 3 (Mar. 8, 2013).

[109] Skype interview, Australian Participant 7 (Apr. 11, 2013).

Exchanging ideas about potential litigation strategies in the courtroom and advocates' legal offices (and also across jurisdictions, a function we hope can be facilitated by a book such as this) can therefore serve as a basis for novel claims in the future.

In the longer term, some Australian interviewees foresaw litigation engaging more closely with big-picture issues of regional planning and urban design rather than just proceeding on a project-by-project basis:

> I think that as climate change becomes a more relevant consideration in how we draw our planning schemes and how we design our cities and the standards that we have, I think there's greater scope for people to say we should be looking for things like urban consolidation, not just because the Regional Plan says so, but we have to understand that in departing from that we are having consequences and those consequences are not only for people's convenience and the economic provision of infrastructure, but it also has consequences in terms of climate change and other things.[110]

Others saw disaster (or a succession of disasters) as a prompt for more robust adaptation litigation extending beyond routine planning issues into the area of liability: "I do think we will see some big tort cases where there's been real damage suffered by somebody with deep pockets."[111]

The other major area mentioned by litigants as a source of future litigation was actions relating to corporations, for instance, "requirements to disclose, misleading statements, investment risk and all that sort of stuff."[112] In general, "there's been some shift to more recognize the importance of economics" in influencing project and investment decisions around coal.[113] Also, emerging among some groups is the idea that it is foolish to place "faith in governments to just be brave for the sake of it because of the power of the fossil fuel companies."[114] For such groups, strategies that focus on promoting risk management by investors and financiers through greater disclosure of climate risk associated with their portfolios and measures to divest themselves of fossil fuel assets offer far more likelihood of transformative change.

Overall, in Australia, like in the United States, litigation looks likely to continue using many of the strategies that have been employed

---

[110] Skype interview, Australian Participant 5 (Mar. 26, 2013).

[111] Skype interview, Australian Participant 8 (Apr. 24, 2013). Also Skype interview, Australian Participant 7 (Apr. 11, 2013), and Skype interview, Australian Participant 9 (May 6, 2013).

[112] Skype interview, Australian Participant 6 (Apr. 5, 2013). Also Skype interview, Australian Participant 7 (Apr. 11, 2013).

[113] In-person interview, Australian Participant 2 (Mar. 8, 2013).

[114] Skype interview, Australian Participant 12 (May 21, 2013).

successfully before, with fewer suits along those avenues that have been less successful or inspired more backlash. However, what continuing along similar pathways means in Australia looks different than in the US context. Future Australian climate change litigation will likely maintain its smaller-scale focus, with a land use planning emphasis, in specialized tribunals. Both mitigation and adaptation suits will probably continue along those lines, though with extra caution around the difficult political environment and the dangers of prompting antiregulatory legislative or local and state government action.

8.4   Conclusion: litigation and our climate change future

Presently, the regulatory approach for climate change emerging at an international level – and its interaction with national and subnational approaches – appears to be headed toward relatively limited voluntary commitments with an unformed and unclear longer-term plan. However, as successive climate science reports have warned, including the most recent report of the Intergovernmental Panel on Climate Change, the next few years are likely to be critical in determining our climate future.[115] If action is taken during this period to initiate deep cuts in global greenhouse gas emissions and to prepare for the climate change impacts that cannot be avoided, then the world may experience a relatively soft landing on climate change.[116] What seems to be emerging as a far more probable scenario, however, is that countries will carry on with their current course of inadequate emissions reductions and investments in adaptation while international negotiators continue to bicker over issues of responsibility for emissions reduction and who should pay for adaptation measures and climate-related damage. An eventual resolution might be reached, triggered perhaps by a series of massive climate-related disasters. But the likelihood is that this will come too late to prevent the globe exceeding emissions levels that lock us into a warming future of 2°C or more and create additional pressure to try geoengineering strategies.[117]

---

[115] For a comprehensive summary of the current state of scientific information on this issue, see IPCC, "Summary for Policymakers" in T. F. Stocker et al. (eds.), *Climate Change 2013: The Physical Science Basis. Contribution of Working Group I to the Fifth Assessment Report of the Intergovernmental Panel on Climate Change* (2013, Cambridge University Press, Cambridge).

[116] IPCC Working Group III, *Summary for Policymakers – Final Draft, Climate Change 2014 – Mitigation of Climate Change* (2014, IPCC, Geneva).

[117] See IPCC Working Group III, "Summary for Policymakers," 15–16; "Estimated global GHG emissions levels in 2020 based on the Cancún Pledges are not consistent with

What role litigation plays in shaping our eventual climate future will also be affected by the choices of governments, corporations, communities, and individuals over the next few years. How quickly climate change creates impacts people care about – particularly in countries, such as the United States and Australia, with the capacity to make a real contribution to reducing emissions and improving adaptive efforts – will be a determinative factor in which lawsuits people are motivated to bring and their likelihood of success. As a general rule, "the less effective we are in addressing the issue of climate change, the more salient these actions will become."[118]

Although most climate change cases to date have been prospective – focused on getting governments and corporations to take action – the litigation has the potential to take on a greater liability focus in the future. For example, if technological measures are employed to mitigate greenhouse gas emissions from coal power or to manage incoming solar radiation, litigation could be expected to engage with questions of liability if these measures fail or are inadequate and damage results.[119] Equally, on the adaptation side, measures such as seawalls and other land defenses against rising seas are likely to generate difficult legal questions about the extent to which private property owners should be compensated for land taken to create them, responsibility for their maintenance over time, and liability for any ensuing environmental impacts.[120] A move from climate litigation as a prospective regulatory tool to one that is retrospectively focused may help to force hard regulatory choices. Overall, as we move toward an uncertain climate future, we can expect more hard choices

---

cost-effective long-term mitigation trajectories that are at least as likely as not to limit temperature change to 2°C relative to pre-industrial levels (2100 concentrations of about 450 and about 500 ppm CO2eq), but they do not preclude the option to meet that goal (high confidence)"; "Delaying mitigation efforts beyond those in place today through 2030 is estimated to substantially increase the difficulty of the transition to low longer-term emissions levels and narrow the range of options consistent with maintaining temperature change below 2°C relative to pre-industrial levels (high confidence)."

[118] William C.G. Burns and Hari M. Osofsky (eds.), *Adjudicating Climate Change: State, National, and International Approaches* (2009, Cambridge University Press, New York), 384.

[119] For a discussion of technological geoengineering measures like solar radiation management, see Catherine Redgwell, "Geoengineering the Climate: Technological Solutions to Mitigation Failure or Continuing Carbon Addiction?," (2012) 17 *Carbon Clim. L. Rev.* 178.

[120] Megan M. Herzog and Sean B. Hecht, "Combatting Sea-Level Rise in Southern California: How Local Governments can Seize Adaptation Opportunities while Minimizing Legal Risk" (2013) 19 *Hastings West Nw. J. Environ. L. Policy* 463.

of this kind, and litigation is likely to play an important role in airing the different options available and reaching solutions on the best way forward.

To date, climate change litigation in the United States and Australia has played a significant role in mainstreaming climate issues in regulatory and decision-making processes but a more limited one in transforming the underlying social, political, and economic structures that support a carbon-intensive system. It is clear that many barriers remain to instituting effective regulatory action to address greenhouse gas emissions and to improve adaptation and resilience to climate change impacts. Mostly, however, these barriers are sociopolitical and institutional in nature, rather than stemming from a lack of technology and scientific know-how. We could initiate the transformation of our energy systems today to put the world on a pathway toward clean energy, but we currently lack the political will and social impetus to do so.[121]

Perhaps the most important role that climate change litigation can serve in this context is continuing to raise the difficult questions that governments and societies would seemingly prefer not to confront head-on. Is an energy system based on fossil fuels sustainable? Should we continue to produce, use, and export coal given its climate change consequences? Are our planning frameworks and insurance systems flexible enough to take account of future climatic change? What are the responsibilities of the present generation to maintain a safe climate for future generations and other species? Courts may not always be the best forum for policy debates of this kind or the most sympathetic to arguments for transformative change. They may follow rather than lead social movements. But in terms of allowing such issues to be aired publicly, thoroughly, and stridently, at least the courtroom doors are open.

---

[121] IPCC Working Group III, "Summary for Policymakers," 10–20. For analyses of how a zero-emissions energy system could be achieved in the Australian context, see Beyond Zero Emissions, *Zero Carbon Australian 2020 Stationary Energy Plan* (2010, Beyond Zero Emissions and University of Melbourne Energy Institute, Melbourne). For an example of similar work in the United States, see Mark Schwartz, "Stanford Scientist Unveils 50-State Plan to Transform U.S. to Renewable Energy," *Stanford Report*, February 26, 2014, available at http://news.stanford.edu/news/2014/february/fifty-states-renewables-022414.html.

INDEX

Books in the series

Climate Change Litigation: Regulatory Pathways to Cleaner Energy?
Jacqueline Peel and Hari Osofsky

Mestizo International Law: A Global Intellectual History 1842–1933
Arnulf Becker Lorca

Sugar and the Making of International Trade Law
Michael Fakhri

Strategically-created Treaty Conflicts and the Politics of International Law
Surabhi Ranganathan

Investment Treaty Arbitration as Public International Law: Procedural Aspects and Implications
Eric De Brabandere

The New Entrants Problem in International Fisheries Law
Andrew Serdy

Substantive Protection under Investment Treaties: A Legal and Economic Analysis
Jonathan Bonnitcha

Popular Governance of Post-Conflict Reconstruction: The Role of International Law
Matthew Saul

Evolution of International Environmental Regimes: The Case of Climate Change
Simone Schiele

Judges, Law and War: The Judicial Development of International Humanitarian Law
Shane Darcy

Religious Offence and Human Rights: The Implications of Defamation of Religions
Lorenz Langer

Forum Shopping in International Adjudication: The Role of Preliminary Objections
Luiz Eduardo Ribeiro Salles

International Law and the Arctic
Michael Byers

Cooperation in the Law of Transboundary Water Resources
Christina Leb

Underwater Cultural Heritage and International Law
Sarah Dromgoole

State Responsibility: The General Part
James Crawford